Britain's Rise to Global Superpower in the Age of Napoleon

Britain's Rise to Global Superpower in the Age of Napoleon

William R. Nester

FRONTLINE BOOKS

First published in Great Britain in 2020 by
Frontline Books
An imprint of
Pen & Sword Books Ltd
Yorkshire – Philadelphia

Copyright © William R. Nester 2020

ISBN 978 1 52677 543 6

Typeset by Mac Style
Printed and bound in the UK by TJ Books Ltd,
Padstow, Cornwall.

Pen & Sword Books Limited incorporates the imprints of Atlas,
Archaeology, Aviation, Discovery, Family History, Fiction, History,
Maritime, Military, Military Classics, Politics, Select, Transport,
True Crime, Air World, Frontline Publishing, Leo Cooper, Remember
When, Seaforth Publishing, The Praetorian Press, Wharncliffe
Local History, Wharncliffe Transport, Wharncliffe True Crime
and White Owl.

For a complete list of Pen & Sword titles please contact

PEN & SWORD BOOKS LIMITED
47 Church Street, Barnsley, South Yorkshire, S70 2AS, England
E-mail: enquiries@pen-and-sword.co.uk
Website: www.pen-and-sword.co.uk

Or

PEN AND SWORD BOOKS
1950 Lawrence Rd, Havertown, PA 19083, USA
E-mail: Uspen-and-sword@casematepublishers.com
Website: www.penandswordbooks.com

Contents

List of Tables

Maps

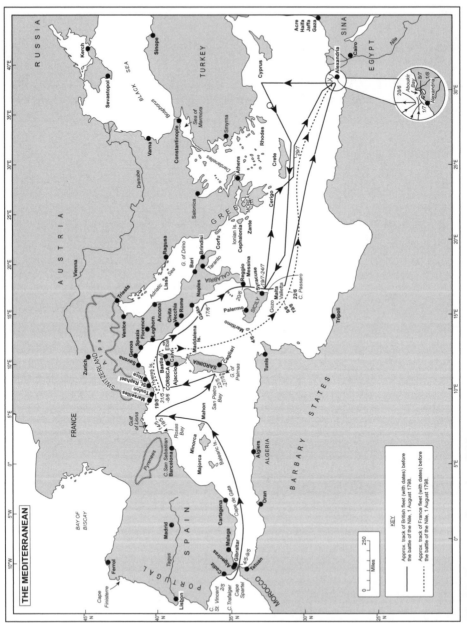

The Mediterranean Campaign, 1798.

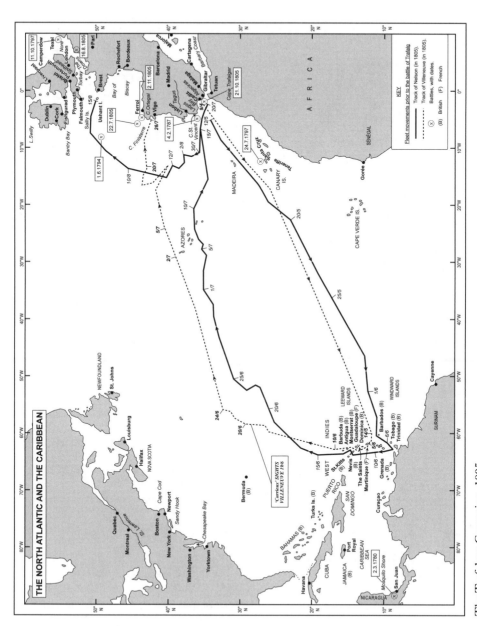

The Trafalgar Campaign, 1805.

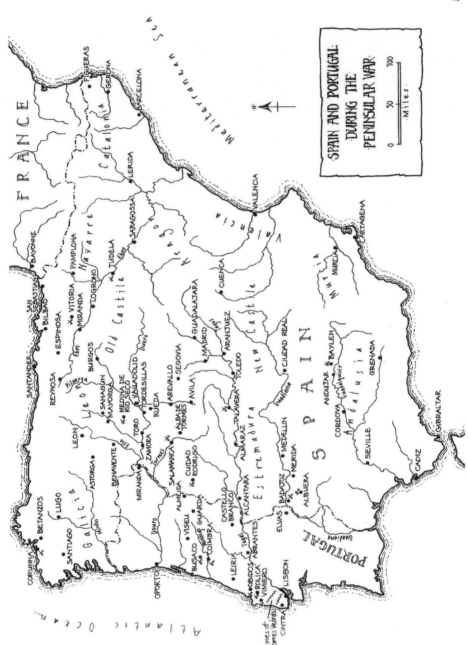

The Peninsula Campaigns, 1807–13.

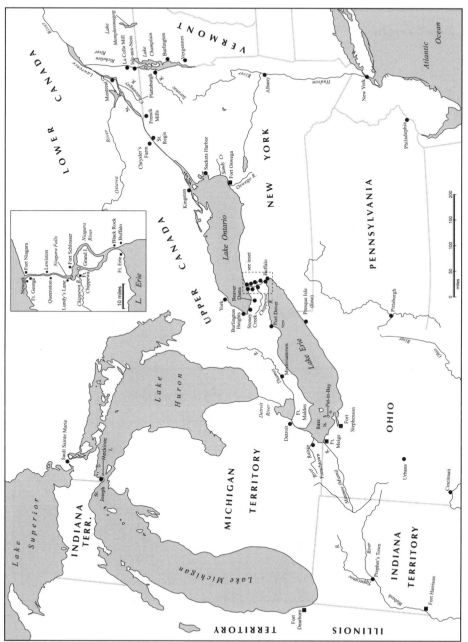

The Great Lakes–Saint Lawrence Campaigns, 1812–14.

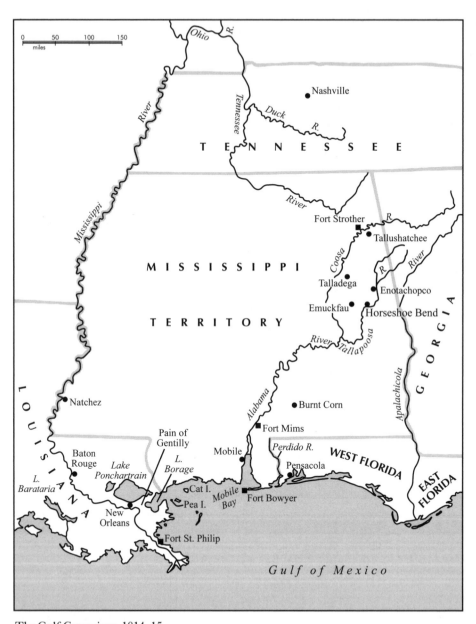

The Gulf Campaigns, 1814–15.

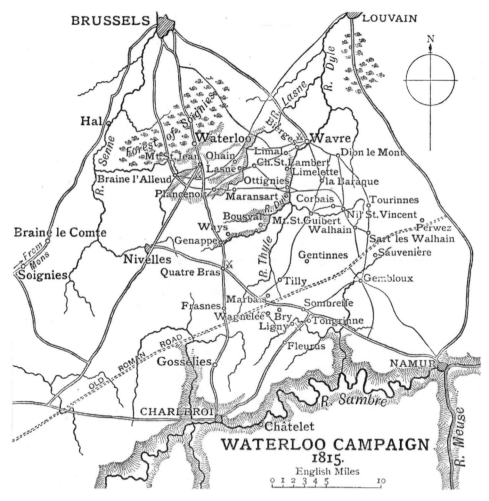

The Waterloo Campaign, 1815.

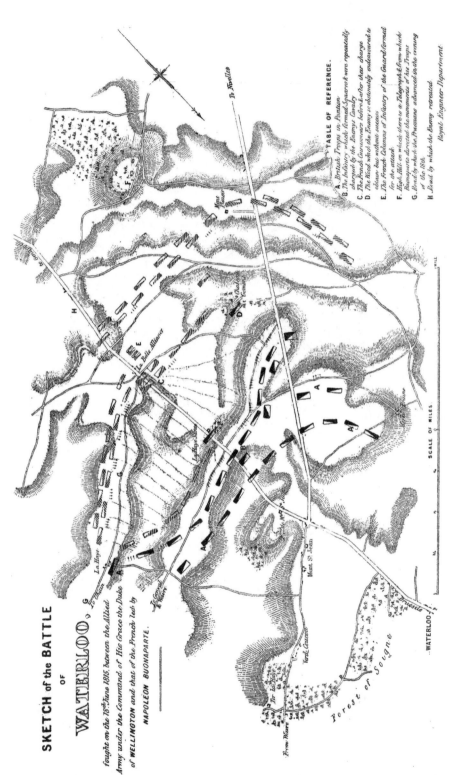

The Battle of Waterloo, June 18, 1815.

Acknowledgements

I want to express my deep gratitude and pleasure at having had the opportunity to work with the outstanding Pen & Sword editorial team of Lisa Hoosan, Alison Flowers, John Grehan, and Martin Mace, who were always as kind as they were professional.

Introduction

The art of power consists of getting what one wants. That is never more challenging than when a nation is at war. Britain fought a nearly non-stop war against first revolutionary then Napoleonic France from 1793 to 1815. During those twenty-two years, the British government formed, financed, and led seven coalitions against France. The French inflicted humiliating defeats on the first five coalitions. Eventually Britain and its allies prevailed, not once but twice by vanquishing Napoleon temporarily in 1814 and definitively in 1815.[1]

Of the many reasons why Britain and its allies suffered defeats during the war's initial two decades, one is crucial. Although war is as old as humanity, the art of war changes with time. Innovations in technology combined with brilliant leadership revolutionize strategy and tactics. French revolutionaries created and Napoleon perfected a new form of warfare. Never before had a government mobilized so much of a realm's manpower, industry, finance, and patriotism, nor, under Napoleon wielded it more effectively and ruthlessly to pulverize and conquer one's enemies.[2]

Britain struggled up a blood-soaked learning curve to master this new form of warfare. With time the British made the most of their natural strategic and economic advantages. Britons were relatively secure and prosperous in their island realm. British merchants, manufacturers, and financiers dominated global markets and exclusive access to an expanding empire.[3] The Royal Navy not only ruled the waves that lapped against the nation's shores but those ploughed by international commerce around the world.[4]

Yet even with those assets victory was not inevitable. Two brilliant military leaders are the most vital reasons why Britain and its allies vanquished France when and how they did. General Arthur Wellesley, Duke of Wellington and Admiral Horatio Nelson respectively mastered warfare on land and at sea. *Britain's Rise to Global Superpower during the Age of Napoleon* reveals how decisively or disastrously Britain's army and navy wielded the art of military power during the Age of Revolution and Napoleon.[5]

Chapter 1

The Art of British Military Power, 1793–1815

A private … of one of our infantry regiments enter[ed] the park, gaping
about at the statures and images – 'There,' he said pointing to the
soldier, 'it all depends upon that article whether we do the business or
not. Give me enough of it, and I am sure.'

> Wellington, when asked how he would beat Napoleon

Some indeed exclaimed that their sufferings were the more aggravated
as being inflicted contrary to the laws of all civilized nations. The
unfortunate sufferers seemed not to reflect that war was will, not law.

> Ensign Robert Blakeney of the 28th, reflecting on the
> British bombardment of Copenhagen[1]

The art of power, or ability to get what one wants, is inseparable from
politics or conflicts between two or more individuals or groups.
Power has 'hard' physical and 'soft' psychological dimensions.
The art of power, or 'smart power,' is the judicious choice and assertion of
appropriate hard and soft resources to prevail in a conflict. The art of power
varies sharply between peaceful and violent struggles. In war, a state or group
musters hard power resources like people, money, weapons, provisions,
and other essentials into military forces. Soft power determines how one
organizes, supplies, and transports those resources, motivates the military
personnel, gets critical information about the enemy's forces and plans,
and implements the strategies and tactics that destroy the enemy's physical
and, most importantly, psychological ability to keep fighting. Strategy,
tactics, and technologies are tightly bound. Occasionally new technologies,
techniques, or outlooks will transform a prevailing art of military power
into something distinctly different. Such inventions as the spear, stirrup,
gunpowder, barbed wire, machine gun, airplane, tank, and computer, to
name a few, revolutionized military power. Obviously the state or group that
first masters the new art will likely triumph over those that persist with the
obsolete version.

In its history, perhaps only one other enemy posed a greater challenge to Britain than France did during the age of first revolution then Napoleon from February 1793 to June 1815. During this time, Whitehall, the seat of Britain's government, helped form, finance, and lead seven military coalitions against France. The French initiated new sources of ideological and organizational power that eventually combined with Napoleon's military genius to defeat the first five coalitions. By 1812, Napoleon's empire of conquered or cowed states stretched across Europe from western Spain to Russia's border. Then, after three years of the largest scale of warfare ever experienced, the British and their allies defeated and exiled Napoleon in 1814, then after his return to power, defeated him again within a mere three months in 1815, this time permanently. Many reasons explain this military seesaw but crucial was the eventual mastery by Britain and its allies of the prevailing art of power that became known as 'total war.'

During the summer of 1789, virtually no Britons could have foreseen that within a few years they would be at war against France let alone that the war would last twenty-two grueling years. Most Britons applauded the French Revolution that transformed King Louis XVI's government from an absolute into a constitutional monarchy. Philosophically, they cheered France for doing what Britain had done a century earlier. Strategically, they assumed that a French government dedicated to political representation and rights would be more divided and less aggressive, which would mean fewer wars. And economically, this meant a lower military burden for Britons to bear. What was there not to like?[2]

Britain did have two war scares from 1789 to 1793, but they were with Spain over the Pacific Northwest America and Russia over the Black Sea. Whitehall resolved each of these crises diplomatically. As for France, the revolutionaries initially lived up to this National Assembly declaration of May 22, 1790: 'The French nation renounces ... any war with a view to making conquests and ... will never use its forces against the liberty of any other people.'[3] Nearly two years later in February 1792, Prime Minister William Pitt confidently assured Britons that: 'Unquestionably there never was a time in the history of this country, when, from the situation of Europe, we might more reasonably expect 15 years of peace than at the present moment.'[4] Pitt, of course, was never more embarrassingly wrong. Yet, that aside, he was Britain's greatest political leader during this era, serving as prime minster from December 19, 1893 to January 1, 1801, and from May 10, 1804 to January 23, 1806.[5]

The French Revolution began in May 1789, when Louis XVI called the Estates General into session to overcome a worsening financial crisis.[6] He hoped to gain the approval of that ancient institution, last convened in 1614, for tax increases to prevent the state from becoming insolvent. The Estates General was composed of three classes, priests, nobles, and commoners, whose respective constituencies elected them. The commoners rejected the king's attempts to make them a rubber stamp for unpopular tax hikes when they convened on May 5, 1789. Instead, on June 17, they transformed themselves into a National Assembly that Louis reluctantly accepted and required the priests and nobles to join. The revolution turned violent on July 14, when a Parisian mob captured the Bastille, a castle that served as an arsenal and prison for political dissidents, and executed its defenders. That violent upheaval made Louis more willing to accept reforms to save his throne. The National Assembly voted to abolish feudal rights on August 4 and assert the Declaration of the Rights of Man and the Citizen on August 26. On October 5, thousands of mostly Parisian women, outraged by the lack of food in the city's markets, marched a dozen miles to Versailles, where the monarchy resided, and demanded relief. The king promised he would do so. The following day, to ensure that the king kept his promise, the protestors forced him and his family to move to the Tuileries Palace in the heart of Paris. Across France, mobs looted chateaus and monasteries. The National Assembly declared that Louis was no longer the 'king of France' but the 'king of the French' on October 10, and nationalized all Catholic Church property on November 3. The revolutionaries began a reorganization of local government that transformed France into 83 departments by January 1790. On May 19, 1790, the National Assembly voted to abolish the nobility, although for now they retained the monarchy. On July 12, the National Assembly issued the Civil Constitution of the French Clergy that transformed priests into civil servants of the French state liable to dismissal.

Although the support for these reforms in the National Assembly was nearly unanimous, the revolutionaries split between the dominant Girondins who defended the constitutional monarchy they had established, and the Jacobins who called for abolishing the monarchy and forming a republic. A worsening foreign threat strengthened the Jacobins. Louis XVI's two younger brothers along with thousands of other nobles fled France and lobbied foreign governments to help restore the king to absolute power. They evoked brotherly love in appealing to Austrian Archduke Leopold II to rescue his sister Marie Antoinette, the French queen. The aborted flight of Louis and his family to safety in the Austrian Netherlands in June 1791 intensified the ongoing debate between Girondins and Jacobins over whether France should be a constitutional monarchy or a republic. Although the Girondins, with a majority in the National Assembly, tried to mask the failed escape as a kidnapping, the Jacobins insisted that the Bourbon family no longer had any political legitimacy and should be deposed.

Leopold unwittingly bolstered the Jacobins when, on July 10, 1791, he issued his Padua Circular calling on all monarchs to unite in destroying France's revolutionary regime and restoring Louis to absolute power. Initially only Prussian King Frederick William II responded. The two rulers met on August 27, 1791, and their Pillnitz Declaration repeated Leopold's previous call to turn France's political clock back before May 1789. This emboldened Louis to defy the revolutionaries by vetoing Constituent Assembly decrees against royalist émigrés in November and priests in December 1791. On January 24, 1792, France's revolutionary leaders warned Austria to retract its appeals for their overthrow or face war.

After vainly awaiting that retraction for nearly three months, France's national assembly declared war against Austria on April 20, 1792. Prussia and the kingdom of Sardinia and Piedmont allied with Austria. Although Whitehall officially declared neutrality, aggressive and brutal French policies steadily drove Britain toward the allies. Karl Wilhelm Ferdinand, Duke Brunswick commanded the main allied army that the Prussians and Austrians massed on France's eastern frontier. On July 25, Brunswick issued what became known as the Brunswick Declaration that the allies would restore Louis XVI to his full power and destroy the revolutionaries if they harmed their rightful monarch and his family. In August 1792, the Jacobins used the interception of Louis XVI's secret correspondence with counter-revolutionary leaders abroad as the excuse to arrest him on treason charges. The revolutionaries declared France a republic on September 22, 1792.

Meanwhile, Brunswick led 42,000 troops into eastern France. The allies were confident that their trained professional soldiers would rout any armed rabbles on their way to crush the revolution and restore Louis XVI to his throne. Then an astonishing event took place. At the battle of Valmy on September 20, 1792, 50,000 French led by Generals Charles Dumouriez and François Kellermann defeated Brunswick's army, diminished to 34,000 troops by illness, desertion, and garrisons that protected the lengthening supply line. Valmy was among history's most crucial battles. Eyewitness Johann Wolfgang Goethe immediately understood its significance: 'From here and today there begins a new epoch in the history of the world.'[7] Dumouriez captured the idealism in Valmy's immediate aftermath:

Liberty is triumphant everywhere; led by philosophy, it will sweep the universe: it will establish itself on every throne, once it has crushed despotism and enlightened the people…. This present war will be the last, and all tyrants and privileged, their criminal plots exposed, will be the only victims of this struggle between arbitrary power and reason.[8]

Brunswick withdrew his army to the Rhine. The French then launched offensives that overran Savoy, Nice, the Austrian Netherlands, and the Moselle valley, and even crossed the Rhine River and captured Frankfort on the Main River. In the Austrian Netherlands, Dumouriez decisively defeated an Austrian army at Jemappes on November 6, 1792. Other French forces marched into Namur on November 6, and Antwerp on November 29. Exhilarated by these victories, the French on November 19 declared a revolution without borders to topple all hated monarchies. William V, the Netherlands' stadtholder or ruler, appealed to Britain for help as France's revolutionary armies neared the frontier in November 1792. While Pitt and the Cabinet mulled this request, Paris announced that the Scheldt River was now open for trade, thus violating the 1648 Peace of Westphalia that closed that river. Foreign Minister William Grenville warned the French either to respect the treaty or prepare for the worst. When Paris upheld its policy, Pitt got Parliament on December 20, to pass a bill authorizing the navy to recruit 20,000 sailors.

Each of these events made war between Britain and France more likely. Then London received the appalling news on January 23, 1793, that two days earlier the revolutionaries had beheaded Louis XVI. On January 24, Pitt and the Cabinet severed diplomatic relations with France. Paris declared war against Britain and the Netherlands on February 1, 1793, Spain on March 26, 1793, and the Kingdom of the Two Sicilies on July 12, 1793.

Pitt and the Cabinet debated how best to mobilize the nation for war and defeat France.[9] The ministers swiftly agreed on such measures as recruiting regiments up to their authorized strength, mustering the militia, stockpiling munitions and provisions, readying the navy, and reinforcing garrisons in the colonies. They then discussed the inseparable issues of developing strategies and allies. Somehow Whitehall had to transform an association of great and secondary powers – Britain, Prussia, Austria, Piedmont-Sardinia, and the Netherlands, and, soon, Spain and Naples-Sicily – that faced a common enemy into a coalition with a common winning strategy. This potential coalition certainly appeared to have overwhelming military and economic power compared with France's revolutionary regime. The challenge was how to coordinate this power to bring about France's defeat as swiftly and decisively as possible. This demanded a prolonged, intense meeting of diplomatic, military, and financial minds among the allies.

This was easier said than done. Each potential ally had its own idea of how to defeat France, and to that end demanded increasing amounts of British money and men with no strings attached. As a latecomer to the war, Whitehall was expected to join the ongoing Austrian and Prussian campaigns. The problem was that these campaigns were failing. An even more critical problem was that the British Cabinet itself split between conflicting strategic visions espoused by Foreign Secretary Grenville and Secretary of State for War Henry Dundas. Grenville's 'continental strategy' would join British forces with allied armies in Europe to fight their way into France with Paris the ultimate objective. Dundas's 'maritime strategy' would destroy the French navy and merchant vessels at sea or blockade them in port, while dispatching armadas to capture France's West and East Indies colonies to be used either as diplomatic bargaining chips or additions to the British Empire.[10]

Circumstances pressured Pitt and the Cabinet into enacting elements of both policies. The previous year, in 1792, royalists on Saint Domingue, France's most lucrative colony, had asked for help in rebelling against France's revolutionary regime; similar requests came from royalists at Martinique and Guadeloupe in early 1793. Then, shortly after Paris declared war against Britain and Holland, Whitehall received a desperate plea from the Dutch government for military aid against a French invasion. The decisions of Pitt and his ministers to agree to these requests married the maritime and continental strategies.

The trouble was that each strategy had its own flaws that the hybrid only complicated. Massing enough redcoats to prevail in Europe or in the colonies was challenging enough, but doing both spread the army to the snapping point. King George III complained to Pitt about this dilemma: 'The misfortune of our situation is that we have too many objects to attend to, and our force consequently must be too small at each place.'[11]

Compounding this problem was the failure of the British and their allies to comprehend the nature of the enemy and the war they were fighting. War radicalized France's revolutionaries and France's revolutionaries radicalized war. They initiated and Napoleon perfected a new type of warfare that took Britain and the other great powers years to understand let alone match. Total war involved mobilizing all the human, industrial, financial, commercial, and cultural forces of one's nation to conquer and transform one's enemies into subordinate versions of oneself. Warfare was as much among peoples as among governments.[12]

France's revolutionary leaders made no secret of the total war they intended to wage. On November 19, 1792, the National Convention declared 'in the name of the French nation, that it will grant fraternity and aid to all peoples who wish to recover their liberty, and charges the executive power to give the generals the orders necessary for bringing aid to these peoples, and to defend the citizens ... for the cause of freedom.'[13] National Assemblyman Edmond Dubois de Crance captured the radical outlook: 'I say that in a nation which seeks to be free but which is surrounded by powerful neighbors and riddled with secret, festering factions, that every citizen should be a soldier and every soldier should be a citizen, if France does not wish to be utterly obliterated.'[14] The Convention embraced this idea when it declared on August 23, 1793, that:

> From this moment until that in which our enemies shall have been driven from the territory of the Republic, all Frenchmen are permanently requisitioned for service to the armies. The young men shall fight; the married men shall forge weapons and transport supplies; the women shall make tents and clothes and will serve in the hospitals; the children will make up old linen into lint; the old men will have themselves carried into the public squares to rouse the courage of fighting of fighting men, to preach the unity of the republic, and hatred of kings. The public squares shall be turned into barracks; the public squares into munitions factories.[15]

The French 'people's war' had two elements, the 'levée en masse' whereby the government mobilized all appropriate human and material resources in a total war against the enemy, and the 'revolution without frontiers' whereby cadres inspired popular revolutions against the regimes that they were fighting.

A maze of institutions and customs impeded the British army's ability to adapt to these revolutionary changes in warfare.[16] The command structure was at once rigid and ephemeral. Legally, the king headed the army. Historically, the last time a British monarch actually joined his army on campaign was in 1744, when George II observed the battle of Dettingen.

Actually, there was no permanent army commander-in-chief – the king only appointed one during wartime.

Whoever served as commander-in-chief somehow had to learn how to deal with a bewildering bureaucratic maze. The Secretary for War was responsible for grand strategy. Once that was determined, the Secretary at War, who headed the War Office with 120 clerks, coordinated and mobilized efforts for specific campaigns. The Home Secretary was in charge of militia and volunteers. The Treasury bought and the Commissariat collected and distributed food and fodder for teamsters and draft animals. The Adjutant-General determined logistics and discipline. The Ordinance Department, headed by a Master General, was in charge of artillery and munitions which it divvied out to both the army and navy. The Storekeeper-General paid for provisions. The Quartermaster-General found and paid for barracks. The Paymaster-General paid the troops. The Transport Board was charged with conveying troops, mounts, draft animals, ordnance, munitions, and provisions by sea. The Medical Board, including a Surgeon General, Physician General, and Inspector General of Hospitals, oversaw the army's abysmal medical system. Of these bureaucracies, the Ordnance Department was the most figuratively and sometimes literally arthritic as its strict seniority system kept elderly men doddering at the top, fearful rather than enthusiastic for new technologies that might enhance British military power.

As if this bureaucratic labyrinth did not sap Britain's potential power enough, there were other handicaps. The initial system for transporting supplies over land was a severe military weakness. Each regiment was responsible for hiring its own transport. Until 1794, private contractors supplied teamsters, wagons, and draft animals. This year, Whitehall asserted a major reform when it established the Corps of Royal Waggoners, renamed the Corps of Royal Artillery Drivers in 1806. An enduring hobble was that an army's commissary general could overrule the commanding general on critical issues. This forced commanders to work very closely with their commissaries, a feat often rendered difficult by clashes of ego and strategy. General Arthur Wellesley, the eventual duke of Wellington, complained incessantly that army politics fouled his military operations. In January 1810, he pleaded with Prime Minister Robert Jenkinson, Earl of Liverpool not to 'send me any violent party men. We must keep the spirit of party out of the army, or we shall be in a bad way indeed.'[17]

The king appointed generals and colonels, choices shaped largely by seniority and politics rather than merit. Each regiment had a colonel, who the king nearly always picked for his political obeisance rather than military experience. The rank was a prestigious and, for the unscrupulous, profitable sinecure whose presence on campaign was not just optional but discouraged. Although most colonels were honest, some milked their regiments by annually supplying uniforms for the troops with government funds from which they palmed huge handling fees and pocketed pay for phantom soldiers on the rolls actually lost from deaths, discharges, or desertions.[18]

Lieutenant colonels actually led regiments on campaign. Ranks from lieutenant colonel down to ensign were for sale to the highest bidder. The commission market varied. Commissions went on sale when officers died, retired, or were dismissed, or the king issued new ones for new regiments. Prices partly reflected the relative popularity of commissions for some regiments or postings. For instance, the death rate for regiments serving in the West Indies was so high that the supply of commissions often far exceeded the demand and the result was sharply lower prices. Commission values plummeted after a war when the king disbanded regiments. Officers went on half-pay which meant generally a consignment to genteel poverty if they had no other income.

Most officers started at or near the bottom and bought their way up as far as their purses and ambitions allowed. Fathers leapt at the opportunity to buy a rank for a son even if the lad was still a child. Indeed, before the 1802 reforms, one in five British officers was under 15 years old, and one of two was under 18 years old![19] Obviously such boy officers inspired little respect from the soldiers. The lads literally grew into the job, essentially acting as apprentices to older officers. There were other less trodden paths to becoming an officer. The king might reward a charismatic man with a commission for recruiting a number of soldiers equal to a rank, say a hundred to captain a company. On rarer occasions – less than one in twenty – officers were promoted for merit and need from the ranks.

No matter whether one bought or earned a rank, being an officer was expensive. Officers had to buy their own uniforms, swords, and other accoutrements, and were expected to entertain and live commensurate with their rank. Salaries underwrote a meager portion of officer lifestyles. Although most came from wealthy families, few were aristocrats. Male offspring of the 500 or so noble families were a sliver of the thousands of army and navy officers. Snobbery, however, was pervasive. This trait hardly endeared officers to their enlisted men or those promoted to officer from the ranks for extraordinary abilities.

Arthur Wellesley, the Duke of Wellington succinctly explained the symbiotic professional relationship between officers and soldiers:

'Subordination and habits of obedience ... can be acquired by soldiers only in proportion as they have confidence in their officers, and they cannot have confidence in their officers who have no knowledge of their profession ... have no subordination among themselves, and never obey an order.'[20] A huge problem was that officers received no formal training, but picked up skills and knowledge through observation and practice. Some supplemented this by reading books and pamphlets on the subject of which the most important was 'Rules and Regulations for the Movements of his Majesty's Infantry,' issued in 1792. Officers led from the front and were more likely to get killed or wounded than their men. For instance, of the six bloodiest Peninsula battles, the officer casualty rate was higher than that for enlisted men in four, the same in one, and less in one.[21]

Wellington, like many of his colleagues, recognized that a merit system would boost the British army's prowess but believed it could never supplant the purchase system: 'It would be desirable, certainly, that the only claim to promotion should be military merit; but this is a degree of perfection to which the disposal of military patronage has never been, and cannot be, I believe, brought in any military establishment.'[22] Nonetheless, midway through this era, the amateur system began to morph toward a merit system. In 1802, Commander-in-chief Frederick Augustus, Duke of York imposed a standard whereby anyone who wanted to purchase a rank had to be at least 16 years old and recommended in writing by a major or someone of higher rank; captain commissions were for sale only to those with two years as a lesser officer; majors needed six years' experience. In 1807, York raised the standard to three years' experience for captains, seven years for majors, and nine years for lieutenant colonels; aides-de-camp required four years as line officers.

Regiments were the British army's organizational backbone. Brigades, divisions, and corps were temporary compositions of regiments designated for a campaign. Usually a brigade held three regiments, a division three brigades, and a corps three divisions. Although the British had used brigades and occasionally divisions throughout most of the eighteenth century, Wellington was the first commander with an army large enough to split into corps in 1813.

When Britain went to war in 1793, the army numbered regiments up to the 76th. Over the next two decades, the army established new regiments from the 77th to the 135th. Most were standard redcoat regiments raised in England. Eight of the oldest regiments were variously designated house, guard, royal, or the king's own, distinguished by blue cuffs and turnbacks on their coats. They were usually among the last to be deployed abroad. Sixteen were Scottish regiments.

Although a regiment could have two to four battalions, most had only one, making them synonymous; the 60th Royal Americans was unique with its eight battalions by 1814. Regiments with two battalions usually fielded the first while the second recruited at a depot in Britain. A full-strength battalion numbered 1,000 troops split among 10 companies, of which 8 were line or center companies, and 2 were elite flank companies, 1 of light infantry and the other of grenadiers. Officers sought swift-footed sharpshooters for the light infantry company that specialized in skirmishing, and the largest, toughest men for the grenadier company that led assaults. A half-dozen exceptionally brave men formed a color guard bearing or protecting the British and regimental flags, which were wedged between the two center companies when the battalion deployed in line. At least eight musically talented men formed the battalion's band of drummers, fifers, and, for highlanders, bagpipers that echoed orders for a specific formation, pace, or manual of arms with a repertoire of rhythms and tunes; in especially bloody battle, the lieutenant colonel might order the musicians to set aside their instruments and act as medics.

Uniforms for line regiments went through distinct changes during the era. In the mid-1790s, regiments began replacing tricorne hats and knee breeches with shakos and trousers; although redcoats persisted, trousers went from white to gray around 1810. Most Scottish regiments lost their distinctive look in 1809 when the government forced them to exchange their kilts for trousers. As for hair styles, in 1808, the men obeyed orders to cut off their long, powdered ponytails; henceforth hair would be close-cropped and unpowdered. All along troops had to shave at least twice a week; only hussars and dragoons could sport moustaches, while sappers could grow beards.

Soldiers received a new coat, waistcoat, pants, three shirts, three pairs of socks, and two pairs of shoes annually; a shako, blanket, and greatcoat every two years; and a canteen and knapsack every six years, all paid for by deducting their own pay. A battalion on garrison duty looked pretty threadbare by a year's end. Campaigns swiftly reduced uniforms to rags patched or replaced with whatever material or clothing a soldier could get his hands on. The first to go were shoes that wore out after a succession of long marches. Like most commanders, Wellington shrugged off his men's ragamuffin campaign appearance as long as they were obedient and ready to fight: 'I think it is indifferent how a soldier is clothed, providing it is in a uniform manner; and that he is forced to keep himself clean and smart.'[23] An officer noted that as far as Wellington was concerned, if 'we brought our men into the field well appointed and with sixty rounds of good ammunition each, he never looked to see whether ... we might be rigged out in the colours of the rainbow if we fancied it.'[24] Indeed, Wellington himself sometimes dressed in civilian clothes for camp, march, and even battle.

Like infantry, British cavalry was split between household and regular regiments.[25] A more important distinction was between light and heavy cavalry or dragoons, with the latter more powerfully armed than the former, and trained to fight on foot as well as horseback; there were no lancers. Before 1796, light cavalry were armed only with pistols and curved sabers, and heavy cavalry with 42in barrel 75 caliber carbines, pistols, and straight swords. From 1796, all cavalry carried sabers, while the dragoon's carbine barrel was shortened to 26in, and light cavalry was issued the Paget 66 caliber carbine with a 16in barrel. In 1803, the Prince of Wales Light Cavalry regiment received the 62 caliber Baker rifle with a 20in barrel. Most regiments included six squadrons of two troops or companies each from 1793 to 1800, and thereafter regiments gradually expanded to ten squadrons. Ideally, a squadron numbered 200 men; few squadrons reached this number in peacetime, while the attrition of men and especially horses often reduced squadrons on campaign to a third or even quarter of that. The British were unique in cropping their horses' tails.

Each cavalry regiment was responsible for training and caring for its own men and horses. Some regiments naturally were better at this than others. An earlier generation of cavalry officers could improve their skills by following such manuals as Captain Robert Hinde's Discipline of Light Horse and Thomas Simes's Military Guide for Young Officers. In 1796, two important manuals appeared, Secretary at War Henry Dundas's 'Instructions and Regulations for the Formations and Movements of the Cavalry' and John Gaspard Le Marchant's 'Rules and Regulations for the Sword Exercise of the Cavalry.' None of these, however, was required reading for officers. Regimental traditions tended to prevail. Troopers enjoyed greater pay than infantry because they had acquired greater skills. They were supposed to spend most of their waking hours either caring for their horses or training. Commissary General August Schaumann observed that the typical British cavalryman 'looks down upon his horse as a machine ... which is the cause of all his exertions and punishments.' As a result he 'mistreats it.... How different things are in the German cavalry regiments' where they much better cared for their horses.[26] Officially each horse should daily consume 14lb of hay, 12lb of oats, or 10lb of corn.[27] Processed feeds were often difficult to get on campaign while grazing was a problem anytime large numbers of cavalry horses and draft animals shared the same fields, especially in the semi-desert conditions for most of the Iberian Peninsula during the five years of war there. Not just forage but horseshoes, nails, saddles, and brindles grew scarce on campaign.

As for artillery, the most fundamental distinction was between field and siege guns. British siege cannons included 18-pounders and 24-pounders which were powerful enough to batter down a fortress's walls and yet mobile enough for draft animals to drag on campaign. Field guns that could keep pace with infantry included 3-pounders, 6-pounders, and, eventually 9-pounders. Before 1793, all British artillery was pulled by horses while the gunners walked alongside. That year, the British established their first 'horse' artillery battalion, with light 3-pounder guns and all gunners mounted on horses or caissons for rapid movement. Through 1803, a British artillery battalion numbered 8 companies or batteries, each with 5 cannons and a 5½in-bore howitzer, manned by a captain, 5 lower officers, 8 non-commissioned officers, 7 bombardiers, 98 gunners, and 3 drummers; a ninth company was added in 1806 and a tenth in 1808. For their skills, gunners received higher pay than infantrymen.

During the era, French artillery outgunned British artillery in numbers. Napoleon tried to keep a ratio of five cannons to a thousand infantry, a ratio two-and-a-half times greater than Britain's two to a thousand. Whitehall never tried to shorten the number gap, but eventually nosed ahead of the French in the range and power of its guns. For most of the era, Britain's standard field gun was the 6-pounder. This changed after British troops found themselves pummeled by French 8-pounders in the Peninsula. In 1809, the army began deploying 9-pounders. Meanwhile, the British army began fielding a new weapon in 1807, the Congreve rocket invented by William Congreve and fired along a 24ft iron pole, with 12-pounders deployed for field battles and up to 32-pounders for sieges. Generally they were effective only against large fixed targets like cities.

The Corps of Royal Engineers consisted solely of officers whose ranks expanded from 73 in 1792 to 262 in 1813. The engineers commanded the Royal Military Artificers and Labourers composed of twelve companies of non-commissioned officers and enlisted men. The Ordnance Department deployed appropriate numbers of its engineers and artificers with armies and key fortresses. Engineers supervised the construction of siege-works, fortifications, roads, bridges, wharfs, and buildings, to name the more common projects. It was hazardous duty. Of the 102 who served in the Peninsula, 24 were killed in combat and 1 died from overwork.[28]

Britain's regular army was nearly all-volunteer. Regiments were responsible for filling their own ranks. Recruiting parties usually consisted of a lower ranking officer, a couple of sergeants, a few enlisted men, and a drummer boy to attract attention and stir passions. Recruiters were chosen for their striking appearances, charisma, and friendliness, less charitably as quick-talking con artists able to get dull-witted, able-bodied men befuddled with enough drink to take the king's shilling often deposited in an ale mug. That shilling soon disappeared as the recruiter cheerfully explained the custom whereby the recruit bought a round for his new mates. No sooner than 24 hours after the recruit took the king's shilling, the party presented him before a magistrate who read the articles of war pertaining to desertion and mutiny. At this point he could still back out if he paid back any money he had received plus 20 shillings to defray the cost of the time spent on him. Otherwise he swore an oath to the king and pocketed a bonus that by 1812 reached £18, 12 shillings, and 6 pence. Until the 1791 Catholic Relief Act, a recruit also had to swear that he was a Protestant; by dropping that requirement, the government eased the challenge for recruiting Catholics.[29]

Before 1807, a man enlisted for his healthy life and was only mustered out after the army deemed him infirm. Then Secretary at War William Windham established a system of three successive seven year periods of enlistments for infantry after which he could retire at half-pay. The periods for cavalry were ten years, seven years, and seven years, and for artillery twelve years, five years, and five years. Desertion rates fell with the new system. Psychologically a soldier could better endure army life with set periods when his enlistment expired and he could either reenlist or leave, rather than decades until the army got rid of him for being too feeble.

Table 1.1: British Army Numbers[30]

Year	Infantry	Cavalry	Total
1793	34,262	4,681	38,943
1794	70,570	14,527	85,097
1795	100,452	28,810	129,262
1804	119,751	16,729	136,480
1806	142,177	23,396	165,573
1809	183,223	27,391	210,614
1813	201,538	28,931	230,469

Keeping the ranks filled was an endless task. The British army lost 80,000 men in just the West Indies from 1794 to 1797; virtually all died from disease rather than battle.[31] Nonetheless, the British army swelled steadily from 38,945 men in 1793 to peak at 230,469 in 1813.

Throughout the war, the army kept one regular British or foreign soldier in the United Kingdom for each two it deployed overseas, and bolstered homeland defense with militia. For instance, in 1811, there were 45,501 infantry, 12,050 cavalry, 3,748 foot guards, 2,745 foreign infantry, 1,568 foreign cavalry, and 77,159 militia at home, and 99,735 infantry, 11,719 cavalry, 3,130 foot guards, 36,735 foreign infantry, and 2,136 foreign cavalry abroad. The attrition from death and desertion was typically devastating with losses of 19,019 British and 3,441 foreign troops.[32]

All able-bodied men from 16 to 45 years old were required to enroll in their local militia company.[33] A lord-lieutenant commanded each county's militia. The Home Secretary could ask each county to draft a quota of militia for the regulars. One could dodge the draft by paying a £100 fine or hiring a substitute. An Act in 1803 established the Army of Reserve Volunteers or Fencibles which was initially composed of 34,000 men in England, 6,000 in Scotland, and 10,000 in Ireland. Each battalion numbered 500 troops in 10 companies. Service lasted five years. Most of these battalions remained garrisoned in the British Isles. Their numbers peaked at 336,404 in 1808.[34] Their utility was more psychological than practical with virtually no chance that Napoleon could successfully invade Britain. Yet the reassuring presence of Fencibles backed by militia let civilian and military leaders stop looking fearfully over their shoulders and instead could focus on genuine threats and opportunities overseas.[35]

The army bolstered its ranks with foreign mercenaries. During 1793 and 1794 alone, Whitehall hired 40,000 troops, mostly from Hanover, Hesse-Cassel, Hesse-Darmstadt, Brunswick, and Baden. The need for foreign troops expanded with British military ambitions. Foreigners numbered one of ten men in 1804, and one of eight in 1813.[36] Most renowned was the King's German Legion of recruits mostly from German states overrun by Napoleon. The King's German Legion began during the British expedition to northern Germany from November 1805 to February 1806, when recruits swarmed hoping to help liberate their homelands from French rule. By 1812, the King's German Legion's strength peaked with 14,000 troops split among 8 regular battalions, 2 light infantry battalions, 5 cavalry regiments, and foot and horse artillery.[37] The Black Legion was the most notorious foreign unit. Frederich Wilhelm, Duke of Brunswick formed the Black Legion after

Austria's defeat in 1809. He led his men to the coast where a British flotilla sailed them to eventual service. The Brunswickers earned a horrid repute for looting, desertion, and rape.[38]

No matter their origin, Wellington had very mixed feelings about his soldiers. His infamous denigration of his men as 'the scum of the earth … who have enlisted for drink' was nearly as accurate as it was cruel.[39] The army offered miserable pay and conditions, seemingly endless spans of tedium broken by terror during an occasional battle, and a good chance of dying well before one's natural lifespan, most likely from disease rather than combat. Why would anyone join? Soldiering usually gave a man steady pay, food, clothing, shelter, companionship, and identity. In such a class-bound age, this was the best that most unskilled men born into poverty could hope for. Wearing the same uniform as tens of thousands of other men and being posted far from one's past also offered a good chance of escaping justice for crimes. However, soldiers accused of crimes rarely evaded punishment.

Discipline was harsh. Soldiers suffered floggings with a cat-of-nine-tails, a nine-stranded, lead-tipped whip, for breaking the rules, with the number of strokes rising with the crime's severity. Deserters could face a firing squad; mutineers almost invariably did. Most soldiers had mixed feelings about floggings. Private Benjamin Harris spoke for countless officers and men alike when he explained: 'I detest the sight of the lash but I am convinced that the British army can never go on without it.'[40] Eventually Wellington ordered his officers to treat their men less harshly. In March 1812, he issued these very astute instructions:

> It requires neither talents nor virtue … to govern by fear. Any fool can be a despot or tyrant … but to govern with gentleness requires wisdom as well as a just mind … he who governors solely by the principle of fear shall cease to govern the moment that fear is overcome by one of those who are under his tyranny.[41]

To varying degrees soldiers, no matter how well supplied, lived off the inhabited land. Although there were standing orders against looting, depending on circumstances an army sometimes strictly enforced and sometimes turned a blind eye to it. Regardless, troops frequently robbed peasants or merchants of food and other valuables. At times desperate armies competed to scour the countryside and cities for provisions. Commissary General Schaumann described a typical operation:

My duty was to clear the ground between us and the enemy of all victuals as quickly and as thoroughly as possible … I was given a detachment of hussars … with which I carried out raids. My people followed us with mules and empty sacks. When we reached a village we sent patrols to the left and right of it; then we would go forward, post sentries, and proceed to plunder the houses and barns … As a rule the owners had concealed their property badly; everywhere one could see from large damp patches on the walls that something had recently been walled up just there; or from hollow sounding places in the gardens that things had been buried.[42]

As for tactics, Britain's officer corps was split between the German and American schools. The German school emphasized massed troops moving slowly in line and unleashing volleys of musket fire followed by bayonet charges that ideally routed the enemy. Advocates were mostly veterans of the Seven Years War in Europe, and especially those who served as liaisons with the Prussian army. The American school was dominated by officers who fought in the French and Indian and American Revolutionary Wars. To fight in often wooded or broken terrain where cavalry were few, the British army adopted tactics that emphasized flexibility, speed, maneuver, and accurate shooting. Light infantry led advances and tried to encircle enemy troops and wear them down with sharpshooting as regular troops marched toward the enemy. The German school dominated British tactics during the first fifteen or so years from 1793. A series of farsighted officers including the Commander-in-chief Frederick Augustus, Duke of York, Adjutant General Major Kenneth Mackenzie, General John Moore, and Lieutenant Colonel David Dundas tried to develop light infantry tactics but failed to implement it for the entire army. It was Wellington who resolved the standoff between the two schools by combining them during his Peninsula campaign from 1808 to 1814.

Tactics are inseparable from technology. The standard infantry weapon was the 'Short Land Pattern' musket, affectionately known as the Brown Bess, with its 42in barrel and 75 caliber bore. Although soldiers were trained to load and fire at least three and ideally four rounds a minute, only light infantry were encouraged to aim carefully before pulling the trigger. Like all muskets, the Brown Bess was inaccurate so that even an aimed musket by a skilled marksman rarely hit its target beyond several score yards. Of the various attempts to access how accurate muskets were in battle, perhaps the conclusion that only about one of twenty shots hit a man a hundred yards off comes the closest to the mark.[43]

Riflemen were the British army's most important innovation during this era. The first rifle-armed battalion was the 60th Royal America's fifth battalion, established in 1797. During the 1799 Flanders campaign, York formed the Experimental Rifle Corps composed of the rifle companies of fifteen regiments. In 1801, the battalion was redesignated the 95th foot, with a second battalion formed in 1805 and a third in 1809. Riflemen wore green coats and either green or gray trousers, and carried Baker Rifles. The first and second light infantry battalions of the King's German Legion were also armed with rifles. A rifle battalion rarely deployed as one, but instead its companies were dispersed by one or two to each brigade.

The limited introduction of rifles did not decisively affect the art of war. Although in the hands of a skilled marksman, a rifle shot several times further and deadlier than a musket, it could not mount a bayonet and took twice as long to load. Charging enemy infantry or cavalry could destroy riflemen as they tried to reload in an open field. General Moore found a way to lessen this vulnerability. In 1803, he received Whitehall's permission to form what became known as the Light Division, which included the 95th Rifle Regiment, the 43rd and 52nd British Light Infantry regiments, the 1st and 3rd Cazadores or Light Portuguese regiments, the 14th and 16th Light Dragoons, and the 1st Hussars, whose combined arms protected one another. The Light Brigade would win a series of laurels in the Iberian Peninsula from 1808 to 1814. The French had no equivalent.

Regardless of the weapons they carried, the best defense was for troops to deploy along hilltops and ridgelines or behind natural or manmade barriers in long lines, two or three deep that concentrated rapid fire against an advancing enemy. Wellington mastered this tactic. He always tried to shelter his troops from enemy fire, usually on the reverse slope of a ridge beyond sight of the enemy's cannons. They would emerge in the open only when enemy attackers neared. The redcoats would fire volleys then often launch a bayonet charge. When enemy cavalry threatened to attack, battalions formed tight, hollow squares bristling hedgehog-like with bayoneted muskets, with front ranks kneeling, backed by at least two other standing ranks. The officers, color guard, and musicians were in the square's center. Cavalry rarely broke infantry deployed in squares.

As for attacks, the debate throughout the era was the relative efficacy of troops advancing in long lines or dense columns. Each had an advantage and disadvantage. Obviously, the longer the line, the more muskets and bayonets that could be leveled toward the enemy. The trouble was that the longer a line, the more it tended to unravel as it advanced over uneven or obstacle-strewn ground. The more concentrated the troops, the less firepower but the greater speed and mass that they could hurl against the enemy. Regardless of whether they attacked in column or line, the British along with most other armies emulated the French tactic of deploying skirmishers to wear down enemy troops by picking them off and provoking them into squandering their ammunition. The British gained the skirmishing edge after deploying large numbers of riflemen, protected by light infantry armed with bayoneted muskets, in the Peninsula.

Commanders usually anchored their flanks with cavalry and kept some in reserve either to exploit a breakthrough by their own troops or to drive off an enemy breakthrough. If the initial charge was repelled and pursued by French cavalry, the reserve could gallop to the rescue and ideally scatter the enemy. On marches, cavalry covered the advances and withdrawals of the infantry, artillery, and baggage train. Cavalry detachments scouted for the enemy's movements and positions, and, ideally got close enough to identify units and count troops or capture stray soldiers or couriers for interrogation. Wellington condemned British cavalry for being 'so inferior to the French from want of order' and 'galloping at everything and ... galloping back as ... fast. They never consider their situation, never think of manoevering before an enemy.' He struggled to get his cavalry commanders 'to charge in two lines, of which one should be in reserve; if obliged to charge in one line, part of the line, at least one-third, should be ordered beforehand to pull up, and form in the second line as soon as the charge should be given, and the enemy has broken and retired.'[44]

Artillery batteries were generally dispersed along the line for defense and then shifted to counter the enemy's attacks, or concentrated to pound the swath of the enemy line where the infantry was going to attack. Wellington and most commanders discouraged their gunners from firing at enemy batteries since they rarely scored enough direct hits to cause significant damage. Gunners fired solid shot at distant targets like fortifications or massed troops. When enemy troops advanced within a couple hundred yards, gunners switched to firing either light (85 1½oz) or heavy (41 3½oz) case shot packed into canisters for a 6-pounder cannon. In 1804, British gunners first began firing shrapnel shells that exploded into fragments and was named after its inventor, Henry Shrapnel. A 6-pounder had an effective range of 628yd.

An army at once reflects and shapes its national character. French officer Thomas Robert Bugeaud vividly recalled a typical French attack in column against a British line:

The men became excited, called out to one another, and increased the speed of their march; the column became a little confused. The English remained silent with ordered arms, and from their steadiness appeared to be a long red wall … Very soon we got nearer, crying 'Vive l'Empereur! En avant! A la baionnette!' Shakos were raised on the muzzles of muskets, the march became a run, the ranks fell into confusion, the agitation became a tumult; shot were fired as we advanced. The English line remained silent … and it appeared to ignore the storm that was about to break … We all felt that … this fire, held for so long, would be very unpleasant when it came. Our ardour cooled … At this moment … the enemy's steady concentrated volleys swept our ranks; decimated, we turned … Three formidable cheers broke the silence of our opponents; at the third they were on us, pushing our disorganized flight.[45]

The Royal Navy was as much of a bureaucratic maze as the army.[46] The Admiralty Board of seven commissioners with the First Lord as president was in overall charge. During wartime, the First Lord worked with the prime minister and other key ministers to develop and implement strategy. Although the First Lord was a Cabinet minister, he reigned over rather than ruled a feudal-like realm of autonomous bureaucracies. Principal Officers headed the divisions of Controller, Surveyor, Treasurer, Victualling, Storekeeper, and Clerk of Acts. The ten-man Navy Board supplied and manned warships, and managed the Royal Dockyards at Portsmouth, Plymouth, Sheerness, and Chatham in England, and Gibraltar, Halifax, and Antigua overseas, along with dockyards at Malta, Minorca, and Lisbon. The Victualling Board provided food and drink. The Commissioners for Sick and Wounded Seamen largely lived up to this duty. The Ordnance Board supplied cannons and munitions to the navy as well as the army. Parliament annually debated and approved the navy's budget known as the Naval Estimate, which was often supplemented during wartime as circumstances demanded.

Fleets were organized into van, center, and rear divisions or squadrons with white, red, or blue pennants streaming from the masts of each squadron's vessels. A commander might also establish a squadron of shallow-draft vessels for close shore operations or a squadron of the fastest vessels for patrol, pursuit, or conveying messages. An admiral's rank was recognizable by which mast carried it, with a full admiral's on the main, a vice admiral's on the fore, and a rear admiral's on the mizzen.

Horatio Nelson quipped, 'We all rise by deaths.'[47] This was an exaggeration. Death from battle or disease was just one way to empty berths. An analysis of the fate of 443 officers who served from 1720 and 1750, found 281 who retired honorably, along with 82 who died from natural causes, 38 who were dismissed or disgraced by court marital, 17 who were killed in action, 15 who drowned, 6 who died from other causes such as duels and murders, and 4 who committed suicide.[48]

Seniority largely determined promotions for officers by the Admiralty and non-commissioned warrant officers by the Navy Board. At times, the navy did award extraordinary merit. An especially enterprising, courageous, and successful captain could be promoted over the ranks of his lessers. But, more frequently, connections or bribes propelled otherwise mediocre men upward. As in the army, some unscrupulous officers pocketed the pay of non-existent sailors on their crew lists. Officers formed cliques to influence decisions of promotion and assignment. Each clique was organized into a patron-protégée hierarchy topped by a senior officer renowned for both his naval service and political connections.

Regardless of whether a promotion was earned or bought, it did not necessarily lead to command. The First Lord could shuffle senior officers in a way that gave fleets to the most competent and shore commands to their lessers. Captain Edward Pelham Brenton expressed the delicate balance between political and military interests in determining these decisions:

I contend that the executive power must ever have the uncontrolled right of selecting its officers; and if it has not that right, it is no longer a government. On the alleged principle of seniority, the command of our armies or fleets would necessarily fall into the hands of imbecility; Nelson never would have commanded at Trafalgar, nor would Collingwood have fought by his side. Promotion by seniority is one thing, selection for command is another.[49]

Admiral John Jervis, Earl of Saint Vincent, expressed this even more succinctly: 'Those who are responsible for measures have a right to choose their men.'[50]

Most officers began as midshipmen, usually as teenagers but sometimes even younger. What followed were years of apprenticeship in how to become a naval officer. This included not just the hard power skills of navigation and gunnery, but also the soft power skills of leadership, of which dignity, erudition, and education were considered essential elements. Who became midshipmen? Each boy's path was unique, but there were some well-worn gangplanks. The most common was for economically hard-pressed families to rid themselves of an excess son. Some boys, starry-eyed from hearing adventurous tales of the sea or restless from drudgery or worse at home, begged reluctant fathers to secure them a berth; Nelson was one of these boys. A captain could have up to four midshipmen for every hundred crewmen. The Royal Navy occasionally accepted officers from four other sources. One was graduates from the Royal Naval College at Portsmouth or Burney's Academy at Gosport, although most captains spurned those who had learned from books rather than hard experience. Another was for a merchant marine officer to apply. Finally, an extraordinary seaman might make his way up first the warrant and then officer ranks. Regardless of his background, each applicant had to pass the examining board for lieutenants. He then joined the officer pool and awaited being hooked by a needy captain. During peacetime the pool expanded with officers of all ranks on half-pay.

A virtuous cycle of soft and hard power explains the Royal Navy's superiority not just during the Age of Revolution and Napoleon but for centuries. Leadership was the key element. During the 1790s, an older generation of brilliant naval commanders such as Richard Howe, John Jervis, George Rodney, and Samuel Hood passed the torch to an even more brilliant younger generation such as Nelson, Edward Pellew, Thomas Cochrane, William Sidney Smith, and Cuthbert Collingwood. The French Revolution widened the chasm between the qualities of British and French naval officers. Hundreds of aristocratic French officers fled into exile; hundreds more who did not escape were cashiered or guillotined. Young, unskilled, inexperienced men filled their ranks and upheld the French navy's culture of timidity.

The soft power of leadership sailed aboard the hard power of sheer numbers. The different sizes of their navies gave the British and French opposing views of battle. With twice as many warships, the British confidently prowled the seas for combats of annihilation. With half as many warships, the French did whatever they could to avoid battle unless the odds overwhelmingly favored them. Different strategies determined different tactics. The British tended to aim low with solid shot at the enemy vessel's waterline in hopes of sinking it or slowing it so they could capture it. The French tended to aim high with chain and dumbbell shot at the enemy vessel's masts and rigging in hopes of crippling it so that they could sail to safety. Finally, the British preferred sailing within 500yd and bombarding the enemy with their array of carronades and longer range guns. The French tried to keep 2,000yd of open sea between themselves and the enemy to make it all the easier to sail to safety. Regardless, when closing for battle, captains always sought to maneuver their vessels to gain the weather gauge or get upwind of the enemy.

Standard battle tactics remained constant for several centuries after ships began mounting cannons. Each fleet sailed single file toward the other with a hundred or so yards between each vessel. Lead vessels generally sustained the most damage. As the lines passed each other the cannon crews fired as long as they viewed an enemy vessel through their gun ports. This tactic was codified when, in 1691, the Admiralty issued the Permanent Fighting Instructions.

A mystery lingers over which came first, the practice or principle of breaking the enemy line by sailing directly toward it.[51] Admiral George Rodney definitely tried to revolutionize naval tactics on April 17, 1780. First, he compacted his line to less than a hundred yards between vessels. As his fleet sailed past Admiral Luc Urbain du Bouexic, comte de Guichen's fleet near Dominica, he ordered his captains to cut toward the strung out French ships. This was a daring and potentially disastrous act. The British vessels were exposed to steady and closer fire until they traversed the French line and fired broadsides point blank at the front or rear of an enemy vessel on either side. Unfortunately, his captains did not understand that Rodney wanted each to square off with a French vessel or two, and instead remained bound by the Standing Instructions. Despite the confusion, Rodney's fleet drove off the French and captured three vessels.

Rodney may have received an unlikely inspiration for his innovation. John Clerk was an Admiralty official who had never been to sea but studied naval history. He advocated the tactic of 'breaking the line' in his manuscript, 'An Inquiry into Naval Tactics,' which he claimed Rodney took with him when he sailed from Britain to the West Indies in January 1780. Rodney and his colleagues denied ever reading the manuscript. After revisions, Clerk's book was published in 1782. The *Naval Chronicle* credited Clerk with the new tactic of forcing 'an enemy's fleet to close engagement, whatever efforts he may make to avoid it, and the breaking through his line of battle and cutting off one division of his fleet from another, so as to prevent the enemy from being able to extricate himself.'[52]

Regardless of where he got the idea, Rodney had two years to think about and discuss the new tactics with his captains before his next big battle. On April 14, 1782, after a 20-day chase his 36 warships closed with 34 French warships led by Admiral François Joseph Paul, Count de Grasse off a cluster of small islands known as the Saints near Guadeloupe and Dominica. This time his captains perfectly executed the tactic, severed the enemy line, and each mauled an enemy vessel or two.

The Royal Navy officially abolished the Permanent Fighting Instructions in 1790. Henceforth, naval commanders could fight battles as they thought best without fear that they could be court-martialed for any deviance from the Instructions. An increasingly sophisticated flag system that let fleet commanders carefully manage their battles accompanied the new tactics. The first step came in 1776, with Richard Howe's simplified flag system for his own fleet. Other admirals and captains adapted Howe's system, including Rodney who wielded it at the battle of the Saints. Admiral Richard Kempenfelt introduced a more complex nine-flag system in 1782. As First Lord of the Admiralty from 1783 to 1788, Howe initiated an array of innovations, of which the most profound was his Signal Book for Ships of War. He cut the number of flags to ten, numbered them from zero to nine, and hoisted them four at a time. This expanded the range of potential messages to an extraordinary 9,999. Admiral Home Popham elaborated the system in 1803, with his book, *Telegraphic Signals or Marine Vocabulary*.[53]

Prolonged tedious blockades were far more common than battles. There were two blockade strategies. A 'close blockade' bottled up the enemy in port by massing warships just beyond cannon shot. For this very reason, Nelson preferred a 'distant blockade' that enticed the enemy to sea and battle; frigates kept watch while the fleet remained beyond the horizon, either riding the waves or in port. A distant blockade's disadvantage was that an enemy fleet might sail, brush aside the frigates, evade the fleet, and strike a vulnerable spot, like Bonaparte's armada did in escaping from Toulon to capture Malta and invade Egypt in 1798.

Ships were 'rated' by their number of cannons. First rates were 3-deckers with 100 to 120 guns and 837-men crews; second rates 2-deckers with 90 to 99 guns and 738-men crews; third rates 2-deckers with 64, 74, or 80 guns and 590-men crews; fourth-rates with 50 to 60 guns and 343-men crews; fifth rates with 32 to 44 guns and 215-men crews; and sixth rates with 20 to 30 guns and 155-men crews. Ships with fewer than 20 guns were unrated, and included brigs, sloops, snows, and schooners with different configurations of masts, sails, and guns.[54] Vessels with 50 or more cannons were ships-of-the-line. The most common of these were 74-gun warships They were usually about 170ft or so long, 45ft or so wide, held up to 1,700 tons, and carried up to 700 men. Sleek and fast-moving frigates with 20 to 40 or so guns were any navy's work-horses. They ranged far ahead of fleets to scout the ocean and report back. They caught up to merchant vessels, checked their papers, and captured them if they were of enemy origin or sailing to or from enemy ports. They sought and fought enemy frigates. Yet they usually observed rather than joined battles between ships-of-the-line.

Cannons were rated by the weight of the balls that they fired. Ships-of-the-line usually carried 32-pounder guns on the lower deck and 24-pounder or 18-pounder guns on the upper deck. Shortly after 1779 when they were invented, snub-nosed 32-pounders called carronades began bristling upper gun decks. What carronades lacked in their range of about 500yd, they made up for with destructive power, the source of their nickname, 'smashers.' The need to near an enemy warship to unleash a carronade barrage accelerated adaptation of the new breaking the line tactic. Like muskets, cannons were loaded with cartridges in which a standard amount of gunpowder was packed into a standard sized sack. The cartridge was rammed in first, followed by the shot, and finally a wad of cloth to hold the load in place. Gunners aimed the largest iron balls to smash enemy hulls, the chained or dumbbell balls to whirl against enemy rigging and masts, and the small clusters of grape or canister balls for shredding enemy sailors and marines. Any of these shots could unleash deadly sprays of splinters.

Once ships closed within 50yd of each other, musket-armed sharpshooters added to the carnage. On rare occasions, ships slammed into each other and sailors hurled grappling hooks at the end of ropes to lock them together. Then one side's marines and sailors armed with pistols, muskets, swords, axes, and spears swarmed onto the enemy ship and cut down the defenders. The easiest prey for a boarding party was a ship crippled from toppled masts or seawater pouring through a shattered hull as dead and dying men littered the decks.

An alarming report circulated through Whitehall in 1793 just as Britain was entering what would become more than two decades of warfare. The Commissioners of Woods and Forests warned that 'such is the present state of the growing timber, and the prospect of future supply, that this country will in all probability experience a fatal want of great oak timber and become dependent on other powers for their means of supporting her navy.'[55] The Royal Navy was increasingly dependent on foreign sources of raw materials to build its vessels. British shipbuilders were importing oak beams and planks from Russia, Lithuania, and Poland, and tall pines for masts, spruce for spars, and pitch to seal cracks from Scandinavia and Canada; most hemp woven into rope was grown in the British Isles.

The reason for the shortages and foreign dependence was simple.[56] For centuries the British had decimated their forests to meet ship, building, cooking, and heating demands. A load of timber took up 50 cubic feet. The Royal Navy alone annually demanded an average 60,000 loads or 40,000 full-grown trees. The merchant shipbuilding industry annually consumed another 72,500 loads. One 74-gun warship devoured 3,000 loads of timber clear-cut from 57 acres of forest. Oak was the most cherished and thus fastest dwindling tree. Thick, curved oak beams formed the ship's skeleton, more slender oak planks formed the sides, and thin oak slabs formed the flooring.[57]

Scarcity bred ingenuity. From 1783, the Royal Navy had thin copper sheets nailed to the hulls of all vessels to prevent rotting by burrowing sea worms or slowing by barnacles and seaweeds. Consequently, British warships tended to move faster and last longer than their rivals. The copper's initial expense paid for itself many times. In 1791, the Society for the Improvement of Naval Architecture was founded to promote more efficient shipbuilding designs and materials. Experiments were conducted to determine a vessel's speed under different arrangements of sails and rigging with the best results adapted by the navy. Innovations resulted in British warship construction costs being 25 percent cheaper than French costs.[58]

The Royal Navy also led the world in navigation techniques. How far one headed north or south along longitude was relatively easy to determine by measuring the sun's relationship to one's position. But determining just where one was east or west along latitude was mostly a calculated guess until 1773, when Parliament awarded John Harrison £8,000 for his device, the chronometer, which accurately measured this. The result was a revolution that gave the Royal Navy a critical advantage until Britain's enemies got their hands on their own chronometers.[59]

Yet, despite the Royal Navy's advantages in leadership, strategy, tactics, seamanship, ship numbers, gunnery, and navigation, it was unprepared for war when the king declared it in April 1793. Although the navy officially counted 304 warships, less than half, 135 warships, were operational, including 26 ships-of-the-line, 32 frigates, 34 sloops, and 43 smaller vessels. Anchored in port for lack of repairs and/or sailors were another 169 warships, including 87 ships-of-the-line, 29 frigates, and 53 sloops or smaller vessels.[60]

The good news was that France's navy was even less well prepared and had far fewer warships. Throughout the war, the Royal Navy would steadily expand its numbers through shipbuilding and the capture of French and other foreign warships, thus widening the power gap with France.

Table 1.2: British and French Naval Power[61]

	British Navy			French Navy		
	Ships-of-the-Line	*Frigates*	*Total*	*Ships-of-the-Line*	*Frigates*	*Total*
1789	147	125	272	71	74	145
1793	131	125	256	63	60	123
1799	159	132	291	49	54	103
1803	120	137	257	40	37	77
1810	185	165	350	56	44	100
1812	180	155	335	72	46	118

A lack of sailors was a critical reason why so many vessels were unready for war. Filling hammocks aboard ship was a constant struggle as desertion, disease, discharge, and, less commonly, combat, emptied them. Desertion was rife, with an average one in twelve sailors annually trying to escape at some port. As for those who died at sea, they were sown with a cannon ball inside their hammocks and, after a chaplain muttered a blessing, dropped over the side into the watery void. Relatively few sailors grew old in the service; more than eight of ten ordinary seamen were less than 25 years old.

Few men joined the Royal Navy for the amenities. Sailors earned a fraction and suffered far more privations than they would aboard a merchant ship or privateer. The navy monthly owed ordinary seamen 19 shillings and able seamen 24 shillings, rates that had not risen since 1665! Even then sixpence was deducted for Greenwich Hospital and a shilling for the Chatham Chest retirement fund. Sea months lasted twenty-eight days or a moon's cycle. Pay, however, was often months and even years in arrears. Only prize money supplemented a sailor's pay and that was sporadic at best and non-existent for most warships. The Admiralty Court determined whether a captured vessel was a proper prize of war. If so, the value of the vessel and its cargo was divvied up among the government, captain, officers, and sailors, with the latter splitting a quarter of the total. The free room and board was miserable. Privacy was non-existent. Sleeping sailors were sardined in hammocks below decks. Three times daily they choked down stale, salty, or rotten rations and foul water. Yet, despite these prison-like conditions, genuine mutinies whereby sailors took over a ship, got rid of the officers, and sailed to a foreign port were rare. The mass 'mutinies' of 1797 that erupted at the Spithead fleet then spread to other fleet were unprecedented, never repeated, and are better understood as labor strikes.[62]

Given the service's unpopularity, the Royal Navy was not terribly finicky about those who volunteered. It took any able-bodied man, including debtors and smugglers. Officially, the navy barred those accused of having committed capital offenses. Of course, this was an era innocent of the means to conduct proper background checks. Unfortunately, volunteers did not fill all the empty berths. To make up the difference, the navy 'pressed' or essentially forced men into the service. The Impress Service was in charge of impressment. Britain's counties were designated districts, each headed by a captain, usually with his headquarters at a wharf-front inn. The captain commanded a score or so tough sailors whose job was to shanghai other sailors into the navy. During wartime about one of two sailors was dragged, often literally kicking and screaming, into the Royal Navy. Any working class man loitering ashore was considered fair game. To escape the press gangs, one could apply for a certificate of exemption and receive one in return for proof that one was already employed in government service on sea or land, or on a privateer. Generally, the Royal Navy could not impress sailors from British commercial vessels at sea. The exemption was a British subject on a foreign vessel. Throughout this era, His Majesty's warships would fire a shot across the bow of merchant vessels and send a marine detachment aboard to scrutinize each seaman's papers. Those who could not prove that they were not British could be forced into the Royal Navy at bayonet point. Impressments at sea soured relations with the United States through the era, and eventually provoked America's war declaration against Britain in June 1812.

On the era's eve, the Royal Navy resolved a major reason for the high attrition rate. Scurvy was a debilitating and even deadly disease caused by the body's lack of Vitamin C. It sapped body strength, rotted gums, and ate away vital organs. The breakthrough in treating scurvy came in 1780 when Admiral Rodney took Dr Gilbert Blane to sea as his personal physician. Blane acted on anecdotes that lemons cured scurvy by making them part of each man's daily ration. This diet eliminated scurvy's usual annual death rate from one in seven to just one death on Rodney's flagship in four months. Although Blane published articles on the effects of lemons and other citrus fruits on combating scurvy, the navy resisted any proposed reforms for another dozen years. The turning point came in 1793, when George III named Blane the Commissioner for Sick and Hurt. It then took Blane until 1795, to talk the Admiralty Board into requiring the infusion of lemon juice into the daily rum ration.[63]

Mercifully, Winston's Churchill's grumpy dismissal of navy life as little more than 'rum, sodomy, and the lash' was a caricature. Although seamen did enjoy a daily tot or two of rum, the other practices rarely occurred. Nonetheless, of the twenty offenses punishable by death, sodomy along with murder were the most common convictions. Executions, however, were as rare as the lash was common. A man's naked back could be whipped with a lead-tipped cat-of-nine-tails up to 500 times for a variety of offenses including stealing, drunkenness, slacking, defying, buggering, fighting, and lying. The worst mass punishments came in 1797 when thirty-six ring-leaders of the mutiny of the Nore fleet swung from yardarms.[64]

Officers were not immune from the navy's justice system, such as it was. A court martial included the second-in-command, who presided, and a jury of from five to thirteen officers of the vessel, flotilla, or port in which the alleged crime took place. The court appointed an officer to act as the prosecutor. The accused could ask an officer to act as his lawyer. The Articles of War was their guide. The most notorious trial in the Royal Navy's history was that of Admiral John Byng, who was, on March 14, 1757, executed by firing squad to, in Voltaire's memorable phrase, 'to encourage the others.'[65] What did Byng do to deserve that fate? He led his fleet from Gibraltar with orders to relieve the British garrison at Port Mahon, Minorca, besieged by a French army. A French fleet of equal numbers of ships and guns blocked and battered Byng's fleet on May 20, 1756. Byng withdrew his fleet to Gibraltar for repairs. The French captured Port Mahon on June 29. The Admiralty ordered Byng court-martialed for cowardice. The court acquitted him of physical cowardice, but convicted him of 'moral cowardice.'[66]

Tedium rather than punishment was a sailor's near constant companion. The day was divided into six 4-hour watches, in which sailors alternated 4 hours of duty with 4 hours of leisure. To keep track of time a watchman rang a bell and turned a half hour glass when the last grain drained from the top to the bottom. There was usually plenty to do. One daily duty was pumping out seawater that seeped in. Cleanliness was another. Sailors scoured the decks. Vinegar was used as a disinfectant. Much time was spent patching tattered sails, splicing frayed ropes, or catching rats. Sailors were trained to perform virtually all the vessel's duties, including clambering up the rigging to adjust or furl the sails in the worst weather or battle. They daily practiced gunnery. The British rate of cannon fire was two to three times that of the French, one crucial reason why they won virtually all the battles between them.[67] Usually the men were organized into eight-man messes that gathered to eat or just socialize together around a table lowered from the ceiling and set between two guns. They slept sausaged in hammocks suspended from hooks side by side. During the day, each man took down his hammock and wrapped his small sea chest packed with other personal effects within it. Dress varied according to rank and duty. Officers wore bicorne black hats and dark-blue coats with white facings over white shirts and knee breeches. Marines wore red jackets with white facings over white shirts and knee breeches. There was no uniform for sailors, who wore whatever clothing they brought with them or bought at some port.

Leadership is the critical element in transforming hard military power into victories or defeats. In a stunning quirk of history, Britain's greatest land and sea military titans, Wellington and Nelson, emerged when they were most desperately needed.

During his life's first quarter century, Arthur Wellesley gave little evidence that he would eventually become one of history's greatest generals.[68] He was born in 1769 as the third of five surviving sons and a daughter to a noble, wealthy, and Anglican family in Trim, Ireland. He seemed little qualified to take advantage of his family's wealth and political power, first in Dublin and later in London. By his own admission, Wellesley was 'a dreamy, idle, and shy lad,' an indifferent student whose only skill was playing the violin.[69] He was a classic middle child lost in the family shuffle, exacerbated by his father's death when he was 15 and his emotionally cold and self-obsessed mother. Indeed, his mother dismissed him as an 'ugly boy' who was 'food for powder and nothing more.'[70] And so, starting when Wellesley was 18, his oldest brother Richard bought him the first of ever higher army officer ranks and sent him to Eton and later to the military academy at Angers, France. After winning a seat in Ireland's parliament in 1790, he seemed to favor a political rather than army career. He lurched back to the military after war erupted between Britain and France in February 1793.

He first experienced war as the 33rd Regiment's 25-year-old lieutenant colonel in the Flanders campaign in 1794. He recalled his first campaign as an eye-opening education in 'what one ought not to do, and that is always something.'[71] Other than that, he saw little fighting beyond a skirmish at Boxtel on September 1794. In all, it was a tedious rather than traumatic introduction to war. Wellesley mastered the strategic, tactical, logistical, diplomatic, and moral dimensions of the art of military power during his five years fighting in India, honed his art during five years fighting on the Peninsula, and brought his art to perfection at Waterloo.

The background of the era's greatest sea captain could not have differed more from that of its greatest general.[72] In 1758, Horatio Nelson became the sixth child and fifth son of a minister in the town of Burham Thorpe near the North Sea in the county of Norfolk. After attending grammar school, he went to sea as a midshipman in 1770, when he was only 12 years old. The highlights of his apprenticeship included an exploration voyage to the Arctic and a journey to India. Amidst America's War for Independence, Nelson passed the exam to become a second lieutenant in April 1777, sailed to the West Indies, was promoted to first lieutenant in September 1778, received command of his first ship, the brig *Badger* in December 1778, and was promoted to captain of the 20-gun *Hinchinbrook* in June 1779. He first experienced combat when he led longboats packed with marines and sailors up Nicaragua's San Juan River to besiege Fort San Juan. The expedition failed and Nelson nearly died of yellow fever. After a year's recuperation at home, he hoisted his pennant atop the 28-gun *Albemarle* in August 1781, and spent most of the next two years protecting convoys; his two notable actions were to evade four French warships off Boston and to join his frigate with another in bombarding a French fort on Turk's Island in the Bahamas. He was transferred to command the 28-gun *Boreas* in March 1784. After Britain signed peace treaties with the United States, France, Spain, and the Netherlands, Whitehall steadily cutback the army and navy; Nelson was shelved ashore on half-pay for five years starting in 1787. The looming shadow of war with France brought Nelson back to sea. In February 1792, he received command of the 64-gun *Agamemnon*. Over the next dozen years, he steadily advanced up the ranks and achieved renown for his battles at sea and on land.

What manner of commander was Nelson? His vessels were renowned for their cleanliness and order. He was a harsh disciplinarian who was quick to have miscreants lashed for minor offenses. Of course, what mattered most is how he fought. What became known as 'the Nelson touch' was his charismatic power to inspire others to emulate his own reckless courage and ruthless, killer instinct. One sentence captures his approach to war: 'When there is a doubt, fight, and you are sure to be right.'[73] He understood the relationship between military and diplomatic power: 'A fleet of British ships of war are the best negotiators in Europe; they always speak to be understood, and generally gain their point.'[74] He also understood that the nature of warfare was changing and he sought to lead that revolution at sea. It was 'annihilation that the country wants, and not merely a splendid victory ... Numbers only can annihilate.'[75] Admiral John Jervis, Earl of Saint Vincent unabashedly admired Nelson, insisting that 'a more able or enterprising officer does not exist.' Yet Jervis was not blind to Nelson's weaknesses: 'The commodore is the best fellow in the world to conduct the naval part; but his zeal does now and then (not often) outrun his discretion.'[76] But it was Nelson's 'zeal' that won Britain decisive victories at Cape Saint Vincent in February 1797 as a subordinate captain, and the Nile in August 1798, Copenhagen in April 1801, and Trafalgar in October 1805 as a fleet commander.

Truly great national leaders like Wellington and Nelson decisively rescue or transform their countries for the better. They do so in the face of seemingly overwhelming challenges that their lessers are incapable of surmounting. Governments can do little to influence those rare perfect marriages of nature and nurture or character and opportunity that produce great leaders. At best, governments can insist that merit determines advancement within and beyond the state. The French revolutionary policy of 'careers open to all talents' offered Britain a model to emulate and one genius who emerged to soar above all others to overcome.

Chapter 2

Toulon, 1793

What an event this has been for Lord Hood; such a one as History cannot prove its equal; that the strongest place in Europe and twenty-two sail of the line should be given up without firing a shot.

Horatio Nelson

The British scored only one significant victory in 1793, and it was limited by the man who eventually became Britain's nemesis, Napoleon Bonaparte.[1] Admiral Samuel Hood commanded the Mediterranean fleet headquartered at Gibraltar. On June 27, Hood sailed eastward aboard his flagship, the 100-gun *Victory*, with 17 other ships-of-the-line, 17 frigates, and smaller warships to blockade Toulon, France's chief naval port in the Mediterranean Sea. The fleet anchored just beyond cannon-shot of Toulon on July 16. Over the next month, Hood's fleet was reinforced by four 74-gun ships-of-the-line, dispatched courtesy of King Ferdinand IV of Naples and Sicily. Although he committed no warships, King Victor Amadeus III of Piedmont and Sardinia sent word that he had opened his ports to the Royal Navy.[2]

Blockade was tedious duty, with day after day rolling with the swells as the men awaited something to happen. This gives officers and sailors alike plenty of time to mull just why they were there and often wish they were elsewhere. Captain Horatio Nelson, then commanding the 64-gun *Agamemnon*, expressed such sentiments in a letter to his wife Fanny: 'I can hardly think the war can last for what are we at war about?'[3]

Meanwhile, extraordinary events unfolded across France that eventually transformed the blockade into an occupation. On June 2, the radical Jacobin party overthrew the moderate Girondin party and seized power. France's government was composed of the 12-man executive Committee of Safety chaired by Maximilien Robespierre, and the legislature then called the Convention. The Jacobins launched the 'terror' that imprisoned or executed thousands of Girondins whose ranks included federalists, who wanted a republic with decentralized power, and royalists, who wanted a constitutional monarchy. In July, the Girondins revolted against the Jacobins and took power in Lyon, Avignon, Aix-en-Provence, Marseille, and Toulon. In August, the Jacobins sent an army led by General Jean François Carteaux down the Rhone River valley to crush the rebels and restore Jacobin rule. Carteaux detached troops to besiege Lyon, and recapture Avignon on July 27, Aix-en-Provence on August 21, and Marseille on August 25.[4]

Just two days before Marseilles fell, its Girondin government sent a delegation to Hood to ask for aid. Talks ended with word that Carteaux's army had captured Marseille and was massacring the defenders. On August 25, Hood sent Lieutenant Edward Cooke, who spoke French fluently, and an escort ashore under a truce flag to meet Toulon's government and request that they render the port in return for the Royal Navy's protection. The Girondins readily agreed, but needed three days to talk the French fleet's captains into capitulating and squeezing their ships in the inner harbor to let the allied fleet anchor in the Great Road or outer harbor.

Hood assembled a force of 1,250 marines and sailors commanded by Captain Keith Elphinstone, and sent them ashore on August 28. Elphinstone deployed his men in the half-dozen forts crowning the surrounding hills. Of them, the most important was Fort Malgue with its 48 cannons overlooking the Great Road. As the British took over Toulon, Spanish Admiral Juan de Langara's fleet of 24 ships-of-the-line arrived. Packed aboard Langara's warships were 3,000 troops commanded by General Frederico Gravina. These troops joined the British and Girondin troops ashore in defending Toulon.

The allies would need thousands more troops to offset the army that Carteaux was massing to retake Toulon. Hood dispatched Nelson first to Oneglia, on Liguria's coast, where he sent a letter to King Victor Amadeus at Turin, informing him that the allies had taken Toulon, and asking him to supply 4,000 troops. Nelson then sailed to Naples to deliver the same message to Ambassador William Hamilton, who requested 6,000 troops from Ferdinand IV. Nelson wrote Fanny:

> I should have liked to have stayed one day longer with the fleet, when they entered the harbor, but service could not be neglected for any private gratification … What an event this has been for Lord Hood; such a one as History cannot prove its equal; that the strongest place in Europe and twenty-two sail of the line should be given up without firing a shot.[5]

Nelson accomplished his missions. Victor Amadeus and Ferdinand eventually sent 800 and 4,000 troops, respectively.

Meanwhile, on August 30, a report arrived that the advanced guard of Carteaux's army had reached Ollioules, just 4 miles northwest of Toulon. Elphinstone led 300 British and 300 Spanish troops to retake the village and rout the French. Although each side suffered only a dozen or so casualties, one among the French would change the course of history. Major Eleazar Dommartin, the French army's artillery commander, was seriously wounded and would need to be replaced.

Elphinstone withdrew his troops back into Toulon's defenses as Carteaux's main army arrived on September 7, and the French general setup his headquarters at Ollioules. Each French republican army had both a general and a political commissar: Antoine Christophe Salicetti oversaw Carteaux who commanded the troops. Salicetti was good friends with a young artillery captain named Napoleon Bonaparte, who reached the siege lines on September 16. Salicetti named Bonaparte the army's artillery chief and asked him to devise a plan for taking Toulon.

Bonaparte toured the lines and carefully observed the dozen or so enemy forts capping the tall hills and ridges around Toulon. He swiftly concluded that the keys were Fort La Malgue and Fort Mulgrave commanding respectively the approaches to the eastern and western horns embracing the inner harbor. Beyond Fort Mulgrave at the twin tips of the western horn were Forts l'Aiguillette and Balguier. Beyond Fort La Malgue halfway down the eastern horn facing the outer Road was Fort Saint Louis. Bonaparte explained which fort was the ultimate objective: 'The moment that we are masters of L'Eguilette, we will force the enemy to evacuate the two anchorages, then we will direct our attacks on the redoubt the closest before Toulon's arsenal.' The effort to take first Fort Mulgrave then Forts L'Eguilette and Balguier would be masked by deploying troops near the other forts on the perimeter, especially Fort Malgue.[6]

Carteaux ordered Bonaparte to fulfill his plan. First, Bonaparte procured all the heavy siege guns, gunpowder, and cannon balls then stored at Marseille's arsenal, and enough men, draft animals, caissons, and wagons to drag them to the siege. After achieving that, over the next three months, he zigzagged entrenchments and batteries closer to Fort Mulgrave and other key forts while scouring the countryside for supplies.[7] As each battery was completed, it opened fire. Captain William Sidney Smith explained the challenges facing Toulon's defenders:

We are building batteries and cannonading those the enemy have raised against us all around ... The nature of the ground ... round this extensive bay [is such] that unless we possess and maintain every height and every point for fifteen miles in circumference, the enemy would be able to force the fleet to relinquish their anchorage. This requires us to have a chain of detached posts, at such as distance from each other that they stand entirely on their own legs without it being possible for assistance ... in case the enemy should determine to force any one ... The deserters from the enemy inform us preparations are making for a general in all quarters at once.... I wish I had a force to land between here and Marseille, to cut off the communication of the republican army that is against Toulon.

Smith was as pessimistic about the political as the military situation: 'This situation does not bid well for a counter-revolution, or a cordial cooperation on part of the French themselves towards their own benefit.'[8]

As reinforcements swelled the allied ranks, Hood replaced as their commander first Captain Elphinstone with Colonel Henry Phipps, Earl of Mulgrave on September 7, and then Mulgrave with General Charles O'Hara on October 27. The Spanish tried to take command on October 23, when Admiral Langara informed Hood that Charles IV had promoted Gravina to lieutenant general, far outranking Mulgrave and even O'Hara when he arrived a few days later. Hood politely rebuffed Langara's assertion. He explained that the British would continue to head allied forces at Toulon because the Girondins had rendered Toulon to the British and the kings of Sardinia and Naples had entrusted their troops to British command. Langara then noted that he had twice as many ships-of-the-line as Hood. To underline this point, Langara actually anchored three of his ships-of-the-line around Hood's *Victory*, hoping to intimidate the British admiral into passing the command to Gravina. But Hood refused to yield. The standoff eventually ended after word arrived that George III had promoted O'Hara to lieutenant general.[9]

The French command also changed three times. Under increasing pressure from Paris to retake Toulon, Jacobin commissar Salicetti fired Carteaux and replaced him with General Amédée Doppet on November 11. After his ineptness ruined a surprise attack against Fort Mulgrave on November 16, Doppet resigned and was replaced by General Jacques François Dugommier.

Nelson, meanwhile, rejoined the armada on October 5. It is one of those fascinating quirks of history that two men whose military genius would change the world were present at Toulon. Neither, of course, had then heard of the other. Toulon was Bonaparte's first military campaign and Nelson was a dim if rising star within the Royal Navy. Nelson did not stay long. Hood dispatched him on another diplomatic mission, this time to the Bey of Tunis.

Although the allied troops defended good positions, their quality varied. Hood condemned the Spanish and Neapolitans as 'dastardly trash,' although he did praise the Piedmontese.[10] The allies kept up an active defense by launching several attacks against French batteries while the fleet bombarded French positions. It was during a sortie on October 1 that a musket ball wounded General Gravina's leg as he led his men against the enemy.

Not to be outdone, O'Hara led an attack on the main battery facing Fort Mulgrave on November 29. Bonaparte was in the thick of the fighting. He later reported that the enemy assault:

> ... overran our advanced posts and reached the battery. They engulfed six of the twenty-four cannons. At that moment, we arrived in force. General Dugommier fought with truly republican courage. We retook the battery and captured the English general, who was wounded in the arm. We chased the enemy with our bayonets at their backs, killing four or five hundred and taking a large number of prisoners ... Our soldiers, transformed by indignation, chased them off the two adjacent heights. We destroyed an earthwork that they were starting to build, and seized a large number of tents. We destroyed what we couldn't carry away. The combat lasted seven hours ... Nothing equals the courage displayed by our men this day.[11]

In all, the British and Spanish suffered 148 and 119 casualties, respectively, while the French lost 179 dead, 68 wounded, and 23 captured.[12] The high number of French dead revealed that the allies took no prisoners in their initial bayonet assault. General David Dundas assumed command of the ground forces after O'Hara was wounded and captured.

The siege settled back into the daily and nightly routine of the French steadily digging forward amidst exchanges of bombardments. The allied army was thinly deployed despite peaking in early December at around 18,700 troops, including 7,000 Spanish, 6,200 Neapolitans, 2,000 British, 2,000 Piedmont-Sardinians, and 1,500 French. They faced more than 38,000 French troops, including 36,000 infantry, 1,650 artillerymen, and 350 cavalry, that stretched around Toulon. Sickness depleted the ranks of both armies. Bonaparte concentrated 11 batteries and 12,700 troops against Fort Mulgrave, which was defended by 400 British, 700 Spanish, 700 Neapolitans, 300 Piedmontese, and 250 French, with a 1,200-man reserve, half Spanish and half Neapolitan, a quarter mile behind the fort.[13]

The decisive battle came at daylight on December 17, when, after an all-night bombardment, two columns of French troops surged across the lines toward Fort Mulgrave. Rain soaked the men's gunpowder so they savagely bayoneted and clubbed each other. The allies repulsed the two columns. Bonaparte led the reserve troops in an assault that surged over the fort and slaughtered or routed the defenders.

Upon learning of Fort Mulgrave's capture, Hood hosted a council of war with his own generals and Spanish leaders Langara and Gravina. They quickly concluded that Fort Mulgrave's loss rendered Toulon indefensible, and thus the allies should immediately begin evacuating the port and heading to sea. The withdrawal was complicated by the thousands of federalists and royalists who begged to be carried to safety. The council agreed to pack the refugees aboard the armada. They would also try to sail away with as many French warships as possible and destroy the rest along with the arsenal and warehouses. Captain William Sidney Smith volunteered to oversee that duty.

Inexplicably, Hood and the allied council never considered transferring French ships, munitions, thousands of allied wounded, and thousands of royalist citizens to safe havens during the three months that the siege lines crept closer and the French army swelled before them. The result on December 18 and 19 was utter chaos as nearly 18,000 soldiers and 6,000 civilians pressed to get aboard vessels tied to wharves or into longboats and rowed to vessels anchored across the harbor. Meanwhile, Smith deployed his men to pack explosives in the arsenal and warehouses that they would detonate after all the refugees were safely aboard and sailing to sea. He selected and manned the best French warships and prepared to burn the rest. Smith and his sailors eventually sailed to safety in the wake of the allied fleet. It was a close escape. Bonaparte reported that 'had the wind delayed them for four hours they would have lost all. A frigate whose sails were poorly unfurled, was late to depart and found itself beneath our batteries at L'Eguilette ... We heated our cannons balls red-hot, and in sight of the entire flotilla, burned it.'[14]

The allied fleet sailed to the Hyères Islands 20 miles eastward to regroup for several days. The fleet then split up. Detachments conveyed the Piedmontese and Neapolitan troops back to their respective countries. Langara and his warships headed first to Port Mahon on Minorca then to Cartagena. Hood led most of his warships first to Elba then to Gibraltar to refit.

Despite their evacuation, the allies scored a significant but hardly overwhelming victory at Toulon. They escaped while sailing away with 3 French ships-of-the-line, 3 frigates, and 7 corvettes, setting fire to 13 ships-of-the-line, and carrying away or burning a portion of supplies packed in Toulon's warehouses. Nonetheless, they not only failed to eliminate the entire French fleet, but abandoned plenty of their own cannons, equipment, provisions, and munitions in the forts.[15] The French recovered intact or doused the flames on 9 ships-of-the-line and 5 frigates; as part of the August deal to occupy Toulon, Hood had previously allowed 4 ships-of-the-line to sail away with republican sailors. So 13 of the original 26 ships-of-the-line at Toulon when Hood arrived remained in French hands. Bonaparte reported that:

> … we found in Toulon the same number of cannons that were there when the enemy entered. It is true that they were spiked but … more than half have been unplugged. They only succeeded in improving the fortifications … and today Toulon is more defensible than ever. In their hasty retreat the enemy left behind most of their tents and baggage, which fell into our hands. They had no time to burn all the vessels, and we recovered fifteen. They did not burn the magazines … Everything they did is repairable … We found in Toulon 40,000 pounds of gunpowder.[16]

The most important result of the Toulon campaign was to transform Napoleon Bonaparte from an unknown artillery captain into a brigadier general and national hero. Through genius and luck he would rise ever higher in power and achievements until his hubris destroyed the empire than he had ruthlessly conquered.

Chapter 3

Flanders, 1793–5

We must if possible retain the Netherlands in the House of Austria, as the only secure Barrier to the [Dutch] United Provinces against the Power and ambition of France.

Henry Dundas

Though the enemy are so near us, we have no certain account ... of their strength or situation ... it is madness, in the present state of things, to think of advancing toward Paris.

Lieutenant Colonel Charles Crauford

I learnt more by seeing our own faults and the defects of our system.

Lieutenant Colonel Arthur Wellesley

The fate of the Low Countries, which included the Austrian Netherlands and the Dutch Netherlands or United Provinces, was crucial to British security.[1] Although England and Holland had fought three wars against each other in the mid-seventeenth century, the Royal Navy's triumph and the decline of Dutch national power transformed a natural foe into a natural friend. French invasions of the Low Countries in the late-seventeenth and mid-eighteenth centuries were among the most important reasons provoking Britain to war against France. In July 1793, Secretary at War Henry Dundas succinctly explained this policy: 'We must if possible retain the Netherlands in the House of Austria, as the only secure Barrier to the [Dutch] United Provinces against the Power and ambition of France.'[2]

A French army led by General Charles François Dumouriez overran the Austrian Netherlands in the fall of 1792 and invaded the Dutch Netherlands on February 16, 1793. Facing the 100,000 troops of Dumouriez and auxiliary French forces were two allied armies. Frederick, Prince of Orange and Dutch Stadtholder Wilhelm V's son, commanded the Dutch army of around 30,000 troops. General Josiah von Coburg-Saalfield commanded an army of 54,000 Austrian, 11,400 Prussians, and 4,200 imperial troops with the mission to retake the Austrian Netherlands.[3] Stadtholder Wilhelm sent a desperate plea for Britain to send a renowned general and troops to help bolster his nation's defense.

Pitt and his ministers agreed on February 20, to dispatch 1,500 troops of the Royal Guard regiments as the first contingent of an expeditionary army. King George III pressured the Cabinet into accepting his son, Frederick Augustus, Duke of York, to lead the expedition.[4] The choice of York was questionable even in an age of nepotism. He was then only 28 years old and had never experienced combat. Yet he was not a complete neophyte to the profession of arms. He had spent seven years as a liaison officer with the Prussian army, and spoke German and French. Most importantly, two much older and experienced men advised him, Adjutant General James Murray (later lord Pulteney) as his chief of staff, and General Ralph Abercromby as his field commander.

The immediate threat to the Dutch Netherlands disappeared by the time York and his expedition's spearhead reached Antwerp in early April.[5] After invading, Dumouriez's troops routed the Dutch at Breda on February 24, but then suffered a series of defeats that drove them back into the Austrian Netherlands. An Austrian and Dutch army led by Coburg defeated Dumouriez at Aldenhoven on March 1, at Neerwinden on March 18, and at Pellenberg on March 23. Dumouriez withdrew nearly to Brussels. Meanwhile, on March 3, the French broke off their siege of Maastricht defended by Dutch and Austrian troops. The French distracted the allies from continuing their offensive by capturing the fortresses of Gertruidenberg and Klundert on March 4. The fighting then ended on this front for nearly two months as each side gathered more troops and supplies.

Whitehall intended for York's army to operate separately but coordinated with the armies of Orange and Coburg. York's mission was to capture Dunkirk, whose port could supply a British advance toward Paris, ideally in harness with other allied armies advancing into northeastern and eastern France. However, for now, the needs of Orange and Coburg for support against the French armies before them overrode the Dunkirk plan. Thus did York's army become an auxiliary to the allied strategy, something Whitehall had wanted to avoid.

York and Coburg first met at Antwerp to discuss strategy on April 7, and Orange soon arrived to join the planning. They agreed to stay on the defensive until they massed enough supplies and reinforcements to resume the offensive. French General Auguste Dampierre launched his 30,000 troops against the advanced Austrian guard at Saint Armand on May

1. After routing them, he marched on to attack the 60,000-man allied army at Raimes on May 8. Despite being outgunned, the French initially repelled the Austrians and Dutch. Coburg and Orange rallied their men and counter-attacked, supported by York's Royal Guards. The allies drove the French from the field, inflicting 1,500 casualties at the cost of about 600 men. The allies then marched on to rout General Jean Lamarque's 27,000 troops at Famars on May 23; the French lost 3,000 dead, wounded, and captured, and 17 cannons to allied losses of 1,100 troops. Finally, the allied army headed to Valenciennes which they besieged on May 25.

A two-month lull settled over Flanders as each side replenished its ranks and depots, and debated what to do next. Reinforcements swelled York's token force into an army that numbered 40,500 troops, including 4,200 British infantry, 2,300 British cavalry, 13,000 Hanoverians, 8,000 Hessians, and 13,000 Dutch.[6] In mid-summer the allies strengthened their grip on the Low Countries by capturing two key fortresses. The 4,300-man French garrison at Conde surrendered on July 12, after an Austrian siege that opened on April 8. At Valenciennes on July 27, York let French General Jean Louis Ferrand march away with his 9,000 surviving troops in return for pledging not to fight again for an entire year.

With these fortresses in their hands, the allies launched a three-pronged offensive, with York's army advancing on the left. Against overwhelming odds, General Charles Kilmaine, the front's latest French commander, hastily withdrew his 25,000 men toward France. The allies caught up and mauled his rear guard at Cesar Camp on August 7; York's men played a crucial role as they marched around the French right flank and the enemy hurried away to avoid being cut off. Orange attacked General Jean Baptiste Jourdan's 5,000 men at Lincelles on August 18, drove them out, and captured 10 cannons. Jourdan counter-attacked and retook Lincelles. Orange asked York for help. York dispatched General Gerard Lake with 1,100 troops who routed the French and seized Lincelles.

With the front apparently secure, York split off from the allies to march to Dunkirk. After detaching forces to garrison fortresses and guard supply trains, York's hodge-podge army numbered 29,700 infantry and 5,400 cavalry when, on August 24, it invested Dunkirk whose 10,000-man garrison was commanded by General Joseph Souham. After encamping most of his men around Dunkirk, York dispatched columns of troops 10 miles or so south on roads along which the 42,000-man French relief force led by General Jean Houchard might approach. Fearing that Dunkirk would surrender before he brought up his entire army, Houchard ordered his advanced guard to attack any enemy forces in their way. An Austrian and Dutch force repelled an attack by 2,200 French at Rexpoede and Oost-Cappel on August 21. At Rosendael, 8,000 Austrian and British troops defeated 5,000 French on August 24. An Austrian garrison in Cysoing drove off a French assault on August 28. With a mixed army of Austrian, Hessian, and Dutch troops, General Jean Daniel Freytag blocked Houchard's main army at Hondschoete, and his troops shattered a series of French assaults on September 6. Over the next two days, Houchard harassed the allied lines with swarms of skirmishers before finally ordering a grand attack on September 8 that routed the allies and inflicted 2,200 killed, wounded, and captured, while suffering 3,000 casualties.

The French victory at Hondschoete forced York hastily to abandon his siege of Dunkirk on September 8. York's army had suffered 2,000 casualties during the two-week operation, and abandoned 32 heavy cannons in the rush to evade being crushed by Houchard. York halted his retreat at Ypres and Furnes.

Houchard shadowed York but refrained from attacking his well-prepared positions. Observing that Orange's 13,000 Dutch infantry and 1,800 cavalry at nearby Menin were fewer and more vulnerable, Houchard attacked there on September 13. The French routed the Dutch, captured the town, inflicted 3,000 casualties, and took 40 cannons. This same day, Austrian General Charles Clerfait captured Quesnoy with its 5,000-man garrison, after opening a siege on August 28. With Quesnoy in enemy hands, Houchard's supply and communications line was vulnerable so he withdrew to Lille in northern France. Houchard paid the ultimate price for his failure to defeat the allied forces before him. France's Committee of Public Safety ordered him arrested and executed. His replacement was General Jean Baptiste Jourdan, who massed troops and supplies for an offensive.

The latest lull to descend on the see-saw Flanders front lasted a month. The French broke it when Jourdan threw his 60,000 troops at Coburg's 30,000 Austrians at Wattignies on October 15 and 16; the Austrians withdrew, having inflicted 5,000 casualties on the French while suffering half their losses. Jourdan's victory forced the allies to abandon their siege of Maubeuge. A severe allied defeat came on October 22, when a garrison of 8,000 Austrian, British, and Hanoverian troops at Menin surrendered to General Joseph Souham's 10,000 troops.

General Ralph Abercromby redeemed a bit of national pride when his British and Austrian troops decimated a 5,000-man French force at Lannoy on October 28. Most of the enemy's losses of 2,000 killed and 1,700 captured took place after Abercromby loosened his cavalry against the fleeing French.

The allies captured a 3,000-man French garrison at Marchiennes on October 30. This ended the war for Flanders in 1793.

Neither side had scored a decisive victory. Indeed after half a year of marching, fighting, besieging, or preparing for the next round the front lines were little changed from the spring. War in the Low Countries favors defenders. The terrain is mostly flat or slightly rolling but is cut by canals, deep streams, and rivers, and checker-boarded with fortress cities and towns linked by roads. This forced generals to fight methodical chess-like campaigns of sieges of fortresses and assaults against field armies. Defeated forces simply withdrew into or behind the nearest friendly fortress. These challenges were compounded for York and his colleagues because they had to command a multinational army and coordinate their strategy with Austrian, Dutch, and Prussian generals who naturally favored their own respective national and army interests. Under such trying circumstances York deserves credit not just for avoiding a disaster but for bravely if unimaginatively leading his army.

Although 1794's first skirmishes flared in Flanders in February, the armies did not stir from their cantonments until the grass thickened for their horses and draught animals in April. The opposing strategies were asymmetrical. The allies massed their forces for a huge assault against the central French army. The French thinned their center to reinforce their flanks for a huge double envelopment of the allies. Victory was most likely for the side that attacked first and blunted the enemy's counter-strategy.

The allied offensive initially succeeded. York, Orange, and Austrian General Graf von Haddik jointly commanded 60,000 British, Hanoverian, Hessian, Dutch, and Austrian troops that defeated nearly as many French led by General Jean Pichegru at Catillon on April 27. The allies suffered 1,000 casualties but inflicted over 2,000 on the French, captured 24 cannons, and drove them back from the Sambre River. An even bigger allied victory came two days later, when a Dutch-Austrian force captured Landrecies with its 9,000-man garrison, at the cost of 1,000 casualties. The winning streak persisted at Villers en Cauchie, when an Austrian force routed 7,000 French, inflicted nearly 2,000 casualties, and captured 5 cannons. York dispatched a division of British infantry and cavalry to join an Austrian attack against 40,000 French at Le Cateau on April 26; once again the French lost 7,000 killed, wounded, and missing, but even worse, over 40 cannons.

The French armies rallied, blunted the allied offensive, and launched their own that regained some ground lost over the previous weeks. Souham's army, now 28,000-men strong, routed the allied advanced guard at Mouscron on

April 26, while 4 days later General Jean Moreau's 14,000 troops captured Menin with its 2,500 defenders. Then York's men scattered a French division at Baisieux on May 10, killing, wounding, or capturing around 2,000 French, while suffering just 325 casualties. Pichegru and his 25,000 troops avenged themselves at Courtrai on May 11, by defeating Clerfait's Austrian army and inflicting more than 2,000 casualties.

Over the next week, reinforcements swelled Pichegru's army to 82,000 men. On May 18, Pichegru attacked the allied army at Tourcoing. Although York and Coburg together had 72,000 troops, they bickered over strategy and committed only 48,000 troops to battle. As a result, the French steamrolled the allied troops that actually got into the fight, killing or wounding 4,000 and capturing 1,500. York and Coburg withdrew their armies in different directions.

Pichegru led 45,000 troops after Coburg's 28,000 Austrian, Hanoverian, and British troops, and caught up at Tournai on May 22. Coburg's well-positioned men and cannons killed or wounded over 5,500 French, and captured 450, while losing about 3,000 men, before Pichegru withdrew. General Franz von Kaunitz-Rietberg's 24,000 Austrian and Dutch troops defeated General Louis Charbonnier's 30,000 troops as they tried to cross the Sambre River at Erqeulinnes on May 24, inflicting 3,000 casualties and taking 30 guns, while losing about 450 killed and wounded, and 250 captured. Orange took over Kaunitz's command and led those men to victory over General Jacques Desjardins's 27,000 troops at Charleroi on June 3; the French suffered 2,000 casualties to little more than 400 Dutch and Austrian killed and wounded.

The latest shift in the seesaw Flanders war occurred after Souham hurled his 20,000 men against Clerfait's 20,000 men at Roulers on June 10, and took the field at the cost of 1,000 casualties to 600 for the allies. Three days later, Souham caught up to Clerfait at Hooglede and won again, this time losing 1,300 men while inflicting 900 casualties. Reinforcements prevented Souham's costly victories from becoming truly Pyrrhic. Pichegru captured Ypres with its 7,000 Austrian and Dutch defenders on June 17, after a two and a half week siege.

Elsewhere, Desjardins led 27,000 troops across the Sambre River and attacked Orange's 28,000 allied troops defending Charleroi on June 3. The allies suffered only 450 casualties while they repelled the French, who lost 2,000 dead and wounded. Jourdan joined forces with Desjardins, and took command of the 73,000 troops. He then side-stepped Charleroi and marched his men toward Orange's rear. Orange withdrew his Dutch and

Austrian army, swelled with reinforcements to 41,000 troops, to Fleurus. Jourdan caught up and attacked on June 16. The allies drove off the French, inflicting 3,000 casualties and capturing 8 guns, while suffering as many killed and wounded. On June 26, Jourdan attacked and lost again. Although Jourdan's 75,000 infantry and 2,300 cavalry outgunned the 32,000 infantry and 14,000 cavalry defenders now jointly led by Coburg and Orange by nearly 2 to 1, the allies held the field, killing or wounded 5,000 French while losing 1,600 men.

The French tactical defeats at Fleurus actually turned out to be strategic French victories, although this was not apparent for months. The battles for Fleurus, atop two months of bloody back and forth fighting that preceded it, convinced Vienna that retaining the Austrian Netherlands was simply not worth the swelling mountain of death and debt. Thereafter each week or so, as Francis II and his advisors debated how to extract themselves honorably from the Flanders quagmire, they received word of the latest loss. After a 2-week siege, the 1,900-man Austrian garrison at Valenciennes surrendered on July 16. Two days later, a couple thousand troops including Austrians rendered the fortress of Nieupoort. Quesnoy's 2,400 Austrian defenders gave up on August 14 after nearly a month-long siege. The 1,700 Dutch and Hanoverians defending Sluis capitulated on August 24, after a five-week siege. On August 29 1,500 Austrians marched into captivity at Conde. These losses culminated when General Barthélemy Schérer's 35,000 troops crushed a wing of General Victor de Fay, Marquis Latour-Maubourg's 18,000 troops at Sprimont on September 18; the French killed or wounded 1,500 Austrians and captured 1,000 men, 36 cannons, and, worst of all, 100 ammunition wagons, at a cost of 1,000 casualties. Each time the French routed an allied army, they reaped a harvest of desperately needed provisions and munitions from captured supply trains. After one typical defeat, Lieutenant Colonel Charles Crauford, a liaison officer with the allies, witnessed 'the road ... as far as the eye could reach, covered with baggage – everything announced an army in deroute.'[7]

Crauford's reports back to Whitehall were increasingly pessimistic about how the campaign was being fought and the ultimate results. In May 1794, he observed that 'this campaign will probably not terminate the contest; but it will certainly show, nearly, how it is to be decided.' The French invasion of:

Flanders has been a most unfortunate circumstance indeed ... The allies find themselves arrested by it ... it has already occasioned great and severe losses; it will probably be the cause of much effusion of blood; and even though the enemy be ultimately ... repulsed, it will retard the great operations of the army for perhaps a month ... Though the enemy are so near us, we have no certain account ... of their strength or situation ... it is madness, in the present state of things, to think of advancing toward Paris, until you are masters of the principal frontier places; but this once effected, every man in France will feel that Paris is at your mercy.

Crauford's pessimism worsened with his experiences. In August 1794, he lamented that 'we have seen so many unaccountable things of late, that I shall no longer be surprised at whatever may happen.'[8]

During this time, York and his men largely sat on the sidelines encamped around Nijmegen. After enjoying a summer-long hiatus, the British briefly got back into the front lines at Boxtel during a battle that raged on September 14 and 15. During the first day, Pichegru's 12,000 troops pushed 1,115 Hanoverians from the town. The next day, Abercromby's attack with four redcoat regiments failed to retake Boxtel. York withdrew his army to Nijmegen.

French armies mopped up allied fortresses through the rest of 1794 and into 1795, capturing 1,800 Dutch and Hessians at Hertogenbosch on October 10; 1,600 Dutch and Germans at Venlo on October 27; 8,000 Dutch and Austrians at Maastricht on November 4; 660 Dutch at Zevenbergen on December 27; 5,000 Dutch and Hessian troops at Bommel on December 28; 1,500 Dutch at Grave on December 29; 1,400 Dutch at Heusden on January 14; and 950 Dutch troops at Geertruidenberg on January 19, 1795. The war's most bizarre battle occurred on January 20, 1795, when French cavalry clattered across the ice-bound Zuyder Zee and captured the Dutch fleet.

Where were the British during this time? York was back in England after Whitehall replaced that lackluster general on November 27 with William, Earl of Harcourt in October. Souham nearly bagged most of the British expeditionary army at Nijmegen on November 7, after a week's siege, but almost all managed to escape the fate of 1,200 Dutch and several score redcoats who surrendered. In a two-day battle that ended on December 30, General David Dundas redeemed some tarnished honor when his 9,000 British and Hessian troops trounced General Herman Wilhelm Daendels's 4,000 troops at Geldermalsen, killing, wounding, or capturing 600 French, while suffering only 60 casualties.

This year-end victory did little to assuage Whitehall's worsening dismay over the campaign. Pitt and his ministers grappled with a cruel dilemma. In two years on the continent the British expedition had suffered 20,000 casualties. Should they commit even more troops, supplies, and money to the campaign in hopes of turning it around, or should they cut their worsening losses and get out as swiftly as possible? The issue was decided after William V, Prince of Orange, and his entourage arrived in London for what would be a two-decade exile. Whitehall authorized Harcourt to retreat with his army's remnants to Bremen. There they wintered until April 1795, then squeezed aboard a flotilla and sailed to Britain.

Many reasons explain the disastrous allied campaign in the Low Countries, but bad leadership was crucial. The generals, including York and Harcourt, were a mediocre lot at best and inept and timid at worst. They blundered as administrators, logisticians, engineers, tacticians, and strategists. Compounding this was the challenge of coalition warfare, whereby every decision became a tug-of-war among each general's ego and national interests.

Lieutenant Colonel Crauford noted several critical reasons for the French victory. He scorned the allied commander, Austrian General Coburg, who 'for more than a month past has been retreating and abandoning some of the best military positions that are anywhere to be found before an army less numerous than his own.' The result was that Coburg had 'fallen into such exceeding great contempt, both with the army and the public that it were better to replace him by a corporal than allow him to remain. It not that he is merely a cipher, but he is the tool of every fool and every rogue who may choose to direct him.'[9] Then there was the contest for hearts and minds that Crauford feared the French were winning:

> Though the people are exceedingly discontented, and even disposed to proceed to violence, yet if the French are allowed to remain there for some months undisturbed, the multitude will be debauched … The most stubborn Fleming and dullest German peasant has conception enough to be pleased with what is held out to him under the words 'liberty and equality.'[10]

Finally, he partly attributed French victories to 'the very alarming discipline … established in their armies. The most implicit obedience is exacted from both officers and men, and almost all officers are punished with death.' He hoped that 'this extraordinary degree of severity' would become a double-edge sword, 'as likely ... to produce desertion and mutiny as order and settled discipline.'[11] Yet, so far, the latter prevailed.

The Low Country campaign was the baptism of fire for Arthur Wellesley, the future Duke of Wellington, but then the 33rd regiment's 25-year-old lieutenant colonel. He and his men arrived among 10,000 reinforcements in August 1794. Much later in his life when he was asked how he learned his profession, he recalled his first campaign: 'I learnt more by seeing our own faults and the defects of our system ... The infantry regiments, taken individually, were as good in proper hands in the campaign of Holland, than anywhere else.... but the system was wretched.' With York anything but a hands-on general, Wellington 'was left ... to myself with my regiment ... thirty miles from headquarters ... a scene of jollification ... I do not think that I was once visited by the Commander-in-Chief.'[12] In sum Wellesley 'learnt what one ought not to do, and that is always something.'[13] Tragically, Wellesley was the only prominent leader who learned any substantive lessons from the Netherlands campaign. Whitehall and its generals would make similar tragic mistakes there and elsewhere in the coming years.

The allied defeat in the Low Countries was total. French armies conquered the Austrian Netherlands and helped transform the Dutch Netherlands. On January 21, 1795, Dutch liberals, backed by French commissars, turned the Dutch Netherlands into the Batavian Republic allied with France. On April 5, 1795, French and Prussian diplomats signed the Treaty of Basel, whereby Prussia withdrew into neutrality; France abandoned its conquests east of the Rhine; the Prussians recognized French conquests west of the Rhine; the French recognized Prussian expansion in northern Germany; Berlin recognized the revolutionary government in Paris and pledged to sever any ties with French royalists and exiled Bourbons. On July 22, 1795, French and Spanish diplomats signed the Treaty of Basel, whereby Spain withdrew into neutrality; France withdrew from Spanish territory, but retained Spain's colony of Santo Domingo; Madrid recognized the government in Paris and pledged to sever any ties with the royalists and exiled Bourbons.

For the foreseeable future, Britain and Austria were the only two great powers leading a diminishing coalition of smaller states dedicated to crushing the French Revolution. At least Prussia stayed neutral. Spain allied with France with the Treaty of San Ildefonso signed on August 18, 1796. Despair rose as Britain's allies succumbed, dropped out, or became enemies. Captain Horatio Nelson spoke for countless of his countryman when he wrote: 'As all the Powers give up the contest, for what has England to fight? I wish most heartily that we had peace, or that all our troops were drawn from the Continent, and only a naval war carried on, the war where England alone can make a figure.'[14]

Nelson's latter wish came true. The costly failure and withdrawal of Britain's Low Countries expedition discredited the 'continental strategy' for thirteen years. Dundas's 'maritime strategy' of devastating France's naval and merchant ships at sea, bottling them up port, and conquering France's West and East Indian colonies persisted until 1808, when General Wellesley led an army back to the continent. During the years when the maritime strategy prevailed, no one waged it more ruthlessly than Nelson himself.

Chapter 4

High and Shallow Seas, 1793–9

My disposition cannot bear tame and slow measures. Sure I am, that had I commanded our fleet on the 14th, the whole French fleet would have graced my triumph, or I should have been in a confounded scrape.

Horatio Nelson

The die is cast and if there are fifty sail I will go through them. England badly needs a victory at present.

John Jervis

Within months of the war's declaration in February 1793, the Admiralty had devised and issued missions to its squadrons deployed around the world, and sent them reinforcements of ships, supplies, and troops. Each squadron was ordered to blockade or, ideally, attack any French forces and conquer French colonies in the region.[1] All this took a long time to implement. In 1793, the only notable operation was at Toulon. Nonetheless, the tightening British blockade atop the Toulon fleet's devastation sharply reduced France's immediate naval threat. The result for now was stalemate. The likelihood of a French armada sailing to attack Britain or its colonies was remote. The chance of another British attack on a French fleet in one of its lairs like Toulon was even more remote. The allies took over Toulon only because counter-revolutionaries had seized the port and invited in the blockading fleet. Revolutionary armies had brutally crushed the southern rebellion, culminating with their recapture of Toulon, and were repressing rebel Chouans in Brittany and Vendeans in the lower Loire River valley. France was most vulnerable in its empire, especially the West Indies.

Revolutionary rhetoric seeped into France's colonies, undermined the planter elite's power, and spread turmoil. Royalists and republicans battled in Saint Domingue, Guadeloupe, Martinique, and Tobago. Delegates from the West Indies appeared at the National Assembly and demanded seats. A handful of liberals advocated abolishing slavery. After slaves rebelled in Saint Domingue in 1791, authorities eventually repressed them, but only after 180 plantations were burned, and 2,000 whites and 10,000 slaves were slaughtered. In Paris, the Convention tried to seal this tense peace by outlawing slavery on February 4, 1794.[2]

Secretary at War Henry Dundas saw great opportunities and dangers in the worsening chaos and violence. Royalists were a rapidly disappearing minority, murdered by republicans and slaves alike. Yet they were Britain's only potential ally, and leaders among them requested British help. Whitehall had to act before the royalists were completely wiped out. The slave revolts were especially disturbing since they could spread to Britain's colonies in Jamaica, Barbados, Grenada, Antigua, and Saint Kitts.[3]

The first step was to rescue the royalists from extinction. Indeed Whitehall acted even before war with France was declared and without consulting the French government. Dundas and the admiralty ordered General Cornelius Cuyler, the Caribbean's senior army commander then headquartered at Barbados, to cram any available troops aboard any available ships commanded by Admiral John Laforey and sail to restore order to France's West Indian colonies. Three days after sending these orders on February 5, Whitehall learned of France's war declaration against Britain on February 1. Dundas and the Admiralty then dispatched Admiral Alan Gardner with seven ships-of-the-line, two frigates, and several regiments aboard, to reinforce Cuyler and Laforey. Only about 500 troops and marines sailed with Cuyler and Laforey. Nonetheless, in April 1793, the expedition was able bloodlessly to seize Tobago, Britain's former colony lost in 1783. In late April, Gardner's flotilla dropped anchor off Port Royal, Martinique. For the next two months, Gardner fought with royalists against republican troops led by General Donatien de Vimeur, Vicomte Rochambeau. Eventually Rochambeau routed the royalists and British. Gardner packed the troops and nearly 6,000 refugees aboard and sailed away on June 22.

Later in the year, General Adam Williamson, Jamaica's governor, established footholds in Saint Domingue by landing troops to link with royalists at Jeremie and fortress Mole Saint Nicolas in September, although the French repulsed a landing at Tiburon on October 4, 1793. After capturing Leogane and Saint Mare in December, the British controlled about one-third of the colony, but lacked the manpower to take the rest. The republicans, led by Léger Félicité Sonthonax, clung to strongholds at Jacmel and Les Caves on the south coast. Then there were black nationalist armies led by the sometimes rivals, sometimes allies Andre Rigaud and Pierre Dominique Toussaint Louverture, who overran most of the interior.

Whitehall launched an expedition in November 1793, designed to conquer France's West Indian colonies. Admiral John Jervis commanded the fleet of 4 ships-of-the-line, 11 frigates, and 6 smaller warships; aboard the transports were 7,279 troops and 379 officers from 9 regiments and detachments from 3 others commanded by General Charles Grey. The armada sailed from Saint Helens on the Isle of Wight on November 26. By the time the armada dropped anchor off Martinique on February 3, 1794, only 6,085 troops were healthy, 224 were in the sick bay, and 970 had been left behind in hospitals on Barbados. This attrition was disturbing enough to Jervis and Grey. It would get much worse.[4]

The troops landed on Martinique on February 6, 1794, and swiftly invested Fort Royal and Fort Bourbon, the island's mightiest fortresses. After putting up a valiant fight, Rochambeau and his troops finally surrendered in the face of overwhelming odds and dwindling supplies on March 25. The British won the island at a relatively low cost in battle casualties – 92 killed, 228 wounded, and 3 missing, but diseases monthly devoured hundreds of lives.[5]

The armada then sailed to Saint Lucia, just a score of miles south of Martinique. The garrison capitulated on April 4 with no losses on either side. The armada's final target was Guadeloupe. The first wave of troops landed and attacked Fleur d'Épée on April 11. The redcoats routed the French, killing 67, wounding 55, and capturing 148, at the cost of 15 killed, 60 wounded, and 2 missing. Grey led his men on to invest Basseterre, the capital. The French commander, General Georges Collot, surrendered his 55 regulars and 818 national guardsmen on April 22. After this initial succession of swift victories, the campaign bogged down and a deadly cocktail of tropical diseases including yellow fever, malaria, and dysentery sickened and killed ever more men. From just April 1 to June 1, Grey's healthy troops plummeted to 4,761, while those in hospitals soared from 1,717 to 2,354, and 1,388 died.[6]

The question for Grey was where to sail next. He mulled then rejected a plan to attack French Guyenne. Instead he sent General John Whyte with a couple thousand troops to reinforce Williamson at Mole Saint Nicolas, Saint Domingue. This briefly boosted British troops on the island to 2,967, but diseases swiftly whittled their ranks. Nonetheless, Whyte launched a campaign to capture Port-au-Prince on May 25. Over the following weeks, the British erected batteries and bombarded the city and its defenses. The French surrendered on June 4. Among the spoils were 131 cannons and 45 merchant vessels, most packed with goods. Yet, as elsewhere across the

Caribbean, the price of victory steadily worsened as disease killed hundreds and prevented the British from attacking elsewhere.[7]

Meanwhile, the French staged a comeback. On April 23, Admiral Corentin Leissegues sailed from Rochefort with 2 frigates, a corvette, and 6 transports packed with 1,100 troops and marines led by Victor Hugues, a revolutionary commissar. The expedition landed at Grand Terre, Guadeloupe on June 3, and two days later captured Fort Fleur d'Épée.

Jervis and Grey were at nearby Saint Kitts when they learned of the French invasion. They mustered as many available ships and men as possible and sailed. Grey landed his troops on June 13, and over the next two weeks built up siege lines against Fleur d'Épée. The steady pounding of the French lines convinced Grey that an assault could capture the fort. He ordered a night attack on July 1. The result was a disaster as the French routed the British, who suffered 543 casualties. These losses atop hundreds dead or sickened from disease forced Grey to break the siege.[8]

This debacle shifted the initiative not just against Grey on Guadeloupe but against the British across the West Indies. Hugues besieged the British in their forts at Berville, Lamentin, Goyave, and Matilda on Guadeloupe, and dispatched agents, money, arms, and, perhaps most importantly, the message that France had abolished slavery, to other islands to foment rebellions against the British. Slave revolts on Grenada and Saint Vincent, rebels on Saint Lucia, and a revolt by free blacks known as Maroons on Jamaica atop devastating diseases undermined British power in the Caribbean basin. General Robert Prescott commanded Britain's dwindling troops and forts on Guadeloupe, and finally evacuated with the remnants of his men from Fort Matilda on December 10, 1794. The British abandoned Saint Lucia on March 18, 1795. The French further boosted their position by pressuring Spain to cede its half of Saint Domingue, and took over the Dutch islands of Saint Eustatius and Saint Martin.

As if all these defeats and deaths were not debilitating enough to Britain, a scandal erupted that further sapped national morale. Unfortunately, temptation got the better of Jervis and Grey, who pocketed commercial and financial plums from various captured ports and ships. After learning of their looting, Whitehall recalled both in disgrace and stripped them of the peerages that the king had granted them for their victories. Jervis and Grey sailed for London on November 27, 1794, The distant West Indies appeared a sideshow compared with potential threats to Britain itself. Whitehall deployed most of the Royal Navy in fleets to blockade and, ideally, intercept and destroy any potential enemy armada sailing toward the United Kingdom. The largest fleet, Admiral Richard Howe's 30 to 35 ships-of-the-line, was naturally concentrated in the English Channel.

The Admiralty ordered Howe to intercept a French convoy of 112 merchant vessels that, in December 1793, had sailed from Brest to supply colonies in the West Indies. Intelligence reports revealed that the convoy would return, laden with grain bought in the United States, sometime in April or May. The French fleet at Brest was expected to sortie, meet the convoy somewhere in the mid-North Atlantic, and escort it home. As if this order was not vague and challenging enough, Howe soon received another. Along the way to intercepting the French convoy, he was to escort 99 British vessels through the Channel to the open ocean, where they would divide into smaller convoys bound for the East Indies, West Indies, and Newfoundland.

Somehow in that vast expanse of ocean, the French and British convoys headed straight toward each other. The French convoy had lifted anchor at Norfolk, Virginia on April 11 and was slowly lumbering eastward across the Atlantic. Howe sailed westward with 34 ships-of-the-line and 15 smaller vessels protecting the convoy from Spithead on May 2. Two days later, the East Indies division split off and headed south, to be escorted as far as Finisterre by six ships-of-the-line and two frigates commanded by Admiral James Montagu. Howe's fleet, now numbering 28 ships-of-the-line and 7 frigates, accompanied the main convoy just another day before heading southwest to zigzag across the enemy fleet's most likely path toward Brest.

The first French naval escort, five ships-of-the-line commanded by Admiral Joseph Nielly, departed from Rochefort on May 6. The main fleet, 25 ships-of-the-line led by Admiral Louis Thomas Villaret de Joyeuse, sailed from Brest on May 16. Villaret de Joyeuse had an added incentive to find and escort the convoy safely to France. The government warned him that he would face a guillotine if he failed. The fleets of Nielly and Villaret de Joyeuse each soon ran into and captured an enemy merchant convoy, then detached smaller warships to convoy the prizes to French ports. On May 15, Admiral Montagu's fleet encountered and liberated Nielly's captives. The next day, Howe's fleet spotted Villaret de Joyeuse's captives, gave chase, and freed 10 vessels. Howe's captains freed three more that the French had taken on May 23, and several more two days later. Howe and his men grew more excited as they neared the enemy fleet.[9]

Lookouts aboard Howe's fleet finally spotted Villaret de Joyeuse's fleet, now with 26 ships-of-the-line and 5 frigates, 400 miles west of Ushant on May 28. Howe immediately had flags hoisted signaling his captains to attack.

Slowly the British fleet closed on the French fleet which turned back toward Brest. The first shots were exchanged around mid-afternoon, but mostly splashed into the sea. Then the 110-gun *Revolutionaire* broke from near the French fleet's vanguard and arched to protect the rear. Five British ships-of-the-line converged and pounded broadsides into the *Revolutionaire* as the sun set and night and gale-force winds arose. Severely damaged, the *Revolutionaire* escaped in the darkness.

Howe's fleet finally caught up to Villaret de Joyeuse's fleet on May 29, and cut off and bombarded five French warships; three managed to escape and two struck their colors. The chase continued for the next two days through churning seas and patches of fog. The decisive battle came on June 1. Seven of Howe's warships broke through the French line, closed for action, and battered four enemy ships-of-the-line into surrendering. The rest of Villaret de Joyeuse's warships sailed on toward Brest. Eleven of Howe's ships-of-the-line were demasted and had to be towed back to England. The next encounter came on June 9, when Montagu's five ships-of-the-line intercepted the French fleet anchored off the Bay of Bertheaume. Villaret de Joyeuse led a chase with eight ships-of-the-line. Outgunned, Montagu and his captains fled to Plymouth.

In all, the Royal Navy had scored a significant if incomplete victory on the 'Glorious First of June' and thereafter. They captured seven and sank two ships-of-the-line but failed to seize the grain convoy that eventually reached Brest. Indeed, Howe called off the chase even though the French escape was slowed as undamaged vessels towed five demasted ships-of-the-line. And Villaret de Joyeuse not only kept his head but enjoyed the government's praise for accomplishing his mission.

Corsica is a mountainous, oval shaped island with a peninsula pointing north. About 3,500 French troops garrisoned various forts and ports, with most either at Bastia, located on the east side of the peninsula's base, or Calvi on the northwest coast. Corsican rebels led by Pascal Paoli controlled much of the island's interior. On September 1, 1794, Paoli sent a letter to George III, requesting British help.[10] The king and the Cabinet instructed Admiral Samuel Hood to assess the viability of Paoli's independence struggle. In January 1794, Hood dispatched three British officers to Paoli. They reported that Paoli commanded several thousand men to assist a British expedition to capture the island.

What ensured was among the more dysfunctional joint operations in British military history. Hood and his right-hand man, Captain Horatio

Nelson, squabbled with a succession of army commanders, Generals David Dundas, Abraham d'Aubrant, and Charles Stuart, over the pace, strategy, and tactics for conquering Corsica. The campaign opened on February 7, when Dundas led 1,600 infantry and 180 gunners ashore near Fiorenzo. Over the next dozen days, the troops constructed siege lines and dragged heavy cannons into place. The French abandoned Fiorenzo on February 19, and withdrew north to Bastia. Hood and Nelson blistered Dundas for letting them get away. D'Aubrant took Dundas's place after he resigned, but was no improvement. When d'Aubrant refused to march against and besiege Bastia, Hood assigned Nelson this mission.

Nelson led ashore 1,183 troops and marines, and 250 armed sailors from his ship, the 64-gun *Agamemnon*, 3 miles north of Bastia on the night of April 3. The following day, they camped atop a hill a mile from the port. It took eight days to build a redoubt and drag eight 24-pounders, and several 10in and 13in mortars inside it. The battery opened fire on April 11. By April 21, Nelson had another battery constructed within a half mile of Bastia. General Jean Pierre La Combe Saint Michel surrendered Bastia's garrison of 1,000 French and Corsican troops on May 22.

Hood then had Nelson sail with his *Agamemnon*, 2 frigates, and 16 transports to take Calvi. Nelson's flotilla dropped anchor 3 miles east of Calvi on June 17. Although only 300 French troops and 247 Corsican militia defended Calvi, its site atop a tall hill with water on three sides made it much tougher to capture than Bastia. It took several weeks for Nelson's men to drag siege guns, munitions, and other equipment atop a hill and construct there a battery. The guns opened fire on July 4. This time the army, led by General Stuart seconded by Colonel John Moore, worked closely with Nelson and the navy. Calvi surrendered on August 10. Although the British controlled Bastia, Calvi, Fiorenzo, and several smaller ports, French garrisons controlled much of Corsica's interior and the island's southern half. A stalemate ensured with neither strong enough to drive off the other.

After the French overran the Netherlands in 1794, Dutch colonies were fair game. The Admiralty organized armadas to capture the Cape of Good Hope and Ceylon. Ideally, seizing those colonies would be bloodless. William V, the Netherlands' rightful ruler, had escaped to Britain. He wrote orders to the governors of those colonies, calling on them to yield to the British commanders. On February 27, 1794, Commodore John Blankett sailed with four ships and the prince's orders bound for Cape Town. Admiral George Keith led the main fleet from Spithead on April 3. It was not until May 15, however, that the transports packed with troops and supplies departed. This piecemeal approach to the mission seemed unwittingly to dare any cruising French squadron to gobble up any one or more segments. Fortunately for the British, that did not happen. Blankett's flotilla dropped anchor beyond cannon shot of Capetown on June 11. The Dutch rejected Wilhelm's order backed by British power to surrender. Keith's fleet finally arrived on July 7, and the transports a few days later. The British went ashore and opened a siege of Capetown, which finally surrendered on September 16.

Admiral Samuel Hood sailed for home in October 1794, leaving Admiral Henry Hotham to command Britain's Mediterranean fleet headquartered at Livorno, Tuscany's port. There on March 6, 1795, Hotham received word that Admiral Pierre Martin's fleet of 14 ships-of-the-line and 3 frigates had sailed from Toulon, escorting transports packed with as many as 6,000 troops to reinforce French garrisons on Corsica. Hotham and 14 ships-of-the-line set forth on March 7, and 3 days later spotted the enemy. Hotham and Martin fought a series of battles from March 11 to March 14, in which two battered French ships-of-the-line struck their colors, one to a Nelson boarding party. Martin signaled his fleet to break off the action and sail back toward Toulon, his mission to reinforce Corsica thwarted. Nelson urged Hotham to pursue. Hotham demurred and tried to sooth Nelson by saying: 'We must be contented, we have done very well.' Nelson held his tongue and later vented his wrath at the admiral's complacency in a letter to his wife: 'My disposition cannot bear tame and slow measures. Sure I am that had I commanded our fleet on the 14th, the whole French fleet would have graced my triumph, or I should have been in a confounded scrape.'[11]

The Mediterranean's naval power balance appeared to shift on April 4, when six ships-of-the-line reached Toulon from Brest. Yet Martin did not immediately sail out to challenge Hotham. When he finally did two-and-a-half months later, his edge in numbers had disappeared. On June 14, the balance tipped back to Britain, when Admiral Robert Mann joined his six ships-of-the-line to Hotham's fleet, now anchored at Fiorenzo, Corsica. The chance to act came on June 29, when a frigate brought word to Hotham that Martin had sailed from Toulon with 17 ships-of-the-line. Hotham dismissed the news as merely a short training exercise. He did assign Nelson the mission of sailing with his 64-gun *Agamemnon* to provide naval cover for an Austrian offensive along the Ligurian coast. Nelson did not get far when, on July 8, he encountered the French fleet that Hotham insisted posed no threat. The French pursued Nelson back to Fiorenzo.

As the chase came into view, Hotham could no longer deny the reality. The trouble was that most of his warships were refitting and unprepared immediately to sail. Yet, rather than attack, the French fleet turned tail at sight of the larger British fleet anchored in Fiorenzo bay. Hotham and eight ship-of-the-line, including Nelson's, gave chase the next day. Over the next few days, the British fleet swelled to 23 ships-of-the-line strung out in pursuit. Near Hyères on July 13, Nelson's *Agamemnon* and Hotham's *Victory* caught up to the rear French warship, the *Alcide*, opened fired, and within an hour battered it into surrendering.

Yet once again Hotham was content with a minor victory. To Nelson's fury, he called off the chase. The French escaped back into Toulon. Looking back, Nelson reckoned that Hotham's failure to pursue and destroy the French fleet at Hyères in July 1795 changed the course of history: 'I say that the British fleet could have prevented the [French] invasion of Italy; and if our friend Hotham had kept his fleet on that coast, I assert ... no army from France could have been furnished with stores or provisions, even men could not have marched.'[12]

Hotham was not the only British admiral who lacked a killer instinct. In mid-June, Admiral Alexander Hood, Lord Bridport led the Channel fleet of 17 ships-of-the-line in search of 12 ships-of-the-line commanded by Villaret de Joyeuse. He found his prey on June 22, and hoisted flags signaling his captains to attack. They failed to catch up before night and finally closed for action early the next morning. After his lead warships pounded two French ships-of-the-line into striking their colors, Bridport called off the chase. Villaret de Joyeuse led the rest of his fleet into the safety of Lorient Bay. The Royal Navy would not have another chance to fight a large French fleet for another three years.

The Admiralty relieved Hotham of command and replaced him with Admiral Hyde Parker, who arrived on November 1, 1795. Nelson was soon disabused of his hope that Parker would hoist more backbone than Hotham. Parker rejected Nelson's plan to lead ships-of-the-line to attack a flotilla of French supply ships anchored in Alassio Bay, Liguria. Nelson was thoroughly disgusted with both his commanders:

Our admirals will have ... much to answer for in not giving me that force which I repeatedly called for, and for at last leaving me with Agamemnon alone. Admiral Hotham kept my squadron too small for its duty; and the moment that Sir Hyde took the command of the fleet he reduced it to nothing – only one frigate and a brig; whereas I demanded two 74-gun ships and eight or ten frigates and sloops to ensure safety to the army.[13]

A French offensive routed the Austrians at the battle of Loano on November 23 and 24, 1795, and captured the Ligurian coast eastward to Voltri, with Genoa only 9 miles away. Nelson sympathized with Austrian complaints that the Royal Navy failed to sufficiently support their army: 'They say, and true, they were brought on the coast at the express desire of the English to cooperate with the fleet, which fleet nor admiral they never saw.'[14]

Nonetheless, Britain was clearly winning its naval war with France. The cumulative disastrous results of two years of war had demoralized France's navy, including its chief. On December 3, 1795, Marine Minister Laurent Truguet reported that 'our fleets are humiliated, blocked in their ports, stripped of resources, and torn by insubordination.'[15]

As far as commanders were concerned, the third proved to be the charm for Nelson. John Jervis arrived aboard the Victory at Fiorenzo, and replaced Parker on November 30, 1795. In complete contrast to his predecessors, Jervis was a bold commander.[16] He was also a strict disciplinarian – he had miscreants harshly punished for any infractions. Yet, for both practical and humanitarian reasons, he constantly looked after his men's health. He issued orders that each seaman was weekly to scrub his hammock, bedding, and clothes. He had the sick and wounded brought up from the dank, fetid bowels of vessels to the forecastle whose gun ports provided ventilation. He insisted that his crews be 'perfect in the use of their guns; I therefore wish that every day, whether in harbor or at sea, a general or partial exercise should take place on board every ship in the squadron.'[17]

In early 1796, Jervis's fleet numbered 25 ships-of-the-line, 24 frigates, and 25 smaller warships.[18] He split his fleet into two divisions, with one blockading Toulon and the other anchored in reserve at a friendly port. He would periodically withdraw ships from the blockade to replenish their supplies and replace them with ships from the reserve.

The French capitalized on their victory at Loano and capture of the Ligurian coast the previous November. The Army of Italy received a new commander on March 27, 1796, when Napoleon Bonaparte arrived at its headquarters at Nice. Bonaparte informed his generals of his campaign plan. The Austrian and Piedmontese troops outnumbered the French, but were separately deployed. Bonaparte intended to attack between them and defeat each in turn. He moved his headquarters to Savona on April 9, and unleashed his offensive on April 12.[19]

Bonaparte's campaign unfolded just as he planned. His divisions marched from the coast over the Maritime Alps and routed the Piedmontese and Austrians in a series of battles. King Victor Amadeus III capitulated with a treaty on April 28, whereby Piedmont-Sardinia withdrew into neutrality, surrendered three frontier fortresses to France, let French troops cross its territory, and ceded Savoy and Nice to France. Bonaparte then relentlessly pursued the Austrians eastward, inflicting numerous defeats and overrunning most of northern Italy. The Austrian army's remnants holed up in Mantua, which the French besieged. During these months, Jervis was unable to significantly aid the Austrians and other allies. British warships occasionally picked off French supply vessels sailing close to the coast but that little affected Bonaparte's army as his troops lived off captured Austrian supplies and local populations. Meanwhile, two more French enemies yielded to Bonaparte's relentless campaign, the kingdom of Naples signed an armistice on June 5 and the Papal States on June 24. French troops marched into Livorno on June 28, and captured British merchants, merchandise, and vessels in the port.

The Mediterranean's naval power balance tipped decisively after Spain allied with France in a treaty signed on August 18, 1796. Secretary at War Dundas explained the consequences to First Lord of the Admiralty Spencer: 'whenever France and Spain are at war ... we must abandon all connection with the Mediterranean, and in truth, with the whole South of Europe.'[20] Dundas ordered British forces to evacuate Corsica and Elba, stop blockading Cádiz, and for now to concentrate at Gibraltar. Admiral Robert Mann and six ships-of-the-line had blockaded Cádiz since October 1795, when he pursued Admiral Richard Richery's squadron there all the way from Toulon. Admiral Juan Langara sailed with 19 ships-of-the-line from Cádiz on August 4, 1796, against Mann's squadron. Mann fled to Gibraltar, then, fearful of being trapped and forced to surrender, on to England.

Jervis maintained that had Mann not sailed with his squadron back to England, but instead joined him, he could have decisively fought the Spanish soon thereafter. Captain Cuthbert Collingwood recalled how:

... we waited in St. Fiorenzo Bay, with the utmost impatience for Admiral Mann, whose junction at one time seemed absolutely necessary for our safety ... The Spanish fleet, nearly double our numbers, were cruising almost in view, and our reconnoitering frigates sometimes got almost among them, while we expected them hourly to be joined by the French fleet.

Collingwood expressed the dire results of Mann's act: 'Our situation is become rather critical: the forces of France and Spain are very superior to ours; and after the evacuation of Corsica, we were left without a port, except Porto Ferrajo, which was ... the most dangerous to be in.'[21] Jervis pointed out that, at the very least, Mann committed very grave fundamental errors: 'He certainly should not have quitted his position before Cádiz until he saw the combined fleet under sail; and even then he should not have passed Gibraltar without filling his ships with provisions and water, and gaining intelligence of the route of the enemy.'[22]

Now Jervis had only 15 ships-of-the-line in the Mediterranean. Langara sailed to Cartagena, where seven ships-of-the-line joined him, then to Toulon, where twelve French ships-of-the-line rested at anchor. If this combined fleet of thirty-nine ships-of-the-line caught up to Jervis and vigorously attacked, it could sweep the Royal Navy from Mediterranean. However, this did not happen. Jervis received orders to transfer his fleet to Lisbon. He first sailed to Gibraltar, stopped briefly to take on supplies and letters on December 11, then on to Lisbon, reaching that safe haven on December 16. Along the way, storms crippled or destroyed five of his ships-of-the-line.

Jervis ordered Nelson to sail from Gibraltar with two frigates, the *Minerve* and *Blanche*, and bring off the garrison at Elba. Four days later, on December 1, Nelson encountered two Spanish frigates, immediately pursued, and battered both into surrender, but had to abandon these prizes when a superior Spanish fleet sailed to the rescue. After reaching Porto Ferrario on December 26, Nelson needed a month to wrap up lingering diplomatic issues and pack all the troops and supplies aboard. They sailed on January 29, 1797, paused briefly at Gibraltar, then on to Lisbon without incident. The Mediterranean basin was now void of British naval power except its Gibraltar toehold.

Whitehall launched a major campaign in late 1795 to regain the edge in the West Indies. On November 16, an armada sailed from Saint Helens, on the Isle of Wight. Admiral Hugh Christian commanded the fleet of 8 ships-of-the-line, 10 lesser warships, and 110 transports packed with 18,742 troops led by General Ralph Abercromby, among that era's better British generals.[23] Storms battered the armada as it reached the open sea with the result that

11 ships ground ashore and several hundred men drowned. The remaining vessels returned to port to repair the extensive damage. When the armada sailed on December 9, it included 218 vessels and 19,284 troops. Storms again battered and dispersed the ships. Most sought shelter back at Saint Helens while the rest sailed for the West Indies. On February 3, Abercromby counted only 11,869 troops with him; as for the missing 7,415 troops, most were at sea but thousands were lost to disease, accidents, and desertions. The losses in port continued. When Christian attempted a third departure on March 20, 1796, Abercromby had only 5,500 troops crammed aboard the 6 warships and 41 transports.[24]

This hard-luck expedition finally reached Barbados on April 26, 1796. Abercromby dispersed reinforcements to Grenada and Saint Vincent, then dispatched General John Whyte with 600 troops to Dutch Curaçao and Demerarra which had asked for British protection. This left Abercromby with 3,238 troops. Then General William Cornwallis arrived with reinforcements, bringing his total to 7,238. A couple thousand local black recruits in pioneer regiments raised Abercromby's strength to 9,584 officers and men. Nonetheless, Abercromby faced formidable enemy forces. Victor Hugues had about 400 white and 8,000 black troops on Guadeloupe, while 4,000 black troops manned Saint Lucia. Compounding these challenges, the rainy, malaria, and yellow fever season had begun.[25]

The armada sailed on April 21 to Saint Lucia. On April 26, Abercromby sent his troops ashore on different beaches to attack two key enemy defenses, Morne Chabot and Morne Fortune that defended the heights overlooking Castries, the capital. Generals John Moore and John Hope respectively led 750 and 550 men in twin assaults against the fortress of Morne Chabot; the redcoats took the fort but most defenders escaped. Meanwhile, Generals William Morshead and James Perry led 1,900 troops ashore at Anse La Raye then marched to besiege Morne Fortune; their attack failed on May 2. Abercromby brought up more guns and munitions to bombard the fort, whose 2,066-man garrison surrendered on May 25. Saint Lucia's capture cost Abercromby 566 casualties up front, but hundreds more to hold. The armada sailed on to Saint Vincent and Grenada, where the troops respectively crushed slave and Carib Indian rebellions by mid-June, while suffering about 250 total casualties. After his short, decisive campaign, Abercromby returned to Britain to enjoy the accolades and receive his latest command.[26]

British efforts elsewhere in the Caribbean had mixed results. General Alexander Balcarres managed to quell the Maroon rebellion on Jamaica by January 1796. General Gordon Forbes brought reinforcements to Saint

Domingue, but his assault against Cap François on March 25, was a fiasco. By July, Forbes had 7,000 British regulars and 10,000 colonial troops but faced perhaps 25,000 enemy troops. François-Dominque Toussaint Louverture and Andre Rigaud, the black rebel commanders, bloodied the British in a vicious guerrilla war.[27] General Donatien de Vimeur, Vicomte Rochambeau had recently arrived to command French troops. The result was a stalemate in which deaths soared from combat and disease. By December 1796, the British had 12,252 fit and 7,302 sick troops in the Caribbean, including 7,133 fit and 4,232 sick in the Windward and Leeward Islands, 3,576 fit and 2,567 sick on Saint Domingue, and 1,543 fit and 516 sick on Jamaica. As always, the most voracious enemy was nature.[28]

Spain's war declaration against Britain on October 8, 1796 widened the potential spectrum of campaigns in the West Indies. The Admiralty targeted Trinidad and Puerto Rico for conquest, with Abercromby to command the expedition's 3,750 troops and Admiral Henry Harvey its three ships-of-the-line, three frigates, two smaller warships, and score of transports. About a thousand miles of sea separates these two islands. Abercromby sailed first to Puerto Rico, reckoning he should attempt the more strongly defended island while his 3,750 troops were still fresh. Then en route he received orders from Dundas to first take Trinidad since the winds and currents were easier from there north to Puerto Rico than the reverse.

The armada appeared off Cariacou, Trinidad on February 15, 1797. Spanish Governor Don Jose Chacon counted only 634 regular troops and 2,300 militia to defend the large island. The Spanish fleet of four ships-of-the-line and a frigate appeared formidable, but its commander, Admiral Sebastian Apodaca was so terrified of fighting the British that he actually burned his warships on February 17. Abercromby led his troops ashore this same day. Low tides and mudflats proved more difficult to overcome than the Spanish soldiers, whose officers kept them in their fortifications. After consulting his naval and army commanders, Chacon surrendered on February 20, 1797.

Abercromby garrisoned Trinidad with 1,000 troops then sailed to Puerto Rico. The troops hit the beach east of San Juan, captured a battery, and routed the defenders on April 18. Unlike his counterpart in Trinidad, Captain General Don Ramon de Castro refused to surrender his 1,200 regulars and 3,000 militia. Abercromby landed siege guns and emplaced batteries. The cannons opened fire on April 23. Castro fought an active defense, sending sorties of his regulars to attack the batteries and his militia to fight as guerrillas behind the British lines. Abercromby gave up the siege on April 30, and began laboriously withdrawing his army to the armada. The Spaniards attacked and captured the siege train, although most redcoats reached safety aboard ship. In all, Abercromby's aborted campaign cost 225 casualties, 7 cannons, and 4 howitzers.[29] In assessing what went wrong, Abercromby concluded that 'the expedition has been undertaken too lightly. We had not sufficient information ... We found them well prepared with a garrison more numerous than us, and with a powerful artillery.'[30]

At Cartagena, Spain, Admiral Josef de Cordova commanded a fleet of 27 ships-of-the-line, 12 frigates, and a corvette; Cordova's flagship, the 136-gun, 4-deck *Santissima Trinidad*, was the world's second largest warship. Yet all these warships packed with cannons that appeared so overwhelming held a secret – they were all severely undermanned and many sailors were new recruits innocent of seamanship and gunnery.

In early February, Cordova led the fleet westward with the mission of reaching Cádiz to shadow Admiral Jervis and his fleet at Lisbon. A storm blew Cordova's fleet through the Strait of Gibraltar and far out into the Atlantic. A Portuguese frigate brought word of the Spanish fleet's location to Jervis. Jervis's fleet included 15 ships-of-the-line, 4 frigates, 2 sloops, and a cutter, or about half the vessels and firepower of the Spanish fleet. Jervis would not know that discrepancy until the day of the battle.[31] He ordered his captains to sail. The two fleets approached each other southeast of Cape Saint Vincent on February 14, 1797. When a lookout reported 27 enemy ships-of-the-line, Jervis quipped: 'The die is cast and if there are fifty sail I will go through them. England badly needs a victory at present.'[32]

Captain Horatio Nelson was largely responsible for the subsequent victory. The battle began with each column sailing pass the other going in the opposite direction, with each warship firing broadsides at each enemy vessel as it appeared through the gun ports. Nelson typically took the decisive initiative. His 74-gun *Captain* was the third from the rear. He sailed the *Captain* directly against Cordova's flagship, the *Santissima Trinidad*. Nelson's audacity provoked three critical events. The other Spanish warships slowed to avoid collisions. Three Spanish warships, the 112-gun *San Josef*, the 112-gun *San Salvador del Mundo*, and the 80-gun *San Nicolas* came to the *Santissima Trinidad*'s rescue and converged on the *Captain*; Nelson and his crew were fighting four ships-of-the-line bristling with five times more cannons. The other British captains veered toward the Spanish fleet and squared off with a warship or two. Despite the overwhelming odds against them, British seamanship and gunnery prevailed. Four Spanish warships struck their colors. The fleets drew apart as night fell.

The next morning the surviving Spanish warships sailed for safety in Cádiz harbor. Officials arrested Cordova as he stepped ashore. Jervis began a blockade of Cádiz. In deep gratitude on behalf of the nation, King George III titled Jervis, Earl of Saint Vincent with a £3,000 annual pension, and made Nelson a Knight of the Bath with a £1,000 annual pension.

The most decisive battle of 1797, took place in English ports rather than the high seas. The elation over the Saint Vincent victory soon wore off, nowhere more swiftly than among sailors. Mutiny was not unknown in the Royal Navy. As recently as 1794, the crews of two ships-of-the-line, the *Windsor Castle* at Fiorenzo and the *Culloden* at Spithead, rebelled against their harsh officers. Officials settled each mutiny differently. They pardoned the *Windsor Castle*'s mutineers and removed its abusive officers, and hanged five of the *Culloden*'s eight mutineer leaders.

The worst mutinies in naval history erupted in April 1797.[33] The sailors had ample cause to complain. They suffered from sadistic treatment from many of their officers, abysmal pay months in arrears, wretched food, and canceled shore leave, with most having been pressed into the service against their will and longing to be free. In February 1797, petitions to ameliorate their conditions began circulating among the crews at Spithead. The officers refused to accept the petitions. On April 15, Admiral Alexander Hood, lord Bridport provoked the mutiny when he ordered the fleet to prepare to sail. The crews of one vessel after another refused to obey any orders. Each crew then elected two delegates to a thirty-two-man assembly that gathered on the *Queen Charlotte* to negotiate.

Prime Minister William Pitt, First Lord of the Admiralty Richard, Lord Howe, and other key government leaders failed to agree whether a conciliatory or uncompromising response was better, so they did nothing. Hope faded that the mutineers would give up and resume their duties. Indeed, the mutineers' demands swelled the longer that the Admiralty dithered. Fear worsened that the infection of mutiny would spread through the Royal Navy. Pitt and the Cabinet finally agreed on appeasement. On April 21, a delegation of admirals met with the assembly and informed them that all their demands would be met, including the king's pardon for the mutiny's leaders. The crews resumed their duties and prepared to sail.

Parliament, however, refused to honor the Admiralty's promises. Bridport's latest order to sail came on May 7, the same day that he received intelligence that the French fleet was about to put to sea. Without the king's pardon or a parliamentary bill granting their demands, the crews again refused to obey their orders. Every warship's officers except one stood by helplessly. On the *London*, Admiral John Colpoys ordered his officers and marines to confine the crew below decks, kill anyone who resisted, and arrest any delegates who tried to come aboard. The crew rebelled. The officers and marines killed two seamen before they were overwhelmed and disarmed. The mutineers locked them in their cabins. The tense deadlock persisted.

Pitt finally got Parliament to pass a bill that increased pay and allowances, and got the king to sign it and issue a pardon on May 9. Howe presented the bill and pardon to the mutineer assembly, then visited each ship to show and explain the documents to the sailors, who cheered him everywhere he went. Bridport's fleet sailed on May 17.

Inspired by the Spithead fleet's example, the Nore fleet mutinied on May 12, with the same demands and organization, followed by those at Yarmouth, Chatham, and Sheerness. The man who eventually emerged to lead the Nore mutiny was Richard Parker, a former lieutenant discharged for unbecoming behavior then pressed into service as a seaman. The Admiralty could have swiftly defused this mutiny by granting the same privileges and pardons that it granted the Spithead fleet. Instead, the officials decided to take a hard line. News that the Dutch fleet at Texel was preparing to sail prompted the Admiralty on May 29, to order all ships to prepare to join Admiral Adam Duncan's blockade. This time one crew after another gave in and resumed its duties. Duncan ordered the remaining mutineers to be arrested. The last defiant crew surrendered on June 12. Parker was the first to be tried, found guilty, and hanged on his ship's yardarm. Of the 442 sailors eventually tried, 59 were condemned to death, 29 actually executed, 29 were imprisoned, 9 were flogged, and the rest were acquitted or pardoned.[34]

Ideally, this brutal crackdown would have nipped any budding mutinies elsewhere, but desperate men are capable of anything. Jervis dealt decisively when the mutiny spread to warships in his own fleet at Lisbon in July. He issued the order to 'fire into that part of his Majesty's ship, the Defense, where … persons [were] resisting or refusing obedience to lawful commands … and continue your fire until they submit.'[35] Facing extinction, the mutineers submitted. The four ringleaders were court-martialed and hanged, the followers suffered varying punishments.[36] Only one mutiny actually got away with murder. In September, the crew of the 32-gun *Hermione* rebelled after two of their mates died at the hands of a cruel captain. The sailors killed the captain and six other officers and cast several others adrift in a longboat. They then sailed to asylum at a Spanish port.

Although word of the mutinies reached Dutch Admiral John William de Winter at Texel, he could not have immediately sailed even if he wanted to do so. The channel leading from Texel to the sea is narrow and shallow so that only one ship can pass through at a time, which would let the blockading fleet pick each off in turn. Winter had to wait until the British blockade was lifted, blown away by a storm, or so remote that he could get all his vessels to sea.

The opportunity came on October 8. Admiral Adam Duncan had withdrawn most of the fleet to Yarmouth for refitting, leaving behind Captain Henry Trollope to command two ships-of-the-line, two frigates, and a sloop. Winter put to sea with 16 ships-of-the-line, 4 frigates, and 4 corvettes. Trollope sailed beyond the Dutch fleet's guns, sent the sloop with word to Duncan, and then shadowed the enemy. The sloop arrived at Yarmouth the next day. Duncan swiftly roused his crews to sail in pursuit. When Duncan joined forces with Trollope, the fleet numbered 16 ships-of-the-line. The British caught up to the Dutch 5 miles off Camperdown, on the Dutch coast, on October 11, and closed for battle. The British took 7 ships-of-the-line, 2 50-gun warships, and 2 frigates, while losing none of their own. The king rewarded Duncan by naming him a viscount.[37]

Meanwhile, Jervis's fleet blockaded Cádiz. Tired of the inaction, Jervis ordered Nelson to lead a flotilla of smaller warships to Cádiz and bombard the city on the nights of July 3 and 5. He hoped to provoke the Spanish fleet out to fight but they stayed safely beyond range while Cádiz was pounded into mass destruction and death. Jervis then detached Nelson with 3 74-gun warships, a 50-gun warship, 3 frigates, a cutter, and a bomb ketch to capture Santa Cruz on Tenerife, Spain's westernmost Canary Island. In doing so, the British would eliminate a key link in Spain's trade empire and seize millions of dollars of gold and silver rumored to be stored there.

This expedition's failure would have merited at best a footnote had not Nelson teetered so near to death or capture. He planned to seize Santa Cruz by leading a night assault of 1,000 marines and sailors against the eastern of the 2 forts overlooking the port. His raging zeal and courage, however, was not enough to take an unbreached hilltop fortress massed with defenders. The Spaniards repelled the attack on the night of July 21, inflicting 40 causalities. A prudent commander would have abandoned all thought of future assaults. Nelson led another attack three nights later, this time into the town itself. The Spanish not only slaughtered 98 of his men but encircled with 8,000 troops Nelson and the 300 survivors who fought their way into the main square. Nelson was among those grievously wounded; surgeons amputated his right arm after a musket ball shattered the elbow.

Astonishingly, Nelson was still full of fight. He sent a message to Governor Juan Gutierrez warning that his gunners would bombard the town to rubble if the British ashore were not allowed to row safely back to their ships. Just as astonishingly, Gutierrez agreed if Nelson promised to sail his fleet away from the Canary Islands and not come back. Nelson agreed. He was philosophical about both the loss of the expedition and his arm: 'My pride suffered, and although I felt the second attack a forlorn hope, yet the honour of our country called from the attack, and that I should command it. I never expected to return, and am thankful.'[38] He needed months to recover from his wound. How different history would read had gangrene rotted him or he languished the war's remainder in a Spanish prison. Instead, he was healthy enough to resume his command of a fleet just in time to make life miserable for Napoleon Bonaparte and his men during their Egyptian campaign.

An intriguing secret message triggered a debate in late March 1799 among Pitt and the inner Cabinet. Surinam Governor Wilhelm de Frederic offered to surrender the colony in return for a knighthood, colonelcy of a regiment, honorary rank of major general, free passage through the British blockade for his good laden ships bound for Hamburg, and, finally, £1 million for him to share among himself and his co-conspirators. To make his surrender appear credible, he insisted that the British send at least 8 warships and 1,000 troops. This was a mighty tall order but Secretary at War Dundas insisted that Surinam's bloodless takeover was worth every penny and honor that Frederic demanded. His argument carried the policy.[39]

Admiral Hugh Seymour and General Thomas Trigge commanded the expedition of 2 ships-of-the-line, 4 frigates, and 2 smaller warships packed with 1,071 troops. They sailed from Martinique on July 31 bound for Surinam, but had a hard time getting there. Faulty charts caused them to lose time among shallows and head up the wrong river before they realized their mistake. They finally reached Fort Amsterdam on August 16, and the diplomatic pantomime unfolded. Frederic insisted on 48 hours to consider the British surrender demand. He finally talked his commanders into giving up on August 20. Over 1,700 defenders were paroled or repatriated, Frederic and his coterie got rich, and the British Empire expanded with its latest acquisition. Word of the swap inspired avaricious Dutch governors in Curaçao, Aruba, and Saint Martin to cut their own deals with British flotillas in 1800.

As the British pocketed Surinam, they finally rid themselves of Saint Domingue. A last-chance offensive in 1797 by General John Simcoe had failed to capture Saint Domingue, and cost him 2,059 of his 4,778 troops.[40] Whitehall authorized Lieutenant Colonel Thomas Maitland, now the senior commander, to strike a deal with Toussaint Louverture. The American envoy asked Maitland to include the United States in any agreement, arguing that there was strength in numbers. On June 13, 1799, Maitland and Toussaint signed an agreement whereby Haitians did not attack the British as they withdrew from their remaining positions and permitted British and American merchant ships to trade freely with Saint Domingue. Now the British could finally find profits in this benighted land.

Chapter 5

Ireland, 1796–8

The very disgraceful frequency of courts-martial and the many complaints of irregularities in the conduct of the troops in this kingdom have too unfortunately proved the army to be in a state of licentiousness which must render it formidable to everyone but the enemy.

General Ralph Abercromby

Arise then, united sons of Ireland; arise like a great and powerful people determined to live free or die.

Proclamation of 1798

Rebels act sometimes in small parties, but often in a considerable body … to at least five thousand men, the greater part of whom are armed only with pikes.

General George Cornwallis

The Irish rebellion of 1798 was the bloodiest and most widespread of all that had erupted against brutal English rule since the conquest began in the fifteenth century.[1] The Irish certainly had good reasons to revolt against their British masters. The 1800 census counted 4,550,000 people in Ireland, of which Anglicans numbered 500,000, Presbyterians 900,000, and Catholics 3,150,000. This was the political, economic, social, and religious power pyramid. Although Ireland had a parliament, only Anglicans served in it. Catholics were denied most political, religious, and economic rights, including being outlawed from attending Mass, voting, or being elected to Parliament. Nearly all Catholics were tenants; only a handful of wealthy 'Papists' were permitted to own land. Catholics along with Presbyterians paid tithes to the Anglican Church. Shortly after the war erupted with France in February 1793, Prime Minister William Pitt got a parliamentary majority to pass the Catholic Relief Act that alleviated many repressive anti-Catholic measures. Catholics could now vote, sit on juries, bear arms, graduate from Trinity College, and hold officer commissions below that of general. They could not, however, sit in Parliament or hold government positions.

The Anglican ruling elite was split between the prevailing conservative view that discrimination, repression, and exploitation of Presbyterians and Catholics should persist, and progressives who advocated equal rights for all. Among the more outspoken liberals was General Charles Cornwallis, who King George III appointed as his viceroy to Ireland in June 1798. Cornwallis cited practical as well as ethnical reasons for enlightened policies. Repression led inevitably to rebellion; the worse the repression, the sooner, bloodier, and more destructive it became. The British government has made 'an irrevocable alliance with a small party in Ireland (which party has derived all its consequences from, and is in fact entirely dependent upon the British Government), to wage eternal war against the Papists and Presbyterians of this kingdom, which two sects, from their fairest calculations, compose about nine-tenths of the community.'[2] Eliminating discrimination would eliminate reasons to rebel.

More than anyone, Wolfe Tone was responsible for the 1798 uprising.[3] Tone was a lawyer, Trinity University graduate, and Presbyterian, who, with a dozen other liberals formed the United Irishmen in 1791, as a movement to pressure King George III and Parliament for reforms including freedom of religious practice and political participation for all men who lived in Ireland. Whitehall viewed such views as sedition and, in 1794, ordered the arrest of the United Irishmen. This oppression radicalized the United Irishmen, transforming them from reformers trying to work within the system to revolutionaries trying to overthrow British rule and liberate Ireland as an independent country.

Tone evaded arrest and reached Paris in February 1796. He promised the French government, whose executive was now a five-man elected Directory, that if a French expedition landed in Ireland, 15,000 Irishmen would join them to drive the English from their land. The directors embraced the idea.[4] The subsequent complex plan involved massing an overwhelming fleet of French and Spanish warships packed with an army at Brest, and then heading to Ireland. Problems plagued the plan at each stage of its implementation. French Admiral Pierre Villeneuve and Spanish Admiral Juan Langara were to sail from Toulon to Brest. When the combined fleet stopped at Cartagena, Admiral Juan de Cordova replaced Langara in command with orders not to venture beyond Gibraltar. Meanwhile, Admiral Richard Richery sailed from Île d'Aix and dropped anchor at Brest on December 11. This brought the Brest fleet to 17 ships-of-the-line, 13 frigates, 8 corvettes, and 7 transports, commanded by Admiral Justin Bonaventure Morard de Galles; General Lazare Hoche led the 13,900 troops crammed aboard. After word arrived that Villeneuve was delayed, Morard de Galles and Hoche decided to sail anyway.

The Admiralty had no advanced intelligence of the pending expedition. When the armada departed, Admiral Richard Howe, the Channel fleet's commander, was enjoying the waters at Bath, having left in charge Admiral Alexander Hood, Lord Bridport, who was with the main fleet anchored at Spithead. A squadron of ships-of-the-line and frigates lay off Ushant. Captain Edward Pellew, aboard the *Indefatigable*, commanded several frigates bobbing off the Brest coast.[5]

The French fleet emerged from Brest on the night of December 16, 1796. Rather than speed away with word of the enemy excursion, Pellew sailed his frigate through the French fleet and ordered broadsides fired at the warships silhouetted against the moonlight. This unexpected attack spooked the French captains. One 74-gun warship smashed into shore. The other warships scattered. The French captains knew that Bantry Bay was their objective, and 14, including 1 with Tone aboard, eventually anchored there. The frigate carrying Morard de Galles and Hoche, however, did not appear. The local Irish peasants viewed their would-be liberators with trepidation rather than enthusiasm and did not rebel. A gale on December 24 forced the captains to cut their cables and head for the open sea back to Brest.

Two days after learning of the French expedition, Bridport sailed from Portsmouth on December 19. Some of his captains displayed even worse seamanship than the French. First two warships collided, then two more. A fifth ship ran aground. The entire fleet anchored while the damage was repaired. Bridport's fleet of 14 ships-of-the-line and 7 frigates finally sailed on Christmas Day but never reached Brest in time to intercept the returning French ships. Pellew, meanwhile, scored another victory when his *Indefatigable* and another frigate, the *Amazon*, caught up to and attacked the 80-gun *Les Droits de l'Homme*. The French captain unfurled all sails for Brest but in the confusion his warship and the *Amazon* wrecked on the Brittany coast. The expedition's denouement came when the Black Legion, a motley crew of 600 French regulars and 800 adventurers and idealists led by Colonel William Tate, landed at Fishguard, Wales on February 22, 1797. Captain John Campbell, Baron Cawdor, gathered 600 reservists, militia, and sailors, and led them to attack the French the following day. Tate surrendered his entire force on February 24.

Whitehall responded to these aborted invasions with measures that actually undermined Britain's grip on Ireland. Martial law and the arrest of thousands of suspects made increasingly likely a rebellion that the British wanted to avoid. Revolutionary leaders, who called themselves the New Irish Executive, developed an underground movement across ever more of the island. Couriers from Paris informed them to prepare their rebellion for some time in the latter half of 1798 when a French expedition would join them in liberating Ireland from England.

Dublin Castle housed Ireland's government which in 1798 split sharply over how best to ensure continued British rule. The initial line-up included Viceroy or Lord Lieutenant John Jeffreys, Earl of Camden and Lord Chancellor John Fitzgibbon, who championed repression, while his secretary Robert Stewart, Viscount Castlereagh and General Ralph Abercromby, the army commander, backed reform. General Gerard Lake, who would replace Abercromby, and subordinate Generals John Moore and James Craig loudly advocated the brutal crushing of any resistance. Charles Cornwallis, who replaced Camden, and subordinate General Ralph Dundas advocated conciliation.[6]

British military power in Ireland consisted of 13,000 infantry, 8,000 cavalry, and 1,500 artillerymen, including both regulars, who could be sent anywhere, and fencibles, who were raised and could only serve in Ireland. All these troops were considered second-rate at best. There were also about 23,000 Irish militiamen. As with militias elsewhere, the Irish militia was little more than an armed mob.[7] Abercromby was appalled by the dismal quality of troops under his command. On February 26, 1798, he issued a General Order condemning the 'very disgraceful frequency of courts-martial and the many complaints of irregularities in the conduct of the troops in this kingdom [that] ... unfortunately proved the army to be in a state of licentiousness which must render it formidable to everyone but the enemy.'[8] Conservatives pilloried Abercromby for this criticism and his outspoken advocacy of progressive policies toward Irish Presbyterians and Catholics; they forced him to resign on March 26.

Meanwhile, the government had penetrated the revolutionary movement with spies and conducted a series of arrests. The crackdown splintered the movement and triggered the rebellion months earlier than when the French expedition could possibly arrive. Fearing arrest, the surviving leaders reasoned that they had better act now rather than later. The first revolt erupted in County Tipperary in late March, then, as word spread, leaders elsewhere led their followers to attack British officials, soldiers, and mail coaches, and seize forts and supply depots, with the largest numbers in Kildare, Wexford, and Leinster, followed by Carlow, Meath, and Wicklow.

The proclamation that the rebels distributed was a model of revolutionary rhetoric:

> Irishmen – Your country is free and you are about to be avenged. That vile Government which has so long and cruelly opposed you, is no more. Some of its most atrocious monsters have already paid the forfeit of their lives, and the rest are in our hands. The national flag, the sacred green, is … flying over the ruins of despotism … Arise then, united sons of Ireland; arise like a great and powerful people determined to live free or die.

What followed were some very practical tactics for destroying the enemy:

> Attack them in every direction by day and by night. Avail yourselves of the natural advantages of your country, which are innumerable, and with which you are better acquainted than they. Where you cannot oppose them in full force, constantly harass their rear and their flanks; cut off their provisions and magazines, and prevent them as much as possible from uniting their forces. Let whatever moments you cannot devote to fighting for your country be passed in learning how to fight for it, or preparing the means of war; for war, war alone must occupy every mind and every hand in Ireland, until its long oppressed soil be purged of all its enemies.[9]

At their peak, the rebels numbered about 13,000 men split among 11 regiments.[10] Their uniforms generally consisted of civilian clothes with green cockades in their hats. Homemade pikes, long poles with knife blades riveted to the end, were their most common weapon. The rebels had few firearms, and those were mostly taken from magazines or dead redcoats. And they were as poorly organized as they were armed and supplied. As for tactics, Cornwallis explained that the 'Rebels act sometimes in small parties, but often in a considerable body … to at least five thousand men, the greater part of whom are armed only with pikes.'[11] Yet these seeming rebel weaknesses were actually strengths, Cornwallis noted, because 'the difficulty of coming up with an army of this kind without artillery and baggage in that wild and mountainous country has hitherto prevented our striking any serious blow.' Compounding these rebel strengths was 'the ignorance of our officers who have commanded small detachments, has afforded the Rebels some encouraging advantages.'[12] A final handicap was the loyal militia, the Orangemen, who 'are totally without discipline, contemptible before the enemy when any serious resistance is made to them, but ferocious and cruel in the extreme when any poor wretches either with or without arms come within their power; in short murder appears to be their favorite pastime.'[13]

Camden proclaimed martial law for Ireland on March 30, and ordered General Lake to mobilize the troops and militia against the rebels. Lord Chancellor John Fitzgibbon, Earl of Clare, advocated the most ruthless means to crushing the rebellion whose 'nature and extent have been so completely developed that no man will now venture to condemn the necessary acts of vigour which have been, and will, I trust, continue to be, exerted for its suppression.'[14] The result was a war without mercy as each side butchered the other. John Beresford, the revenue commissioner, wrote vividly of the vicious fighting, pillaging, raping, and murdering that he witnessed: 'The most wanton murders are being committed ... the cry is for instant trial and execution ... they want actually to hang every person taken, some even without trial.'[15] Cornwallis grieved at the vicious cycle of violence whereby 'the deluded wretches who are still wandering about in considerable bodies and ... committing still greater cruelties than they themselves suffer.'[16]

At his Knockallen Hill headquarters, General Dundas received a delegation of Kildare rebel leaders under a truce flag on May 28. The rebels promised to lay down their arms and return home if the government released and pardoned all prisoners. Dundas sent to Camden a report on what transpired along with the recommendation that Camden sign a document acknowledging that 'the rebels had taken up arms for the redress of their wrongs ... and they were willing to forgive and forget what had passed, and to lay down their arms, on condition of indemnity to them and their friends.' This provoked Camden immediately to gallop an order to Dundas 'not to accept any terms short of unconditional submission by the rebels, and the surrender of their leaders to be punished as they deserve.'[17]

The campaign's turning points came in May and June. First came the arrests of most of the movement's leadership, including John Sheares, John Lawless, and, the chief, Lord Edward Fitzgerald.[18] Then came the surrender of 3,000 rebels at Knockallen Hill on May 26, and the battles of New Ross on June 3, Antrim on June 7, Ballynahinch on June 13, Arklow on June 9, and, most decisively, Vinegar Hill on June 21, when British troops routed and slaughtered thousands of rebels. Lake unleashed his men to exterminate any Irish men and many women and children they found regardless of their proclaimed religion or loyalties.

Whitehall replaced Camden with Cornwallis as Ireland's Lord Lieutenant on June 22. Cornwallis pardoned all rebels except the top leaders, who would be tried and executed for treason. In doing so, he hoped to reverse the practice whereby the 'principal persons of this country, and the Members of both House of Parliament' for being 'averse to all acts of clemency ... and too much heated to see the ultimate effects which their violence must produce.'[19] He insisted that only reconciliation and forgiveness could break the vicious cycle of violence. Yet he understood that would only mitigate violence for a while. Rebellions would erupt as long as the government's religious, economic, political, and social repression of Catholics persisted. Cornwallis called for a policy that could 'soften the hatred of the Catholics to our Government. Whether this can be done by advantages held out to them from a union with Great Britain, by some provision for their clergy, or by some modifications of tithe, which is the grievance of which they complain.'[20] Labels matter because they shape perceptions and thus behavior. Cornwallis insisted that British officials, officers, and soldiers recognize that a political rather than religious creed motivated the rebels: 'I shall use my utmost exertion to suppress the folly which has been too prevalent in this quarter of substituting the word Catholicism instead of Jacobinism for the foundation of the present rebellion.'[21]

By the time the French invaded, the British had smothered the rebellion. The Directory did not officially order the expedition until July 13, 1798. Two forces would land on different parts of the Irish coast then rally and arm the rebels as they marched inland and joined forces. The British blockade prevented any precise departure date. Each force would sail whenever the varying weather conditions and array of enemy warships hovering off the coast appeared the most advantageous. At La Rochelle, General Joseph Humbert and 1,099 French troops boarded 3 frigates that sailed on August 6. At Brest, Wolfe Tone, General Gerald Hardy, and 3,000 troops crammed aboard a flotilla of one ship-of-the-line and eight frigates commanded by Admiral Jean Baptiste Bompart. A fiasco ensued when this armada first tried to slip past the blockade on August 20; two frigates collided, British warships converged, and the French warships reversed course for the safety of Brest's harbor.

Humbert and his troops disembarked at Killala, a tiny port on Donegal's remote north coast on August 22. The French distributed arms and munitions, and gave rudimentary training to rebels who gathered. Three days later, Humber led his troops and rebels inland. After learning of the invasion, General Francis Hutchinson, the region's commander, massed his forces at Castlebar and called on General Lake for reinforcements. Lake hurried to Castlebar and took command of the 1,700 troops and militiamen. Upon reaching Castlebar on August 27, Humbert positioned his guns and troops, then ordered a bombardment. After the French gunners blasted swatches of dead and wounded through the enemy ranks, the infantry charged and routed the British. In all, the British lost 9 cannons, 53 killed, 36 wounded, and 278 missing. Lake and the remnants of his troops fled 20 miles south to Hollymount.[22]

Cornwallis had marched with several thousand troops from Dublin and, on August 27, reached Athlone, where he learned of Lake's debacle at Castlebar. Cornwallis split the 10,000 troops in the region into 3 columns to converge on Humbert. On September 8, Cornwallis caught up to Humbert at Ballinamuck, and hurled his 5,000 troops at Humbert's men, now reduced to 750 French and several hundred Irish. Facing overwhelming odds, Humbert surrendered. Cornwallis dispatched columns to capture the remaining French troops at Killala, which fell on September 23. The terms for Humbert and his troops could not have been more lenient – they were given honors of war, paroled, and shipped back to France. In stark contrast, the fate of the rebels who joined the French was harsh. Scores of leaders were tried and executed, and hundreds of their followers were imprisoned.

The campaign was not yet done. The expedition of Bompart and Hardy managed to sail past the blockade on September 16. Admiral John Warren's squadron of 3 ships-of-the-line and 6 frigates closed with the French armada off Ireland's north coast on October 12, and after a fierce battle captured 6 warships packed with 2,500 troops and Wolfe Tone. Hardy's troops received the same terms as Humbert's, pardon and repatriation. Tone, however, was tried and sentenced to death for treason. He cheated the hangman by slitting his throat on November 10.

Just how many people died during the 1798 rebellion will never be known, but the standard number is over 30,000. Perhaps a thousand political prisoners were imprisoned or deported to Botany Bay, Australia or Prussian salt mines. Thousands more fled to America and other foreign safe havens. The figures are precise for the number of captured arms, including 48,109 muskets, 1,756 bayonets, 4,463 pistols, 4,183 swords, 248 blunderbusses, 22 cannons, and 70,630 pikes. As for property damage, government claims amounted to £1,023,337, but this was just a fraction of the value of thousands of destroyed houses, churches, offices, and warehouses, and their contents.[23]

The Pitt government tried to follow up this military victory with conciliatory policies to placate Irish Presbyterians and Catholics. On January 1, 1800, the Union Bill took effect. The Irish Parliament was dissolved and 100 seats were opened to Irish Anglicans in Britain's House of Commons, and 28 peers and 4 Anglican bishops in the House of Lords. This reform, of course, failed to alleviate the plight of Irish Catholics or even Presbyterians in any way. For this, Pitt tried to push through a Catholic Relief Act that would have granted full religious, political, and economic rights to all Irish men, but King George III rejected it. Pitt resigned. The oppression of Catholics persisted. The British kept nearly 50,000 regulars and fencibles in Ireland for the war's duration to deter and, if necessary, crush other rebellions.

Chapter 6

Egypt and the Mediterranean, 1798–9

The ... appearance of a British squadron in the Mediterranean is a
condition on which the fate of Europe may ... depend ... if, by our
appearance in the Mediterranean, we can encourage Austria to come
forward again, it is ... probably that the other powers will seize the
opportunity of acting at the same time.

George, Lord Spencer

I feel that I have the zeal and activity to do credit to your appointment,
and yet to be unsuccessful hurts me most sensibly. But if they are above
water, I will find them out, if possible bring them to battle.

Horatio Nelson

It was Napoleon Bonaparte who broke the back of what came to be
known as the First Coalition. After capturing most of northern Italy in
the summer of 1796, he defeated in succession four Austrian offensives
designed to retake the region and relieve the Austrian garrison besieged
in Mantua. In January 1797, he launched an offensive that over the next
three months pushed the Austrians back to within 80 miles of Vienna.
The Austrians desperately signed the preliminary Treaty of Leoben on
April 17, and the elaborate Treaty of Campo Formio on October 18, 1797,
both imposed by Bonaparte. Austria recognized France's acquisition of its
Netherlands province (modern Belgium) and the Ionian Islands, territorial
expansion to the Rhine, free navigation of the Rhine, Mosel, and Meuse
Rivers, and the Cisalpine and Ligurian Republics established as French
protectorates in northern Italy. In return, France accepted Austria's takeover
of the Venetian Republic. The First Coalition essentially died when Austria
dropped out of the war.

Despite these discouraging events, King George III, Prime Minister
William Pitt, and the other ministers were deadset to fight on. Pitt and the
inner Cabinet made a crucial policy decision on April 6, 1798.[1] The Royal
Navy would reenter the Mediterranean and square off with the French and
Spanish for its control. Many reasons shaped this decision. The decisive

victories of Saint Vincent and Camperdown shifted the naval power balance and freed more warships for a Mediterranean fleet. The Channel and Lisbon fleets numbered 34 and 24 ships-of-the-line, respectively. A powerful portion of these vessels could deploy in the Mediterranean Sea.

The catalyst for returning to the Mediterranean now rather than later was word that France's Toulon fleet was preparing a major expedition, destination unknown. A Mediterranean fleet could nip this expedition in the bud, either through blockade or, ideally, by destroying it at sea. First Lord of the Admiralty, George, Lord Spencer instructed Admiral John Jervis, Earl of Saint Vincent, who commanded the fleet based at Lisbon, to send a squadron to Toulon. He explained why:

> The … appearance of a British squadron in the Mediterranean is a condition on which the fate of Europe may … depend … [I]t is as this time to run some risk, in order, if possible, to bring about a new system of affairs in Europe, which shall save us all from being overrun by the exorbitant power of France … it is impossible not to perceive how much depends on the exertions of the great Continent powers … if, by our appearance in the Mediterranean, we can encourage Austria to come forward again, it is … probably that the other powers will seize the opportunity of acting at the same time.'[2] Spencer then advised: 'If you determine to send a detachment into the Mediterranean (instead of going in person with the fleet), I … suggest … putting it under the command of Sir. H. Nelson, whose acquaintance with that part of the world, as well as his activity and disposition, seem to qualify him in a peculiar manner for the service.[3]

Jervis had actually reached the same conclusions weeks before he received Spencer's instructions on May 19. On April 20, after hearing of the expedition assembling at Toulon, he asked Nelson to see if there any truth to the rumor. Nelson's flotilla included 3 74-gun ships of the line and 3 32-gun frigates. On May 19, a storm raged in and for nearly two days and nights walloped Nelson's flotilla and demasted his flagship, the *Vanguard*. The men managed to sail to the tiny island of San Pietro, Sardinia, where they repaired their vessels. Nelson learned on May 28, that an expedition led by Bonaparte had sailed from Toulon, destination unknown. Meanwhile, Jervis was once again ahead of the game. He designated 10 ships-of-the-line and smaller warships led by Captain Thomas Troubridge to reinforce Nelson. One of Nelson's frigates brought word of his squadron's whereabouts. The reinforcements dropped anchor at San Pietro on June 5.

Nelson now commanded a powerful fleet. The alarming question was just where Bonaparte's armada was heading. By June 15, Nelson reckoned that 'they are going on their scheme of possessing Alexandria and getting troops to India.'[4] He ordered his captains to spread sail for Egypt. Nelson's hunch was absolutely right.

During the first few months of 1798, the French government, now called the Directory for its executive council of five directors, debated how to follow up its decisive 1797 victories with an expedition that carried the war to Britain or its empire. They asked General Bonaparte to assess the possibility of invading the British Isles or Ireland. Bonaparte concluded that Britain's Channel fleet and home defenses were too strong to overcome. He then suggested a target that he and Foreign Minister Charles Maurice de Talleyrand-Perigord had discussed for months – Egypt. On March 5, the Directory approved the Egyptian expedition and asked Bonaparte to organize and lead it.

Bonaparte got to work in a typical frenzy of 18-hour days that exhausted everyone except himself.[5] He launched his expedition just two-and-a-half months later. His armada included 276 officers, 28,000 infantry, 2,800 cavalrymen, 2,000 gunners manning 180 cannons, 1,158 engineers, and 900 civilians, of whom 151 were scientists, historians, and artists, packed into 278 transports. Protecting this flotilla were 13 ships-of-the-line, 8 frigates, and 18 smaller warships commanded by Admiral François Paul de Brueys aboard his flagship, the 120-gun *L'Orient*.[6] Bonaparte sought more than Egypt's conquest; he wanted to unleash his experts on that ancient land to reveal every possible secret and wonder. As he explained to his soldiers, 'you are about to undertake a conquest, the effects of which on the civilization and commerce of the world are immeasurable.'[7]

Only the Royal Navy could possibly thwart Bonaparte's ambitions. Four British frigates watched Toulon on the horizon. A storm blew them far away on May 18. Bonaparte took advantage of the storm's aftermath to ride its tailwinds southward. The armada sailed on May 19, with most vessels departing from Toulon and contingents from Marseilles, Genoa, Ajaccio, and Civita Vecchia. The flotillas converged at Malta.

The island of Malta is the Mediterranean Sea's strategic linchpin, splitting the basin between western and eastern halves. Bonaparte's armada anchored off Valletta, Malta's port and capital, on June 9. Ferdinand von

Hompesch, Grand Master of the Knights of Saint John that ruled Malta, rejected Bonaparte's request to squeeze his entire fleet in the port for safety and to replenish its water barrels. Bonaparte used the rebuff as the excuse to land 4,000 troops on June 11, march them to the base of the peninsula with Valletta at its head, and demand that Hompesch surrender. After a short exchange of artillery fire, Hompesch yielded the next day. On June 19, after garrisoning Malta's fortresses with 3,053 troops and requisitioning supplies and money, Bonaparte ordered the expedition to sail eastward.[8]

The armada anchored off Alexandria on July 1. Bonaparte led his army ashore beyond cannon shot of the city. After the governor rejected his demand to surrender, he ordered his troops to attack the next day. The French captured Alexandria after suffering several hundred dead and wounded. Bonaparte had triumphed in his campaign's first two stages. He had taken Malta bloodlessly and Alexandria with minimal casualties. He garrisoned Alexandria with 2,000 men, and led the rest of his troops on a 140-mile march south up the Nile River valley to Cairo. Defending Egypt's capital were Ibrahim Bey and Mohammed Murad Bey, the head chiefs of the Mameluk class that governed Egypt under Turkish suzerainty; they commanded an army of perhaps 3,000 cavalry and 10,000 infantry.

Before leaving on July 5, Bonaparte warned Brueys not to stay exposed at Aboukir Bay any longer than was absolutely necessary. Brueys should either crowd his fleet into Alexandria's cramped, shallow harbor or sail to Corfu. Brueys not only disobeyed this order, he failed to deploy a picket of frigates beyond the horizon to warn of any approaching British fleet.[9]

The French army routed the Egyptian army near the Pyramids on July 21, and entered Cairo three days later. After dispatching troops to secure the rest of the country and his scientists to explore it, Bonaparte launched administrative, legal, and economic reforms designed to transform Egypt from a feudal into a modern country. Horrifying news interrupted his efforts on August 14. Nelson's fleet had destroyed Bruey's fleet at Aboukir Bay two weeks earlier. Bonaparte and his army were now marooned in Egypt.

In retrospect, it was far more challenging for Nelson to find than destroy the French fleet.[10] After Troubridge joined him, Nelson sailed his warships south in desperate hope of somehow locating and battling a vast enemy armada that enjoyed a few weeks' head start. The British fleet was off Naples on June 17, when Nelson learned that Bonaparte's expedition was last seen at Malta. A few days later Nelson's fleet anchored off Malta where he was told that the French armada had sailed east, but no one knew where.

Nelson sailed to Alexandria, arriving on June 28, but to his chagrin found not a single French vessel let alone the armada. This was because Nelson had gotten there first. His fleet had sailed straight to Egypt while the lumbering, overloaded French armada sailed closer to North Africa's coast.

The next day Nelson headed toward Constantinople, reasoning that if Bonaparte was not going to conquer Egypt then perhaps he had instead targeted the Ottoman Empire. After a few days Nelson abruptly changed his mind. The idea of Bonaparte trying to conquer the Ottoman Empire by attacking its capital seemed farfetched. He headed westward and reached Syracuse, Sicily on July 19. No one there was any wiser about Bonaparte's whereabouts. In despair, Nelson wrote Jervis:

> Yesterday I arrived here, where I can learn no more than vague conjecture that the French have gone eastward ... I feel that I have the zeal and activity to do credit to your appointment, and yet to be unsuccessful hurts me most sensibly. But if they are above water, I will find them out, and if possible bring them to battle.[11]

He led his fleet east from Syracuse on July 25, bound once again for Alexandria.

Aboukir Bay is a shallow crescent starting about a dozen miles east of Alexandria. A small fort crowned the crescent's western horn and 3 miles northeast of that point was tiny Aboukir Island. Starting 3 miles east of there, Brueys anchored his warships bow to stern with a about 160yd of water between them. In doing so, he violated Bonaparte's instructions to choose between the ports of Alexandria or Corfu. He compounded his disobedience by violating elementary rules of security. None of the cables anchoring the vessels were springed to turn the vessels swiftly to broadside an approaching enemy warship. There was plenty of deep water on the landward side of the vessels that enemy warships could exploit. Most sailors either lolled in makeshift camps ashore or were fetching supplies from Alexandria. Worst of all, Brueys failed to post a series of swift frigates at intervals beyond the horizon to warn of an enemy fleet's approach.

With the wind at its back, Nelson's fleet approached Alexandria around midday on August 1, but his lookouts spotted no French vessels massed in the port.[12] The fleet reached Aboukir Bay's west end in late afternoon. What Nelson saw through his spyglass astounded him. The entire enemy fleet was strung out over 2 miles and seemingly unprepared for battle. Nelson signaled his captains to attack in two lines, with one passing seaward and the other landward to rake the French warships from both sides.

French lookouts sounded the alarm but the captains had trouble rousting their sailors to their battle stations. Toward sunset the lead British warships sandwiched and opened fire on the first French warship then steadily passed down the line blasting each in turn. One by one the British warships dropped anchor beside a French warship and fired broadside after broadside into it. About 9.30 that evening Brueys's flagship *L'Orient* exploded when fire detonated the magazine. The battle continued through the night and into the next day until every French warship had either been blown up, surrendered, or fled. In all, the British suffered 218 dead and 678 wounded, and lost no ships, while killing 5,235 and capturing 3,305 French, and destroying 2 ships-of-the-line and taking 9 others. Only two French ships-of-the-line managed to cut their cables and escape. As for the French future in Egypt, Nelson noted grimly: 'I have little doubt but that they will be destroyed by plague, pestilence, and famine, battle and murder, which that it may be soon, God grant.'[13]

Nelson reorganized the battered warships. Four of the French prizes were damaged beyond salvation; he ordered them stripped of anything useful then blown up. He had Captain James Saumarez lead the six least ravaged British and French warships back to Gibraltar. He then split the remaining warships into three divisions. He assigned two ships-of-the-line and three frigates each to Captains Samuel Hood and Alexander Ball to blockade, respectively, Alexandria and Malta. He sailed to Naples with his flagship the *Vanguard* and the *Culloden*, each with 74 guns.

Several reasons drove Nelson to Naples. There was the practical – it was a secure site to repair his warships, revive his exhausted crews, and personally recover from a head wound and malaria. There was the sensual – he was smitten with Emma, British ambassador William Hamilton's enchanting wife.[14] Admiral John Jervis, Earl of Saint Vincent, the Mediterranean fleet commander, had no inkling of how ironic his words were when he showered Emma Hamilton with 'ten thousand most grateful thanks … for restoring the health of our invaluable friend … Pray do not let your fascinating Neapolitan dames approach too near him, for he is made of flesh & blood & cannot resist their temptation.'[15] Most importantly, there was the strategic – the kingdom of Naples spanned southern Italy and the island of Sicily in the heart of the Mediterranean basin.

That kingdom was an enthusiastic British ally. King Ferdinand IV and Queen Maria Carolina were unabashed Anglophiles. The queen's love for England had swelled with their feverish hatred for France after its revolutionaries guillotined her younger sister, Marie Antoinette. Their prime minister, John Acton, was an expatriate Englishman. The royal couple's closest friends were William and Emma Hamilton.

The alliance's strength was only as secure as the royal couple was upon their throne. Severe problems afflicted the Kingdom of Naples. Ferdinand IV and Maria Carolina reigned over a realm renowned for its incompetence, corruption, and sloth. The army and navy were poorly led and manned. The royal couple itself was incapable of comprehending let alone implementing reforms that might strengthen their rule. The queen had a backbone wanting in her milquetoast husband, but zeal unguided by reason would lead to disaster. Exacerbated with her own inept generals, Maria Carolina convinced her husband to bring in an outsider to transform the army's discipline and morale from dismal to professional. Austrian general Karl Mack arrived at Naples in 1798 for this daunting challenge. Mack might have succeeded had he not received orders to test his army in war before it was ready.

Nelson was the worst influence on this catastrophic decision. After he reached Naples on September 22, the Hamiltons threw a banquet and ball to celebrate his decisive win at the Nile and 40th birthday. His nearly unbroken record of victories and the fawning adulation bloated his hubris. Nelson and Maria Carolina pressured a reluctant Ferdinand to provoke war with France.

Ferdinand finally succumbed. On November 22, 1798, he issued an ultimatum that the French must withdraw from Malta and the Papal States. He did not await a reply. The next day, Ferdinand and Mack led 20,000 Neapolitan troops northward to drive the French from the Papal States. Nelson sailed with 5,000 Neapolitan troops packed aboard a flotilla to Livorno to cut off the French retreat and block reinforcements. The outnumbered French withdrew from Rome and Livorno. The king and his army marched into Rome on November 29. Nelson triumphantly disembarked the troops at Livorno on November 28, left Captain Thomas Troubridge in charge, then sailed back to Emma in Naples. The campaign appeared to have met the hopes that inspired it. Actually nothing could have better advanced France's strategic goals.

After massing troops and supplies, General Jean Championnet launched an offensive that routed the Neapolitans at Civita Castellana on December 4, at Otricoli the next day, and marched unopposed into Rome on December 6; the French had killed, wounded, or captured more than 7,000 Neapolitans while suffering only about 1,000 casualties. Upon learning of these debacles and facing a swelling French army before Livorno, Troubridge reembarked his troops at Livorno and sailed to Naples. On Christmas Day, Championnet marched south toward Naples. One of his columns captured Gaeta with its 3,600-man garrison on January 5, 1799. The Neapolitan army's remnants fled to Naples. As the French army marched toward them, the king and queen tearfully abandoned half their realm for the other half, with its capital at Palermo. The royal couple, the Hamiltons, Acton, and the rest of the elite sheltered aboard Nelson's *Vanguard*, while hundreds more members of their court packed aboard other vessels that sailed to Sicily from December 23 to 26.

The Neapolitan army held out nearly a month before surrendering on January 23, 1799. Two days later, Championnet joined the city's liberals in declaring the establishment of the Parthenopean Republic. This government did not last long. A very charismatic and fierce 60-year-old priest began its destruction. Ferdinand asked Cardinal Fabrizio Ruffo to cross the strait from Messina to Silla, and preach the overthrown of the godless regime in Naples. After massing an army of ill-armed peasants, Ruffo marched toward Naples. Learning of his success, Ferdinand sent General Antonio Micheroux with 10,000 Sicilian troops to join him. Nelson had Troubridge blockade Naples.

As royalist and British forces besieged Naples, the liberals were mostly on their own. On April 22, 1799, faced with overwhelming Austrian and Russian offensives in northern Italy, General Etienne Macdonald, who had replaced Championnet as France's commander in southern Italy, withdrew northward with all his forces except 500 troops at Fort Saint Elmo in Naples and small garrisons at Brindisi and Bari. A Russian squadron forced the French troops at Brindisi and Bari to withdraw northward on May 4 and 13, respectively.

Determined to administer the *coup de grâce* to the Parthenopean Republic, Nelson sailed on June 21, and dropped anchor before Naples on June 24. There he was enraged to learn that on June 20, Ruffo and Captain Edward Foote, who commanded the British blockade flotilla, had cut a deal with the 1,500 republican rebels whereby if they capitulated they would be amnestied and transported along with the French garrison to France.

What followed was one of history's more vicious crackdowns before the twentieth century, and among the more notorious betrayals of all time that has forever partly blackened Nelson's name. After British marines and Neapolitan troops secured Naples, Nelson had the French garrison in Fort Saint Elmo besieged and thousands of rebels arrested. He justified doing so by obeying the king's instructions to be merciless to the rebels. During the subsequent treason trials, of the 105 found guilty, 96 were hanged and 5 pardoned. Among them was Commodore Francesco Caracciolo who committed treason against Ferdinand IV by becoming a rebel leader. Meanwhile, British marines and Neapolitan troops captured Capua on July 29 and Gaeta on July 31. King Ferdinand and Queen Maria Carolina returned to Naples to reign again over their entire realm. The allies did not stop there. They marched into Civitavecchia on September 29 and Rome on September 30.

Meanwhile, Admiral George Elphinstone, Viscount Keith, replaced Saint Vincent as the Mediterranean commander.[16] He sent orders on June 27, for Nelson to cover Minorca against a possible attack by a combined Spanish and French fleet under Admiral Eustache Bruix that had sailed from Cartagena for an unknown destination. After receiving the order on July 13, Nelson chose to disobey it, reasoning that Minorca was not threatened while the political situation at Naples remained uncertain. Keith repeated his orders on July 9 and 14, but Nelson remained defiant. Eventually Keith learned that Bruix had sailed not to Minorca but the opposite direction, to Cádiz and later on to Brest. This, however, did not excuse Nelson's blatant insubordination. Keith's subsequent protest to Whitehall provoked a heated debate among the ministers over just how far to tolerate the transgressions of the Royal Navy's star captain.

Bonaparte's conquest of Egypt and Nelson's destruction of the French fleet profoundly transformed the Mediterranean basin's strategic landscape. No change was more surprising than the alliance between Turkey and Russia.[17] These empires had warred against each other off and on for centuries. For now they shelved their hatreds, fears, and ambitions to act on that venerable law of power – the enemy of my enemy is my friend.

Paul I was among the more eccentric, cruel, and erratic of Russia's tsars.[18] His mother, Catherine the Great, so loathed him that she disinherited him and instead bequeathed the throne to his son and her grandson Alexander. But when Catherine died in November 1796, Paul managed to destroy her will and seize the throne. He purged his mother's advisors and replaced them with those who proclaimed their devotion to him. He invited the would-be Louis XVIII and his entourage to install themselves in a palace at Mittau. Intelligence reports that France's Toulon fleet was preparing an expedition excited Paul's paranoia. He jumped to the assumption that France's revolutionary government had targeted Russia for an attack to retaliate against him for sheltering the Bourbons. In May 1798, Paul ordered Admiral Feodor Ushakov to ready his Black Sea fleet to repel a possible French expedition.

It was Paul's devotion to the Order of the Knights of Saint John that would propel a Russian fleet and army into the Mediterranean. After becoming tsar, he offered the Knights protection and money. Bonaparte's conquest of Malta and pensioning of the Knights enraged Paul, who considered these acts personal assaults on himself. He had his ambassador in Constantinople get Sultan Selim III's permission for Russia's Black Sea fleet to sail through the Bosporus and Dardanelles Straits to the Mediterranean to liberate Malta from the French. When word arrived that Bonaparte had invaded Egypt, Paul wrote Selim calling for an alliance and joint expedition against France. Later this year, in November, the Knights rewarded Paul for all his efforts by declaring him their Grand Master.

Paul's letter to Selim sailed with Ushakov's fleet of six ships-of-the-line and seven frigates from Sevastopol on August 23. Meanwhile, Selim III and his advisors had spent over a month debating how to respond to Bonaparte's invasion of Egypt.[19] The stalemate had persisted even after they learned on August 12 of the battle of Aboukir Bay. It continued even after the Turks and Russians signed an alliance treaty on August 20. It took the arrival of Ushakov's fleet at Constantinople to decide the matter. On September 8, Selim ordered Admiral Kadir Bey to devise with Ushakov and British Captain William Sidney Smith, who commanded a small flotilla then at Constantinople, a strategy for their Mediterranean campaign. Selim declared war against France on September 9.

The plan was for the combined fleet to retake the French-held Ionian Islands while sending a small flotilla to blockade Alexandria. The combined fleet sailed on October 1, captured the Ionian islands of Cerigo on October 9, Zante on October 24, Cephalonia on October 28, and Santa Maura on November 13, along with Nicopoli, Albania on November 1. The only significant French resistance was on Corfu, where the siege lasted from November 5 until the garrison surrendered on March 1, 1799. As Russian and Turkish officials got to work jointly ruling the Ionian Islands, the allied fleet split up. Bey's Turkish fleet headed to Rhodes eventually to transport the Turkish army there to invade Egypt. Ushakov's Russian fleet protected transports packed with 12,000 troops sailing to reinforce General Alexander Suvorov's army that was fighting with the Austrians against the French in northern Italy.

These Russian and Turkish diplomatic and military initiatives appeared to complement Whitehall's strategy and ongoing operations in the Mediterranean. Nelson, however, saw a Russian fleet and troops in the Mediterranean as rivaling British interests and his own ambitions: 'Malta, Corfu, and those islands are my object after Egypt, and therefore I hope that the Russian fleet will be kept in the East, for if they establish themselves in the Mediterranean, it will be a bad thorn in the side.'[20]

The French government sought to relieve French forces at Malta, Corfu, and Egypt by sweeping the British from the Mediterranean Sea. In March 1799, the Directors ordered Admiral Eustache Bruix to sail with his fleet from Brest to join Spain's squadrons. There were 5 Spanish ships-of-the-line at Ferrol, 17 at Cádiz, and 17 at Cartagena. This combined allied fleet would dwarf any British squadrons in its path. The largest was Admiral George Keith's 16 ships-of-the-line at Cádiz, followed by Admiral John Jervis's 8 at Gibraltar, Admiral John Duckworth's 4 off Minorca, Captain Thomas Troubridge's 4 off Naples, Captain Alexander Ball's 3 off Malta, Smith's 2 at Acre, and Nelson's 1 at Palermo.

Bruix waited until Admiral Alexander Hood, Lord Bridport, moved his blockading fleet of 22 ships-of-the-line off Ushant, leaving just a frigate behind. On April 25, Bruix led 25 ships-of-the-line, 5 frigates, and 2 corvettes from Brest. Three British frigates carried news of this expedition the following day to the Channel fleet. Bridport's first fear was that Bruix was heading for Ireland so he signaled his captains to sail in that direction. After cruising for several days without spying an enemy fleet, Bridport reasoned that Bruix had headed south, and so sent a fleet of 10 ships-of-the-line led by Admiral Charles Cotton in that direction.

Bruix intended to engage the British squadrons blockading Cádiz, but a storm blew both side's warships far southward. Rather than beat back against the winds, he sailed directly into the Mediterranean. Jervis watched astonished as the French fleet glided pass on May 5. He sent word to Keith to weigh anchor and join him, warned the other squadron commanders to be on the lookout, and dispatched frigates to trail the French fleet and report back its directions. After Keith reached Gibraltar on May 10, Jervis and Keith sailed with their combined fleet to Minorca to join forces with Duckworth. Learning that Bruix was headed to Toulon, Jervis sailed the fleet in that direction. Ill-health forced Jervis to turn over command to Keith on June 12.

With the blockade lifted, Admiral Jose Massaredo y Salazar's fleet of 17 ships-of-the-line at Cádiz put to sea on May 17, and reached Cartagena on May 20. Meanwhile, on May 13, Bruix anchored at Toulon where he found conflicting orders to aid French forces in Italy and Egypt. He sailed to Vado, Italy where he put ashore supplies. Then, fearing that Britain's scattered squadrons had by now gathered to outgun him, he sailed to Cartagena to join the Spanish fleet. After arriving on June 22, Bruix could not convince Massaredo to join him in heading to Alexandria. Instead Massaredo talked Bruix into jointly sailing for Cádiz. The combined fleet spread sails on June 24, then split on July 7 as Massaredo turned into Cádiz and Bruix forged north. Bruix finally dropped anchor at Brest on August 8.

For nearly four months Bruix led the Royal Navy on the war's wildest non-violent goose chase. It could have resulted in a decisive French and Spanish victory had Bruix attacked rather than bypassed Keith's fleet at Cádiz in early May. The French alone outnumbered the British by 26 to 16 ships-of-the-line. And had the Spanish sortied with their 17 ships-of-the-line, the odds against Keith would have been overwhelming. This combined fleet could then have sailed to scour Britain's scattered squadrons from the Mediterranean. And this, in turn, would have empowered Bonaparte to conquer Palestine, thus decisively changing the course of history.

All along Napoleon Bonaparte was going stir crazy at Cairo. He had routed the Mameluks, crushed a rebellion, and implemented reforms designed to transform Egypt into a modern country. But he was cut off from the outside world and he longed to break free. For him the only way out was eastward to the Holy Land, ideally by diplomacy, if necessary by conquest.

The region was split among five pashaliks or Ottoman states, with capitals at Acre, Aleppo, Damascus, Tripoli, and Jerusalem. Acre's realm extended down the coast to El Arish at the Egyptian border, and thus was the most important to Bonaparte. Acre's governor was Ahmed Pasha, also known as Djezzar, 'the Butcher.' A British visitor to Acre the capital, reported that Djezzar was 'cruel and oppressive in the extreme … he had put to death the whole of his officers of his customs, whom he suspected of defrauding him … lately, in a fit of jealously, he had put to death all his wives after' a Frenchmen penetrated his harem; the Frenchman escaped.[21]

Bonaparte sent Djezzar three letters filled with flowery praise asking him for peace and the expulsion of the Mameluk leaders, Ibrahim Bey and Murad Bey, who had taken refuge there.[22] Djezzar ignored the first two letters but his reply to the last letter could not have been more pointed – he ordered the messenger decapitated. Bonaparte seized this as an excuse for war. He imagined that if he conquered Palestine and defeated any Turkish attempts to retake it, he might convince the Ottomans to sue for peace and perhaps even ally with France. He marched with 10,000 troops eastward from Cairo on February 10, captured El Arish on February 20, Gaza on February 25, Jaffa on March 7, and opened a siege of Acre on March 19. It was at Acre that his campaign ground to a halt and where, two months later, he was forced into his military career's first retreat. One man above all was responsible for that.

Captain William Sidney Smith was a flamboyant, courageous, imaginative sea warrior.[23] Captain Edward Brenton described Smith as 'ever present in danger, and the last to retreat from it; equally gallant and enterprising.'[24] Smith exceeded Nelson in at least two ways that vitally affected his career. Smith's ego was even more bloated than Nelson's and alienated most of his fellow officers. Both men received independent commands because they enjoyed powerful patrons. While Nelson enjoyed Admiral Jervis's backing, Smith had not one but two patrons at the very pinnacle of British power, Prime Minister William Pitt and First Lord of the Admiralty George, Earl Spencer. Nelson and Smith excelled in the respective independent commands entrusted to them, and simultaneously aggravated resentments among other captains whose seniority they leapfrogged.

Smith joined his 80-gun *Tigre* to the blockade squadron off Alexandria on March 3, 1799, and relieved Captain Thomas Troubridge of that command four days later. Learning that Bonaparte had invaded Palestine, Smith sailed eastward to help Djezzar defend his realm. What Smith did after reaching Acre on March 15, shifted the course of history. Acre was a walled town but poorly armed. Smith supplied Djezzar with vital amounts of cannons, munitions, and gunners, and assigned engineers to inspect and strengthen Acre's defenses. As crucially, his flotilla captured the convoy packed with Bonaparte's siege guns sailing from Egypt. Without Smith's decisive acts, Acre would have soon suffered the same fate as other Palestinian citadels in Bonaparte's path.

Bonaparte deployed his army in a crescent just beyond cannon shot of Acre on March 19, and set his men to work zigzagging siege lines toward the city. Meanwhile, Abdullah, the pasha of Damascus, was marching with 25,000 troops to Djezzar's aid. Learning of his approach, Bonaparte dispatched General Jean Baptiste Kleber with 2,000 troops to block his advance. The French routed the pasha's advanced guard at Canaan on April 11, and his main army at Mount Tabor on April 16. For now, Bonaparte could concentrate on besieging Acre without constantly looking over his shoulder toward Damascus.

A French supply convoy sailed from Alexandria when the blockading squadron briefly left for Cyprus to fill its empty water casks, reached Jaffa on April 15, and unloaded six siege guns and munitions. It took another three weeks before these guns and munitions could be dragged and placed in Acre's siege lines. The guns opened fire on May 7. Over the next two days the bombardment toppled one of the towers and opened a high rubble-strewn breach. Bonaparte ordered an assault on May 10. Anticipating this attack, Smith landed all his marines and armed sailors to join the Turks and Arabs on Acres' walls. The allies repelled the desperate French attack. Bonaparte renewed the bombardment, hoping to bury the defenders beneath their fortress's rubble. But the walls largely held up as the number of French dead, wounded, and sick steadily climbed. On May 21, Bonaparte finally lifted the siege and began his army's long march back to Egypt, having left the rotting bodies of over 2,000 of his troops in Palestine.

In a tone half-adulatory, half-mocking, Smith fired a parting shot against Bonaparte:

> I, who ought not to love you, should say nothing more; but circumstances remind me to wish that you would reflect on the instability of human affairs ... I ... your antagonist ... have compelled you, in the midst of the sands of Syria, to raise the siege of a miserable, almost defenseless town ... Believe me, general, adopt sentiments more moderate, and that man will not be your enemy, who will tell you that Asia is not a theatre made for your glory. This letter is a little revenge that I give myself.[25]

Bonaparte's demoralized army stumbled into Cairo on June 14. He tried literally to paper over his debacle with a Bulletin claiming a triumphal return after a glorious victory: 'I have razed the palace of Djezzar and the ramparts of Acre. Not a single stone remains.'[26]

Where was Nelson during this time? Nelson's heart rather than head commanded his movements. He mostly dallied with Emma at Palermo and later Naples. He and the Hamiltons resigned their official duties and sought to return to England by an extraordinary route. Queen Maria Carolina wanted to pay a prolonged visit to her family in Vienna. Nelson repeatedly asked Keith for permission to escort them there. Keith finally yielded on July 13. So Nelson, Emma, pregnant with his child, and her husband

William Hamilton joined the queen's entourage. The result was an unofficial honeymoon tour for Nelson and Emma. At each court along the way, Nelson was feted and awarded with medals and money. The trio eventually made their way to the North Sea and from there sailed to England. They reached Yarmouth on November 6, and took the stagecoach to London, arriving in a snowstorm on November 9, 1800. The celebrations for Nelson there began only after the Londoners dug themselves out of the largest snowfall in a century.

Meanwhile, Smith helped organize an Egyptian bound armada with Turkish admiral Hassan Bey whose combined British and Turkish fleet included 13 ships-of-the-line, 5 frigates, and 58 transports or smaller warships packed with 8,000 Turkish troops from Rhodes. They sailed to Aboukir Bay and landed on July 11, but, rather than immediately march on Alexandria, they camped on the beach as supplies were unloaded.

Upon learning of the landing, Bonaparte mustered 8,000 of his troops and quick-marched them from Cairo to Aboukir Bay. He launched his attack on July 25. The result was slaughter as the French charged the Turks and cut down or drove around 5,000 of them into the sea where they drowned. The French lost about 200 killed and 750 wounded. The French captured large stores of munitions and provisions.

Bonaparte sent a delegation to Smith aboard his flagship, the *Tigre*, to request a prisoner exchange. Smith was happy to talk. Meanwhile, he handed the French officers a bundle of British and French newspapers. In doing so, he seized the latest chance to wage psychological warfare against a foe he at once admired and loathed. It had the desired effect. The newspapers revealed all the disasters that French armies had suffered over the previous year.

Bonaparte despaired: 'The scoundrels! All the fruits of our victories have disappeared! It's essential that I leave.'[27] He secretly prepared to escape back to France at the first opportunity. He had two frigates and two corvettes readied with ample provisions, water, and crews. He tapped a score of his most trusted officers and esteemed scientists to accompany him. He returned to Cairo to wrap up his affairs then hurried back to Alexandria. The opportunity came after August 17, when Smith's flotilla sailed away to Cyprus to replenish its water and supplies, leaving only a Turkish warship to carry on the blockade. Leaving Kleber in command of the 20,000 surviving French troops, Bonaparte and his inner circle packed into the 4 vessels, and, on August 20, sailed toward France.

Bonaparte stepped ashore at Frejus on October 9, reached Paris on October 16, and for the next three weeks enlisted a coterie of generals and politicians behind the Directory's overthrow. The coup unfolded on November 9 and 10, as Bonaparte and his followers forced the directors to resign and the legislature to name him the First Consul, assisted by two subordinate consuls. Bonaparte had a constitution written that justified these changes and granted him extraordinary military and political powers.

Bonaparte's priority was peace. He appealed to King George III for negotiations to settle all problems between France and Britain. The king and the Cabinet rejected the offer. Pitt justified this policy as 'security against a danger the greatest that ever threatened the world – a danger such as never existed in any past period.' The war would grind on until Bonaparte and the French republic was destroyed, followed by the 'restoration of the French monarchy' which 'would afford the best security to this country and to Europe.'[28] What Pitt could not know was that victory was 15 blood-soaked years away.

Chapter 7

Holland, Denmark, and Egypt, 1799–1801

The measure may be thought bold, but I am of the opinion the boldest
measures are the safest.

Horatio Nelson

I don't care a damn which passage we go, so that we fight them.

Horatio Nelson

Well, I have fought contrary to orders and perhaps I should be hanged.
Never mind, let them!

Horatio Nelson

Russia rather than France inspired British invasions of Holland in
1799 and Denmark in 1800. Britain was allied with Russia in the
former and against it in the latter. This turnabout was swift and
largely unexpected.

An Anglo-Russian alliance naturally followed Paul's dispatch of a fleet to
the Mediterranean and alliance with Turkey against France in September
1798. For Whitehall, the challenge then was how to coordinate their efforts
to bolster the odds of defeating France. The easiest step was to forge a
formal alliance among Britain, Russia, and Turkey. Under the Convention of
Saint Petersburg, signed on December 29, 1798, Whitehall pledged to help
underwrite Russia's military efforts with £225,000 upfront and £75,000 a
month thereafter for the war's duration. In return, Paul promised to send
two Russian armies westward, one of 45,000 troops to join a British army
invading the Netherlands, and another of 60,000 to join an Austrian army
in northern Italy. Under a separate agreement they committed themselves
to a joint British, Russian, and Neapolitan expedition to capture and occupy
Malta, and restore the Knights of Saint John to power there.

This in turn emboldened the Austrians back onto the field. Whitehall
devised and underwrote a grand strategy with the Austrians, Russians, and
Neapolitans to overwhelm France's armies in 1799.[1] The offensives opened
in early March. Austrian Archduke Charles was the first to attack. He led

the Austrian army across the Rhine on March 1, and defeated General Jean Baptiste Jourdan's army at Ostrach on March 21. At Stockach, Jourdan turned his army on the pursuing Austrians and defeated them in a two-day battle that ended on March 26. The war in the Rhine Valley stalemated.

In northern Italy a succession of allied commanders including Austrian Generals Paul Kray and Michael Friedrich, baron Melas, and Russian Generals Alexander Suvorov and Peter Bagration defeated in succession four French commanders, including Generals Barthélemy Schérer, Jean Moreau, Jacques Macdonald, and Barthélemy Joubert. Macdonald commanded the French army occupying southern Italy, but the successful Russo-Austrian offensive in northern Italy forced him to evacuate the entire region except for a garrison in Naples. The decisive battles came after Suvorov took command of the Russo-Austrian army in northern Italy, and led it to victory over the French in an epic three-day battle at Trebbia from June 17 to 19, then again at Novi on August 15.

The allies failed to punch through in Switzerland. General Andre Massena blunted a series of enemy offensives around Zurich, which he besieged. The decisive battle came on September 25, when Massena launched an attack that routed the Russo-Austrian army now commanded by Alexander Korsakov-Rimski. Meanwhile, Suvorov was leading his army north across the Alps to relieve the allies at Zurich. Upon learning of Massena's victory, he turned eastward and lost most of his men who starved and froze to death while crossing the mountains to Austria.

Meanwhile, Whitehall succumbed to allied pressure to donate men as well as money to the continent. The idea was for an Anglo-Russian army to invade the Netherlands to divert French attention from the Austrian and Russian offensives in Germany, Switzerland, and Italy.[2] Somehow Pitt and the Cabinet believed that they could succeed where they had failed miserably from 1793 to 1795. Secretary at War Henry Dundas typically acted as the Cabinet's Cassandra, warning that 'unless the Dutch cooperate with us cordially and actively, I do not believe it possible to do as much by force of arms as we flatter ourselves.'[3] Once again nepotism determined King George III's choice of the expedition's commander. His second and most esteemed son, Frederick, Duke of York, would be in overall charge, seconded by General Ralph Abercromby. Admiral Adam Duncan led the British fleet. Tsar Paul contributed 6 ships-of-the-line, 5 frigates, 2 transports, and 17,593 troops. This was hardly an act of generosity. Whitehall hired the ships and troops, respectively, for £48,927 and £88,000 upfront, and £19,642 and £44,000, respectively, each month thereafter as long as they were on 'active duty.'[4]

The 1799 Low Country campaign would be much shorter than the previous campaign but would end just as dismally. The expedition sailed from Yarmouth on August 13; headwinds kept it from anchoring off Den Helder until August 27. The campaign opened with victories on land and water. The riskiest military operation is landing troops on a beach before numerous and well-armed defenders. If the assault fails a counterattack could capture or kill everyone ashore. After landing on August 27, General James Murray, Lord Pulteney's 8,000 British troops pushed inland and routed General Herman Daendels 10,300 Dutch troops near the village of Groet-Keetbun; the Dutch suffered 1,400 casualties to British losses of 63 killed and 404 wounded. The Dutch retreat opened the Dutch naval base of Den Helder to capture. By August 30, the Dutch surrendered without a fight 9 ships-of-the-line and 15 frigates.[5] York was content with these victories and resisted Abercromby's urgings to swiftly advance. Instead, he insisted that all supplies and the Russian contingent be disembarked first.

This let French General Guillaume Brune march and mass ever more French and Dutch troops to block routes leading from the enemy toehold. On September 10, Brune launched his 14,000 Dutch and 7,000 French troops against Abercromby's 17,000 British at Zyper-Shais. Abercromby chose his position well. His redcoats killed, wounded, and captured over 2,000 of the enemy, while suffering only a couple hundred casualties.[6]

York then ordered a cautious advance after the retreating enemy. The campaign turned against the allies at Bergen on September 19, when York sent 23,000 Anglo-Russian troops against Brune's 22,000 Franco-Dutch troops. The plan was for the allies to advance in four columns, two British and two Russian. Russian General Ivan Hermann von Fersen jumped the gun. Captain Herbert Taylor, the British liaison officer with the Russians, painted a vivid account of the resulting chaos and carnage:

> General Herman said that although the attack was certainly beginning too soon, the impatience of the troops was such that he could not delay it. When the front reached the enemy's work, they gave a great shout, which was repeated by the whole of the Russian troops, and succeed by a most violent and irregular fire, which appeared to be as much from the rear division as the front.

Taylor was horrified to see 'the Russians ... lying dead or wounded' and 'I observed to General Herman that the troops in the rear must have fired upon those in front.' This did not faze Herman, who admitted the tragedy 'was more than probable.' Then the Russian artillery was 'brought forward and began to fire' even though it was 'too dark to derive the least benefit.' Nonetheless 'the Russians loudly and constantly called for their guns as they moved forward, and these were fired without a possibility of pointing them at any object.'[7] A horse was shot beneath Herman, who mounted another and cantered forward to lead a charge. The Russian troops fired away their cartridges. The French counterattacked and captured hundreds of them, including Herman. Meanwhile, the French blunted Pulteney's attack while Abercromby's column stalled without reaching the battlefield after an exhausting all-night march that swung too far in an attempt to reach the enemy's rear. Although Brune lost 1,000 killed and 2,000 wounded, his men held the field and inflicted 133 dead, 440 wounded, and 840 captured on the British, and 1,792 killed or captured, and 1,275 wounded on the Russians.[8]

In assessing the battle, York blamed Russian incompetence for obliging the British army 'to give up the advantages which we had gained, and almost the whole of the poor fellows we have lost in covering their retreat.' Although he lauded the Russians for their bravery, 'their discipline is terrible.' As for Herman, York saw him as 'a well-disposed, and, in some degree, well-informed man' and popular with his troops, but questioned his competence.[9] The British valued Herman mostly for his manners, and they deeply felt that loss after his capture. General David Dundas pointed out that 'so long as General ... Herman remained at the head of the Russian troops, there was a perfect cordiality between the armies, and a perfect zeal for cooperation on the part of the Russian general; but from the moment of ... Herman being unfortunately taken, the very reverse has been the case.' To York and his generals, Herman's replacement, General Ivan Essen was petulant, obstinate, and ill-tempered. The campaign ground to a halt as the British and Russians failed to forge a common strategy. The British faced the dilemma that to complain about Essen to Tsar Paul might worsen a bad relationship. Yet, 'if we do not publicly state to the Emperor our dissatisfaction with the conduct of this general, are we not responsible for all the mischievous consequences like to result from it?'[10]

York redeemed himself four weeks later on October 2, at the battle of Egmond-an-Zee. The attack by 21,000 British and 9,000 Russian troops drove 20,000 French and Dutch from their line at Bergen, Egmond, and Alkmaar. Both sides suffered heavily, with 1,300 British and 467 Russian casualties to 3,000 French and Dutch dead, wounded, and captured. Brune deployed his army around Castrium further down the peninsula. After finally catching up, York hesitated to attack, seeing how powerful the enemy's position was. Once again the Russians triggered a battle. Essen launched an attack then, after it faltered, called for British support. York reluctantly sent the rest of the army forward. Brune's troops, now 24,000 strong, repelled York's attacks. The French and Dutch suffered 1,142 and 242 casualties while inflicting 95 killed, 732 wounded, and 612 captured on the British, and 383 killed, 735 wounded, and 8 cannons captured on the Russians. York ordered a withdrawal up the Helder Peninsula to shelter behind the Zype Canal. Brune's troops hounded York's retreating army, capturing hundreds of stragglers, mostly Russians.[11]

York faced a conundrum. He lacked enough men to overwhelm Brune. If he stayed put, his men would just consume supplies and accomplish nothing. If he withdrew to the fleet, Brune could attack and destroy him. York grimly concluded that only a deal with Brune could save his army, but at a humiliating price. By signing the Convention of Alkmaar on October 18, York could retain the Dutch fleet captured at Den Helder but had to release 8,000 French and Dutch prisoners; then he and his men were free to sail away. This was actually a good deal given the likelihood that Brune could have eventually destroyed part or all of his army. After all, it was the Dutch navy rather than a Franco–Dutch army that posed a potential threat, and that was now in British hands. All those prisoners were competing with Anglo–Russian troops to consume rapidly diminishing provisions.

But many Britons rejected York's rationale. George, Lord Buckingham exaggerated but spoke for many when he insisted that the Convention of Alkmaar as 'the most disgraceful to the British character of any document I ever read.'[12] Buckingham obviously had not read many British surrender documents. Plenty were just as humiliating. Foreign Secretary William Grenville put this gloss on the debacle in a letter to General Henry Philipps, Lord Mulgrave: 'You will have heard of the result of our Dutch campaign. It has not been ultimately successful as to all its objectives, but it has produced much honor to our troops, and much advantage to the country; and the public spirit will, I trust, remain unabated, and enable us to persevere.'[13]

Searing rage filled Tsar Paul in autumn 1799. He was incensed by reports that the Austrians were snubbing his generals and using his troops as cannon fodder in Italy and Switzerland. He was just as enraged at the British who had entangled Russian troops in a humiliating surrender in the Netherlands. His anger boiled at reports that Ambassador Charles Whitworth was conspiring with officers and officials against him. All this was atop years of enduring British depredations against Russian shipping.

Paul finally could not take any more humiliations. On November 3, 1799, he announced Russia's withdrawal from the coalition and ordered all Russian armies and fleets to return home as soon as possible. He expelled Whitworth in May 1800. Paul became increasingly enamored of French First Consul Napoleon Bonaparte after he defeated the Austrians at Marengo, returned without strings attached 7,000 Russian prisoners captured in the Netherlands with York's expedition, and offered Malta to Russia. Then came word that the British had captured Malta on September 5, 1800, but refused to let Russian troops ashore for the joint occupation as promised by the Anglo-Russian alliance treaty of December 1798.

Despite all this, Paul was not yet ready to ally with France against Britain. Seeking an intermediary step, he set his diplomats to work forming the League of Armed Neutrality among Russia, Prussia, Sweden, and Denmark. Under the treaty signed on December 16, 1800, the members committed themselves to resisting Whitehall's policy of stopping their France-bound ships and confiscating them and their cargos, and imprisoning their crews. Paul ordered all British vessels in Russian ports confiscated and British subjects across his realm arrested. Prussian and Danish troops marched into Hanover.

The result was a crisis for Britain. If the League transformed itself from neutrality into outright hostility, it could muster over 50 ships-of-the-line against Britain. But the trade embargo was potentially disastrous enough. Britain's shipyards depended on the Baltic basin for critical supplies of oak beams and planks, tall pines for masts, fir trees for spars, hemp for rope, and pitch to caulk seams.

Pitt and the Cabinet issued its own trade embargo against the League on January 14, 1801. They debated following up economic with military retaliation but a political crisis shelved that discussion. Pitt and most of the Cabinet resigned when King George III rejected a Catholic emancipation law that they supported. It was not until February 5, 1801, that a new government formed with Henry Addington as prime minister and John Jervis, Earl of Saint Vincent as First Lord of the Admiralty.[14]

Addington and the inner Cabinet agreed that the League of Armed Neutrality threatened Britain's vital interests and thus only war could destroy that threat. They targeted Denmark first because it was the League's weakest military link.[15] By making a brutal example of Denmark, they hoped to intimidate the other members. The attacking fleet would include 18 ships-of-the-line and 35 smaller warships. Only one regiment led by Lieutenant Colonel William Stewart accompanied the expedition since the object was to destroy Denmark's fleet, not invade and conquer the realm.

To head this mission, Whitehall chose Admiral Hyde Parker. Seniority and politics rather than combat prowess determined the choice. Parker was obese, genial, and rich, best known for his administrative skills and elaborate dinners. Captain Cuthbert Collingwood dismissed him as 'full of vanity, a great deal of pomp, and a pretty smattering of ignorance.'[16] Fortunately, Horatio Nelson was Parker's second-in-command. Nelson would furnish the expedition with the backbone and brains lacking in its commander. Typically, he disdained what he considered half measures and advocated total war. He urged Parker to simultaneously attack Denmark's fleet at Copenhagen and Russia's fleet at Reval, today's Tallinn. When Parker wondered if that plan might be too ambitious, Nelson insisted that the 'measure may be thought bold, but I am of the opinion the boldest measures are the safest.'[17] Parker gently explained to Nelson that ideally diplomacy would render an attack unnecessary and the first step would be with the Danes.

The fleet sailed from Yarmouth on March 12 and anchored just above the 3-mile strait between Kronenbourg, Demark and Helsingborg, Sweden, 50 miles north of Copenhagen on March 18. Sailing on a fast frigate ahead of the fleet was diplomat Nicholas Vansittart, whose mission was to talk the Danes into breaking with the League or else suffer the consequences. He rejoined the fleet on March 19 after Frederick, Denmark's prince regent, rejected the ultimatum. Nelson had opposed the policy of sending an envoy to Copenhagen, insisting that the best policy was. 'Beat the enemy first and negotiate afterward.'[18]

So war it would be. Yet, to Nelson's mounting fury, Parker squandered a week as he worried how to pass the Scylla and Charybdis-like fortresses guarding the strait. He fruitlessly tried to convince the commander of Denmark's Kronenbourg castle on the strait's western side to let the British fleet pass without firing. Parker finally signaled his fleet to sail through the strait on March 26. The Danish guns opened fire but the Swedish guns remained silent. Parker signaled his fleet to hug the Swedish shore, praying that the Swedes would not seize the chance to bombard the British at point-blank range. The Swedish gunners did not receive orders to fire. The British fleet sailed safely past as Danish cannon balls splashed into the sea a few hundred yards away.

The British fleet anchored about 7 miles north of Copenhagen. What followed were five days of Parker's irresolution and Nelson's resolution over what to do. Parker convened daily councils of war in which the captains mulled the latest intelligence reports and debated various options. The core issue was how many warships should attack. Crowding too many warships into such a narrow strait would reduce the effectiveness of their fire, make them easier targets for Danish gunners, and raise the chances of collisions and running aground. As if those were not reasons enough, what if the Russian fleet appeared? At one point, fed up with the seemingly endless debate over the niggling details, Nelson exclaimed, 'I don't care a damn which passage we go, so that we fight them.'[19] He tried to shame Parker into action: 'On your decision depends whether our country shall be degraded in the eyes of Europe, or whether she shall rear her head higher than ever.'[20] Nelson finally prevailed during the March 31 council, when he pledged to destroy the Danes if Parker lent him 10 ships-of-the-line. Parker conceded then added a couple of 50-gun warships, 7 frigates, and 9 smaller warships. Parker would command the remaining eight ships-of-the-line in reserve far beyond cannon shot. For Nelson, that was just as well.

The Copenhagen Strait has inner and outer channels split by a broad shoal. Nelson's plan was to sail down the outer channel then up the inner channel. The strait's winds, tides, and currents were tricky for navigators. It was not until late on April 1, that Nelson's flotilla anchored at the bottom of the strait. Once again, Nelson would sail against a fleet anchored bow to stern in a long line, but now with 18 ships-of-the-line ready for action backed by 6 shore batteries. The most formidable guns were in Trekonner fortress built on shallow waters where the harbor waters mingled with the inner channel.

Shortly after sunrise on April 2, Nelson signaled his captains to attack with 'close action.' The three lead ships-of-the-line soon ran aground. Danish batteries and warships rained an increasingly destructive deluge of iron balls upon the vessels. Nelson directed his flagship, the 74-gun *Elephant*, to sail around the stranded warships but it also ground to a halt. Parker panicked at the sight and announced that he would recall Nelson. Captain Robert Otway protested that the admiral should let Nelson himself make that decision and offered to be rowed to consult with him. Parker reluctantly agreed but, as Otway's boat made slow progress against the headwind, he hoisted flags signaling 'Discontinue the action.'[21] Nelson was furious when someone urgently pointed out the flags. Allegedly he exclaimed: 'Leave off action? Now damn me if I do! … I have only one eye – I have a right to be blind sometimes.' He then put his spyglass to his blind eye. 'I really do not see the signal.'[22]

Parker's message was not just for Nelson but for all captains to obey. The result for each was confusion over what to do. Most followed Nelson's signals for 'close action' and some Parker's 'discontinue the action.' The Danish fire inflicted worsening damage on the British fleet. After Otway finally reached the *Elephant*, Nelson agreed to withdraw. The question now was how? He sent a messenger in a long boat to Copenhagen to ask for a ceasefire but the man was killed. He sent a second messenger who somehow safely reached the shore along with his rowers. Prince Regent Frederick sent Adjutant General Hans Lindholm to the *Elephant* to negotiate. Nelson pointed him to Parker's flagship several miles north. The respite let Nelson and the captains of the other stranded warships get their vessels afloat. The British suffered 941 casualties and the Danes around 1,700 killed and wounded.[23]

Parker assigned Nelson the mission of negotiating peace with the Danes. The following day, Nelson went ashore and strode to Amelienborg Palace, where Prince Regent Frederick cordially greeted him. Although Nelson was polite, he did not mince his words. Denmark must withdraw from the League of Armed Neutrality or he would destroy Denmark's fleet and capital. At this, the 'prince seemed to quake.' Frederick thanked Nelson for his candor and promised to discuss the demand with his royal council. Nelson arrived the next day for an answer, this time accompanied by Lieutenant Colonel Stewart. The Danes explained that they feared Russian retaliation if they left the alliance. Would Britain stand by Denmark? They agreed to a two-week armistice as they negotiated the terms for a lasting peace and possible alliance.[24]

Tragically both sides lost the battle of Copenhagen. All the death and destruction would have been avoided had the campaign somehow been delayed a few days. A coterie of high-ranking nobles and generals murdered Paul on March 25, and installed his son Alexander as tsar. Word of Paul's death reached Copenhagen on April 8. The question then was whether the new tsar would uphold or dissolve the League of Armed Neutrality. To find out, the British and Danish diplomats agreed to extend the ceasefire another two weeks. Then, on April 9, the Danes reasoned there was no point in waiting and agreed to a fourteen-week armistice as diplomats negotiated an enduring treaty.

The fleet sailed into the Baltic on April 12. Parker was worried that if he advanced against the Russian fleet at Reval, the Swedish fleet at Karlskrona might strike him from the rear. He decided to blockade that port and pressure the Swedes into an armistice. It was there on April 22, that word arrived that Tsar Alexander had ordered his warships not to attack the British. This was good enough for Parker, who was ready to call off the campaign. Nelson insisted that the fleet had to force a formal declaration from Russia along with the other League members.

Meanwhile, Pitt and his colleagues had mulled with mounting frustration reports of Parker's indecisiveness. They finally decided to recall Parker and elevate Nelson to head the fleet. The order reached the fleet on May 5. Nelson officially took command the next day, and two days later ordered his captains to seek out the Russians. The fleet reached Reval on May 12, but found the harbor empty. Learning of Nelson's approach, the Russian fleet withdrew to the safety of Kronstadt, Saint Petersburg's naval base. Then word arrived from Alexander that he hoped to reestablish the alliance between Russia and Britain, but would never negotiate as long as a British fleet threatened Russia. Nelson flared at this threat but calmed the more he pondered it. He finally decided that this was a face-saving way for all sides to stand down militarily and let the diplomats take over. He ordered his captains to head for home. The fleet dropped anchor at Yarmouth on July 1.[25]

Alexander was good to his word. He had actually withdrawn Russia from the League of Armed Neutrality on May 19. Under a treaty signed on June 17, Britain and Russia resumed trade and diplomatic relations; Britain publicly promised to resolve Russian merchant claims against the Admiralty for confiscations and secretly to withdraw its remaining warships from the Baltic Sea. As for the other League members, Britain signed similar agreements with Denmark, Sweden, and Prussia, and eventually restored the West Indian islands of Saint Thomas, Saint John, and Saint Croix to Denmark, and Saint Bartholomew to Sweden that the Royal Navy had bloodlessly taken.

General Jean Baptiste Kleber, the French commander of Egypt, was as demoralized as most of his men. He wrote:

> I know all the importance of the possession of Egypt. I used to say in Europe that this country was for France the fulcrum by means of which she might move ... the commercial system of every quarter of the globe; but to do this effectively, a powerful lever is required, and that lever is a navy. Ours has ceased to exist ... the only expedient that holds out to us [is] ... getting rid of an enterprise no longer capable of attaining the object for which it was undertaken.[26]

Kleber asked Captain William Sidney Smith, who commanded the blockade of Alexandria, for negotiations in October 1799. After receiving permission, Smith opened talks aboard his flagship, the *Tigre*, on December 22, 1799. Smith and Kleber signed the Treaty of El Arish on January 28, 1800, whereby the French army would be repatriated to France. In signing the document, Smith officially disobeyed orders. Although initially Pitt and the inner Cabinet supported Smith's request to negotiate, they changed their mind. They came to believe that the French were so desperate that they would soon surrender unconditionally. If so, Kleber and his army would spend the war's duration as prisoners rather than receive a free pass back to France. On December 17, the Admiralty sent that policy to Keith to forward to Smith. After Smith received the instructions on January 8, 1800, he begged Keith to reconsider. He argued that returning Kleber and his army to France would likely provoke political conflict because Kleber is Bonaparte's 'most decided opponent' who bluntly confronts him with 'criticism of his absurdities.'[27] He signed the treaty gambling that his commanders would change their mind. He lost the gamble when he received another letter from Keith adamantly rejecting any compromise.

Kleber's army was embarking when Smith told him the deal was off. Kleber and his men returned forlornly to shore. When Kleber did not surrender as Pitt and his ministers predicted, the British pledged to support an invasion of Egypt by the 40,000-man Turkish army commanded by Grand Vizier Yussuf Pasha on Rhodes. The Turkish army landed near Alexandria in early March. Yussuf left part of his army to besiege Alexandria and marched up the Nile with the rest. Kleber launched his 12,000 troops against Yussuf's army at Heliopolis a half-dozen miles from Cairo, on March 20. The French routed the Turks, killing, wounding, and capturing as many as 9,000 while suffering only 600 casualties. Yussuf fled with his army's remnants to the coast, embarked, and sailed away.[28]

The French would rest unmolested in Egypt for another year until they faced the next enemy invasion. After an Egyptian murdered Kleber in Cairo on June 14, General Jacque Menou assumed command. Meanwhile, the allied noose around Egypt tightened. Joint British navy and army operations captured two vital French citadels in the Mediterranean. After enduring more than a year of blockade, the French surrendered Malta to Captain Alexander Ball on September 5, 1800. Little more than 2 months later, General Charles Stuart and his 3,000 troops captured Spanish Minorca in a whirlwind, virtually bloodless campaign. On November 6, the redcoats rowed ashore from two ships-of-the-line, two frigates, and two smaller warships commanded by Commodore John Duckworth. The following day Stuart led his army to Mahon, whose garrison surrendered on November 6. Stuart then marched his men to Ciudaella at the island's other end, arriving on November 13, and 2 days later Ciudaella's 3,600 defenders capitulated. Minorca was a perfect base for operating in the western Mediterranean basin.

Egypt was the remaining French stronghold. Secretary at War Dundas, backed by Prime Minister Pitt, talked the Cabinet into approving on October 5, 1800, an invasion of Egypt.[29] The hope was to use the anticipated conquest of Egypt and capture of the French army as bargaining chips in peace negotiations with Bonaparte. Ideally, there would be a three-pronged invasion, with an army led by General Ralph Abercromby landing in December 1800, a British army from India in February 1801, and a Turkish army marching overland from the Holy Land at some point. These invasions did take place, but long after they were scheduled.

Upon receiving his orders, Abercromby sailed to Malta where, after arriving on November 19, he began organizing his expedition with Admiral George Elphinstone, Viscount Keith, who commanded the flotilla.[30] Abercromby sent an envoy to coordinate offensives with Grand Vizier Yussuf, who now commanded the roughly 15,000-man Turkish army in Palestine, with his headquarters at Jaffa. Yussuf promised to cooperate and encouraged Abercromby to move his headquarters to Marmaris, in southwestern Turkey. That site was obviously much closer to Egypt but, more importantly, was convenient for procuring draft animals to haul cannons and wagons, and horses for cavalry.[31]

Abercromby ensured that his troops were as well trained as they were supplied. The most crucial operation would probably be seizing a beachhead from defenders. He had the sailors and troops frequently practice embarking and disembarking. The 3 types of landing craft included 58 flatboats that drew only 9in of water even when loaded with 50 fully equipped troops, a naval officer, a gunner, and 20 rowers; 37 flatboats that carried 25 troops and 10 rowers, and 84 boats that carried 10 men and 6 rowers. For artillery, barges had special runners to draw the guns in and out; each barge could hold a cannon, ammunition caisson, 15-man gun crew, and 25 rowers.[32]

Storms, adverse winds, and turbulent seas kept the expedition anchored at Marmaris through most of February even after all the troops, supplies, and draft animals were gathered. The winds finally shifted on February 22. Keith and Abercromby quickly agreed that the time had come to sail. The expedition included 22 ships-of-the-line, 37 frigates and sloops, and

80 transports, with 14,144 infantry, 1,063 cavalry, 603 artillerymen, 627 horses, and 500 mules crammed aboard.[33]

The armada anchored 5 miles from shore in Aboukir Bay on March 1, but the sea churned too wildly for a landing. Abercromby, Keith, and their men cursed the delay. Each day that the weather straitjacketed the expedition gave the French more time to mass more troops to fight the invaders on the beach. Word arrived that 10 French ships-of-the-line had escaped the blockade at Brest, entered the Mediterranean, and were likely heading to Aboukir Bay.

The French were indeed preparing to resist a landing but with far fewer troops than Bonaparte might have rushed to Aboukir Bay were he in charge. General Menou had converted to Islam and changed his given name from Jacques to Abdullah. He did so inspired by the religion's teachings sweetened by his love for a beautiful Muslim woman. Although Menou's conversion puzzled his officers and men, his indecisiveness infuriated them. Menou was at Cairo on March 2, when he learned of the invasion from the last of a series of couriers galloping from Alexandria. He dismissed the report as exaggerated before succumbing to his officers' urgings to send reinforcements, but believed he could spare only 460 troops. Rather than hurry to Aboukir Bay to see for himself, he tarried with his wife at their mansion at Cairo. There were currently 23,493 healthy French and auxiliary troops split among Egypt's cities and forts. General Jean Reynier urged Menou to strip every garrison to the bone and quick-march all other troops to Aboukir Bay. Menou refused.[34]

General Louis Friant, who commanded the French troops near Aboukir Bay, shrugged off the lack of reinforcements. He was confident that his 2,000 men would easily rout a British attack.[35] The assault finally came on March 7, when the seas calmed enough for Abercromby, Keith, and their officers to agree that it was now or never. The first wave included 5,500 redcoats crammed into 320 boats. It took a half-dozen hours to get everyone aboard before they rowed to shore.

The French gunners not only failed to decimate that huge slowly approaching target but managed to sink only three boats. The redcoats jumped into the surf and trudged ashore where their officers formed them then led them inland. After a sharp fight, the British overwhelmed the French. Friant withdrew his brigade a half-dozen miles to a ridge on the road to Alexandria. In all, the British army and navy suffered 625 and 97 casualties, respectively, and the French between 200 and 300 men, along with 7 cannons.[36] The landing and battle revealed that the weeks of training paid off as each level of the British army and navy flawlessly executed its mission. Captain Thomas Grenville reported to Foreign Minister Grenville that 'the most perfect good understanding' prevailed 'between Keith and Abercromby, and that ... gallantry of our troops at their first landing exceeded all that had been seen ... in former actions.'[37]

The rest of the British troops along with artillery, supplies, draft animals, and cavalry mounts disembarked over the next week. On March 13, Abercromby led his army forward until they were just beyond cannon shot of the French position at Mandara. General François Lanusse had superseded Friant in command and had massed 4,470 and 19 cannons along a low ridge. Lanusse parried Abercromby's attempt to turn his right flank, then counterattacked. The redcoats advanced and routed the French, who fell back to another low ridge, where they were routed again. Both sides lost heavily, with the British suffering 1,240 casualties and the French about 700 killed, wounded, and captured. Lanusse fell back toward Alexandria.[38]

Although the British celebrated their two victories, Abercromby and others soon worried that they may have been pyrrhic. Within a week, combat had killed or wounded nearly 2,000 British troops, while disease sickened another 3,500, of whom 1,000 were hospitalized.[39] Meanwhile, the French force before them was intact and being reinforced.

Abercromby pushed his army forward. The third battle erupted on Alexandria's outskirts on March 21. Menou had finally reached Alexandria and took command of 11,600 troops. His officers talked him into attacking Abercromby, who now fielded about 11,900 troops. The plan was to overwhelm the British right and left, then engulf the center. The redcoats held steady and poured volleys into each French wing, eventually breaking them. Menou withdrew his army into Alexandria. Once again the British paid heavily for their victory, 1,436 casualties to 1,700 for the French.[40] Abercromby was eventually counted among the dead; he 'received a mortal wound early in the action, but continued to direct it till the close, when he was carried off, having fainted through loss of blood.'[41]

General John Hely-Hutchinson took command of the British army. He and his officers debated a terrible dilemma. The French troops in Egypt actually outnumbered the British. If the British besieged Alexandria, the remaining French troops across Egypt could mass and surge against their rear. If the British left a covering force at Alexandria and headed to Cairo, they might not have enough troops to prevail in either direction. Although Grand Vizier Yussuf had promised to march his army from Palestine to Egypt, there was no word whether he was on the way or even intended to come. Likewise, when or even whether a British army from India would land at Suez was another unknown. Atop these uncertainties and inadequacies were continued reports of a French naval squadron possibly sailing toward Aboukir Bay.

These dilemmas eased considerably on March 26, when Captain Pacha arrived at Aboukir Bay with 3 warships and several transports packed with 3,600 Turkish, Albanian, and Greek troops. He also brought word that Yussuf was marching his 15,000 troops across the Sinai Peninsula.

Hutchinson and his advisors made a bold decision. Half of the British army would entrench to besiege Alexandria, while the rest along with the Turkish force marched toward Rosetta where they would join with the fleet's gunboats, then together they would ascend the Nile to Cairo. Meanwhile, Yussuf would capture Damietta then ascend the Nile's east branch to join them below Cairo. Hutchinson led the march that overcame limited French resistance to take Damietta on April 19; routed a French force upstream at Eft on May 5; and scattered another at Rahmenieh on May 9, capturing the city the next day. Meanwhile, Yussuf took Damietta and ascended the Nile to Bilbeis, where his men repelled an attack by General Augustin Belliard on May 16. Belliard withdrew into Cairo. On June 9, the armies of Hutchinson and Yussuf camped on opposite sides of the Nile just above where the river split into its two branches. They advanced to Cairo's outskirts on June 16, and summoned Belliard to surrender. Over the next few days Hutchinson ferried most of this army across the Nile to Cairo's side and erected batteries for a siege. This was enough for Belliard, who rendered his 13,672 troops and the city on June 22.[42]

Meanwhile, First Consul Bonaparte was doing what he could to rescue his army in Egypt. Anticipating a British invasion, he ordered Admiral Honore Ganteaume to sail from Brest to Toulon with seven ships-of-the-line and two frigates in January 1801. After Ganteaume anchored at Toulon in February, he received Bonaparte's orders to head to Alexandria. Finding Keith's fleet blocking his way, Ganteaume returned to Toulon. Bonaparte was furious when he found out and ordered Ganteaume to try again. Ganteaume sailed on April 27, again found overwhelming British naval forces before Alexandria, and sailed home.

After learning of the British invasion, Bonaparte ordered one last rescue attempt. His complex plan was designed to divert British attention from its object. Admiral Charles Durand de Linois sailed from Toulon on June 13, with three ships-of-the-line to Cádiz, where he joined forces with Admiral

Pierre Dumanoir le Pelly's two ships-of-the-line. They were to sail to Italy, pick up troops, and then head to Alexandria. Linois departed Toulon on June 13, and sailed past Gibraltar on July 1, but anchored at Algeciras when he learned that Admiral John Saumarez's blockade at Cádiz included seven ships-of-the-line. Upon receiving word that Linois was at Algeciras, Saumarez sailed there with five ships-of-the-line and attacked on July 5. For once, the French fought well and repelled the British attack. Although no ships were sunk on either side, all were battered and Saumarez withdrew his vessels across the bay to Gibraltar for repairs.

Admiral Jose Massaredo y Salazar at Cádiz dispatched Admiral Bonaventura Moreno with six ships-of-the-line to join Linois. Although his warships outnumbered Saumarez by nine to five, Moreno simply sought to escort Linois to a safer haven at Cádiz. As the combined fleet put to sea on July 12, Saumarez attacked. The battle raged all that afternoon and into the night. In one of the most bizarre tragedies in naval history, 2 112-gun Spanish warships mistook the other for the enemy and bombarded each other at close range until each exploded after fire reached its magazine; the captain of another ship-of-the-line surrendered. The surviving three Spanish warships and Linois's three escaped to Cádiz. The battle was the latest instance of superior British seamanship, daring, and gunnery defeating superior numbers of enemy warships and cannons.

After the fall of Cairo, Alexandria's fate was merely a matter of time. Allied forces swelled. The British expedition from India finally reached Egypt but by a roundabout route with losses along the way. Storms dispersed transports carrying 8,000 troops so that only 5,822 men led by General David Baird disembarked. They landed not at Suez but at Kosseit, then trekked the camel track across the desert 120 miles west to the Nile and down it to Cairo, arriving July 10. It was at once an epic march and sideshow in Egypt's conquest.

To his credit, Menou held out the rest of the summer as the siege lines tightened and the bombardment destroyed more of the city and his men. He surrendered on September 2, 1801, only after receiving the same terms that Kleber and Smith had agreed to in January 1800. Menou and 11,209 French, of whom 10,524 were troops and the rest civilians, could simply sail home, courtesy of the Royal Navy.[43]

As such, the British may have won militarily but lost economically and, thus, strategically. Whitehall squandered enormous amounts of lives and money in operations related to Egypt between the aborted surrender in

January 1800 and the actual surrender in September 1801. The combat casualties in Egypt alone were 633 dead and 3,058 wounded; disease killed another 1,000 troops and crippled hundreds more, including 160 blinded by ophthalmia and 200 who lost an eye.[44] The British, however, did extract something positive from the tragedy. Many Egyptian campaign officers like John Moore, David Baird, William Beresford, John Hope, Thomas Graham, Rowland Hill, Brent Spencer, Lowry Cole, and John Cradock made excellent use of their Egyptian experience later fighting in the Peninsula. Finally, astonishing as it may seem, the 1801 Egypt campaign was the first time a British army had defeated a French army in the eight years since the war began in 1793. And, for many British, the pride they took in that justified all the sacrifices.

Bonaparte diplomatically demolished the latest coalition through a series of peace treaties in 1801, with Austria on February 9, the Kingdom of Naples on March 28, Portugal on June 6, the Papal States on July 15, and Bavaria on August 24. Prime Minister Henry Addington and the Cabinet reluctantly concluded that fighting alone against France was self-destructive. Why not give peace a chance? They reckoned that Britain had captured enough prizes so that it could keep the most lucrative and trade off the rest.[45]

After agreeing to an armistice on October 1, 1801, the diplomats needed another five months to work out the details. Under the Treaty of Amiens signed on March 25, 1802, the Addington government bought a generous peace by returning to France, Spain, and Holland all the colonies that British arms had taken except Ceylon and Trinidad. It acknowledged the expansion of French territory to include Belgium, the Rhine's west bank, Savoy, Piedmont, and Nice. It recognized France's 'sister republics' or satellites, depending on one's point of view, known as Cisalpine (northern Italian), Helvetian (Swiss), and Ligurian (Genoan). The concessions did not end there. The British promised to withdraw from Malta and restore the Order of Saint John to power.[46]

If some Britons grumbled at giving away so much after sacrificing so many lives and so much treasure, they could at least take pride in the Royal Navy's astonishing exploits. From 1793 to 1801, British sea captains captured or destroyed 50 French ships-of-the-line, while losing only 5. The navy expanded from 135 to 202 ships-of-the-line and from 133 to 277 frigates. France's navy, meanwhile, declined from 80 to 39 ships-of-the-line and from 66 to 35 frigates.[47]

The army, however, had a much more mixed record. Although York's campaign did capture a Dutch fleet, Brune fought him to a standstill then generously let him sail away rather than forced him into a humiliating surrender. Abercromby proved to be a first-rate general at organizing, supplying, and leading the Egyptian campaign, and won three battles before being mortally wounded. Stuart captured Minorca in a decisive campaign against an outnumbered enemy. The most astonishing reports of British generalship, however, came from the other side of the earth.

Chapter 8

India, 1799–1805

The best thing you can do is … dash at the first party … If you … succeed in cutting up, or in driving to a distance one good party, the campaign will be your own. A long offensive war will ruin us, and will answer to no purpose whatever.

Arthur Wellesley

The French influence in India, thanks be to God! is now nearly extirpated.

Richard Wellesley, Lord Mornington

B ritish imperialism in India began as a private venture and preceded piecemeal.[1] In 1600, Queen Elizabeth I granted the East India Company a charter for a trading monopoly with South and Southeast Asia. The East India Company cut deals with local rulers to establish trading posts in India and elsewhere around the Indian Ocean basin where English manufactured goods could be exchanged for a variety of local products including spices, fabrics, tea, and opium. Profits were enormous and swelled steadily even after the Company lost its monopoly in 1694. For instance, the combined trade of the East India Company and private merchants with Bengal alone rose from £527,818 imports and £2,828,930 exports in 1796 to £776,605 imports and £3,382,581 exports in 1798. This trade did not just enrich businessmen. Revenues skimmed from the Indian trade contributed about 40 percent of Exchequer receipts during this era.[2] The Company's political clout in England and India alike expanded with its economic clout.

The East India Company ruled its colonies with governors armed with plenipotentiary powers of diplomacy and war. Of its expanding empire, the East India Company governed some realms directly and others indirectly through local rulers. To protect its territories and get more, the East India Company developed an increasingly larger army of both European and native or sepoy troops that periodically fought threatening Indian states and imperial rivals like France and Holland. Precipitation determined India's campaign seasons. Marching and fighting was nearly impossible during the monsoon season that swelled rivers until they were unfordable and transformed roads into quagmires. Yet the dry season could be just as formidable. Too little rain and a campaign could be canceled for lack of water for men and beasts. These conditions varied considerably in degree and season across the tropical south, subtropical north, and desert northwest.

Although commerce remained more important than territory, the logic of empire prevailed. The more land one leased, bought, or conquered, the more vulnerable its frontiers became so new frontiers had to be taken to protect existing frontiers. All along there was no grand plan to guide policy, only successful or failed reactions to commercial and political opportunities and threats. 'The enemy of my enemy is my friend' largely determined the diplomatic and military strategy of the East India Company, its European rivals, and the Indian states. In London, 24 directors organized themselves in 13 committees, of which the most important was the Secret Committee that directed army operations. Ideally, wars paid for themselves. The victorious British imposed reparations of money or land on the defeated that underwrote the last campaign and part of the next. Governor Richard Wellesley, lord Mornington explained: 'Reasonable indemnification for our expense in the war and an adequate security against the return of that danger which originally provoked us to arms.'[3]

For the first century or so, the British government's role was largely to cheer the East India Company's efforts, reap revenues from the trade, and occasionally dispatch small flotillas of warships and troops when wars erupted. Yet, the East India Company's bloating wealth and power boomeranged against the British government. The East India Company was increasingly notorious for wielding portions of its enormous profits to corrupt politicians and officials in London. Parliament first attempted to reign in the company's powers with the 1784 India Act, which made all military and civil appointees subject to Whitehall's approval. Overseeing the East India Company was a Board of Control which included the secretary of state, Chancellor of the Exchequer, and four privy councilors. Greater government oversight led to an even greater government commitment to help the East India Company defend and expand its Indian colonies. In 1798, the British army supplied 22,000 of the 80,000 troops in India.[4]

When war erupted with France in 1793, the East India Company had four patchworks of territory in India. The largest was Bengal with its capital at Calcutta. The Northern Sarkars stretched midway along the east coast with its capital at Masulipatam. Madras governed four separate territories in southern India. Finally, there was the city-state of Bombay on the northwest coast. The governors of Bombay, Masulipatam, and Madras were subordinate to Calcutta's governor. By 1815, the British controlled most of southern and central India and the Ganges River valley.

After learning that Paris had declared war in February 1793, the East India Company governors organized a campaign that captured Pondicherry, Chandermagore, and Mahe along India's southeast coast in 1794, thus eliminating France's last holdings on the subcontinent. The French clung to Isle de Bourbon, Isle de France, the Seychelles, and Reunion in the Indian Ocean; from these lairs they preyed on British shipping but posed no real threat to Britain's Indian empire. After the French conquered and converted the Netherlands into the Batavian Republic, the East India Company and Royal Navy captured the Dutch colonies of Ceylon and Java in 1796. Thereafter British efforts focused on blunting threats and exploiting opportunities on the subcontinent.

Three great Indian powers contested the British. In the far south lay Mysore with his capital at Seringapatam. In south central India was a large realm with its capital at Hyderabad. Stretching across central India was the Maratha Confederacy with its capital at Poona. Tipoo, Mysore's Sultan, was the most formidable British foe. Tipoo carried on a struggle initiated by his father, whom the East India Company defeated in wars that lasted from 1766 to 1769 and 1780 to 1784. British army and East India Company troops led by General Charles Cornwallis crushed Tipoo in a war that lasted from 1789 to 1793. Over the next half-dozen years, Tipoo rebuilt his wealth and military power, partly thanks to French advisors and arms. He allied with the Nizam, Hyderabad's leader, who also bolstered his army with French advisors and arms.

Meanwhile, a trio of formidable British leaders who happened to be brothers arrived in India. Richard, Arthur, and Henry Wellesley would win fame and fortune on the subcontinent.[5] Arthur stepped ashore at Calcutta in February 1797 as the 33rd Regiment's lieutenant colonel; Richard, Lord Mornington, and Henry arrived there as the governor and his aide, respectively, in May 1798. Their arrival's timing could not have been more fortuitous for them and Britain. Pitt and his colleagues correctly interpreted Bonaparte's invasion of Egypt in July 1798 as the first stage of a campaign to join forces with Indian leaders and drive the British from India. After receiving a warning from Whitehall, Mornington and his military advisors decided to launch a preemptive strike, but against Hyderabad rather than Mysore, which was more distant. The campaign was bloodless. In October 1798, several thousand East Indian Company troops marched to Hyderabad and demanded that the Nizam eject his French advisors and sign a treaty of alliance with Britain. The Nizam complied. This prompted Mornington to crow, 'The French influence in India, thanks be to God! is now nearly extirpated.'[6]

This assertion of British power was designed to intimidate Tipoo to follow the Nizam's lead. It had the opposite effect. Tipoo redoubled his efforts to strengthen his army, denied employing French advisors, and rejected an alliance with Britain. Mornington issued orders to invade Mysore on February 3, 1799.[7] Two British armies converged on Seringapatam: westward from Vellone marched 4,300 redcoats and 13,900 sepoys led by General George Harris, seconded by General David Baird, with Lieutenant Colonel Wellesley; eastward from Cannore marched 1,600 redcoats and 4,800 sepoys led by General James Stuart. On February 18, Meer Allum, who was probably the Nizam's son, and 20,000 Hyderabad troops joined Harris's army at Amboor. Harris appointed Wellesley and his 33rd regiment to help Allum better organize, equip, and train the Hyderabad army. Although Tipoo had 33,000 infantry, 15,000 cavalry, and 2,000 gunners manning 100 cannons, the training, equipment, arms, and morale of his troops was abysmal compared with that of the British and their sepoys. Hundreds of elephants and thousands of water buffalos dragged carts packed with supplies and siege guns. Against a superior enemy, Tipoo could only fight delaying actions as he withdrew his forces to Seringapatam. His light cavalry skirmished with the advanced guards or raided the supply trains of the British columns. He imposed a scorched earth policy of carrying away all food or draft animals, and poisoning the wells. At one point Tipoo vented his rage by ordering 12 captured British troops murdered by strangling or having nails driven into their skulls. His hope was to stall the British columns until the rainy season rendered the rivers impassible. This hope died when the British forces reached Seringapatam in early April nearly six weeks before the rainy season began.

Harris had batteries emplaced and probing attacks launched at vulnerable points around the walled city. Wellesley recalled 'a series of successful attacks upon the enemy's posts, particularly one which I made upon his posts close to the river and within about 400 yards of the fort … enabled us to erect our breaching batteries at a very short distance, and to complete our breach.' The final assault came on May 4. The city 'was in our possession in about two hours after the troops first began to move out of the trenches. Tipu was killed in one of the gateways, and to complete our good fortune his body was found among the 500 others piled … in a very narrow compound.'[8]

This victory came at a huge cost – the British forces suffered 181 dead, 622 wounded, and 2 missing Europeans, and 119 dead, 420 wounded, and 100 missing sepoys. Although most of the more than 20,000 defenders surrendered, 9,000 died in the fighting.[9]

To the victors went the spoils. Tipoo's treasure was mindboggling – £1,143,216, of which Harris pocketed £150,000, Wellesley £4,000, and the troops about £5 each.[10] These were not the only plums. Seringapatam needed a governor. Baird was the natural choice as the second-in-command who had led the assault. The trouble was that Baird had, as Wellesley noted, 'strong prejudices against the natives' having 'been Tipoo's prisoner for years.'[11] So Harris instead tapped Wellesley to serve temporarily which Mornington made official in September. Baird naturally resented this, complaining that 'I was superseded by an inferior officer.'[12] To Arthur, Mornington justified the reasons for and consequences of his rather blatant act of nepotism: 'Great Jealousy will arise among the General Officers in consequence of my employing you; but I employ you because I rely on your good sense, discretion, activity, and spirit; and I cannot find all these qualities united in any other officer in India who could take such a command.'[13] Mornington wrote proudly that:

> My brother Arthur has distinguished himself most brilliantly in an expedition against an insurgent, who had collected a great force of predatory cavalry – the wreck of Tipoo's army. We have now proved – a perfect novelty in India – that we can hunt down the lightest footed and most rapid armies as well as we can destroy heavy troops and storm strong fortifications.[14]

The British had no sooner crushed the Mysore threat when a new one arose. Dhoondiah Vagh, Tipoo's son, had escaped and gathered an army to reconquer his inheritance. He got crucial secret support from the Maratha Confederacy and Hyderabad's Nizam. Mornington assigned the mission of crushing Dhoondiah to his younger brother. Wellesley did not launch his campaign until he received hard intelligence of his enemy's military, economic, and political strength gathered by sepoys who infiltrated Dhoondiah's forces. By April 11, 1800, Dhoondiah's army included 5,000 infantry, 6,000 militia, and 15,000 cavalry. Given the superior quality of British forces, Dhoondiah's only sensible strategy was a hit-and-run campaign. Wellesley split his 8,000-man army among 3 columns and set off in pursuit of Dhoondiah in June 1800. Each column slowly diminished in numbers as men deserted or died from disease, and units were hived off to garrison key positions. The first victories came on July 10, 14, 28, and 31, when British forces captured the fortresses of Savanore, Koondgul, Dummul, and Gudduck. Dhoondiah, however, always managed to slip away without suffering a decisive defeat. Learning that Dhoondiah and his army were encamped near the fortress of Manowly, Wellesley quick-marched his troops there, where they slaughtered nearly 5,000 enemy troops. Once again Dhoondiah escaped. It took another five weeks before Wellesley discovered his elusive enemy's latest lair. The British attack at Conaghul on September 10, killed Dhoondiah and most of his 5,000 troops.[15] With mingled pride and weariness, Wellesley reported 'the complete defeat and dispersion of the enemy's force, and above all, the death of Dhoondiah, puts an end to this warfare ... At the same time I must inform you that all the troops have undergone, with the greatest patience and perseverance, a series of fatiguing services.'[16] Wellesley resumed his governorship of Mysore.

Meanwhile, the Maratha Confederacy's current chief or Peshwa, Baji Rao II, was contested by Jawswant Rao Holkar of Indore, Maharaja Daulut Rao Sindia of Gwalior, and Raja Bhonsla of Berar. In retaliation for the murder of his brother, Holkar attacked and routed the combined forces of Baji Rao and Sindia at Poona, the Martha capital. Baji Rao fled to Bassein near Bombay and requested British help in restoring him to power. Mornington reported: 'The crisis of affairs appeared ... to afford the most favorable opportunity for the complete establishment of the interest of the British power in the Maratha empire.'[17] On December 31, 1802, Baja Rao and Barry Close, signed the Treaty of Bassein that committed the British to restore Baji Rao to his throne for one-third of his territory. Mornington assigned Arthur Wellesley that task. Wellesley commanded his own army of 14,700 troops and a separate force of 8,856 troops led by Lieutenant Colonel James Stevenson.

The campaign opened on March 12, 1803. Holkar ordered his general, Amrit Rao, to withdraw his army from Poona. On April 20, Wellesley's troops marched unopposed into Poona, escorted Baji Rao back to his throne, and in the following weeks asserted order over the region. However, the threat to the Peshwa's power lingered. Holkar allied with Sindia and Bhonsla Raja to oppose Baji Rao's rule; together they commanded over 52,000 troops. Mornington organized a campaign to converge and destroy those defiant rival chiefs. General Gerard Lake would march with 4,500 troops from Bombay, General James Stuart with 5,000 troops from

Madras, and Wellesley, seconded by Stevenson, with 7,700 troops, including 1,500 redcoats, 6,200 sepoys, and 22 cannons, from Poona.[18]

Wellesley launched his latest campaign on August 7. With a much shorter distance to the enemy, he and his troops soon racked up victories. Guarding the frontier was the hilltop fortress of Ahmednuggur, which Wellesley and his troops reached on August 7. The next day, Wellesley ordered an attack that captured the outer fortifications. It took just two more days before heavy cannons were emplaced to blast a breach through the fortress walls. The garrison surrendered on August 11. An allied Indian chief offered a mythic account that spread widely in the minds of Indians and thus enhanced British power: 'These English are a strange people. They came here in the morning, surveyed the wall, walked over it, killed the garrison, and returned to breakfast.'[19]

The region's most formidable Maratha chief was Sindia with 40,000 troops and 100 cannons. Wellesley caught up to Sindia at Assaye on September 23, 1803. Having detached troops to defend depots and his supply lines, Wellesley had with him only 4,500 troops, including 1,300 British infantry, 2,000 sepoy infantry, and 1,200 cavalry. Nonplused, Wellesley was determined to attack. The trouble was that the enemy was on the Kaitna River's far side. Native guides insisted there were no undefended fords across the river. Wellesley was just as adamant that there must be a way across. He found it after scanning the landscape with his spyglass. Two villages faced each other on opposite banks a mile downstream from the Maratha's left flank. He reasoned that 'men could not have built two villages so close to one another … without some habitual means of communications either by boats or a ford – most probably by the latter.' After dispatching a scout who confirmed his hunch, Wellesley promptly led his army across the river.

Sindia shifted his army against Wellesley's men and ordered his gunners to open fire. The Maratha barrage killed or wounded many men, including Wellesley's aide whose head was shattered by a cannon ball. Wellesley deployed his troops between the Kaitna River and the Juah River a mile north, then ordered an attack. The British and sepoys routed the Marathas who did not stop running until they faced the Juah River. Sindia and his officers managed to rally their men to face their pursuers. Wellesley ordered an attack that shattered the Marathas. Looking back, Wellington reckoned the battle of Assaye 'the bloodiest for the numbers that I ever saw.' In all, his men suffered 1,584 casualties, including 428 dead, but inflicted 1,200 killed and 4,800 wounded, and captured 102 cannons. Wellesley himself had one horse shot beneath him and another speared.[20]

Sindia escaped with thousands of troops and joined forces with Bhonsla. Wellesley and his men spent two months pursuing before they caught up to the Maratha chiefs. Along the way they captured the fortresses of Burhanpur and Asirghar. Wellesley and Sindia's envoy signed a suspension of hostilities on November 22. Wellesley led his army into Berar on November 25. When Sindia refused to withdraw from nearby Argaum, Wellesley marched his army there. On November 29, 1803, Wellesley ordered his advanced guard to capture a massed battery of fifty cannons. The Marathas repulsed the attack. Wellesley rallied his troops. They shattered 2 Maratha assaults then attacked and routed the enemy, slaughtered over 3,000 troops and captured 38 cannons, while suffering 562 casualties. The victorious army marched to Sindia's capital at Gwalior and opened a siege on December 13. Two days later the defenders surrendered. Wellesley won that fortress at a cost of only 14 killed and 112 wounded. Sindia had fled Gwalior before Wellesley's army arrived and now withdrew his army's remnants to the Deccan. Short of men, munitions, provisions, and pay, Wellesley's campaign ended at Gwalior.[21]

Lake's campaign, meanwhile, was just as successful. Lake and his troops captured Aligarh fortress on September 4, and defeated Holkar's 19,000-man army at Dehli on September 11. Yet Holkar escaped with most of his army. Lake marched on to Agra, taking that fortress on October 17. The decisive battle came at Lasswary on November 1, when Lake's army crushed the Maratha army. Yet it was not until late the next year that Lake finally ran Holkar to ground. His army defeated Holkar at Furruckabad on November 17, 1804, slaughtered 3,000 Indians at the cost of 2 British dead and 26 wounded. Holkar surrendered at Amritsar on December 24, 1805.[22]

Britain's empire in India more than doubled in size during the seven years from Mornington's arrival in 1798 to Holkar's surrender in 1805. Arthur Wellesley worried about imperial overstretch: 'The extension of our territory and influence has been greater than our means. Besides, we have added to the number and description of our enemies ... Whenever we spread ourselves, particularly if we aggrandize ourselves at the expense of the Marathas, we increase this evil. We throw out of employment, and of means of subsistence, all who have hitherto managed the revenue, commanded or served in the armies, or have plundered the country. These people become additional enemies at the same time that, by the extension of our territory, our means of supporting our government, and of defending ourselves, are proportionately decreased.'[23] To maintain and eventually enhance the empire, he insisted that mild rather than harsh treaties with the vanquished were most likely to endure: 'The war will be eternal if nobody is ever to be forgiven. When the empire of the Company is so great, little dirty passions must not be suffered to guide its measures.'[24]

Henry Wellesley offered his own prescription for imperial rule:

> If the Indian Empire be a great stake to the Nation ... the advantages which Great Britain ought to derive from what has been declared the brightest jewel in the Imperial diadem, will never be realized until the ... Government of India shall be revised and general principles shall superseded the miserable policy of temporary expedients. We may then hope to see the interests of the people of India more liberally considered, and on pervading power, watching over and directing the ways and means and their applications.[25]

Inevitably, wars would erupt. For Arthur Wellesley, the crucial strategic and tactical lesson was 'light and quick movements, and we ought always to be in that state to be able to strike a blow as soon as a war might become evidently necessary.'[26] Experience taught him that after catching up to the enemy 'the best thing you can do is ... dash at the first party ... if you ... succeed in cutting up, or in driving to a distance one good party, the campaign will be your own. A long offensive war will ruin us, and will answer to no purpose whatever.'[27]

Having experienced war on two continents, Wellesley clearly understood that what worked well in defeating one enemy would not necessarily work in defeating another. Indian armies were little more than armed mobs that were easily scattered and slaughtered by a swift ruthless bayonet assault. The opposite tactic, of deploying his troops in excellent defensive positions, awaiting an attack, and then unleashing concentrated musket and artillery fire worked best against the French. If tactics varied with one's enemies, logistical skills were universally applicable. The lessons in how best to supply his troops with provisions and munitions that he learned in India served him well in Iberia. Likewise India taught him vital lessons about how to keep men physically and emotionally healthy anywhere. Finally there was diplomacy. The byzantine nature of Indian politics and culture prepared Wellesley for similar challenges with the Portuguese and especially the Spaniards. After returning to Britain in September 1808, Wellesley would have nearly three years to ponder all this before his first campaign on the Peninsula in August 1808.

Chapter 9

Trafalgar, 1805

If we could master the straits for six hours, we would be masters of the world.

Napoleon

I do not say the French cannot come. I only say they cannot come by sea.

John Jervis, Earl of Saint Vincent

Thank God I have done my duty.

Horatio Nelson

The peace of Amiens did not last long, less than fourteen months from the treaty's signature on March 24, 1802, until Britain declared war against France on May 18, 1803.[1] Ample blame can be heaped on both sides for resuming war. Each violated the Amiens treaty as British troops remained in Malta and Egypt, and French troops in Holland, Italy, and Switzerland. Each insisted that it would end its occupations only after the other departed first.

What most alarmed Whitehall were spy reports that Bonaparte had launched a naval build-up by constructing 32 ships-of-the-line at French and Dutch shipyards.[2] He seemed to be preparing another Egyptian expedition. He sent special envoy General François Sebastiani on a diplomatic and intelligence-gathering mission to Egypt. Three days after Sebastiani returned to Paris on January 25, 1803, the *Moniteur*, the French government's quasi-official newspaper, published his report revealing that Britain's occupation force was weak and could be defeated by just 6,000 French troops. The British force was indeed weak because Whitehall had ordered it steadily diminished as the Turks established a government in Cairo. The last British troops sailed from Egypt on March 17, although word did not reach Paris for a couple of months. Regardless, the redcoats stayed firmly put in Malta.

A classic 'mirror image' trapped Paris and London as each accused the other of violating the Amiens treaty and preparing an attack. Bonaparte summoned ambassador Charles Whitworth on March 13, 1803, and demanded why his government wanted to resume war. Whitworth replied that Britain did not want a war that French treaty violations were making increasingly likely. This enraged Bonaparte who castigated the British for bad faith. Whitworth conveyed Bonaparte's remarks to London. Whitehall instructed Whitworth to issue Bonaparte an ultimatum to withdraw all French troops from Holland, Switzerland, and Italy; if the First Consul did not comply within a week, Whitworth was to return to London. Bonaparte angrily rejected the ultimatum. Whitworth's carriage clattered out of Paris on May 12 and he was back in London three days later. On May 16, George III informed Parliament that diplomatic relations had ended, and, on May 18, the king formally declared war against France.

What followed for another two-and-a-half years was a 'phony war.' Asymmetrical power kept the enemies from each other's throats. The French with their overwhelming land power could not attack Britain and its empire. The British with their overwhelming sea power could not attack France or its warships that mostly kept to port. All Bonaparte could do was confiscate any British ships and imprison any British subjects then in French ports, and order French forces to occupy Hanover, the British monarch's ancestral home, and Naples, Taranto, and Brindisi in the Kingdom of the Two Sicilies, a British ally. Meanwhile, the Royal Navy and British privateers swept the seas of any French vessels they caught. Whitehall also backed an attempt by a group of French royalist exiles led by George Cadoudal to assassinate Bonaparte; French police learned of the plot and rounded up Cadoudal and his men before they could act.

Bonaparte hoped to break the stalemate by invading England. In all, he contrived eight distinct plans to do so, with the first expressed on July 26, 1803. To this end, he established an army headquartered at Boulogne on August 23, 1803. A successful invasion depended on the French fleet dominating the 22 miles of English Channel between Boulogne and Dover long enough for the army to cross and land safely.[3] Over the next two years, he amassed more troops along the coast straddling Boulogne, accelerated a warship and landing craft building campaign, and through treaty acquired operational control over Spain's navy.

The biggest changes in Napoleon's plans concerned how long a successful invasion depended on his navy controlling the Channel. He was initially confident that: 'If we could master the straits for six hours, we would be masters of the world.'[4] Eventually he doubled that time to 24 hours, then extended it to days, a week, and, finally, several weeks. The longer the needed time, the more warships had to mass there to fight off the Royal Navy's inevitable onslaught.

Most of the invasion craft fleet harbored a fatal flaw. With no keels, the flatboats packed with troops and their weapons and equipment could only be rowed on days with no winds and calm seas. Napoleon witnessed the disastrous consequences of attempting a crossing without optimum conditions on July 20, 1804. During a visit to Boulogne, he ordered a long-planned exercise of flatboats packed with troops to proceed even through his naval officers begged him to cancel it before a worsening gale and a hovering British flotilla of two sloops and two brigs. Before his eyes 200 men drowned as the winds and waves capsized their boats or crushed them against the rocky shore as they fled before the gale and British cannon shots.[5]

Seemingly nonplused by the disaster, Napoleon reviewed 80,000 troops on the plain near Boulogne on August 16. His observation of 146 boats packed with troops on August 25, was interrupted as British warships approached, although at least this time no one died. The British flotilla threatened Napoleon himself on August 26, when the emperor and his entourage were aboard the imperial barge in Boulogne bay. The rowers beat a hasty retreat to the inner harbor.

Napoleon issued on September 29, 1804, the naval campaign plan that ended at Trafalgar.[6] To raise the odds of dominating the Channel, he sought to divert as many British warships as far away from it as possible: 'The English will find themselves at the same time attacked in Asia, Africa, and America.'[7] The worst threat would be against Britain's West Indian colonies. Three fleets would depart from French ports, unite in the West Indies, drop off troops in French colonies, capture any vulnerable British colonies, then sail to the Channel while leaving much of the alerted Royal Navy far behind in their wake.

Whitehall's decision to war against Spain boosted the odds of Napoleon's plan succeeding. The Admiralty ordered Captain Graham Moore to lead four frigates to intercept and capture Spain's annual treasure fleet sailing from the New World to Cádiz. Moore's flotilla spotted and closed with four Spanish frigates on October 5, 1804. When the Spanish captains refused to heed his warning shots to yield, Moore signaled his captains to attack. The battle did not last long. British broadsides sank one of the frigates and battered the others so severely that they struck their colors. Unfortunately, the frigate most packed with treasure sank, but the British took £1 million worth of silver, copper, and tin from the other three. Despite this blatant act of war, King Charles IV did not declare war against Britain until December

12, 1804. It was another month, on January 4, 1805, before Napoleon's diplomats convinced Charles IV to accept a treaty whereby he ceded operational control of Spain's fleet to France for the invasion of Britain.[8]

If the French and Spanish fleets somehow united, they would outgun the Royal Navy. This was a huge 'if' given how scattered two navies were. The French fleet included 21 ships-of-the-line at Brest, 6 ships-of-the-line at Rochefort, 5 ships-of-the-line at Ferrol, and, finally, 11 ships-of-the-line at Toulon. The Spanish fleet included 15 ships-of-the-line at Cádiz, 5 ships-of-the-line at Ferrol, and 6 ships-of-the-line at Cartagena.[9] Spain's alliance with France stretched the Royal Navy's blockade to near the snapping point with flotillas led by Admirals James Montagu off Flushing and Calais, William Cornwallis off Brest, Cuthbert Collingwood off Rochefort, Edward Pellew off Ferrol, and Horatio Nelson off Toulon.

The British enjoyed more than a numerical advantage over the enemy fleets. More vital was the superiority of British admirals and captains. Napoleon recognized this, lamenting that the French navy 'lacked men of superior merit,' that he 'could not find … a single enterprising, cold-blooded man.' The man who commanded France's main fleet, Admiral Pierre de Villeneuve, appeared the best of a mediocre lot. Was Villeneuve prudent or cowardly when he cut his cables and sailed away to safety rather than staying and fighting during the battle of the Nile? Napoleon quipped that 'Villeneuve is one of those men who needs much more a spur than a bridle.'[10]

Britain eventually enjoyed another advantage in its war against France. Bonaparte's aggressive and grandiose policies steadily alienated Saint Petersburg and Vienna to the point where they joined Whitehall in coalition against him. The first provocation was the French rendition of Louis de Bourbon, duc d'Enghien from his home in Ettenheim, Baden, and, on March 20, 1804, his execution at Vincennes chateau near Paris on charges of being a leader in a conspiracy to overthrow Bonaparte's regime. Saint Petersburg and Vienna protested the execution but remained neutral. Then Bonaparte had the Senate declare him France's emperor on May 18, 1804, subject to approval of the French people by a plebiscite. From now, he was technically Napoleon I and signed his orders and decrees as such, although his coronation did not take place until December 2, 1804. Napoleon had himself crowned king of Italy in Milan's cathedral on May 26, 1805.

The Russian and Austrian monarchies did more than sneer at Bonaparte's presumption to elevate himself to their ranks. Tsar Alexander severed diplomatic relations with France on October 5, 1804, and allied defensively with Vienna on November 6, 1804, with Whitehall on April 11, 1805, and with Berlin on May 4, 1805. Although the Prussians opted out, the British, Russians, and Austrians intensified talks over transforming their defensive alliance into an offensive alliance after learning that Napoleon dissolved the Republic of Liguria and annexed it to the kingdom of Italy on June 4. Russia and Austria jointly declared war against France and openly joined the coalition on August 9, 1805. Although tempted, Prussian king Frederick William III resisted entreaties by the British, Russians, and Austrians to link arms.

The allies developed a two-stage plan to defeat Napoleon by first conquering his satellites then France itself. An Austrian army, led by Archduke Ferdinand, seconded by General Karl Mack, would overrun Bavaria, then wait as Russian armies marched to reinforce it. Meanwhile, the allies would invade France's Kingdom of Italy from two directions, Archduke Charles's Austrian army from the east, and a mixed army of Russians, British, and Neapolitans from the south. In the Tyrol a third Austrian army led by Archduke John would march to either front as needed. Britain would underwrite much of the expense of these campaigns with monthly payments to Saint Petersburg, Vienna, and Naples. Meanwhile, although Neapolitan King Ferdinand IV and Queen Maria Carolina had publicly signed a neutrality treaty with France on September 23, 1804, they secretly signed an alliance treaty against France on September 11, 1805. After the war erupted, British and Russian troops would land at Naples, then, with the Neapolitan army, march north to join the Austrians in driving the French from Italy. Ideally, the allied victories would entice Prussia to join them. Once Bavaria and Italy were secured, the allies would march against France itself.

Until the Russian and Austrian war declarations against him, Napoleon remained committed to his plan to invade Britain. The French admirals received orders to implement Napoleon's plan as soon as possible after New Year's Day 1805.[11] The first French fleet to venture forth was Admiral Edouard de Missiessy's 3 ships-of-the-line, 3 frigates, and 2 transports packed with 3,500 troops from Rochefort on January 11, 1805. After reaching Martinique on February 20, and after dropping off the troops, Missiessy headed back to Rochefort. Villeneuve sailed with 11 ships-of-the-line, 7 frigates, and transports packed with 6,330 troops from Toulon on January 17, but storms battered his vessels so badly that he had to return to port. Honore Ganteaume led his 21 ships-of-the-line from Brest on January 18, then abruptly turned back before Admiral Alan Gardner's 21 ships-of-the-line.

Villeneuve sailed again on March 30, chased away the British flotilla blockading Cádiz on April 9, and there joined Admiral Frederico Gravina's 16 ships-of-the-line. The combined fleet reached Martinique on May 14. During his month in the West Indies, Villeneuve did win one battle, although it was on land. He sent a force ashore to capture the British fort atop Diamond Rock on Martinique on June 2.

Nelson learned of Villeneuve's escape and direction on April 19, but was unable to unite 15 ships-of-the-line at Gibraltar and pursue until May 10. Nelson's fleet reached Barbados on June 4. This same day Villeneuve received Napoleon's orders that he sail to Ferrol, attach those warships to his fleet, then on to Brest, collect the warships there, and, finally, head to the straits between Boulogne and Dover and hold it as long as possible.[12] Villeneuve turned his fleet eastward. Upon getting word of Villeneuve's direction, Nelson pursued. Napoleon ordered Admiral Zacherie Allemand, who had replaced Missiessy as the Rochefort fleet's commander, to join Villeneuve at Ferrol. Allemand's 5 ships-of-the-line and 3 frigates sailed from Rochefort on July 14, but eventually turned back after sighting Admiral Robert Calder's fleet of 10 ships-of-the-line.[13]

The Royal Navy squadrons on the French and Spanish Atlantic coasts included Admiral George Keith's 21 ships-of-the-line off Dover; Admiral William Cornwallis's 25 ships-of-the-line off Brest; Admiral Charles Stirling's six ships-of-the-line off Rochefort; Admiral Robert Calder's 10 ships-of-the-line off Ferrol; and Captain Cuthbert Collingwood's 6 ships-of-the-line off Cádiz. Learning of Villeneuve's approach, Calder intercepted and attacked the strung-out allied fleet as it neared the Spanish coast on July 22. Two Spanish ships-of-the-line struck their colors as the rest of Villeneuve's fleet safely reached Ferrol. After leaving some frigates to observe Ferrol, Calder sailed north to join Cornwallis. Together they had 35 ships-of-the-line to pummel any attempt by Villeneuve to sail to Brest and join Ganteaume.

Villeneuve dutifully sailed northward with a combined fleet of 29 ships-of-the-line on August 11. A swift blockade vessel at Ferrol took word to Cornwallis who stayed with 17 ships-of-the-line at station off Brest, while he sent Calder with 18 ships-of-the-line to seek out and ideally destroy Villeneuve. Learning of Calder's approach, Villeneuve reversed course and fled to Cádiz, entering that safe haven on August 22. Collingwood and Calder blockaded him there. It seemed that the French naval campaign for 1805 had ended without a major battle.

Napoleon left Paris on August 2, and the following day reached his headquarters at Boulogne. There he mulled the threats facing France and the options for thwarting them. Spies reported that the Austrians and Russians were massing and marching armies that would invade Bavaria and Italy. He heard the news of Calder's attack on the allied fleet and Villeneuve's refuge in Ferrol. He ordered Villeneuve to attack 'wherever the enemy appears before you with less than 24 ships-of-the-line.'[14] Yet he figured the odds of ever seizing the Strait of Dover even briefly were a chimera. Britain did not directly threaten France but the Austrians and Russians posed a worsening threat eastward. The emperor finally abandoned his dream of invading England, and instead, on August 26, decreed that henceforth the Army of England would be known as the Grand Army. On August 29, he ordered his troops to march toward the Danube River valley.[15]

Nelson, meanwhile, had sailed to Portsmouth for a well-deserved leave. He enjoyed only 25 days ashore before receiving orders that would carry him to his final and greatest triumph. He sailed aboard the 110-gun *Victory* on September 14, and joined the fleet before Cádiz on September 28.

Napoleon sent his latest orders to Villeneuve on September 14. His mission now was to ready his fleet to sail into the Mediterranean, join with Spain's Cartagena fleet, head to Naples, land his 4,000 troops there, then sail to Toulon and await further orders. Napoleon sent Admiral François Rosily-Mesros to replace Villeneuve in command and actually fulfill this mission.[16]

Villeneuve typically dallied after getting Napoleon's orders on September 27. He was not eager to sortie against the blockading British fleet. Atop this the quality of the French and Spanish crews was even worse than usual. Disease and desertion had devoured their ranks. Tallies of the French fleet alone listed 1,731 hospitalized and over 300 deserters. Gravina was also short a couple thousand men. This loss severely affected the fleet's seamanship and rate of fire in the battle ahead.[17] It was the unofficial word on October 11 that Rosily was at Madrid and coming to replace him that finally spurred Villeneuve to action.

Villeneuve sailed with 33 ships-of-the-line, including 18 French and 15 Spanish, along with 5 frigates and 2 brigs, with 2,568 cannons, on October 18. The two fleets met 21 miles northeast of Cape Trafalgar on October 21, 1805. Nelson's fleet included 27 ships-of-the-line, 4 frigates, a schooner, and a cutter, with 2,148 cannons. Nelson split his fleet into 2 parallel columns, with Collingwood commanding one with 14 ships-of-the-line to cut into the enemy line's center, and Nelson the other with 13 ships-of-the-line to sail toward its head. He had signal flags hoisted first declaring 'Close for action,' then 'England confides that every man will do his duty.'[18]

The battle of Trafalgar lasted 6½ hours. When the smoke cleared, the French and Spanish fleet had suffered 5,860 killed and wounded, and 4,799 captured of the 29,000 allied sailors, including 16,000 French and 12,900 Spaniards. The British captured 17 ships-of-the-line and sank one; much to his regret, Collingwood ordered the 130-gun *Santissima Trinidad*, the second largest warship, sunk as the pumps failed to keep up with the water pouring through all the holes in its hull. In all, the French lost 10 of their 18 ships-of-the-line, and the Spaniards 9 of their 15 ships-of-the-line or 55 percent of the allied fleet. The British lost 449 killed and 1,214 wounded or 10 percent of the 17,256 men present. No ships sank but eight were bashed so severely they had to be towed to Gibraltar repairs.[19] Nelson was among the dead; a musket ball tore down through his shoulder, severed an artery, and shattered his spine, and he slowly bled to death. Upon hearing of the British victory and prizes taken, Nelson muttered, 'Thank God I have done my duty.'[20]

Only nine French and six Spanish ships-of-the-line sailed away. Ten of these warships reached Cádiz. In the pursuit, Commodore Richard Strachan's flotilla of 5 ships-of-the-line and 2 frigates caught up to Pierre Le Pellet's 4 ships-of-the-line off Cape Finistere on November 4, and battered all of them into surrender, bringing the enemy fleet's losses to 23 ships-of-the-line. Villeneuve was among the Trafalgar prisoners. He was taken to England, treated well, and exchanged in April 1806. Villeneuve was found dead with a knife in his chest on April 22. Whether it was suicide or murder will probably never be known.

Napoleon did not learn of Trafalgar until November 17. The tragedy briefly darkened what had been an unbroken string of French victories. An army of 40,000 Austrian troops led by Archduke Ferdinand and General Karl Mack invaded Bavaria on September 8 and overran the realm. Napoleon's corps encircled most of the Austrian army at Ulm. Ferdinand escaped but Mack surrendered 25,000 troops on October 18. Napoleon then sent his corps down the Danube valley. The Austrian and Russian armies withdrew before the French onslaught. Francis II abandoned Vienna and joined Alexander I at Olmutz in Moravia. Napoleon triumphantly entered Vienna on November 13, and began preparing his campaign's next phase against the allied armies in Moravia. The decisive battle came at Austerlitz on December 2, when Napoleon's army devastated the Russians and Austrians, inflicting nearly 30,000 casualties while suffering around 10,000. Alexander withdrew his army's remnants to Russia while, on December 26, Francis signed the

Treaty of Pressburg, whereby he ceded Tyrol, Voralberg, Venetia, Istria, and Dalmatia.

After Austerlitz, Britain essentially faced France alone for the next ten months. Francis had signed a humiliating peace treaty with France. Alexander led his army back to Russia. Frederick William clung to neutrality. Faced with overwhelming French forces marching against them, the British and Russian troops that landed in Naples hastily reembarked and sailed away; Ferdinand, Maria, and their court fled to Palermo.

Yet, Britain remained secure. Without Trafalgar, Napoleon could have swiftly massed another army on the Channel and threatened Britain with invasion. With his navy devastated, Napoleon riveted most of his attention on Germany and Prussia. Nonetheless, Whitehall needed four years to figure out how to exploit its naval hegemony. The answer came with Napoleon's attempt to conquer the Iberian Peninsula. British naval power kept Portugal and Spain in the fight, and, most vitally, General Arthur Wellesley's army in the field. The result was to transform Napoleon's ambitions into a cancer that steadily devoured his empire.

Chapter 10

High and Shallow Seas, 1806–9

We now observed that the Spaniards were collecting in great numbers … and upon our appearance commenced firing alarm guns. About four o'clock p.m. we began to disembark the troops, which we accomplished by midnight, without any … accident, we had a heavy surf to wade through.

Lieutenant John Fernyhough

The spectacle was lamentable and well calculated to rouse every feeling of sympathy. Many houses were still smouldering and in part crumbled to the ground; mothers were bewailing the melancholy fate of their slaughtered children, and there was not one but deplored the loss of some fondly beloved relative or dearly valued friend.

Ensign Robert Blakeney

We must not disguise the fact from ourselves – we are hated throughout Europe, and that hate must be cured by fear.

George Canning

The naval war persisted year after year. Despite Trafalgar, Napoleon did not cancel a mission for two squadrons to sail from Brest to the West Indies and ravage British shipping. In December 1805, Admiral Corentin Leissegues led to sea five ships-of-the-line, two frigates, and a corvette, and Admiral Jean Baptiste Willaumez six ships-of-the-line, two frigates, and two corvettes. Upon learning of Leissegue's expedition, Admiral John Duckworth abandoned the Cádiz blockade and pursued with his six ships-of-the-line. His fleet caught up to Leissegues off Saint Domingue. There his captains wiped out Leissegue's fleet by capturing three ships-of-the-line and driving two ashore to their destruction; the British suffered 64 killed and 294 wounded to over 760 French dead and wounded.[1] Willaumez's ships-of-the-line escaped battle in the West Indies. Although his fleet spotted Willaumez, Duckworth reckoned his warships were too shot up for a fight. A hurricane battered and scattered Willaumez's ships on August 18. This made one of them prey for Admiral Richard Strachan's squadron patrolling America's coast; in the pursuit, the French captain drove his vessel onto Chesapeake Bay's shore to avoid capture.

The sea war shifted to the South Atlantic. On September 1, 1805, an expedition sailed from Cork, Ireland to capture the Cape of Good Hope. Admiral Home Popham commanded the 4 ships-of-the-line, 2 frigates, a sloop, and a brig, along with a score of transports packed with 6,300 troops led by General David Baird. Popham rose to admiral by an unusual route. He was born into a British expatriate merchant family in Tetuan, Morocco, studied at Cambridge, was fluent in several languages, and was a merchant ship captain. During the 1794 campaign, Frederick, Duke of York rewarded his services by granting him a naval captain's commission. Popham devised a sophisticated version of the flag signal system. During a diplomatic mission, Popham so impressed Tsar Alexander that he received a Russian knighthood and Royal Society membership.

Nature proved to be a worse enemy than man to the Cape Hope expedition. On January 4, 1806, the armada anchored in Table Bay with Cape Town on the south horn. Heavy surf against rocky shores thwarted an attempted landing by the Highland Brigade on January 6. Two days later, the British tried again, this time on a beach at Lospord's Bay; forty-one soldiers drowned trying to get ashore. The Dutch opened fire then retreated as overwhelming numbers of redcoats massed on the beach and marched inland. Marine Lieutenant John Fernyhough recalled how it was:

> ... astonishing to me how we did land through such a tremendous surf ... The nearest point we could get to shore was forty or fifty yards, so that we were obliged to wade that distance ... The Diadem, Leda frigate, and gun-brig covered our landing; and just as we were leaving the boats, some of the enemy advanced down the hill towards us, but gun-brig opened a fire of grape shot among them that killed two, and the rest retreated. Another part of the enemy ... attempted to get a ... cannon upon an eminence, but a well-directed fire from our ships completely baffled the attempts.[2]

As the troops marched inland, Lieutenant Samuel Walters observed 'most of the enemy's cavalry kept on the Heights during the action. The flank companies of the respective Regiments were sent after them, and a smart action took place ... Our killed and wounded about two hundred, that of the enemy double the number.'[3]

The Dutch withdrew into Cape Town. The British followed on January 9, and deployed in a crescent around the city. The Dutch capitulated the following day. In all, the British had captured one of the world's most strategic sites at a relatively light cost.

Popham was restless for more conquests. He talked Baird into lending him troops to take Buenos Aires, Argentina, which was a shipping point for gold and silver mined in the distant Andes Mountains and whose people were said to long for liberation from Spain's inept, corrupt, and repressive rule.[4] On April 20, 1806, Popham sailed aboard a flotilla of 4 ships-of-the-line, a brig, and 4 transports packed with 1,400 troops led by General William Beresford. En route the expedition picked up another 200 troops at Saint Helena Island.

Diverse winds and currents slowed the armada's progress across the Atlantic then up Platte River Bay. Lieutenant Fernyhough and his comrades were frustrated by being:

> ... frequently obliged to anchor on account of foul wind and the strong tides which were continually running against us ... In approaching Buenos Aires the navigation became extremely difficult and dangerous ... We arrived of Buenos Aires on the 25th [June], near Quilmes, about fifteen miles from the city. Here General Beresford deemed it prudent to land. We now observed that the Spaniards were collecting in great numbers ... and upon our appearance commenced firing alarm guns. About four o'clock p.m. we began to disembark the troops, which we accomplished by midnight, without any ... accident, though we had a heavy surf to wade through.[5]

The British scattered a Spanish force on June 27, and appeared before the city. Beresford sent a demand to surrender. While Governor Rafael de Sobremonte fled with the colony's million dollar treasury to Cordoba, the officials he left behind capitulated. Beresford and Popham triumphantly led their men into the city. Learning of Sobremonte's escape, they sent a force in pursuit. Sobremonte abandoned his treasure in galloping with his aides to safety. Popham sent the million dollars to London.

Most Argentinians viewed the British as hated invaders rather than liberators. Buenos Aires, with 40,000 mostly resentful inhabitants, proved to be impossible to hold. Sobremonte put General Santiago de Liniers in command of the several hundred regular Spanish troops while Martin de Alzaga and Juan de Pueyrredon gathered the militia. Nearly 10,000 troops fought their way into the outskirts of Buenos Aires on August 10. Revolts erupted inside the city against the redcoats. Beresford surrendered on August 12.

Popham promptly sailed across the Platte River Bay, dropped anchor before Montevideo, and demanded that it surrender. He hoped to trade Montevideo for Beresford and his men. The Spaniards rejected his demands. It was not until late October that Popham landed a force of marines and armed sailors led by Lieutenant Colonel Thomas Backhouse at Maldonada, where they established a fort and awaited enough reinforcements to actually besiege and take Montevideo, which was defended by 5,000 militiamen and several hundred Spanish regulars.

Meanwhile, Whitehall learned of Popham's unauthorized conquest and Beresford's humiliating capitulation. The Admiralty usually turned a blind eye to rogue captains if they brought success. Failure, however, could result in harsh punishment for the miscreant. The debacle in Buenos Aires prompted Whitehall to look for a scapegoat. Who would be better than Popham, whose outspokenness and untraditional upward path had alienated so many brother officers. Admiral Charles Stirling arrived at Montevideo on December 3, to relieve Popham of command and send him to a court martial at Portsmouth. Stirling withdrew the force from Maldonada, combined them with 6,000 troops led by General Samuel Auchmuty he had brought with him, and directly attacked Montevideo. The British captured the city on February 3, 1806. Meanwhile, back in England a court martial reprimanded Popham for withdrawing naval forces without orders for an unauthorized campaign. He might have suffered a harsher penalty without the Duke of York's support.

General John Whitelocke arrived at Montevideo on May 10, and took command of British forces. After reinforcements arrived, Whitelocke resolved to avenge Beresford's humiliating surrender of the previous year. Leaving behind 1,350 troops to garrison Montevideo, he sailed with 7,800 troops to Buenos Aires. The expedition landed and marched inland on June 27, 1807. General Liniers and his men put up a desperate fight outside the city, but were routed back inside on July 1. Three days later, Whitelocke launched his men against Buenos Aires. The redcoats fought their way into the suburbs of Retiro and Residencia, but at the cost of over 1,000 casualties. Liniers rejected Whitelocke's request for an armistice, and ordered his men to attack. When the Argentinians threatened to completely overwhelm him, Whitelocke sent another desperate request for an armistice. In nearly two weeks of fighting, Whitelocke's army had suffered 311 killed, 679 wounded, and 1,808 captured or missing. This time Lanier agreed, but only after Whitelocke promised not just to abandon Buenos Aires but Montevideo as well. The two leaders signed the armistice on August 12. Whitelocke embarked the remnants of his troops and sailed back to England, where a court martial would cashier him. In all, Britain's Platte River campaign was a humiliating debacle that obscured a genuine victory the previous year.

In the summer of 1806, General John Stuart led a British expedition against the French in Calabria in southern Italy.[6] The aim was to divert French forces from their siege of Gaeta, King Ferdinand's IV's last mainland stronghold. Captain William Sidney Smith commanded the flotilla that conveyed Stuart and 5,300 troops across from Messina, Sicily to deep waters near Eufemia, Calabria where they were rowed ashore on July 1.

From his headquarters at Reggio, General Jean Reynier commanded French forces in southern Italy. Upon learning of the invasion, he marched 6,000 troops toward the invaders. Scouts brought word to Stuart of Reynier's presence at nearby Maida on July 3. Early the next morning, Stuart led his men to Maida. As Stuart's column marched into view, Reynier and his men crossed the shallow Lomato River to intercept them. Stuart deployed his column into line with the right flank anchored on the river. Reynier deployed his regiments in individual columns to attack. Stuart spread his Corsican and Sicilian rangers before the advancing French skirmishers. The three British cannons opened fire, first with round shot then canister as the French columns closed. Stuart ordered his regiments to fire volleys as the French got within a hundred yards. The cannon and musket fire devastated the French ranks which faltered, broke, then fled. Stuart ordered his men to pursue. At a cost of 45 dead and 282 wounded, the British killed 490 French, wounded 870, and captured 722 along with 4 cannons. Stuart then marched down the coast mopping up French garrisons and taking nearly 1,500 more prisoners. Most notably, the British captured Tropea on July 7, Reggio on July 9, Scilla on July 23, and Cortone on July 28. The campaign's only shadow was the unrealistic hope that it would somehow divert French forces from the siege of Gaeta, which fell on July 18.[7]

A demoralizing surprise greeted Stuart when he returned triumphantly to Palermo. General Henry Fox, the brother of Whig leader Charles Fox, awaited to relieve him of command. Nonetheless, a jubilant Ferdinand IV named Stuart the count of Maida, while George III made him a Knight of the Bath after he returned to London. Those honors were well earned. Stuart's campaign was a critical success. It damaged the French in southern Italy and boosted British morale. Stuart's tactics would serve as the template for other British generals, especially Wellington. The mass firepower of a line of troops proved superior to the intimidating power of a column of fast-moving troops.

Had Horatio Nelson, Thomas Cochrane, or the actual second-in-command, William Sidney Smith, rather than Admiral John Duckworth led the expedition that sailed against Constantinople in February 1807, the result might have been a resounding British victory rather than a humiliating setback. Duckworth failed to sail his eight ships-of-the-line and dozen smaller warships decisively against Constantinople when his flotilla first appeared at the Bosporus Strait's mouth. For several weeks Duckworth rejected the pleas of Smith and most other captains to boldly pass through the gauntlet of batteries leading to Constantinople. Finally, Duckworth ordered an advance through the Bosporus Strait and the Marmara Sea, only to halt before the Dardanelles Strait where Turkish batteries and warships battered his fleet. Duckworth detached Smith with three ships-of-the-line to attack enemy batteries and warships. Smith's flotilla destroyed a 31-cannon battery, 9 warships, and 2 gunboats.[8] The fleet then sailed eastward to anchor beyond cannon shot of Constantinople on February 20. Rather than attack, Duckworth spent two weeks trying to talk the Turks into peace negotiations. Meanwhile, Smith and most of the captains tried to convince Duckworth that the Turks would only yield after suffering a devastating bombardment. Duckworth was not willing to chance this and on March 3, ordered his fleet to sail westward back to Gibraltar. In all, although only 1 ship-of-the-line and 250 men aboard had been lost and that was from an accidental fire, Duckworth's expedition was a dismaying defeat.

The expedition against Copenhagen revealed how that against Constantinople might have turned out if a decisive rather than dilatory commander had led it.[9] As in 1801, Whitehall claimed compelling reasons for attacking Copenhagen. Napoleon's power on the continent had expanded enormously with his latest round of conquests and subjections. On October 1, 1806, Prussian king Frederick William III foolishly issued an ultimatum to Napoleon to withdraw all his troops west of the Rhine and dissolve the Rhine Confederation of German states allied to France. The subsequent war's initial phase lasted only a couple of weeks, culminating with the French army's decisive twin victories at Jena and Auerstadt on October 14. Over the next month Napoleon's corps mopped up most of the Prussia's army's remnants and captured Berlin along with nearly all other major cities and fortresses. The king, his court, and about 20,000 troops fled to East Prussia where Tsar Alexander sent an army to their rescue. On November 21, Napoleon issued the Berlin Decree that proclaimed a trade embargo or Continental System against the British Isles. After French forces marched into Warsaw on November 28, Alexander sent more troops westward and ordered his generals to expel the French from Poland and East Prussia. An initial round of fighting in December north of Warsaw was indecisive, as was an even bloodier round in early 1807 that climaxed with the battle of Eylau on February 6 and 7, with around 20,000 Russian and 25,000 French casualties. Both armies then went into prolonged winter encampments to rest, resupply, and reinforce the troops.

The campaign reopened in May as the French and Russian forces along with their respective allies maneuvered for position. Alexander sent an urgent request to Whitehall to land an expedition somewhere along the Baltic coast to divert Napoleon's attention. Whitehall dispatched General William Cathcart with 8,500 mostly King's German Legion troops to join Swedish forces on Rugen Island. Then came word of the battle of Friedland, where Napoleon devastated General Levin Bennigsen's Russian army on June 14.

As Napoleon's corps pursued the Russians, Alexander pleaded for a ceasefire and peace talks. The two emperors met on a barge on the Niemen River near the town of Tilsit. The result was two Tilsit treaties. Under the treaty signed between Napoleon and Alexander on July 7, Russia abandoned its alliance with Britain, joined the Continental System trade embargo against Britain, agreed to mediate peace with Britain, and pledged to ally with France against Britain if Whitehall refused to accept peace by December 1, 1807; Russia received Prussia's share of Poland and Napoleon's support for Alexander's ambitions to conquer Finland from Sweden; Napoleon secretly agreed to support Russian ambitions against the Ottoman Empire if Constantinople did not accept French mediation and a favorable peace after three months of negotiations; France received Cattaro on the eastern Adriatic shore, and the Ionian Islands from Russia; Alexander recognized Napoleon's brothers as existing or future monarchs including Louis as king of Holland, Joseph as king of Naples, including both southern Italy and Sicily (Ferdinand IV and Maria Carolina would be compensated with the Balearic Islands), Jerome as king of Westphalia, and Saxon king Frederick Augustus I to head of the Duchy of Warsaw; Alexander would back Napoleon in pressuring Denmark, Sweden, and Portugal to join the Continental System.[10] Under the treaty signed between Napoleon and Frederick William on July 9, Prussia pledged to cede half its territory, cap its army at 42,000 troops, pay a huge indemnity to France, and permit French troops to occupy key fortresses in Prussia.[11] The Tilsit treaties atop the 1805 Pressburg treaty revolutionized Europe's distribution of power. Napoleon's empire extended into central Europe, the Italian Peninsula, and the Adriatic Sea. The military power of Austria and especially Prussia was sharply reduced. Napoleon backed Alexander's ambitions for Russia to expand west into Poland and northwest into Finland.

Once again Britain was shorn of significant allies in its war against France. Whitehall feared that Napoleon's next step would be to take over Denmark and seize the Danish fleet. Foreign Minister George Canning sent an ultimatum to Denmark's crown prince Frederick, who replied that he considered an enemy any nation that threatened Denmark.

Denmark was a secondary power with 17 ships-of-the-line, 11 frigates, an army of 35,000 troops, scores of merchant ships, Norway as a province, and the West Indian islands of Saint Croix and Saint John's as colonies. Although King Christian VII reigned over Denmark, crown prince Frederick actually ruled that realm because his father was mentally and physically incapable of doing so. Frederick and Foreign Minister Joachim von Bernstorff were careful to do nothing that the British could interpret as an excuse for repeating their devastating attack of 1801. They did not back with any threats their protests at Britain's policy of confiscating any Danish and other neutral vessels that they accused of carrying war 'contraband' to France. Indeed the Danes had actually massed and mothballed their entire fleet at Copenhagen, stripping the sails and spars from nearly all of their warships except for two ships-of-the-line, two frigates, and three brigs. As for the army, 20,000 troops were deployed in northern Holstein to defend that province against a possible French attack; Frederick commanded that army from his headquarters at Kiel.[12]

Despite all this, Whitehall eventually decided to issue an ultimatum to Copenhagen either to surrender its entire fleet or suffer its destruction. Led by Foreign Secretary George Canning, the ministers convinced themselves that Denmark posed an imminent threat of allying with France. They did so by cherry-picking the one intelligence report that warned of Danish preparations for war while turning a blind eye to numerous others that maintained the Danes posed no threat. In a classic psychological case of projection, the British accused the Danes of aggression for protesting Britain's aggression against Danish shipping. The debate over what to do about the 'Danish threat' opened on July 10 and concluded on July 19, when army and navy commanders received orders to capture or destroy Denmark's fleet if Frederick did not peacefully render it. Canning dispatched the abrasive Francis Jackson as his envoy to issue the ultimatum to Frederick at Kiel.[13]

The military plan was for two forces to converge on Copenhagen. General William Cathcart would embark his 8,500 men at Rugen and take command of the British army at Copenhagen. At Yarmouth, Admiral James Gambier led the armada that included 16 ships-of-the-line, 7 frigates, 16 smaller warships, and 377 transports packed with munitions, provisions, and 18,000 troops headed by Major General Arthur Wellesley. It took days for all those vessels to put to sea during August's first week.[14]

Copenhagen is sited on Zealand Island's east coast. The strait between Zealand and Sweden are tight, only a half-dozen or so miles across. The Great Belt is the waters lapping Zealand's northern, western, and southern shores. The armada's lead warships reached the top of the strait on August 2. There Gambier sent a squadron of 4 ships-of-the-line, 3 frigates, and 10 smaller warships commanded by Commodore Richard Keats to sail counter clockwise around the Great Belt and drop off vessels to block key crossings between ports on the mainland and Zealand. At the top of the strait, Gambier awaited the rest of the armada sailing from Britain, Cathcart's flotilla sailing from Rugen, and Jackson's diplomatic mission from Kiel.

The Danes remained blissfully unaware that they would soon be the victims of one of the more blatant and destructive acts of aggression in British history. As late as August 7, Frederick wrote General Heinrich Peymann, who commanded Danish troops on Zealand, that 'we are not at war with England and do not expect to be.'[15] Then Jackson appeared at Kiel later that day and demanded that Bernstorff surrender the Danish fleet by August 14 or face war, then repeated it to Frederick the following day. Dumbfounded and enraged, Frederick angrily rejected the ultimatum, slipped away, and managed to sail in a small vessel that evaded British warships patrolling the Great Belt. Upon reaching Copenhagen on August 11, he conferred with Peymann over military strategy, then withdrew to the mainland with his father and the crown jewels.

Jackson reached Gambier on August 13 and informed him that his 'diplomacy' had failed. On August 16, Wellesley and part of the army landed without opposition at Vedbaek, a dozen miles north of Copenhagen, then marched inland and deployed around the city. Cathcart arrived to take command. Over the next several weeks the British unloaded supplies and zigzagged trenches and batteries toward Copenhagen. While most of the 27,000 troops were deployed around the city, Wellesley commanded a reserve of 6,000 troops near Kioge a half-dozen miles behind the line's central sector. Defending the city were about 5,500 troops, 7,300 militiamen, and 7,000 sailors manning warships and land batteries. The Danes launched several sorties by land and sea against the British, but were repulsed.[16]

The campaign's only large-scale battle was fought at Kioge on August 29, when a Danish relief force of 7,270 militia gathered by General Joachim von Castenschiold from the rest of Zealand tried to break through the British siege lines. Wellesley deployed his 6,000 troops to block their advance. British volleys then a charge shattered the Danes, killing 152, wounding 204, and capturing over 1,700 men; the British suffered light losses of 28 killed, 122 wounded, and 21 missing.[17] Although pleased with his victory, Wellesley later reckoned he could have captured far more of the enemy had the Danes not 'concealed the direction of their march and evaded pursuit.'[18]

The bombardment began on September 2, after the Danes rejected the latest surrender demand. Supplementing the cannon fire were Congreve rockets, named after their inventor William Congreve. Of the 6,000 projectiles that devastated Copenhagen over the next 3 days, 300 were rockets.[19] Charles Chambers, a fleet surgeon, recalled:

> ... the incessant roaring of guns ... resembled ... an unremitted peal of thunder ... they fired red-hot shot, the distinct hissing of which through the air was awful indeed. Our mortar boats sailed forth ... but were shortly obliged to return, being unable to cope with the enemy's heavy metal, especially of Copenhagen's Crown Battery ... I saw several of our shells burst over the city ... shot and shells dropped on both sides; those which fell in the water produce an extraordinary splashing, and those on shore raised immense clouds of dust ... the action continued till 4 in the afternoon, when the firing of each party ceased, as if reciprocally.[20]

Ensign Robert Blakeney of the 28th Regiment was both appalled and resigned to the horrors:

> The spectacle was lamentable and well calculated to rouse every feeling of sympathy. Many houses were still smouldering and in part crumbled to the ground; mothers were bewailing the melancholy fate of their slaughtered children, and there was not one but deplored the loss of some fondly beloved relative or dearly valued friend ... some indeed exclaimed that their sufferings were the more aggravated as being

inflicted contrary to the laws of all civilized nations. The unfortunate sufferers seemed not to reflect that war was will, not law.[21]

After enduring three days and nights of devastating bombardment, Peymann asked for and received a ceasefire for peace negotiations. As envoys Cathcart dispatched Generals Wellesley and George Murray, and naval Captain Home Popham. Under the treaty on September 7, the Danes bitterly agreed to surrender their entire fleet, naval supplies, and Helgoland Island at the Elbe River mouth. Over the next five weeks, the British readied then sailed away with 16 ships-of-the-line, 9 frigates, 14 smaller warships, and 31 gunboats; destroyed 3 ships-of-the-line being built, 2 older ships-of-the-line, and 2 frigates; and emptied warehouses full of beams, planks, spars, masts, rope, cannons, munitions, and provisions, and sent that astonishing haul back to England. In contrast, the soldiers and sailors garnered few victory spoils. Although eventually £300,000 in prize money was distributed, the commanders and officers grabbed the lion's share, leaving token amounts for the men.[22] Captain Harry Ross-Lewin of the 32nd expressed the prevailing anger:

> The ships and stores brought off from Copenhagen were valued in England at four millions and a half sterling, and it was supposed cost the Danes about ten millions; but as no formal declaration of war had been made, it was decided that the captors were not entitled to prize money, and a sum of only eight hundred thousand pounds was granted by way of compensation to that portion of the army and navy which had been engaged in the siege of Copenhagen.[23]

Wellesley was among many Britons who questioned the campaign's morality. As a loyal soldier, he literally and figuratively went along with the war against Denmark although 'we have no grounds of justification' for what he saw as a naked act of aggression. Yet his sense of duty forced him to accept orders 'to arrange the capitulation,' something 'I shall ever regret.' He obeyed his instructions to secure Britain's occupation of Zealand even though he viewed the island as a strategic liability rather than asset. Defending Zealand diverted an enormous amount of British naval and army power from genuine threats and opportunities. He estimated that the island could only be defended with 30,000 troops, and only then with a huge naval flotilla to ensure that it was supplied. If the fleet is called away, 'it is very obvious that 30,000 Men cannot hold the island against three or four times that number which may be brought against them.' These objections aside, he recognized that the war's results protected British commerce in the Baltic, shielded the Swedes, and checked the Russian navy.[24]

The right of states to defend themselves against an attack or to preempt a pending enemy attack by launching the first blow was then as now a fundamental principle of international law and morality. Whitehall justified its war against Denmark on a hypothetical rather than a real threat. Although Denmark showed no signs of declaring or even preparing for a war against Britain, Prime Minister William Bentinck, Duke of Portland and the Cabinet assumed that it would and acted on that assumption. In reality, Britain's short but destructive war against Denmark in September 1807, grossly violated international norms of law and morality. Foreign Secretary Canning vividly express the war's logic: 'We must not disguise the fact from ourselves – we are hated throughout Europe, and that hate must be cured by fear.'[25]

The latest French naval escapade began on February 21, 1809, when a storm blew off Admiral James Gambier's fleet blockading Brest. This was the opportunity that Admiral Jean Baptiste Willaumez had impatiently awaited. He ordered the captains of his eight ships-of-the-line and two frigates to lift anchors and spread sail. His mission was to drive off the blockading fleets from Lorient and Rochefort, then sail to Toulon and join forces with Admiral Honore Ganteaume's fleet.[26]

Several days later Willaumez's fleet sailed within sight of Commodore John Beresford's four ships-of-the-line off Lorient. Although outgunned two to one, the British commander typically gave chase. Although he outgunned the enemy two to one, the French commander typically fled. As Willaumez's squadron sailed past Admiral Robert Stopford's squadron blockading Rochefort, Stopford pursued two lagging frigates until their captains wrecked their vessels ashore to avoid capture. The rest of Willaumez's squadron dropped anchor in Basque Roads, a wide bay that spread before La Rochelle and Île de Ré northward and Île d'Oléron westward, with the small Île d'Aix in the middle shielding the approach to the Charente River mouth with Rochefort a half-dozen miles upstream. When Stopford's squadron approached, Willaumez led his vessels southwest of Île d'Aix, but along the way a ship-of-the-line wrecked on a shoal. After joining his remaining vessels to those already anchored there, his fleet included 12 ships-of-the-line split in 2 parallel lines of 6 each, screened by 3 frigates.

So far Willaumez's cruise had been a disaster. It would get much worse. Willaumez had his sailors erect a boom across the channel leading to his anchorage which offered little protection while trapping him as thoroughly as he had been in Brest. Outraged that Willaumez had fled rather than fought Beresford and Stopford, Napoleon had Marine Minister Denis Decrès replace him with Admiral Zacharie Allemand.[27] The new commander would be just as inept as the man he replaced.

Gambier arrived with his fleet on March 7, but did not attack despite his overwhelming numbers. He later explained:

> The enemy's ships are anchored in two lines very near to each other in a direction due S from the fort on the Isle d'Aix ... [S]hips ... as might attack the enemy would be exposed to be raked by the hot shot ... from the Island; and should the ships be disabled in their mast, they must remain within the range of the enemy's fire until destroyed, there not being sufficient depth of water to allow them to move ... out of distance.[28]

Yet, there was a viable alternative. During a war council, Gambier rejected Captain Eliab Harvey's suggestion that they panic the French to ground ashore or to open sea with fireboats. Harvey erupted in rage and, according to Captain Thomas Dundonald, criticized Gambier 'to his face such as I had never before witnessed from a subordinate.'[29]

Learning of both the plan and Harvey's tongue-lashing of Gambier, the Admiralty embraced the former and court-martialed the latter. Harvey was later found guilty and cashiered for using 'vehement and insulting language' against his commander. Meanwhile, the Admiralty ordered Captain Thomas Cochrane, who happened to be in London, to gather fire-ships and sail them against the French fleet. Cochrane was an excellent choice.[30] He was among the Royal Navy's most daring and aggressive captains. He was also an impassioned radical Parliamentarian. He was the son of a sea captain, Thomas Cochrane, Earl of Dundonald, and the nephew of Admiral Alexander Cochrane, himself a first-rate commander. Yet these connections would not be influential enough to get Cochrane out of trouble for speaking his mind and offending far more powerful people.

Cochrane joined Gambier's fleet on April 3. He selected three small, aging supply vessels for fireboats, had them emptied then filled with combustibles and gunpowder kegs. Another 18 fireboats soon arrived from England. The plan was to sail the fireboats on a moonless night when the tide and wind would carry them directly to the French fleet. Quarter of an hour before the vessels reached the enemy, the skeleton crews would light the fuses, clamber into longboats, and row swiftly to safety.

That night came on April 11. Cochrane led the way. Enemy lookouts spotted the dark shadows moving toward them and shouted the alarm. Cochrane and the other captains lighted their fuses and escaped. One by one the flames engulfed the 21 boats steadily approaching the French fleet. The French captains ordered their men to cut their cables, unfurl sails, and flee. The fireboats broke through the boom and began exploding, showering flaming debris for hundreds of yards in all directions. All the fireboats blew up or ran aground without sinking a single French vessel. But that did not matter. In their panic, most French captains wrecked their warships ashore.

The next morning, Cochrane was astonished to see only 2 ships-of-the-line afloat while 7 were beached, including Admiral Allemand's 120-gun flagship. Cochrane signaled Gambier, whose fleet was safely anchored 10 miles away, that he was going to attack and asked for support: 'Half the fleet can destroy the enemy. Seven on shore.'[31] Cochrane sailed his 38-gun *Imperieuse* directly at the 2 French ships-of-the-line and opened fire. Rather than turn and fight, the French captains tried to escape but soon ran aground. Those two vessels and a third already stuck struck their colors. Cochrane had those ships burned.

Meanwhile, Gambier did bring his fleet forward but halted his 11 ships-of-the-line, 7 frigates, 5 sloops, 2 bomb ketches, and smaller vessels 3 miles away beyond cannon shot of Île d'Aix's fortress and watched the battle. Eventually he sent a bomb ketch supported by three brigs but they did little fighting and withdrew before nightfall.

Cochrane remained alone with his battered *Imperieuse*. As the new day dawned, he was preparing to attack Allemand's flagship when he received Gambier's order to withdraw: 'You have done your part so admirably that I will not suffer you to tarnish it by attempting impossibilities, which I think … any further effort to destroy those ships would be. You must, therefore, join us as soon as you can.'[32] Cochrane had won a glorious if limited victory. Had Gambier reinforced him with all his warships, they could have destroyed the entire French fleet. Cochrane strongly made this point and asked for permission to resume his attack.

Instead, after designating a small blockading flotilla, Gambier ordered the rest of his captains including Cochrane to sail for Britain. There King George III awarded Cochrane by making him a Knight of the Bath. Cochrane took his seat in Parliament and wielded his position and prestige to deny a vote of thanks to Gambier, who he accused of cowardice. Gambier insisted upon a court martial to clear his name. He argued that for him to have attacked would have exposed his warships to destruction by enemy forts and warships. In this, he was supported by Admiral Stopford. No one pointed out that fear of being destroyed did not prevent Cochrane from sailing amidst the French fleet and fighting at point-blank range.

Politics as usual rewarded connections over courage and competence. The court martial acquitted Gambier of cowardice on July 26, 1809. The Admiralty punished Cochrane, not just for his barbed criticism of Gambier, but his outspoken radicalism by sidelining him from active command for the rest of the war. This was at once politically correct and a blow to Britain's war against the French empire.

Chapter 11

Portugal, 1808

We gave the French an unmerciful beating yesterday.

Arthur Wellesley

If things go on in this disgraceful manner I must quit them.

Arthur Wellesley

We shall be in Lisbon in three days!

Arthur Wellesley

Portugal was England's oldest ally, with the first treaty binding them dating to 1373. Shared economic and strategic interests linked them.[1] The exchange of Portuguese wine for British fabrics mutually enriched each realm. Lisbon, Oporto, and other Portuguese ports were excellent anchorages for British merchant and war vessels or stepping stones toward the south Atlantic, Gibraltar, and Mediterranean. As small realms at different ends of Europe they often faced larger, neighboring threats, especially when France and Spain were allies. They now faced just such a threat.

After defeating in succession the Austrians, Prussians, and Russians to dominate Germany, Napoleon turned his ambitions toward Portugal. On July 19, 1807, he had Foreign Minister Charles Maurice de Talleyrand-Perigord demand that Portugal sever trade with Britain, confiscate all British ships and arrest all British subjects then in Portugal, and ally with France. Lisbon rejected these demands. Napoleon presented Portugal a last chance to be an ally or suffer conquest. The governments of France and Spain jointly issued an ultimatum to Portugal on August 12. Once again Lisbon, backed by Whitehall, refused.

This stance was at once courageous and foolhardy. Portugal suffered debilitating military and political weaknesses; its army numbered only 25,000 troops and its navy only 11 decrepit ships-of-the-line, while no king sat on the throne, only mad queen Maria with her son João acting as her prince regent.[2] And Britain lacked the military power to defend its venerable trade partner and ally. The thin red line was stretched to the snapping point. There simply were not enough available troops, provisions, munitions, and transports to muster and sail an army large enough to Portugal to repel a mass French and Spanish invasion. Nonetheless, Whitehall sent a fleet to Lisbon.

Two days after receiving the latest rejection on October 15, Napoleon ordered an army commanded by General Andoche Junot to march from Bayonne across the Iberian Peninsula to Lisbon. Meanwhile, Charles IV mobilized part of Spain's army to join forces with Junot and invade Portugal. Napoleon and Charles IV designated who got what of the spoils with the Treaty of Fontainebleau signed on October 27. Portugal would be carved up into regions, of which Charles IV's daughter and the Kingdom of Etruria's queen and her husband would take the north; Foreign Minister Manuel de Godoy would take the south; and France would occupy the center. To conquer Portugal, France would supply 25,000 infantry and 3,000 cavalry, and Spain 8,000 infantry and 3,000 cavalry; a reserve army of 40,000 French would mass at Bayonne to march against Portugal should the initial invasion fail. The French could garrison towns across northern Spain to protect their supply and communication lines between Bayonne and Lisbon. Finally, to reassure Charles of his good faith, Napoleon included treaty clauses that guaranteed Spain's territory and recognized Charles as the 'emperor of the two Americas.'[3]

Incapable of defeating this invasion, Portugal's royal family, court, and treasure packed onto a flotilla of 8 ships-of-the-line, 4 frigates, and 24 merchant ships that sailed from Lisbon to exile in Brazil on November 29, 1807; Admiral William Sidney Smith and his fleet of 9 ships-of-the-line escorted the Portuguese flotilla as far as Madeira then returned to blockade Lisbon. Meanwhile, Junot led 1,500 troops into Portugal's capital on November 30. Over the next few weeks 26,500 other French troops and 13,000 allied Spanish troops deployed across central Portugal, and General Domingo Belesta with 16,000 Spanish troops spread across northern Portugal. On January 1, 1808, Napoleon declared deposed the Braganza dynasty that had ruled Portugal since 1640, but for now did not name a successor.[4]

Portugal's unopposed foreign occupation represented the latest failure of British policy and disaster for British security. Napoleon's Continental System now excluded Britain from all of Europe except Sweden and Sicily. Yet eventually spy reports lightened some of Whitehall's gloom. Apparently the French were experiencing worsening indigestion trying to consume Portugal. Riots erupted against voracious French indemnity, requisition, and anti-clerical policies in Lisbon on December 13. Although the French brutally suppressed the uprisings, the tensions simmered. General Belesta withdrew his troops from northern Portugal back to Spain. Junot and his 26,000 troops held only Lisbon, Elvas, Almeida, Setubal, Abrantes, Peniche, Faro, and Evora. Portugal's leaders reasserted their power in the wake of that Spanish army and dispersal of the French army. Bishop Don Antonio de Castro of Oporto formed a Supreme Governing Junta and called on the Portuguese to revolt against the French. The Junta sent Whitehall a desperate plea for help in liberating their country.

Whitehall eventually responded. General Arthur Wellesley commanded a 7,000-man expedition preparing at Cork, Ireland, to sail to the West Indies. On June 14, 1808, Wellesley received orders to sail instead for Portugal where 5,000 troops under General Brent Spencer at Gibraltar would reinforce him, with Governor General Hew Dalrymple eventually taking command. The mission was to unite with any Portuguese troops and drive the French from Portugal.

The campaign suffered from three weaknesses. France's 2,500 cavalry far outnumbered the 400 British dragoons. France's 8-pounder cannons outgunned Britain's 6-pounders. Most importantly, first Sir Harry Burrard then Dalrymple would supersede Wellesley in command; although Burrard had fought in America, Flanders, and Denmark, Dalrymple had never led troops in combat.[5] Wellesley was confident that he could surmount the first two handicaps but despaired at the third. He complained that Whitehall's decision to make him the third-ranking general put him in the 'awkward' situation of serving 'in subordinate capacity in an army which one has commanded. However, I will do whatever they please. I think they had better order me home.'[6] The prospect of being replaced in command shortly after he entered the field naturally angered him. Yet he reassured Secretary at War Robert Stewart, lord Castlereagh that the strictest professionalism would guide his behavior despite the unfortunate circumstances: 'whether I am to command the army or not, or am to quit it, I shall do my best to insure its success ... I shall not hurry operations or commence them one moment sooner than they ought to be commenced in order that I may acquire the credit of the success.'[7] Wellesley would typically be true to his word. As for the French, he reckoned them a formidable foe but was confident he would beat them:

I am thinking of the French that I am going to fight. I have not seen them since the campaign in Flanders when they were capital soldiers, and a dozen years of victory under Bonaparte must have made them better still. They have, besides, a new system of strategy which has outmaneuvered and overwhelmed all the armies of Europe. It's enough to make one thoughtful; but no matter, my die is cast; they may overwhelm me, but I don't think they will outmaneuver me. First, because I am not afraid of them, as everybody else seems to be; secondly, because if what I hear of their system of maneuver be true, I think it a false one as against steady troops. I suspect that all the continental armies were more than half beaten before the battle was begun. I, at least, will not be frightened beforehand.[8]

The flotilla dropped anchor briefly at Oporto on July 24, as Wellesley went ashore to negotiate a joint strategy with Portuguese General Bernardino Freire. Wellesley would sail south and disembark at Mondego Bay where Freire would join him with 5,000 Portuguese troops. Wellesley explained to Castlereagh that 'to effect a landing in front of the enemy is always difficult, and I shall be inclined to land at a distance from Lisbon.'[9]

The flotilla anchored off Mondego Bay, 80 miles from Lisbon, on August 1. It took until August 8, before all the troops and supplies were disembarked, including those of General Spencer packed aboard a small flotilla that appeared on August 5. The biggest challenge was rounding up enough carts and draft animals to carry all the provisions and munitions.

Wellesley was outraged to learn that Freire had changed his mind and was marching south on a road through the mountains rather than along the coast. Freire did, however, dispatch to Wellesley 1,600 Portuguese light infantry trained and led by British Colonel Nicholas Trant. Wellesley vented his disgust: 'Freire will have to justify himself with the existing government of Portugal, with his Prince, and with the World, for having omitted to stand forward … and for having refused to send me the assistance.'[10] This was the first of countless frustrations that Wellesley and the allied cause would suffer over the next six years from backstabbing or cowardly Portuguese and Spanish generals. Such potential pitfalls of coalition warfare are why Napoleon preferred to fight than join them.

When Wellesley led his army on the road to Lisbon on August 9, he commanded 14,000 British troops, 1,600 Portuguese troops, and 18 cannons. His chief weakness was cavalry, with only 254 of 390 dragoons mounted.

Spearheading the advance were the dragoons, four companies of the 95th rifle regiment, and the light infantry companies of the other regiments.[11]

Meanwhile at Lisbon, Junot was unruffled as he read reports of Wellesley's landing. He assumed that Britain was incapable of launching more than a spoiling raid against him. So, rather than mass his forces and quick-march to Mondego Bay, he dispatched General Henri Delaborde with 4,400 men to chase the raiders into the sea.

The advanced French and British guards skirmished near Obidos on August 15. Learning that Wellesley's men far outnumbered his own, Delaborde withdrew toward Lisbon. On August 17, Wellesley caught up at Rolica, and launched a diversionary attack on Delaborde's front while curling a column around each French flank. A British sergeant recalled that they:

> ... rapidly approached the field of battle and found a difficulty at first getting within range. The hills on which the enemy were posted were ... too perpendicular to attempt a direct ascent. Our staff officers, however, discovered certain chasms of openings made ... by the rain up which we were led ... the enemy playing on us all the time.[12]

Delaborde skillfully extracted his men from the trap, but suffered 700 casualties while inflicting 485 British casualties.[13] In analyzing the battle, Wellesley lamented three mistakes that prevented the enemy's complete destruction. The first two were crucial, the failures of General Ronald Ferguson and Lieutenant Colonel George Lake to carefully follow his instructions. Ferguson did not turn the enemy's left but instead attacked directly, while 'Lake went up the wrong road. He ought to have gone up that on his right; he hurried his Men, [but] did not clear the pass of the Enemy by his Light Infantry before he entered with his column.' Less important was the delay in the artillery and infantry reserves in getting to the front because they 'could not find the road.'[14]

Wellesley resumed his small army's march toward Lisbon. The decisive battle came at Vimeiro on August 21. The day before word reached Wellesley that Burrard and 4,000 reinforcements were disembarking at a beach near the Maceira River mouth a dozen miles away. Burrard instructed Wellesley to await his arrival. Wellesley deployed his army along a string of hills south of Vimeiro.

Junot, meanwhile, had arrived with reinforcements at Delaborde's camp, bringing the French force to 13,890 men and 24 cannons compared with

Wellesley's 18,781 men and 18 cannons.[15] Although Junot knew that he was outnumbered, he ordered his artillery to bombard the redcoats while massing most of his troops in columns to assault each enemy flank. As the French guns opened fire, Wellesley withdrew his exposed troops atop the hills to their rear slopes, his first use of this tactic. The French believed that they had the British on the run when most disappeared from sight. As the French got within musket range, Wellesley ordered his troops back to the hilltops. The British fired volleys into the French until they broke and ran. Private Benjamin Harris, of the 95th Rifles, recalled 'lanes torn through their ranks as they advanced ... and we pelted away at them like a shower of leaden hail.'[16]

In all the British repelled four French attacks. Wellesley then ordered his dragoons to charge a French squadron. After watching the British cavalry scatter the French, Wellesley excitedly implored Burrard: 'Sir Harry, the French are completely beaten; we have a large body of troops that have not yet been in action ... You take the force here straight forward; I will bring round the left with the troops already there. We shall be in Lisbon in three days!'[17] Burrard demurred then and again when word arrived that 2,000 French troops were cut off and could be captured if the reserves marched forward.

Wellesley rendered a bittersweet account of Vimeiro. He was proud that his men 'gave the French an unmerciful beating yesterday' when the 'Enemy came ... & attacked ... Sir Harry not being in the field till one of the attacks was completely beaten off & the other begun & all the dispositions made for defeating it.'[18] Yet he felt cheated of a greater victory. Although Burrard did not interfere with Wellesley's handling of the battle, he refused to let him follow up his victory by pursuing the French 'by which he saved them from total destruction.'[19] Nonetheless, Wellesley's men killed 450 French, wounded 1,200, and captured 350 men and 13 cannons, while suffering 135 killed, 534 wounded, and 51 missing.[20]

After Dalrymple appeared the day after Vimeiro, Wellesley 'did everything in my power to prevail upon him to march.' But Wellesley was appalled to discover that Dalrymple 'has no plan, or even an idea of a plan, nor do I believe he knows the meaning of the word plan.'[21] Instead Dalrymple welcomed General François Kellermann who appeared under a truce flag and carrying Junot's request for an armistice and negotiations.

Wellesley insisted that his victories at Rolica and Vimeiro had Junot on the ropes and thus a knockout blow should precede any negotiations. Dalrymple and Burrard worried that the French enjoyed superior numbers and positions, making the campaign's outcome uncertain; regardless, a settlement could prevent senseless bloodshed on both sides. Private John Leach shared their view of the strategic situation: 'The enemy then had possession of all the defensible positions between us and Lisbon, independent of the citadel and different forts near the capital. This would have enabled General Junot to protract the contest for a length of time, whilst the game of the British clearly was to root out their opponents with as little delay as possible.'[22]

Wellesley 'entirely disapproved of the indefinite terms given to the suspension of hostilities' which the French used to strengthen their position. He was thoroughly frustrated and disgusted with being subordinate to Dalrymple and Burrard. It was maddening enough that they 'ask my opinion about everything, & never act according to it.' He feared 'that my friends in England will consider me responsible for many things over which I have no power.' He grumbled that 'if things go on in this disgraceful manner I must quit them.'[23]

Junot may have been a mediocre general but was a crafty diplomat. On August 31, he got the British commanders to sign the Convention of Cintra whereby the Royal Navy would sail Junot and his army with all their guns and loot back to France. The deal infuriated Wellesley who 'did everything I could to prevail upon' Dalrymple 'not to agree to the objectionable parts of the agreement but in vain.' He then agonized over whether to sign the document. He finally did so, reasoning that refusing to do so 'could not have prevented it' and 'would have placed me at the Head of a party against the Comr. in Chief ... & created a breach between us.'[24] He fired off a letter to Castlereagh, explaining: 'Although my name is affixed to this instrument, I beg that you will not believe that I negotiated it, that I approve of it, or that I had any hand in wording it.'[25]

The Royal Navy conveyed back to France Junot and 25,747 troops. Junot left behind nearly 3,000 troops, with most in graves, while most of his Swiss and German contingents deserted.[26] Nothing in the Convention prevented Junot's troops from being redeployed in the Peninsula. Shortly after their arrival, Napoleon sent Junot and most of his regiments back to fight in Spain.

Whitehall shared Wellesley's view of the Cintra Convention and recalled Dalrymple, Burrard, and Wellesley to explain their decisions. While Dalrymple sailed immediately, Burrard and Wellesley embarked for home only after General John Moore arrived to command the British army. In the end, all three commanders were vindicated. On December 22, 1808, the Court of Inquiry voted six to one to approve the armistice and four to three to approve the Convention of Cintra. This close professional call for Wellesley would have profound consequences for the fate of Britain and the world.

Chapter 12

Spain, 1808–9

I was risking infinitely too much, but something must be risked for the honour of the Service, and to make it apparent that we stuck to the Spaniards long after they had given up their cause as lost.

General John Moore

Sir John Moore ought to be hung his conduct has been infamous.

Captain Alexander Gordon

lthough Wellington had liberated Portugal, Napoleon steadily transformed neighboring Spain from an independent country into the French empire's latest satellite. Under the Treaty of Fontainebleau signed on October 27, 1807, the French could garrison key cities and fortresses across northern Spain. The initial rationale for this was to support their joint operations in Portugal. In fall 1807, this rationale gave way to another more pressing. Those French troops helped maintain order and support Spain's monarchy. A third reason arose by May 1808. The French army was poised to takeover Spain and impose Napoleon's brother as the realm's king. Marshal Joachim Murat commanded 90,000 troops concentrated mostly near cities like Irun, San Sebastian, Vitoria, Pamplona, Burgos, Toledo, and Madrid that led back to Bayonne, just across the French frontier. Murat's headquarters was at Madrid, where he deployed 20,000 troops either within the city or in the nearby countryside.

How did it come to this? Napoleon typically took advantage of his latest opportunity for conquest. Charles IV, his chief minister Manuel de Godoy, and the rest of his administration were notoriously inept, corrupt, greedy, and brutal, and thus widely despised. When people protested or outright rebelled against his misrule, the king ordered his troops to mercilessly crush them. Hatred of the king was not confined to the masses of overtaxed, down-trodden, poverty-stricken subjects in villages or cities. Disdain permeated Spain's elite. Many liberals, known as afransecados, admired Napoleon and the progressive reforms he imposed on France and his empire. Others, especially army officers, prayed for the day that Crown Prince Ferdinand took the throne. Ferdinand seemed progressive and vigorous alongside his reactionary, doddering father. Indeed, paranoia that Ferdinand sought to overthrow them provoked his parents to incarcerate him on October 27, 1807. They released him only after he pledged loyalty to them. He soon broke his promise. On March 19, 1808, Ferdinand, backed by a Royal Guard regiment, forced his parents to abdicate at the palace of Aranjuez, 20 miles south of Madrid. Charles secretly appealed to Napoleon for help.

Napoleon summoned the royal family to meet him at Bayonne where he promised to resolve all their problems. They were stunned when they learned his solution, but nonetheless acquiesced. Charles and Ferdinand signed treaties on May 5 and 10, respectively, whereby each renounced the throne and entrusted it to Napoleon in return for huge pensions and exile at separate French chateaux.[1] Napoleon then talked his brother Joseph, currently the king of Naples, to yield that throne to Joachim Murat, married to their sister Caroline, and hurry to Madrid to become Spain's king.

With enormous trepidation, Joseph accepted Spain's crown from a rump assembly of Spanish afransecados at Bayonne on June 6. He faced a worsening anti-French rebellion. The first resistance actually erupted in Madrid on May 2, before the royal family signed away their realm to Napoleon. After mobs murdered several French soldiers, Marshal Murat unleashed his troops against them; they restored order after slaughtering as many as 500 people. The most important step came on May 28, when the military commander of the Asturias region declared war against France; within weeks most of the other 14 military regions each led by a general, 32 provinces each led by an intendant, and cities each led by a magistrate announced their own defiance.[2]

Spain's army numbered 100,000 men on paper, but virtually all regiments mustered far fewer than its official number. Even worse the regiments were scattered across Spain and the overseas empire. Spain's king, of course, was the commander-in-chief. His abdication abruptly ended the army's unity of command. The subsequent void took a long time to fill. Communications among the regional commanders was tenuous and coordination virtually nonexistent as each largely followed his own strategy out of ambition, jealousy, fear, and ignorance.

Napoleon's awareness of the Spanish army's debilitating weaknesses typically fed his hubris. In ordering his commanders to secure the entire country, the emperor forced them to do too much with too little. General Pierre Dupont advanced with 13,000 troops as far as Cordova on June 13, then hastily withdrew as General Francisco Castanos approached with

34,000 troops. Castanos caught up, cut off, and began a series of attacks against Dupont at Baylen from July 14. After suffering 2,200 casualties, Dupont surrendered not just his troops but 7,000 nearby reinforcements on July 19.

The war seesawed abruptly with Dupont's surrender of 17,635 French troops.[3] Although Marshal Jean Baptiste Bessières's 14,000 troops routed 25,000 Spaniards under the fumbling joint command of General Antonio Cuesta and Joaquin Blake at the battle of Medina de Rio Seco on July 14, he could not follow up his victory as French forces elsewhere beat hasty retreats. News of the Dupont disaster greeted Joseph days after he entered Madrid on July 20. More bad news followed. General Adrien Moncey abandoned his siege of Valencia and withdrew with his 20,000 men to Madrid. Outgunned, General Philibert Duhesme called off his campaign to conquer Catalonia and withdrew into Barcelona. Astride the French communication line between Barcelona and Perpignan, Spain's garrison at Gerona refused to surrender. At Saragossa, General José Palafox also defied a French siege that would ground on for months. On August 1, Joseph, the would-be Spanish king, panicked and fled to Burgos with Moncey's corps and other detachments.

Spain's military and civilian leaders struggled to retake their country. The scattered armies advanced in the wake of the French retreats. Delegates from the regional juntas met to form a national Junta at Aranjuez on September 25. They eventually reestablished a council of ministers, ministries, a secretariat, and a Supreme War Council, and elected Jose Monino y Redondo, conde de Floridablanca the president. On November 10, they announced the restoration of Spain's traditional political and legal system. As for a king, they did not openly endorse either Charles IV or Ferdinand who were luxuriously pensioned at French chateaux.

A king was the least of Spain's wants. The generals were mostly vain, squabbling, jealous, and inept. Competent officers and noncommissioned officers were rare. Soldiers were wretchedly trained, equipped, provisioned, motivated, and led. Ironically, despite Spain's proud caballero heritage, the cavalry was the worst mounted in Europe; centuries of breeding mules degenerated horses.

Spain fielded about 90,000 troops split among 4 armies, with General Joachim Blake's 32,000 at Espinosa, General Francisco Castanos's 30,000 at Tudela, General José Palafox' 10,000 at Saragossa, and General Juan Vives's 20,000 in Catalonia. Reinforcements arrived from an unusual direction. In 1807, Charles IV had dispatched General Pedro Romano with 14,000 troops to join operations against Sweden as Napoleon led his army against the

Russians and Prussians in Poland. After learning that Napoleon had deposed Charles and enthroned Joseph, Romana was determined somehow to escape and return home to fight the French. He managed to extract 9,000 troops and rendezvous with a British flotilla at the island of Langeland, where they embarked on August 21. On October 21, Romana proudly led his men ashore at Santander.

Napoleon characteristically responded to these reverses with a burst of plans, orders, and movements of troops and supplies. Reinforcements streamed south along roads leading to northern Spain and Catalonia. On November 6, Napoleon reached Vitoria to take command. In the region, his army numbered 130,000 troops split into 7 corps, the Imperial Guard, and 4 cavalry divisions. His plan was simple. He sent four corps in different directions to rout the Spanish before them and seize key cities, while he led three corps and the Imperial Guard toward Madrid, which he captured on December 1. Elsewhere Marshal Nicolas Soult captured Burgos and Marshal Laurent Gouvion Saint Cyr secured most of Catalonia. Napoleon called a halt to let his corps rest and resupply.

Meanwhile, belated help to Spain from Britain was on the way. General John Moore had commanded the 20,000-man British army in Portugal since September 1808. On October 6, he received orders to combine forces at Astorga with a division led by General David Baird that Whitehall sent to Corunna. Once together, they would march to join Generals Romana and Blake against the French. Moore mulled then rejected the notion of sailing his army from Lisbon to Corunna. It would take weeks just to embark, sail, disembark, and march 133 miles to Astorga. The longer a sea voyage took, the worse its effects on a regiment's morale, cohesion, and energy. So Moore announced that they would march instead. Reports that the most direct route was impassible to artillery and wagons caused Moore to split his command. The infantry marched northeast over the mountains while the artillery and cavalry headed east into Spain and then north.

Baird and his 12,000 troops sailed from Falmouth on October 8 and anchored at Corunna on October 13. The trials of campaigning in Spain began immediately. Any elation at such a swift voyage vanished when Spanish authorities refused to let Baird and his men disembark until they received the Supreme Junta's permission. A courier was sent galloping off to Madrid. He returned with permission granted on October 22. Even then red-tape prevented the redcoats from stepping ashore for another four days as Spanish bureaucrats debated where the troops could camp. It then took until November 4, before the vessels disgorged all the troops, supplies, and cannons onto the docks. On November 8, another flotilla appeared packed with General Edward Paget and his cavalry; all these horses and men, and their equipment were ashore five days later. Whitehall had not given Baird enough money to buy crucial supplies. Fortunately, John Frere, Britain's ambassador to Spain, lent Baird £50,000 to tide over his division's needs for the next few weeks until he received £100,000 on November 9.[4]

The dilemmas of operating in Spain worsened the deeper the British marched into the interior. Major Alexander Gordon castigated the Supreme Junta as 'a pack of fools' and 'idiots,' and General Romana for 'deceiving us from the beginning.'[5] Most damning of all was this pervasive British sentiment: 'Nowhere have the Spaniards fought at all to entitle them to the name of soldiers.'[6] This posed an insurmountable dilemma: 'We can only act on the defensive without the Spaniards, and I fear unless things wear a more favorable aspect with them we must retreat.'[7] Gordon saw potential for mobilizing Spain's people for war, but castigated Spain's leadership for the problems:

> This Country is lost from the want of Exertion in the higher classes, from the want of heads to direct that spirit which rose up so nobly among the common people, who ... alone show any spirit or activity. But this spirit is dying away for want of direction ... from the Clergy & nobility who are sunk into the most profound Apathy.[8]

The British recognized that their sojourn in the country depended on the ability of the Spanish to delay and ideally blunt Napoleon's offensive:

> I know not whether Madrid will quietly fall when the French are under its walls ... If this bubble breaks, and the City quietly surrenders, we must have a run for it. If, on the contrary it acts the part of another Saragossa the most beneficial effects may be expected ... Upon the fate of Madrid depends that of the Nation.[9]

This view, of course, could not have been more wrong. Madrid was largely indefensible.

By November 22, Baird and Moore were at Astorga and Salamanca, respectively, separated by 105 miles. It was only then that Moore learned that the French had routed Spain's armies, Soult had captured Burgos, and Madrid's fall was inevitable. Napoleon, meanwhile, learned of the British advance. He fired off orders for several corps commanders to march against Moore and hurried the army under his immediate command northwestward.

Moore sent orders on November 28, for Baird to withdraw to Corunna. Baird and his officers were exultant when they received Moore's orders. Gordon noted: 'This intelligence has caused Sir John to give up his foolish plan of advancing (a plan he never ought to have adopted after the dispersion of the Spaniards) and determined him to fall back.' Indeed, 'Sir John has already advanced too far, and what is the object of defeating a Corps of French – none.'[10]

This exultation soon turned to rage. Moore once again changed his mind. General John Hope led the artillery and cavalry into Salamanca on December 4. With his army reunited, Moore's confidence returned. He decided that honor demanded that he advance against Burgos and try to rout Soult despite the overwhelming odds against him. He admitted that 'I was risking infinitely too much, but something must be risked for the honour of the Service, and to make it apparent that we stuck to the Spaniards long after they had given up their cause as lost.'[11]

Moore sent orders to Baird to about-face and head east to Valladolid where they would join forces. Baird and his staff reacted angrily to this command. Gordon expressed the general condemnation of Moore for putting his desire to win glory before his duties: 'I never can agree to a man entrusted with a command giving way to these feelings and risking the safety of the army for personal considerations.'[12] The anger of Baird and his men was not confined to attacking Moore. The sickening fear was that they were sacrificial lambs, dispatched by Whitehall to assert power even if it led to disaster: 'I think Ministers deserve to be turned out if this Army is sacrificed. Why in God did they not send a man of Rank & talents to know the real State & Situation of things before they committed themselves.'[13]

Moore read a captured French dispatch on December 14 that prompted him to change his plans once more. Soult's advanced forces were further west than he anticipated. Moore sent a courier galloping to Baird with orders to unite at Majorca. Moore and Baird joined forces there on December 20. All along the conflicting orders, short rations, cold, and rain ate away the British army's morale and discipline. Moore deplored 'the extreme bad conduct of the troops of late … it is disgraceful to the officers, as it strongly marks their neglect and inattention.' He condemned 'officers who neglect … essential duties; or … soldiers who disgrace their country by acts of villainy towards the country they are sent to protect.' He implored his troops to have faith in his leadership:

It is impossible for the General to explain to his army the motives of the movements he directs ... When it is proper to fight a battle, he will do it, and he will chuse the time and place ... He begs officers and men of the army to attend diligently to discharge their parts, and to leave him, with the other General Officers, the decision on measures which belong to them alone. The soldiers may rest assured that he has nothing more at heart than their honour.[14]

The first clash was a British victory. On December 21, General Paget led his cavalry in a charge against a French cavalry regiment near Sahagun, where his men killed 20, wounded 19, and captured 170 of the enemy.[15] More importantly, Moore learned how close the French corps were and ordered his army to withdraw to Astorga. Romana led 9,500 men into Astorga on December 30. Together the allies had nearly 35,000 troops, but shivering, starving, ragged, and limping, they could barely stumble westward let alone fight. Private Benjamin Harris of the 95th Rifles recalled:

The shoes and boots of our party were now mostly either destroyed or useless to us from foul roads and long miles, and many of the men were entirely barefooted with knapsacks and accoutrements ... dilapidated ... The officers were also ... in a miserable plight. They were pallid ... their feet bleeding and their faces overgrown with beards ... Many of the poor fellows, now near sinking with fatigue, reeled as if in a state of drunkenness, and ... looked the ghosts of our former selves.[16]

Moore recognized that he faced being annihilated by overwhelming French forces. He ordered his army to retreat from Astorga to the coast to embark on vessels and sail to safety. Ever more redcoats dropped behind too exhausted and malnourished to continue. The French captured 900 stragglers on January 4 and 500 more on January 9. At Lugo on January 9, Moore split his forces, sending half to Vigo, while he led the rest to Corunna.

Napoleon led the pursuit as far as Astorga, where he turned over command to Soult and hurried back to Paris. He did so animated by rumors that a conspiracy was brewing against him in his capital while the Austrians were preparing their army for the latest war against France. Whether Napoleon would have relentlessly pursued, caught, and destroyed the British expedition will never be known. What did happen was that most British troops escaped. But it was a very close shave. Facing the crossroads where the British army split, Soult chose to keep his army united and snapping at the heels of Moore's troops.

The grueling retreat demoralized the army and made the soldiers increasingly desperate. Romana was appalled that the British:

> ... seized the mules and oxen that drew our army's artillery, munitions, and baggage train; they have insulted and mistreated ... our officers ... They have ... killed and eaten the oxen that pulled these carts and have not paid ... They have killed three magistrates and various other inhabitants ... In a word the French themselves could not have found agents better calculated to whip up hate of the British than the army commanded by General Sir John Moore.[17]

Romana eventually turned his back on the British and marched toward Oviedo. The British were just as scathing of the Spanish. Augustus von Schaumann, the British commissary general, condemned the:

> ... apathy with which the inhabitants ... have witnessed our misery is revolting. They were to be seen in large armed hordes far away from us in the mountains ... when ... they might have been of use to us and covered our retreat. But not only did these puffed-up patriots ... remove all cattle and all foodstuffs out of our way ... [but] murdered and plundered our own men who fell out.[18]

The remnants of the British columns reached Corunna and Vigo on January 11 and 12, respectively. Moore's troops staggered into Corunna to view the bay empty of British vessels that could sail them to safety. Storms had battered and delayed the transports' arrival. Facing the likely prospect of spending the war in a French prison, Gordon asserted that 'Sir John Moore ought to be hung his conduct has been infamous.'[19]

The flotilla finally appeared on January 14. As Moore prepared his men to embark, he ordered them to destroy anything of military value that they could not carry off. Thomas Howells of the 71st Highlanders 'witnessed a most moving scene. The beach was covered with dead horses and resounded with the reports of pistols ... [The horses] appeared frantic, neighed and screamed ... Many broke loose and galloped along the beach.'[20] This horror was eclipsed when sappers detonated 4,000 barrels of gunpowder to deny it to the French. The series of explosions was deafening and shook the ground.

Soult's 24,200 troops reached Corunna's outskirts on January 15, and they attacked early the next morning. The British repelled the French in desperate fighting, suffering 900 to the enemy's 1,400 casualties. General Hope took command after Moore was killed and Baird was grievously wounded. That night and the following day, Hope managed to embark 26,000 troops on the vessels. The survivors left behind 7,000 dead or captured comrades on the roads they had marched and the places they had fought, culminating with Corunna.[21]

Within weeks the transports began disgorging the men at English ports. For some shame mingled with the elation at having survived and come home. For Subaltern Robert Blakeney:

> … on quitting our ships we presented an appearance of much dirt and misery. The men were ragged, displaying torn garments of all colors; and the people of England, accustomed to witness the high order and unparalleled cleanliness of their national troops, for which they were renowned throughout Europe, and never having seen an army under the termination of a hard campaign, were horror-struck.[22]

The immediate reaction of the survivors to the campaign they had endured was searing. Gordon condemned 'the shameful conduct of Sir John Moore against whom the whole Army talks loudly … His acts have been one continued scene of imbecility & folly.'[23] He lamented that the 'Government as well as the Nation were so foolishly deceived by the first impulses of the moment, without weighing the Causes and state of this movement of a Nation the true Character of whom is little known.'[24]

History is kinder to Moore. His campaign disrupted Napoleon's plan to conquer all of Spain. Much of the French army turned northwest rather than fanned out toward not just Corunna and Vigo but south to Valencia and southwest to Seville and Cádiz, the seat of government and most important port, respectively. Then there is the contribution of Moore's campaign for British identity. His epic retreat has become Britain's version of Xenophon and his Greek army evading the Persians 2,300 years earlier. And the losses of men and materiel, while severe, were soon overcome. A new commander would appear to lead the war against the French in the Iberian Peninsula, and he would eventually triumph.

Chapter 13

Portugal and Spain, 1809

If we can maintain ourselves in Portugal, the war will not cease in the Peninsula, and, if the war lasts in the Peninsula, Europe will be saved.

Arthur Wellesley

Never was there such a murderous battle.

Arthur Wellesley

Despite the devastating results of Moore's campaign, Whitehall deepened its commitment to rescuing the Peninsula from French imperialism. General Arthur Wellesley succinctly explained why: 'If we can maintain ourselves in Portugal, the war will not cease in the Peninsula, and, if the war lasts in the Peninsula, Europe will be saved.'[1]

Yet the responses of the Portuguese and Spanish governments to Britain's commitment differed sharply. Most Portuguese leaders were grateful, pragmatic, and humble; they recognized the British as their nation's saviors and subordinated their troops to superior British military skills. Britain's alliance with Portugal gave Britain's commanders leeway to wage war as they saw fit. They could march, camp, and fight wherever military necessity drew them. British officers trained, equipped, paid, and led the Portuguese troops. Colonel Nicholas Trant created a brigade of light infantry, known as cazadores. The Junta appointed General William Beresford to command Portugal's army on March 8, 1809. Overall, the choice was fortunate. Although Beresford was a mediocre field general, he was outstanding at organizing, training, supplying, and motivating the Portuguese army. Wellington called Beresford 'the ablest man I have yet seen with the army … I know of no one fitter for the purpose.'[2]

Britain and Spain's Junta, now ensconced in Seville, formally allied with a treaty on January 14, 1809, signed by Foreign Minister George Canning and Ambassador Juan de Apoda. The alliance, however, was cramped. The Junta wanted the British to supply them with unending amounts of money, arms, and troops while giving nothing or little in return. Whitehall opened its treasury and magazines to the Junta. Before the campaign season opened in May 1809, the Spaniards received 20,000 uniforms, 200,000 muskets, and 155 artillery pieces. Yet the Spanish barred British officers from commanding Spanish troops, British soldiers from setting foot in Cádiz, and British merchants from trading in Spanish colonies.

Nonetheless, the Junta did take some positive measures to fight the French and establish legitimacy for itself. On December 28, 1808, the Junta issued a proclamation that had an important impact on the war. It at once encouraged and tried to regulate the guerrilla bands mushrooming across Spain. All bands would be subject to the region's regular military commander. The Junta would issue officer commissions. No band could accept deserters from the draft or regular regiments. The Junta also tried to transform itself into a more elaborate and legitimate government. On May 22, 1809, the Junta announced that it would hold elections for a Cortés or national assembly within a year.

Meanwhile, in early 1809, French troops were busy conquering or exploiting most of Spain. Pockets of Spanish guerrillas or regular troops resisted across the country, but the largest armies defended the southwest where Seville and Cádiz stood. For now Napoleon ignored that region and ordered a campaign designed to conquer Portugal. French armies would invade Portugal from the north and east. Marshal Nicolas Soult's 24,000 troops and 20 cannons were deployed around Orense in Spain's northwestern Galicia region, while Marshal Claude Victor's 17,500-man corps was deployed around Merida in western Spain. A third force of 9,000 troops led by General Pierre Lapisse screened the Spanish fortress of Cuidad Rodrigo.

Soult opened his campaign first. He swiftly captured the fortress of Chaves, scattered 25,000 militia commanded by General Bernadino Freire at Braga on March 25, then headed west down the Douro River valley toward Oporto. Outgunned nearly two to one, General Francisco da Silveira struggled to keep his 12,000 troops beyond Soult's relentless advance, but stopped to defend Oporto. The French routed his army and occupied Oporto on March 29. Freire crossed to the Douro River's south bank then headed up the valley to shelter in the mountains. Soult did not pursue Freire but instead sent forces south to secure positions about midway between Oporto and Coimbra. Soult had about 17,300 troops in and south of Oporto. He deployed General Louis Loison with 6,500 troops at Amarante to guard his eastern flank against Silveira, and garrisoned about 1,500 in key towns leading back to Galicia.

Victor, meanwhile, was stalled at the frontier where he faced Spain's fortresses of Badajoz and General Antonio Cuesta 23,000-man army. Cuesta attacked Victor at Medellin on March 28, but lost 10,000 troops and retreated far south. This cleared the way for Victor to besiege first Badajoz then Portugal's fortress of Elvas a score of miles beyond. The trouble was that Victor lacked enough heavy cannons for a proper siege and had to await their arrival. Once he got them and captured those frontier fortresses, he could lead his men down the Tagus River valley and join forces with Soult at Lisbon. That junction never took place.

King George III named Arthur Wellesley to command British forces in Portugal on March 26, 1809. Two key reasons lay behind his choice. First, Wellesley had spearheaded the successful campaign in August 1808 that forced Junot's capitulation. Second, at Minister for War Castlereagh's request, Wellesley had penned an analysis on how to defend Portugal that would cost the treasury only £1 million while draining the French empire.[3] This bargain price convinced the king and the Cabinet that Portugal was worth fighting for and that Wellesley was the man to lead the effort. Although the actual cost of Britain's Peninsular War would skyrocket far beyond the estimate, having Wellesley in command proved to be priceless.

Wellesley could not have been happier with Castlereagh's campaign instructions:

> The defense of Portugal you will consider as the first and immediate object of your attention. But, as the security of Portugal can only be effectually provided for in connexion with the defense of the Peninsula … his Majesty … leaves it to your judgment to decide when your army shall be advanced on the frontier of Portugal, how your efforts can be best combined with the Spanish, as well as the Portuguese troops, in support of the common cause.[4] Essentially Wellesley was free to do as he pleased, constrained only by circumstances beyond his control such as the relative troop numbers, supplies, and plans of his allies and enemies.

Wellesley stepped onto the Lisbon waterfront on April 22, 1809, and three days later relieved General John Cradock of command of Britain's 16,000 troops. He enjoyed unity of command when, on April 27, the Junta named him commander-in-chief of Portugal's army. He got to work transforming the hodgepodge of British and Portuguese regiments into an army. He reorganized his forces into brigades with one Portuguese and two British regiments, and established two brigade divisions commanded initially by Generals John Sherbrooke, Edward Paget, and Rowland Hill, with Stapleton Cotton commanding the 1,500-man cavalry brigade. Wellesley was determined to beat the French at their own tactic of skirmishing by assigning a rifle company to each brigade and ensuring that each regiment's light infantry company was well trained in marksmanship.

Wellesley assessed the twin threats. Soult's army appeared to be slowly moving south from Oporto, while Victor's army had stalled near Badajoz. To block Victor's advance down the Tagus River valley to Lisbon, Wellesley posted General John Mackenzie with 4,575 British and 7,425 Portuguese troops at Abrantes, while Portuguese troops garrisoned the frontier fortresses of Almeida and Elvas. Wellesley led the rest of his army north to Coimbra, which he reached on May 2. After four days of massing supplies, on May 6, Wellesley ordered Beresford to march northeast with his 4,175 Portuguese and 1,875 British troops toward Viseu in the mountains, where he would turn north. Two days later, Wellesley led 12,821 British and 2,400 Portuguese troops, including 3,134 cavalry, directly north to Oporto. The plan was for Wellington to pin Soult on his front while Beresford arced behind and cut him off.[5]

The advanced British and French guards clashed at Albegaria Nova on May 10, then at Grijon on May 11; the allies won these skirmishes and inflicted 300 casualties while suffering only half as many. Soult withdrew his outnumbered forces by a pontoon bridge into Oporto on the Douro River's north bank then dismantled the bridge and brought the components to the north bank.

The allied army reached Vila Nova on the Douro River's south bank across from Oporto early on May 12. Wellesley lined his 18 cannons atop the high bank to bombard the French positions. A mile upstream a cavalry patrol found a man with a skiff who told them of four wine barges hidden in a cove just across the river. The enterprising troopers sent word to Wellesley, while several scrambled into the skiff and rowed across to retrieve the barges. Wellesley ordered the 3rd Infantry to pack into the barges, cross, and occupy a nearby walled seminary on Oporto's eastern outskirts. When Soult noticed the redcoats in the seminary, he launched four different attacks against it but the British repulsed each in turn. Scouts found a ferry 4 miles upstream. Wellesley ordered thousands more troops to march there to cross the river. Outflanked, Soult withdrew his army northward.

The following day, Wellesley and his army pursued. Beresford, meanwhile, crossed the Douro River upstream at Lamego on May 10, linked with General Silveira, then veered northwest toward the French army's rear. Wellesley and Beresford hurried their troops forward to converge on the French. Soult and his men barely escaped the jaws of this trap as they fled to the fortress of Orense in Galicia. Wellesley called off his pursuit.

The triumph of chasing a defeated enemy was soured by stomach-turning scenes along the way. The French were bitter losers. Wellesley and his men were appalled to view 'many persons hanging in the trees by the sides of the road, executed for no reason that I could learn, excepting they had not been friendly to the French invasion … the route of their column on their retreat could by traced by the smoke of the villages to which they set fire.'[6] Yet Wellesley would repeatedly condemn his own troops for looting and worse crimes: 'They have plundered the country most terribly … They are a rabble.'[7] To curb those crimes, he ordered any man caught committing robbery or rape to be hanged 'some place where they might be seen by the whole column in its march the next.'[8]

Wellesley had fought a masterly campaign. In a mere two weeks, his forces liberated northern Portugal, won several skirmishes and the battle of Oporto, and inflicted 4,000 casualties, mostly prisoners, on the enemy. The butcher's bill for all that was astonishingly light. Oporto's capture cost Wellesley only 23 dead, 98 wounded, and 2 missing; he suffered a couple hundred casualties in the advance toward Oporto and a couple hundred more afterward pursuing Soult. Beresford also lost a few hundred casualties.[9] Yet Wellesley lamented not bagging Soult's entire army, a failure he attributed to subordinates who failed to strictly follow his orders, push their troops forward hard enough, or seize opportunities.[10]

Wellesley secured Portugal's northern frontier by garrisoning its fortresses and Oporto with Portuguese troops. On May 22, he led his army south to Abrantes to join forces with McKenzie. From there he intended to march east up the Tagus valley and join Cuesta against Victor. A lack of money or even credit to buy supplies halted Wellesley and his army for nearly a month.[11] Then, after finally receiving an infusion of gold and resuming his march, Wellesley had to shed his Portuguese troops at the frontier. The Junta was adamant that they not set foot outside the homeland. It would take more than a year for Wellesley to convince the Junta that France's threat to Portugal would end only after the allies drove them back over the Pyrenees, and that was most likely if Portuguese troops joined British and Spanish troops against the French anywhere they could find them.

Wellesley led his army from Abrantes on June 24, crossed into Spain on July 4, and rode ahead to meet Cuesta at Almaraz on July 10. His first impressions of his ally were not favorable. Wellesley's Spanish guides got lost and he was 5 hours late. Cuesta struck Wellesley as frail even for his 70 years, but haughty and boastful. Cuesta was probably overcompensating from shame at being routed by Victor at Medellin, and resentment at British ambassador John Frere's pressure on the Cádiz Junta to appoint Wellesley commander-in-chief of all Spanish forces. They agreed to join forces at Oropesa, then attack Victor at Talavera, a day's march eastward. It was vital to decisively strike Victor's 20,000 troops before General François Sebastiani joined him with 26,000 troops from Madrid, just 70 miles to his rear.

Wellesley returned to his army at Plasencia and led it eastward. Cuesta was waiting at Oropesa when he arrived on July 21. In parallel columns the allied armies marched toward Talavera, which they reached the following evening. After reconnoitering the French position, Wellesley devised a plan whereby the British and Spanish armies crushed the French army between them. Early the next morning, Wellesley deployed his divisions but Cuesta's were nowhere to be seen. Wellesley angrily postponed the attack. The delay enabled Victor to hastily withdraw.

When Cuesta finally arrived later that day, Wellesley struggled to contain his rage: 'I find General Cuesta more and more impracticable every day. It is impossible to do business with him, and very uncertain that any operation will succeed in which he has any concern.'[12] Cuesta was only the tip of Spain's institutional, cultural, economic, and social obstacles to Wellesley's operations. He fumed that 'the people in this part of Spain are either unable or unwilling to supply [us] and ... till I am supplied, I do not think it proper, and indeed I cannot continue my operations in Spain.'[13]

Having failed to keep his word, the Spanish conception of honor compelled Cuesta to overcompensate in some dramatic fashion. Typically, the results were nearly disastrous. While Wellesley wanted to await reinforcements and supplies at Talavera, Cuesta insisted on seeking the French for battle. When Wellesley demurred, Cuesta led his army eastward on July 24. Cuesta got his wish near Toledo on July 25, when he ran into the combined forces of Victor and Sebastiani, accompanied by King Joseph and Chief of Staff Jean Baptiste Jourdan. With the French hot on his heels, Cuesta hurried his army back to Talavera.

Wellesley, meanwhile, deployed his 20,641 troops with his right flank anchored at Talavera on the Tagus River's north bank and his left on a low plateau a mile-and-a-half distant. He lined most of his infantry behind a shallow stream that began northeast of the plateau and ran down to the river. Several hundred yards to their rear, he posted the cavalry with orders to charge any French infantry or cavalry that broke through. Batteries studded the front, with most positioned atop the plateau with its sweeping view and cannon-shot range of most French approaches. When Cuesta arrived, Wellesley had him split his 34,800 troops, with most defending Talavera and the rest massed in the valley between the plateau and the foothills of the mountains half a mile beyond.[14] Although with 53,000 allied troops to Victor's 46,138 French, Wellesley enjoyed a manpower edge, he was outgunned 55 to 80 in cannons. More important was the vast quality gap between the first-rate French troops and Wellesley's British, whom he deemed second-rate, and Cuesta's Spaniards whom he condemned as little more than an armed mob.[15]

Victor did not exploit that gap when he ordered his army to attack on July 27, but instead hurled most of his divisions in repeated attacks against the British in the center and on the plateau. He did charge some of his cavalry against the Spanish in the valley. Although the Spanish broke and fled, Victor lacked the reserves to exploit the breakthrough.

Wellesley micromanaged the battle, scribbling orders and thrusting them into the hands of couriers to gallop off to his commanders. General Rowland Hill's division defended the plateau. Wellesley had him conceal his troops beyond sight and accurate cannon shot of the French, then suddenly emerge, fire a volley, and charge at the enemy struggling up the slope. The French troops broke and ran, leaving 1,300 dead, wounded, and captured behind.

A common need and humanity united the enemy soldiers that evening. One British soldier recalled:

> The water in the stream, which in the morning was clear and sweet, was now a pool of blood, heaped over with the dead and dying. There being no alternative, we were compelled to close our eyes and drink the gory stream. The French troops were equally ill off and ... came down in thousands ... We shook hands with them in the most friendly manner.[16]

The following day, Victor launched a series of attacks, but the allies managed to repel each. In all, the British lost 5,365 or 1 in 4 men killed, wounded, or missing, the Spanish perhaps a thousand, and the French 7,268.[17] Wellesley himself 'was hit but not hurt & my coat shot through. Almost all the staff are wounded or have had their horses shot. Never was there such a murderous battle.'[18]

Victor wanted to stay put and await Marshal Soult who promised to sever Wellesley's supply line at Plasencia. But he received two dispatches that forced him to abruptly change his plans. Soult explained that Spanish resistance and supply shortages delayed his advance on Plasencia. Toledo's governor reported that Spanish General Francisco Venegas was marching with his army against Madrid. Joseph and his generals reluctantly agreed to withdraw toward the capital.[19]

Wellesley could not follow up his victory by pursuing Victor 'because the Men were so fatigued ... the want of Provisions is extreme & very distressing, ... and I heard of the advance of a French Corps,' namely Soult. Perhaps worst of all, he lacked confidence in his own men: 'this is the Worst British Army that ever was in the field.'[20] He was even more scathing of his allies, enraged that countless Spanish troops 'threw away their arms, and ran off in my presence, when they were neither attacked nor threatened with an attack, but frightened, I believe, by their own fire ... When these dastardly soldiers run away they plunder everything they meet, and in their flight from Talavera they plundered the baggage of the British army.'[21] The Light Division's arrival the day after the battle was not enough for Wellesley to advance. He had over 4,000 wounded to tend, while severe shortages of forage and food caused 'the loss of many horses of the cavalry and artillery ... [and the] sickness of the army ... has increased considerably ... Indeed, there are few ... officers or soldiers ... who ... are not more or less affected by dysentery.'[22]

Cuesta, whose losses were light, did cautiously shadow the French army eastward. Typically he did not get far. He withdrew to Talavera when he learned that Venegas had halted his own advance. Meanwhile, reinforcements swelled French forces guarding approaches to Madrid.

Word reached Wellesley on August 2, that Soult had captured his depot and severed his supply and communication lines at Plasencia. Wellesley quick-marched 18,000 troops westward to Oropesa near Plasencia. Although Soult had only 12,000 troops immediately with him, he was in a powerful position and intelligence reports claimed he had 50,000 troops. When Cuesta joined him, Wellesley called for crossing to the Tagus's south side at Arzobispo, then hurrying westward to sever Soult's supply line. Cuesta preferred waiting for Soult to attack them. Wellesley followed his own plan, tailed by Cuesta when Soult's army approached.

Victor, meanwhile, returned to Talavera then marched on to Arzobispo. Soult found a ford across the Tagus, caught up to Cuesta, and routed him on August 8, killed, wounded, or captured 1,400 Spanish troops and recaptured

14 of the 18 cannons lost at Talavera. Then, on August 11, Sebastiani routed Venegas at Almonacid, inflicting 5,500 casualties while suffering 2,400. Shorn for now of his ally, Wellesley led his battered army's remnants back to Portugal.

Parliament, desperate for any victory, awarded Wellesley by naming him baron Wellington of Douro and viscount Wellington of Talavera, and granted him £2,000 for each of the next three years. Although pleased by the honor, Wellington was haunted by the campaign's shortcomings. He was thoroughly disgusted with his Spanish allies, who 'do not consider … military operations so much as political intrigue and the attainment of petty, political objects.'[23] To this, he might have added, except when pride consumed them. He warned the Spanish generals not to attempt and refused to join offensives that fall. He later muttered I told them so after the French routed the separate armies of Generals Antonio Cuesta, Carlos Areizaga, and Vicente Canas y Portocarrio, Duque del Parque, and captured Seville, forcing the Junta to flee to Cádiz. The Spaniards, in turn, insisted that they would have vanquished the French had not Wellington refused to support them. Now the French controlled virtually all of Spain except Cádiz and the western frontier fortresses of Badajoz, Cuidad Rodrigo, and Astorga. And in spring 1810, the French would try to eliminate those holdouts and once again conquer Portugal. Wellington and his army would be waiting.

Chapter 14

Walcheren, 1809

The multiplicity of ships to be seen almost as far as the eye can carry, forms a beautiful sight, and highly gratifying to the feelings of an Englishman.

Surgeon W. Cullen Brown

If the Walcheren expedition is to pass unmarked by the general censure, then can no calamity happen on which the British nation will deserve to be heard?

The London Times

You had too many and too few men; too many for a coup de main and too few for a regular siege.

Napoleon Bonaparte

He may be a very able statesman, but I am afraid he is a d——d bad general.

Captain James Seton

In early 1809, Whitehall received a stunning secret message. Vienna intended to war against Napoleon, and asked the British for £2.5 million and a second front to distract and divert French forces. This set off a debate within the inner Cabinet over how far to honor either request, if at all. Eventually Prime Minister William Cavendish-Bentinck, Duke of Portland, and his ministers agreed to help underwrite Austria's war against France. As for a second front, they first discussed landing a British expedition at the mouth of the Elbe or Weser Rivers, but eventually shelved the notion when estimates of the time and cost to do so seemed too much. The discussion shifted to the Scheldt River mouth. They soon concluded that capturing Antwerp, the French empire's largest naval base after Toulon, would inflict a sharp blow, act like a magnet for Napoleon's forces in that region and beyond, and prevent the French from using that port to invade England.[1]

The key questions were how many ships, men, and supplies were needed to seize Antwerp and whether Britain could muster that power. On March 24, the Cabinet agreed that 15,000 troops would be enough, and asked David Dundas, the army's commander-in-chief, to marshal those forces. Then new intelligence reports questioned whether 15,000 troops would be sufficient. On May 8, Secretary for War Castlereagh asked Dundas to assess the feasibility of raising the expedition to 25,000 infantry and 5,000 cavalry, backed in England by 10,000 infantry and 5,000 cavalry to act as a second wave to seize an opportunity or counter a threat. Dundas reported on May 31, that it could be done but would delay the expedition for at least a couple of months. Castlereagh authorized him to mass those forces.[2]

Morale among those charged with planning the expedition undoubtedly suffered as once again Napoleon seemed invincible. He defeated the Austrians in a series of battles down the Danube River valley and captured Vienna on May 15. Then came word on May 21 and 22, that the Austrians had defeated Napoleon's attempt to cross the Danube at the villages of Aspern and Esling. Castlereagh wrote that the news 'had a preponderating influence with His Majesty's Government' to launch the expedition as soon as possible.[3]

Getting to Antwerp, let alone taking it, would be a challenge. The port is nearly a hundred twisting river miles from the North Sea. The Scheldt River, 20 miles below Antwerp, splits into west and east channels that flow first around South Beveland Island then Walcheren Island before reaching the open sea. The West Scheldt is the main channel and was protected by the fortress towns of Flushing on Walcheren, Batz on South Beveland, and nine small fortresses from the forks to Antwerp. Large stretches of shallow waters, mudflats, sand dunes, and marshes along the estuary bolstered the man-made defenses. Flushing itself was a major naval base with seven ships-of-the-line then anchored there. Fortunately for the British, the troops defending the lower Scheldt estuary were severely deficit in numbers and quality. Napoleon had stripped all the first-rate regiments from Holland for his campaign against Austria. The 8,400 troops scattered across the region included second-rate French, Dutch, Spanish, Prussian, Irish, and Colonial regular battalions, and Dutch national guard battalions.

Whitehall's plan called for three simultaneous landings. Two would secure the West Scheldt mouth by overrunning Walcheren and Candsand islands, with the capture of Flushing on Walcheren's southern shore vital for success. The third force would sail along the East Scheldt, land on South Beveland, and quick-march to seize Batz at the southeast tip. These three forces along with reinforcements would then mass at the Scheldt's forks for landings on the mainland and a march to Antwerp.[4]

Speed was the key to victory. The British had to make a series of moves that swiftly captured one position after another culminating with Antwerp before the French could mobilize and march reinforcements. A related reason for speed was avoiding bad weather. Admiral Home Popham knew the waters that would swirl around the expedition, and shared his worries with Castlereagh: 'I see the season advancing fast; and, if we are imperceptibly led on till the midsummer fine weather is past, we shall have the most dreadful of difficulties, the weather to encounter.'[5] Stagnant rather than turbulent water posed the worst danger. Walcheren fever, a cocktail of diseases such as typhus, dysentery, and malaria, would devastate the army's ranks.

When it came to speed, the men that Whitehall chose to lead the expedition could not have differed more. Commanding the fleet and army were, respectively, Admiral Richard Strachan and General John Pitt, Earl of Chatham. Strachan was a good choice. Captain Graham Moore lauded Strachan as 'extremely brave and full of zeal and ardour ... [and] an excellent seaman, and tho' an irregular, impetuous fellow, possessing ... an uncommon share of sagacity and strong sense.'[6] In stark contrast, Chatham, the older brother of now deceased Prime Minister Pitt, had a well-deserved reputation for being lethargic, unimaginative, and timid, and for having received such a vital command from the triumph of connections over competence. No one may summed up Chatham better than Captain James Seton of the 92nd Highlanders: 'He may be a very able statesman, but I am afraid he is a d—d bad general.'[7]

By July 9, all the regiments had reached the embarkation ports of Portsmouth, Ramsgate, Dover, Deal, Chatham, and Harwich. On July 12, the government ordered all merchant vessels to remain in port to prevent any word reaching the enemy of the expedition's imminent departure. As the troops squeezed aboard their vessels, they encountered a minor but annoying hazard:

> The decks had been newly caulked, the heat of so many bodies had drawn the pitch and tar so that we were stuck fast in the morning. It was the most ludicrous sight imaginable, some were fast by the head, others had got an arm secured, those who had laid on their backs were completely fast, some who were wrapped in their blankets came off best, but their blankets were completely spoiled. It was a fine treat for the blue jackets [sailors] to see the lobsters [soldiers] stuck fast to the decks.[8]

Then, amidst the expedition's fevered last-minute preparations, came word on July 19 of Napoleon's victory at Wagram on July 5 and 6, and the armistice signed at Znaim on July 12. This killed the expedition's goals of opening a new front and diverting Napoleon's forces. Yet no one in Portland's government openly called for canceling the expedition. Too much money had been spent and hopes raised to stand down now. The armada would sail.

A new strategy, however, channeled the expedition. A report from a frigate observing the Scheldt revealed that the French had moved their fleet of 11 ships-of-the-line close to Flushing. This caused Strachan and Chatham to scrap the plan of landing on Walcheren's south side where Flushing was sited; to avoid all that French firepower, the troops would hit the island's northern beaches.

The nation had never before mounted a larger expedition. In all, there were 616 vessels, including 264 warships and 352 transports. The warships included 27 ships-of-the-line, 5 ships of 40 to 50 guns, 23 frigates, 32 sloops, 5 gun-brigs, and 130 smaller vessels. Crowded aboard were 1,888 officers and 44,600 men, including 1,888 officers and 42,712 troops along with 4,501 horses and 206 cannons, 110,000 artillery shells, and 10 million musket cartridges. The army included 5 divisions, with General Eyre Coote commanding 13,666 troops known as the Army of Walcheren; George Gordon, Lord Huntley the Second Division of 5,377 troops; General Thomas Grosvenor the Third Division of 5,347 troops; James Saint Clair Erskine, Earl of Rosslyn the Light Division of 6,528 troops; and General John Hope the Reserve Division of 7,779 troops.[9]

The sailors lifted the anchors and unfurled the sails of the armada's vessels scattered among a half-dozen ports on July 28. Powerful winds conveyed the armada swiftly to the Scheldt estuary mouth. But the same winds churned the sea so violently that the commanders postponed the landings along the East Scheldt until July 30, and canceled Huntley's landing on the beaches near Candsand. That day and well into the next, Coote's troops disembarked on Walcheren and Hope's on South Beveland, followed over the rest of the week by the other three divisions. Each force fanned out and rapidly took its respective objectives, encountering little or no resistance along the way. Fort Ter Veere on Walcheren surrendered on August 1. Hope's troops marched into an abandoned Fort Batz on August 2. Coote massed most of his troops and cannons for a siege of Flushing.

So far the campaign had been brilliantly executed. But the failure to capture Candsand left British forces on West Scheldt's north side and ever more French troops on the south side. Rather than try to land a massive force on the south bank, Chatham concentrated on capturing Flushing. By August 12, the batteries were emplaced and opened fire.

Being subjected to such a bombardment was hellish, a seemingly endless series of deafening explosions and showers of debris, stones, screams, and body parts, never knowing when a direct hit would bury or blow oneself to smithereens. Captain Thomas Howell of the 71st Highlanders was:

> stunned and bewildered by the noise; the bursting of bombs and falling of chimneys, all adding to the incessant roar of the artillery. The smoke of the burning houses and guns ... at every cessation from firing ... by the piercing shrieks of the inhabitants, the wailings of distress, and howling of dogs ... The enemy had set fire to Old Flushing, whilst the New Town was kept burning by the shells and rockets. The dark flare of the burning, the reflection on the water and sky, made all the space, as far as the eye could see, appear an abyss of fire.[10]

It was horrible enough just being near the cannons as they fired. Surgeon Cullen Brown, on the appropriately named HMS *Aetna*, recalled:

> By stuffing my ears with cotton, and pressing them with my fingers ... I find no manner of inconvenience from the concussion ... My ears have continued ever ringing. At the very first firing of the mortar, the lock of my cabin has been forced off, and the boards of the bulkhead have drawn their nails. This ... is but the prelude ... The tide is now turning; and such a force of bomb-vessels, gun-brigs, and flat-bottomed boats will slowly assail the place ... The multiplicity of ships to be seen almost as far as the eye can carry, forms a beautiful sight, and highly gratifying to the feelings of an Englishman.[11]

After three days of bombardment that silenced nearly all his guns, Monnet asked for terms. Coote granted General Louis Claude Monnet's request for honors of war or being allowed to march out with flags flying before being sent for internment in England. Although the agreement was signed on August 15, the French did not evacuate Flushing until August 18. On Walcheren, the British captured 5,539 troops at Flushing, 519 at Fort Ter Veere, 127 at Ramakins, and killed, wounded, or captured another 2,100 men either during the siege of Flushing or in other operations. In doing so, the British army suffered only 103 killed and 443 wounded, and the navy 9 killed and 55 wounded. In all, the British had won a relatively swift and cheap victory.[12]

Mather Brown's work illustrating The Glorious First of June of 1794. This was the first and largest fleet action of the naval conflict between Great Britain and the First French Republic during the French Revolutionary Wars. (*Anne S.K. Brown Military Collection, Brown University Library*)

The Battle of Aboukir Bay (the Battle of the Nile) of 1798, as seen in a painting by Giuseppe Pera. (*Anne S.K. Brown Military Collection, Brown University Library*)

The Assault of Seringapatam by Allan Alexander. This battle, of 4 May 1799, was the final confrontation of the Fourth Anglo–Mysore War between the British East India Company and the Kingdom of Mysore.

The famous scene of Lord Viscount Nelson's death at the Battle of Trafalgar in 1805. (*Anne S.K. Brown Military Collection, Brown University Library*)

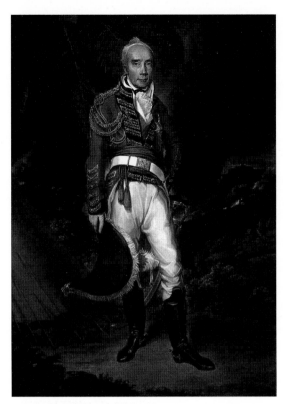

A full-length portrait of His Excellency Lieutenant General Sir George Beckwith KB, the Governor of Barbados and Commander of His Majesty's Forces in the West Indies. (*Anne S.K. Brown Military Collection, Brown University Library*)

The Battle of Maida, as depicted here by Philip James de Loutherbourg, was fought between a British expeditionary force and a French force outside the town of Maida in Calabria, Italy, on 4 July 1806. (*Anne S.K. Brown Military Collection, Brown University Library*)

This engraving by George Robinson depicts the storming by British forces of the fortified city of Monte Video on 3 February 1807. (*Anne S.K. Brown Military Collection, Brown University Library*)

Johan Lorenz Rugendas' depiction of the Bombardment of Copenhagen by British forces in 1807. (*Anne S.K. Brown Military Collection, Brown University Library*)

An etching by George Thompson showing the British invasion of Isle de France, now Mauritius, underway in 1810. (*Anne S.K. Brown Military Collection, Brown University Library*)

The death of General Brock at the Battle of Queenston Heights in October 1812. A British victory, it was the first major battle in the war of 1812. (*Library and Archives Canada*)

William Heath's depiction of the Battle of Vittoria underway on 21 June 1813. This was a British victory that ultimately led to Wellington's success in the Peninsular War. (*Anne S.K. Brown Military Collection, Brown University Library*)

A scene showing the Battle of the Pyrenées on 28 July 1813, that was the work of the renowned British war artist William Heath. (*Anne S.K. Brown Military Collection, Brown University Library*)

The Battle of Lake Erie was fought off the coast of Ohio on 10 September 1813, and saw nine vessels of the United States Navy defeat and capture six British warships. (*Library of Congress*)

A graphic depiction of the capture and burning of the US capital, Washington, by the British in 1814. (*Library of Congress*)

The Battle of New Orleans of January 1815. General Andrew Jackson can be seen on horseback in the foreground commanding the US troops. (*Library of Congress*)

By Friedrich Campe, this scene depicts some of the last moments of the Battle of Waterloo on 18 June 1815. (*Anne S.K. Brown Military Collection, Brown University Library*)

That was where it ended. Chatham did not even try to win the campaign's ultimate goal, Antwerp's capture. Indeed Chatham did not land on South Beveland until August 20, did not establish his headquarters at Batz until August 24, and did not conduct his first war council with Strachan and the other leading admirals and generals until August 26. The council agreed to suspend operations and withdraw from South Beveland Island, starting the following day. Thereafter the biggest challenge for the British commanders was figuring out how to evacuate Walcheren Island without being slaughtered by pursuing French.

The British expedition came as little surprise to the French. For months, Napoleon and his brother, King Louis of Holland, had mulled intelligence reports that the British were massing naval and army forces for an expedition most likely targeted against Antwerp. Louis repeatedly asked Napoleon for reinforcements, only to be told that he had to make do with what he had until the emperor crushed the Austrians.

Upon learning of the landings, Louis ordered his Dutch troops to muster and march to the Scheldt, and galloped off couriers with pleas to Napoleon in Vienna and War Minister Henri Clarke in Paris for reinforcements. Clarke ordered Marshal Jean Baptiste Bernadotte, then in disgrace at Paris for his failures in the Austrian campaign, to hurry to Antwerp and take command. Napoleon had Marshall François Kellermann at Strasbourg send all troops passing through or stationed in the region north on the long march to Antwerp. Louis ordered General Monnet at Flushing to open the dykes and flood the countryside. That latter act hurt the British the most since those sea waters at once bogged them down, ruined their fresh water sources, and spread mosquito-borne disease among them.

Bernadotte reached Antwerp on August 15. Within 2 weeks, he had massed 27,380 troops, including 14,800 regulars and 13,000 National Guard troops, in the lower Scheldt estuary.[13] He was no more interested in attacking Chatham, than Chatham was in attacking him. Bernadotte and his men settled in for a long wait as nature defeated the British expedition.

Walcheren fever began devouring the British ranks shortly after they landed. The fever was actually a deadly combination of malaria, dysentery, and typhus.[14] Of all the reasons why Chatham justified ending the campaign, none matter more than Walcheren fever when the time the last British troops embarked and sailed away on December 9, 1809. An official report released in February 1810 revealed that of the 39,219 troops, 106 died in action, 84 deserted, 25 were discharged, 3,960 died of disease either on the expedition or after its return, and 11,513 were still sick.[15]

The House of Commons conducted an investigation into the Walcheren campaign in March 1810. After mulling the evidence, the Commons conducted votes on four motions. The first to censure the Cabinet for the campaign lost by 275 to 227. The second not to single out any minister for blame passed by 272 to 232. The third to condemn the Cabinet for not retaining Walcheren lost by 275 to 224. The fourth to approve retaining Walcheren until a peace treaty was signed between France and Austria passed by 253 to 232. *The London Times* condemned the refusal of a parliamentary majority to censure the government for mishandling the campaign: 'If the Walcheren expedition is to pass unmarked by the general censure, then can no calamity happen on which the British nation will deserve to be heard?'[16] Years later on Saint Helena, Napoleon had the last word: 'You had too many and too few men; too many for a coup de main and too few for a regular siege.'[17]

Chapter 15

Portugal and Spain, 1810–11

Depend upon it, sooner or later this general determination of resistance
will take place & … the fair example of Spain will be followed by other
powers. You will then see that overgrown Empire of France fall to pieces
in a far shorter time than it was erected.

Major Alexander Gordon

If Boney had been there we should have been beaten.

Wellington

By mid-January 1810, Napoleon had massed 324,996 troops in Spain
and ordered his marshals to launch knock-out blows against the
remaining resistance.[1] On paper this should not have been difficult.
Spain's largest army, about 20,000 men, defended the toehold of Cádiz, where
the government now holed up. Three other fortresses, all in western Spain,
held out – Badajoz, Cuidad Rodrigo, and Astorga. Elsewhere Spanish generals
found remote refuges for their army's remnants and tried to rebuild them.
Although guerrilla bands wiped out ever more isolated French detachments,
they could never drive the French from their land on their own.

The French would likely have crushed Spain this year had not the largest
French army been siphoned off to invade Portugal. Marshal Andre Massena
received orders in April 1810 to take command of three corps led by Generals
Michael Ney, Jean Reynier, and Jean Junot deployed around Salamanca, and
to lead this 68,000-man Army of Portugal to destroy Wellington. Massena
reached Salamanca on May 28, and prepared for campaign.

Wellington anticipated a French invasion of Portugal in 1810. In assessing
his chances of defending Portugal, he concluded: 'I think that if the
Portuguese do their duty, I shall have enough to maintain it; if they do not,
nothing that Great Britain can afford can save the country.'[2] He understood,
of course, that Portugal's fate depended on far more than this. He explained
the interdependence of allied operations in Spain and Portugal, with defeats
or victories in one country leading to likely defeats or victories in the other:

'If they should be able to invade, and should not succeed in obliging us to evacuate the country, they will be in a very dangerous situation; and the longer we can oppose them … the more likely are they to suffer materially in Spain.'[3]

Wellington's assessment was widely shared. Major Alexander Gordon expressed the prevailing pessimism about future operations:

Lord Wellington has undertaken to defend against the approaching invasion of the Enemy … We may protract the war for a few months, but it is I think impossible to hinder Portugal from eventually falling. And although this move of Lord Wellington's is most unpopular in the army, I … think he could not … do otherwise. Portugal is fully committed with the cause of Britain … We have put arms in the hands of the people, we have taken upon ourselves the management of her Government, her Army, her defense; we cannot desert her in danger, we must sacrifice ourselves for her.[4]

Wellington counted on four layers of defense. The first included the Spanish fortresses of Cuidad Rodrigo and Badajoz. If these capitulated the defense fell back to the corresponding Portuguese fortresses of Almeida and Elvas. If the French took these, Wellington planned to defend the mountains astride the invasion route, ideally at the fortress of Abrantes. Finally, if the French broke through, Wellington would withdraw his army within the fortified Lines of Torres Vedras running from Alhandra on the Tagus River upstream of Lisbon to where the Zizandre River flows into the Atlantic Ocean. The previous October, he had ordered 23,000 Portuguese militia to construct and garrison what became 53 miles of forts, redoubts, and entrenchments in two parallel lines with the front 29 miles and rear 22 miles long. Royal Navy warships bristling with 24- and 18-pounder cannons guarded each flank. A series of hilltop posts could convey semaphore messages from one end of the line to the other in 7 minutes. Wellesley would reach this sanctuary leaving nothing but scorched earth behind.[5]

Wellington's field army numbered 24,796 British and 24,649 Portuguese troops in 5 line divisions, the Light Division, and the cavalry division. Each division included two British brigades and one Portuguese brigade. Generals Brent Spencer, Rowland Hill, Thomas Picton, Lowry Cole, and James Leith led the line divisions, General Robert Craufurd the Light Division, and Stapleton Cotton the cavalry division. General William Beresford's 5,000-man Portuguese division was detached to guard the frontier south of the

Tagus River, although Wellington recalled him after the French invasion. In addition, around 25,000 militia were deployed in detachments at strategic spots around the rest of the country. It was mostly the militia that destroyed anything of military value that refugees could not cart or herd beyond the advancing French army.[6]

If his number of troops generally satisfied Wellington, their quality troubled him: 'I have ... terrible disadvantages to contend with. The army was, and indeed is, the worst British army that was ever sent from England. Then, between ourselves, the spirit of party ... prevails here ... There is a despondency among some; a want of confidence in their own exertions, an extravagant notion of the power and resources of the French, and a distaste for the war in the Peninsula, which sentiments have been created and are kept up by a correspondence with England, even with Ministers and those connected with them.'[7]

Indeed, the prime minister and many other Britons feared the worst. War Secretary Robert Jenkinson, Lord Liverpool informed Wellington 'that a considerable amount of alarm exists within this country respecting the safety of the British army' and 'you would rather be excused for removing the army ... than by remaining in Portugal too long.'[8] The Cabinet debated whether Lisbon was actually worth defending, and mulled concentrating their forces to defend Cádiz.

A lesser general might have seized this excuse to cut and run, and thus would have drastically shifted the course of history. Wellington was made of sterner stuff. He reassured Liverpool that 'I am perfectly aware of the risks that I incur ... All I beg is that if I am to be responsible, I may be left to the exercise of my own judgment, and I ask for the confidence of Government upon the measures which I am to adopt.'[9] He explained that the ability to defend Cádiz and ultimately drive the French from Spain depended on the ability to defend and drive the French from Portugal, and vice versa; likewise, France's conquest of one realm would lead to the other's conquest: 'As long as we shall remain in a state of activity in Portugal, the contest must continue in Spain ... The French are most desirous that we should withdraw from the country.'[10]

Massena launched his campaign in late May. Ney spearheaded the advance, and by May 30 reached the first objective, Cuidad Rodrigo. It took nearly four weeks to zigzag siege parallels forward enough for French batteries to open fire on June 25. Cuidad Rodrigo's 4,000-man garrison surrendered on July 9. Massena's losses were light, about 500 casualties and were easily replaced. What he could not replace was time – the Spanish had held up the French advance for six crucial weeks. Throughout the siege, Wellington resisted pressure to march to the fortress's relief. He admitted that 'however unreasonable it may appear … the people of Spain are by no means satisfied that His Majesty's troops have taken so active a share … in the war as might have been expected from them.'[11]

As Massena consolidated his victory, he sent Ney west to invest Almeida, just a day's march away. Wellington dispatched General Robert Craufurd's Light Division to probe Ney at the Coa River, a mile west of Almeida. Unfortunately, Craufurd committed a fundamental military error when he crossed the bridge and deployed his troops with an unfordable river behind them. Ney detached a division and hurled it against Craufurd on July 24. The Light Division fought valiantly against overwhelming odds, then, during a lull, streamed across the narrow bridge to safety, suffering 36 killed, 189 wounded, and 83 missing, while inflicting 117 dead and 404 wounded on the French.[12]

Colonel William Cox commanded 4,500 Portuguese troops defending Almeida. They had held out for over a month when a freak accident forced them to surrender on August 27. The previous day a leaking gunpowder keg left a trail as soldiers carried it from the magazine to one of the bastions. A stray spark ignited the trail which fizzled rapidly back to the magazine and detonated the scores of gunpowder barrels packed within. The explosion killed or mangled about 500 men and stunned the survivors.

Once again, Massena won a relatively inexpensive victory, having suffered only about 400 casualties. And once again his most significant loss was time. The two sieges consumed the entire summer. Massena hurried his troops toward Wellington's advance guard, which withdrew as they neared. With reinforcements Massena now had 65,000 troops, with 3,500 detached and split to garrison Cuidad Rodrigo and Almeida.

Wellington halted his 52,000 troops and deployed it along 10 miles of the Bussaco mountain range that ran north from the Mondego River. Two switch-backing roads traversed the range along his line, with one on the center and the other on the left flank; both led to Coimbra, a dozen miles west in the coastal lowlands.

Massena deployed his army along the foot of these mountains on September 26. After scanning the ridgeline, he ordered Ney and Reynier to attack, respectively, up the roads at dawn the next morning. The result was slaughter as the defenders poured volleys into the troops struggling up the slope, then launched short charges with bayonets lowered to rout the survivors:

The instant the attacking columns were turned back, they were exposed to the fire of our whole division; whilst our battalion and some cazadores were ordered to pursue, and to give them a flanking fire, and the horse artillery continued to pour on them a murderous fire of grape. [They were] trampling each other to death in their great haste to escape.[13]

During the battle, Wellington and his staff cantered along the line to whichever French attack seemed the most menacing. Wellington issued orders 'in a loud voice … short and precise' with 'nothing of the bombastic pomp of the commander-in-chief surrounded by his glittering staff. He wears … simply a low plain hat, a white collar, a grey overcoat, and a light sword.'[14] After 3 hours of fruitless bloodbath, Massena called off the attacks without committing Junot's corps or divisions of Ney or Reynier held in reserve. The French lost 4,473 troops, including 535 dead. The British and Portuguese each suffered exactly 626 casualties, bringing their total to 1,252 men.[15]

Only then did Massena bother to send cavalry squadrons northward to search for an undefended pass around the allied line. When a courier galloped back with word that his detachment had scattered militia at Sardao Pass, Massena hurried his army there. The pass was lightly defended through no fault of Wellington's. He had ordered Colonel Nicholas Trant to plug it with his Portuguese light infantry regiment, but somehow the orders never reached him in time.

Learning of Massena's advance, Wellington withdrew his army through Coimbra to the Torres Vedras Line. Massena followed hard on his heels, leaving his wounded and supplies in Coimbra. Trant, meanwhile, withdrew his regiment and several thousand militia north. On October 7, Trant led his men in a lightening advance against Coimbra, overwhelmed the defenders, and captured 4,500 French and a caravan of supplies critical for Massena's army. He then withdrew with his spoils to Oporto.

Massena drew up his army before a central swath of the Torres Vedras Line on October 11, and pondered what to do. Before him was a daunting array of earthen forts and redoubts, studded with sharpened logs, surrounded by deep ditches, and packed with enemy troops, cannons, and provisions. His army was exhausted and diminished by disease and battle. In all, he now had 10,000 fewer men than before Bussaco, while Wellington had 10,000 more. The winter rains began and turned trenches, camps, and roads into churned quagmires. He lingered a month in indecision as the weather, supplies, and morale worsened.

During this time, Wellington chose not to attack his dwindling enemy. He explained to Liverpool that 'if I should succeed in forcing Massena's position, it would become a question whether I should be able to maintain my own, in case the enemy should march another army into this country.' This possible future threat aside, Wellington faced a more immediate problem: 'I observe how small the superiority of numbers is in my favour, and know that the position will be in favor of the enemy. I cannot but be of opinion that I act in conformity with the instructions and intentions of His Majesty's government, in … incurring no extraordinary risk.'[16]

Massena sent back his sick and cavalry to Santarem, then led the rest of his army there on November 14. Wellington gingerly followed a week later. He was astonished that:

> … the enemy have been able to remain in this country so long; and it is an extraordinary instance of what a French army can do [since] … they brought no provisions with them … With all our money, and having in our favour the good inclinations of the country, I assure you that I could not maintain one division in the district in which they have maintained not yet less than 60,000 men and 20,000 animals for more than two months.[17] Evidently the allies had not 'scorched' the entire 'earth' accessible to French foragers.

At Santarem Massena received reinforcements and supplies, most notably General Jean Baptiste Drouet, comte D'Erlon's 11,000-man corps. But even then Massena prudently was no more eager to attack Wellington than Wellington was to attack him. So the stalemate dragged on dreary month after month until Massena finally abandoned Santarem on March 4 and withdrew to Celerico, shadowed by Wellington.

When Massena turned his army south toward the Tagus valley, Wellington's Light Division, now commanded by General William Erskine, caught up to Reynier's corps at Sabugal on the Coa River, and attacked on April 3. Fog and intermittent rain fouled eye-sights and muskets. Commanders were uncertain just where the enemy was until they marched or rode right before them. Then victory mostly went to the more numerous side that most savagely thrust bayonets or swung sabers. The British routed the French, and inflicted 760 casualties while suffering 179.[18]

Massena hastily retreated with his surviving 44,000 troops and reached his supply depot at Salamanca on April 11, finally ending a campaign that began eleven months earlier. In all, the French suffered about 25,000 casualties, including 2,000 killed in battle, 8,000 prisoners, and 15,000 who perished from disease and starvation. The allies lost only about half as many. Wellington's scorched earth strategy inflicted devastating losses, and not just on the French. Perhaps as many as 50,000 Portuguese died from starvation, disease, and exposure over the winter.[19]

Wellington's campaign was decisive in that he drove the invader from Portugal, aside from a French garrison in Almeida. Yet, could he have done more? Neither Wellington nor Massena was ever powerful enough to crush the other. Death, desertion, and reinforcements caused each army's troop numbers constantly to seesaw with the other, but the general power balance prevailed. Although Wellington won a large-scale battle at Bussaco and a small-scale battle at Sabugal, he lacked the manpower to turn either into a crushing victory. So Wellington never pondered such a possibility. Instead he was obsessed with denying Massena any opportunity to crush him. Aside from his disastrous attack at Bussaco, Massena was just as cautious. The result was a stalemate decided not by battle, but by who suffered the worst attrition of troops, supplies, and morale.

Some prominent British politicians and newspaper editors criticized Wellington for not destroying Massena. Word of the criticism of their chief and, by extension, themselves, angered the soldiers. Major Gordon condemned:

> ... the language of the people with regard to Lord Wellington ... [as] ... infamous & one cannot but deplore to what a length the liberty of the Press has arrived. People now are not satisfied because Lord Wellington has not utterly destroyed Massena and his army ... Yet these same people some months ago declared that nothing was equal to [his] rashness ... in attempting even to defend this country, that it was useless even to attempt to resist Massena and his army.[20]

As Wellington drove off one threat, another loomed that had been a long time steadily building. On December 31, 1810, Marshal Nicolas Soult marched north with 20,000 troops from Seville to clear the border of Spanish forces and possibly link with Massena. He forced 4,161 Spanish troops to surrender Olivenza on January 23, 1811. When General Francisco Ballesteros neared within a day's march, Soult dispatched a division that routed him at Villanueva de los Castillejos back into Portugal. Soult opened a siege of Badajoz on January 27. General Gabriel Mendizabal advanced with 15,000 troops, drove off the French on the Guadiana River's north side, and sent 4,000 troops across the bridge into Badajoz on the south side, bringing its garrison to 7,000 defenders, then withdrew to a ridgeline. Soult could never take Badajoz as long as Mendizabal dominated the north bank and supplied the city. On the night of February 18, Soult's engineers constructed a pontoon bridge across the river a few miles upstream, and sent 7,500 to outflank and rout Mendizabal. Badajoz's garrison surrendered on March 11; in all the Spaniards suffered 1,851 killed and 8,980 captured.[21]

Soult had fought a masterly campaign. Over 2½ months, his men had inflicted 20,000 Spanish casualties while losing one-fifth that number, and captured the minor fortress of Olivenza and the major fortress of Badajoz. The brilliance of Soult's campaign contrasted with the ineptitude of the Spanish generals and soldiers that opposed him. This provoked Wellington to quip that the string of humiliating defeats 'would certainly have been avoided had the Spaniards been anything but Spaniards.'[22]

The campaign's next phase was for Soult to march north, join forces with Massena, and overwhelm Wellington. But word of a French defeat near Cádiz and a march by Ballesteros against Seville forced Soult to leave General Adolphe Mortier with 11,000 troops at Badajoz and hurry south with rest of his army.

The French siege of Cádiz opened in February 1810 and ground on for a year with no end in sight. The stalemate persisted not just because the defenders outnumbered the besiegers. Within Cádiz were 21,000 Spanish troops led by General Manuel de la Pena and 5,000 British and Portuguese troops led by General Thomas Graham, while Marshal Claude Victor commanded the 19,000 French deployed in the countryside. There was no chance of a battle. Since Cádiz crowned an island, the French could not assault the city even if their artillery breached the thick walls, and for the same reason the defenders could not massively attack the besiegers. At most, skirmishes erupted when the Spanish launched sorties from their redoubts on the mainland defending approaches to Cádiz. Nor could the French starve out the defenders since a powerful Royal Navy squadron kept the sea lanes open. Although the French could not take Cádiz, their artillery fire systematically destroyed the city while their very presence insulted Spanish pride.

Graham conceived a bold plan to break the siege and talked Pena into reluctantly joining him in carrying it out. They would embark Graham's 5,000 troops and 8,000 of Pena's on ships, leaving 13,000 troops to defend Cádiz, sail to Algeciras, land, then march against Victor's rear. They disembarked at Algeciras on March 1. The following day, with Graham's troops leading, the allies headed toward Cádiz, 60 miles away. Learning of the landing, Victor hurried 10,000 troops and deployed them across the road at Barrosa on March 5. Victor ordered his men to attack as Graham's division deployed before them. As the battle raged, Graham galloped off couriers with pleas to Pena to hurry his troops forward in support. By the time the Spanish arrived, Graham's men had driven off the French, inflicting 2,400 casualties while suffering 1,740. An emboldened Pena then urged Graham to pursue the French back to Cádiz. But with thinned ranks, empty cartridge boxes, and hundreds of wounded, Graham could not immediately follow up his victory. This deflated Pena's enthusiasm. The following day, the allies headed back to Algeciras.[23]

Wellington, meanwhile, learning of Soult's siege of Badajoz, dispatched General Beresford to join Spanish troops in opposing him. Concerned that Beresford's force was not large enough, Wellington hurried General Cole's division after him. Finally, worried that Beresford might not be able to defeat Soult, Wellington left General Spencer in command, and cantered south with his staff and a cavalry escort on April 16.

By now, Soult had marched south to defend Seville, leaving Mortier behind. Mortier captured the small fortress of Campo Mayor, 10 miles north of Badajoz. Beresford's advanced guard surprised and routed Mortier's troops outside Campo Mayor on March 25. Beresford, however, did not follow this up with a massive attack despite outnumbering Mortier by 18,000 to 11,000 troops. The battle seesawed as each commander fed in his reserves to counter the other's threatening advances. Facing overwhelming odds, Mortier finally withdrew into Badajoz. There he received orders to transfer his command to General Fay Latour-Maubourg, who garrisoned Badajoz with 3,000 troops and withdrew south to Olivenza. With reinforcements Beresford had 27,000 troops when his army surrounded and besieged Badajoz on May 6.

Massena, meanwhile, replenished his ranks and supplies at Salamanca then advanced to break the British siege of Cuidad Rodrigo. Learning of Massena's advance, Wellington promptly raced north, reached Almeida on April 29, then spent several days searching the region for the best site to defend. He finally decided to defy Massena a dozen miles west of Cuidad Rodrigo on a ridgeline behind the shallow Dos Casar River and overlooking the village of Fuentes de Oñoro.

When Massena appeared on May 3, his army outnumbered Wellington's by 48,268 to 37,614 troops (23,026 British, 11,471 Portuguese), but for lack of draft animals was outgunned in cannons by 38 to 48.[24] By early afternoon, he deployed his army and decided on a plan. Massena's tactics could not have been more unimaginative – he tried to steamroll Wellington's army with a series of piecemeal, direct assaults. He hurled a division against Fuentes de Oñoro then watched dismayed as enemy musket volleys and canister shot decimated it. He ordered a second division to march into that maelstrom. This time the French took the village, but only after suffering devastating losses. Wellington ordered a counterattack that retook the village, pursued the routed French infantry, and then formed squares to repel French cavalry attacks. In all the battle for the village cost the French and the allies 652 and 259 casualties, respectively. Fog gathered that night and blanketed the battlefield the next morning. As the sun slowly burned off the fog, each side waited for the other's attack. Massena sent cavalry to probe for a way around the enemy's right flank, but the allies repelled them. The enemy commanders agreed on a truce to remove the wounded between their lines.

The battle resumed on May 5, when Massena launched an assault of infantry, cavalry, and artillery against Wellington's right. The allied line was about to break when Wellington threw in General Craufurd's Light Division. Craufurd's men drove off the French infantry then formed squares as the French cavalry charged. Wellington ordered General Cotton to rescue them. As the British and French cavalry battled, Craufurd withdrew his troops to the allied line. Massena then sent 22,000 troops against Wellington's army, which repelled it with severe losses. Massena hurled 10,000 reserves against Fuentes de Oñoro. After savage fighting, the French took the village, only to be driven off by a British counterattack. Massena massed his artillery and again sent forward his exhausted troops. When the allies drove the French infantry back, the French guns bombarded the exposed British and Portuguese troops. As Wellington withdrew his troops behind the ridge, he cantered batteries to the ridgeline where they bombarded and finally silenced the enemy cannons. Each side spent the next day readying his position for an attack that never came. Massena tried to arc his cavalry around Wellington's right but the British infantry and cavalry repelled them.

The waiting game ended on May 10, when Massena withdrew his army on the long road back to Salamanca, leaving Cuidad Rodrigo to its fate. In all, the French suffered 2,844 casualties and the allies 1,711.[25] The heaps of dead and dying were especially thick in the village, where the fighting was hand-to-hand: 'Among the dead that covered the street ... it was quite ... common ... to see an English and a French soldier with their bayonets still in each other's bodies, and their fists convulsively grasping the butt ends of their muskets, lying on top of each other.'[26] Although Wellington had once again defeated Massena, he was anything but exultant. Instead he noted grimly: 'If Boney had been there we should have been beaten.'[27]

The latest French threat came from the south. Soult routed Ballesteros's advance toward Seville, gathered reinforcements, and marched north to rescue Badajoz. Beresford's siege was not going well. His supplies were dwindling, he had lost around 500 troops including most of his engineers in various sorties and bombardments, and his lines were still far from pounding range of the city's walls.

Learning of Soult's approach, Beresford marched 20,310 men, including 8,738 British and 9,131 Portuguese infantry, and 1,995 cavalry, and 446 artillerymen, 20 miles south and deployed them behind a shallow stream straddled by the village of Albuera. There he was joined by 14,644 Spanish troops, including 12,593 infantry, 1,886 cavalry, and 165 gunners jointly led by Generals Joaquin Blake and Francisco Castanos. The allied army numbered 34,954 troops. Soult's army of 24,260 troops, including 19,015 infantry, 4,012 cavalry, and 1,233 artillerymen, marched into view on the afternoon of May 15.[28]

Although grossly outnumbered by the enemy in a strong position, Soult ordered a massive attack the following morning on the Spanish troops on the allied right. As that flank crumbled, General William Steward diverted much of his division against the French attack and blunted it. Soult arched his cavalry around the Spanish and routed them. Beresford charged his cavalry against the French and drove them off, then sent Cole's division against Soult's center at Albuera. Although Cole's men captured Albuera, they could not advance beyond. A cartridge-soaking rain ended the battle. The enemies suffered nearly equal numbers of casualties, the French 5,936 and the allies 5,956, including 4,199 British, 389 Portuguese, and 1,368 Spanish. But Soult lost nearly one-quarter of his army to the allied loss of less than one-fifth. Severely outnumbered, Soult withdrew the next day to Badajoz.[29]

The allied failure to capitalize on their superior troop numbers and crush Soult provoked heated recriminations. As usual, the redcoats expressed contempt and loathing for the people they were sent to save. A sergeant condemned the 'Spaniards' who 'soon gave way in great disorder, leaving the brunt of the battle to the British … It was always a bother to get them to stir forward during a battle, but retreating was what they were best at, and then it was always in confusion.'[30] Major Gordon blistered a British general: 'The Battle of Albuera was certainly gained by Cole's division but it was entirely owing to the gallantry of his men, and not to any merit of his … Cole has no more head than a Child, is quite lost, and confused, and without the least confidence in himself.'[31] Beresford's account of the battle dismayed Wellington who replied: 'This won't do – write me down a victory.'[32] Privately, Wellington was scathing of how Beresford and his staff handled the battle: 'They were never determined to fight it; they did not occupy the ground as they ought; they were ready to run away at every moment from the time it commenced till the French retired.'[33]

With Massena and Soult now far away, Wellington ordered resumptions of the sieges of Cuidad Rodrigo and Badajoz, and personally took command of the latter. Auguste Marmont relieved Massena of his army's command at Salamanca. Soult replenished his army at Seville. Couriers raced between Marmont and Soult as they distantly worked out a campaign to relieve Badajoz. With 35,000 troops Marmont marched first to Cuidad Rodrigo. Outnumbered, Spencer broke off his siege and withdrew to Almeida. When Marmont approached Almeida, Spencer abandoned that fortress and hurried south to join Wellington at Badajoz.

Perched high on a mesa surrounded by rocky ground and on the Guadiana River's south bank, Badajoz was extremely difficult to besiege. San Christobal fortress on the north bank protected the bridge across the river. Although the British began digging siege lines against Badajoz and San Christobal on May 29, neither was making much progress. Word arrived of the convergence of Marmont and Massena toward Badajoz. Wellington ordered night assaults on San Christobal on June 6 and 9, but the French repulsed each. The fighting was especially hellish for the British:

> We advanced up the glacis … The top of this wall crowded with men hurling down shells and hand grenades … Add to this some half a dozen cannon scouring the trench with grape … heaps of brave fellows killed and wounded, ladders shot to pieces and falling together with the men down upon the living and the dead … But in the midst of all these difficulties … we should have taken the fort, but for an unforeseen accident … The ladders were too short … as soon as this was discovered … the order was given to retire.[34]

Wellington ended the siege on June 10, and deployed his army in line on ridgelines anchored by Elvas and Campo Mayor.

Soult and Marmont joined forces at Merida on June 18, then advanced with their 60,000 troops to Badajoz. There they ended their advance even though they outnumbered Wellington's 44,000-man army. After resupplying Badajoz, Massena and Soult withdrew to their respective bases of Salamanca and Seville. Soult hastened his march after learning that Spanish General Blake was marching against Seville. Blake withdrew to Portugal as Soult neared and barely escaped destruction as he embarked with his men aboard British transports that sailed for Cádiz.

Wellington abandoned any notion of successfully besieging Badajoz. Instead he led most of his army back to invest Cuidad Rodrigo. This prompted Marmont to advance and reunite before Cuidad Rodrigo with General Jean Dorsenne who arrived with 20,000 troops from Astorga. Once again Wellington broke off a siege before superior numbers and withdrew into Portugal.

The advanced French guard caught up and attacked Wellington's rear guard at El Bodon. The British formed squares to repel French cavalry attacks:

> ... until, at last the French infantry being brought up, we were ordered to retreat in squares ... The French cavalry ... rushed furiously ... but they halted and we repulsed them with the utmost steadiness and gallantry. The French suffered severely ... We were much annoyed by shot and shell from the heights where the French artillery were posted, some ... falling in the squares ... killing and wounding several of our men, and blowing up our ammunition. We had about six miles to retreat ... before we reached the body of the army, with the French cavalry hanging on our flanks and rear.[35]

The next day, on September 25, Wellington deployed his army along a ridgeline above Fuenteguinaldo. When Marmont approached on September 27, Wellington withdrew that night to a stronger position further west. Marmont scanned Wellington's line and decided that any attack would only fail with senseless slaughter. Marmont and Dorsenne withdrew their men to their respective bases.

While this ended Wellington's operations for the year, General Hill launched a small campaign. On October 22, he led his 11,000-man division toward Merida to disrupt the main road linking Salamanca and Seville. Although Hill did not get that far, he wiped out a 2,500-man French detachment at Arroyo Molinos, mopped up another 800 French scattered in posts on his route, then returned to Portugal having suffered only a hundred casualties.[36]

Wellington's series of victories over French armies in 1810 and 1811 transformed perceptions of the Peninsular War by most politicians, newspaper editors, and the public from pessimism to optimism. Foreign Secretary Wellesley expressed the new outlook: 'The wisdom of maintaining the war in Spain and Portugal has been fully proved by the shade it has cast on the military and political character of Bonaparte.'[37] Certainly Wellington and his staff saw the Peninsula campaign in a broad strategic vision that embraced the rest of Europe. Major Gordon captured his vision: 'Depend upon it, sooner or later this general determination of resistance will take place & ... the fair example of Spain will be followed by other powers. You will then see that overgrown Empire of France fall to pieces in a far shorter time than it was erected.'[38] Gordon's vision was prescient.

Chapter 16

The Great Lakes, 1812–14

The American war has excited a great sensation and is doubtless a most calamitous thing; people imagine everything will be right when the Americans hear of the repeal of the orders in Council, I scarcely think this will be the case.

George Hamilton-Gordon, Lord Aberdeen

It is far from intention to join in a war of extermination, but you must be aware that the numerous body of Indians who have attached themselves to my troops, will be beyond control the moment the contest begins.

General Isaac Brock

President James Madison signed a congressional war declaration against Britain on June 18, 1812. The subsequent war lasted over two-and-a-half years, cost both countries vast amounts of blood and treasure, and ended with neither side victorious. Why did the United States and Britain fight a second war against each other just a generation after the Americans won independence?[1]

Madison cited two long-term British policies – one at sea, the other on land – for justifying the war. The most important was Whitehall's policy of confiscating American ships and cargos sailing to enemy ports, and impressing into the Royal Navy sailors without documents proving they were American citizens. British arms, munitions, and incitement of resistance to Northwest and Southwest Indians tribes in American territory was a secondary issue.

Yet the 1812 War was not inevitable. President George Washington was able to alleviate chronic tensions with the 1795 Jay Treaty, whereby the British agreed to open their markets to American goods and abandon their forts on American territory. Informally, they promised to curtail their seizures of American ships, cargos, and sailors. The threat to the United States then shifted to France, whose depredations against American shipping soared. The result was the Quasi-War from 1798 to 1800, when American and French warships battled on the high seas.[2] This ended with the 1800 Treaty of Mortefontaine, whereby Napoleon Bonaparte also agreed to stop preying on American shipping if the United States waived seeking compensation for previous losses.

During the next dozen years, Britain revived its Orders in Council that authorized seizing American ships and goods bound for Britain's enemies, and impressing men into the British navy. From 1796 to 1812, Royal Navy warships forced 9,991 sailors from American vessels into British service, with around 6,000 pressed after 1803.[3] How did the British justify this policy of essentially kidnapping thousands of sailors from American and other foreign ships, even when the prisoners protested that they were no longer or never were British subjects? Whitehall insisted that nationality and thus duty to one's country was life-long, that no one could legally shed the land of their birth. Atop this was the claim, expressed by Captain Edward Brenton, that 'the Americans have made a practice from the beginning of hostilities … to entice the crews of his Majesty's ships to desert, and have even given them large bounties.'[4] Actually, while about one of four American sailors was originally from Britain, relatively few were deserters. Finally, the British argued that the United States government could have alleviated this problem and raised revenues simply by issuing citizenship documents to the sailors who manned America's merchant fleet, but for reasons of economy and national pride did not.

With his Berlin Decree of November 21, 1806 and Milan decrees of November 23, 1807, Napoleon established the Continental System designed to sever Europe's trade with Britain.[5] This provoked the latest Whitehall policy shift. The British issued new Orders in Council that authorized the Royal Navy to prey on any ships bound for Europe. Prime Minister Spencer Percival later justified this policy by insisting that the 'object … was not to destroy the trade of the Continent, but to force the Continent to trade with us.'[6] Not all British officers and politicians favored the policy of essentially robbing, humiliating, kidnapping, and occasionally murdering Americans and others. Admiral Cuthbert Collingwood criticized the policy that 'may involve us in a contest which it would be wisdom to avoid. When English seamen can be recovered in a quiet way, it is well; but when demanded as a national right, which must be enforced, we should be prepared to do reciprocal justice.'[7]

The distinction between hardliners and moderates was not confined to Britain's leadership. President Thomas Jefferson had a chance to resolve the conflict, but his idealism trumped a deal.[8] He rejected a treaty negotiated by Charles Pinckney and James Monroe in 1806, whereby the British would stop preying on American shipping and, as a side understanding, sharply cut back impressment. In return, Washington had to prevent foreign privateers from using American ports and Americans from serving in foreign armies and navies warring against Britain. Jefferson rejected the treaty solely because the impressment curb was not stated, but simply understood. Jefferson's decision to spurn rather than embrace the treaty did not make war certain, but certainly made it more likely.[9]

To add insult to injury, the Royal Navy actually committed many of its depredations in American waters. The British committed a homicide in New York Bay on April 25, 1806, when the *Leader* fired a warning shot across one vessel's bow and the cannon ball decapitated a sailor on another American vessel. Although the British callously dismissed this as an accident, they committed not just outright murder but an act of war on June 22, 1807, when the *Leopard* fired three broadsides into the *Chesapeake*, killing 3 Americans and wounding 18 others. The British excuse for this atrocity was Captain James Barron's refusal to let aboard a party of marines to search for deserters. With his ship crippled, Barron had no choice but to strike his colors. British marines swarmed onto the *Chesapeake*, interrogated the crew, and dragged away four suspects. The *Leopard* then sailed to Halifax to put the four men on trial. Three could prove that they were Americans that had deserted the Royal Navy after being impressed, and Admiral George Berkeley ordered them to receive 300 lashes; although none were actually whipped, one man died in prison and the other two were eventually released broken in health and mind from the hellish treatment. The fourth man was found to be British and a deserter, and was hanged.

The *Chesapeake* atrocity, however, did not lead to an American war declaration. Jefferson instead ordered on July 2, all British warships from American waters. When the British disdainfully refused to do so, Jefferson took a drastic step, but one that harmed America rather than Britain. He believed that he could bring the British Empire to its knees without a shot being fired in anger. He launched a trade rather than military war against Britain. He zealously insisted that Whitehall would eventually bow to all of Washington's demands if British merchants could neither sell to nor buy from the United States, and if British warships could not confiscate American ships, cargoes, and crews. This was the 'logic' behind the Embargo Act that Congress passed and Jefferson implemented on December 22, 1807.

The Embargo Act, which outlawed Americans from foreign trade, was among the more authoritarian and self-destructive policies in American history. Just to engage in coastal trade within the United States, a merchant had to post a bond that cost six times his cargo's value, to be redeemed only when he returned with a certificate from the port where he sold his goods. Only foreign merchants in foreign ships could trade with the United States. This policy certainly prevented American vessels, cargoes, and crews from being confiscated by British and French warships. The trouble was that the policy devastated the economy by transforming otherwise thriving American ports into ghost towns with ships rotting at anchor and countless jobless sailors and stevedores milling about listless or angry. From 1807 to 1808, American exports plummeted from $108 million to $22 million, and imports from $138 million to $57 million.[10]

Mounting protests finally forced Jefferson reluctantly to change the policy. The Non-Intercourse Act that took effect on May 20, 1809, let American merchants trade with all countries except Britain and France. American-conducted trade slowly nudged upward in relatively minor markets, but remained a sliver of previous volumes while the economy remained depressed. Macon Bill Number Two, which took effect on May 1, 1809, permitted Americans to trade with any country, but would resume a cutoff with either Britain or France if the other agreed to end its depredations against American shipping. Napoleon did so with the Cadore letter of August 1810, issued by Foreign Minister Jean Baptiste Champagny, duc de Cadore. Hoping that Whitehall would follow suit, the Madison administration waited until February 2, 1811, before severing trade with Britain.

Ironically, neither the Jefferson nor the Madison administration wielded the one trade weapon that just might have forced Whitehall to yield. The British army could not have fought the Peninsular War for five years without American grain and other provisions. American grain shipments rose from 80,000 bushels in 1807 to 900,000 in 1812.[11] Had the Americans threatened to sever this supply, then done so if Whitehall refused to compromise, the British most likely would have soon yielded. But Republican Party presidents Jefferson and Madison did not want to alienate farmers, the backbone of their political support. Indeed the Madison administration let these shipments persist throughout the War of 1812!

Nearly four years after the *Chesapeake* atrocity, the Americans finally avenged themselves.

After the *Guerriere* impressed a sailor off an American vessel in New York Bay, the *President* sailed in pursuit. On the night of May 16, 1811, the *President* neared the *Little Belt*, mistaken for the *Guerriere*. The British captain ordered a broadside that hit the *President* but hurt no one. The *President* replied with its own broadside that killed 9 men and wounded 23 aboard the *Little Belt*, which struck its colors. Word of this combat did not spark war between Britain and the United States, but raised passions on both sides to a fever pitch.

Atop Britain's depredations against American trade, the British supplied muskets and munitions to the Indians, and not so secretly incited them to fight the Americans. This resulted in bloodshed in the Northwest Territory. Tecumseh and his brother Tenskwatawa, the Prophet, were Shawnee chiefs who sought to unite all the tribes in a confederacy against the Americans. In fall 1811, William Henry Harrison, the Northwest Territory's governor, tried to preempt this threat by marching a thousand troops against their village, known as Prophetstown. The army was encamped at Tippecanoe Creek, when the Indians attacked on the night of November 7, 1811. The Americans repelled the attacks, then marched the next day to destroy the now abandoned village. Many of the refugees fled to Canada where they received arms, munitions, and provisions to avenge themselves on the American frontier.

If the Americans had a long list of burning grievances against the British, there were no concrete causes to cite for declaring war when they did. Greed powerfully motivated many of those who wanted war. The War Hawks believed that the Americans could easily conquer Canada to exploit its land and other rich resources. Jefferson insisted that, while the British 'will have the sea to herself … we shall be equally predominant on land, and shall strip her of all her possessions on this continent.' Indeed, Canada's conquest was 'a mere matter of marching.'[12]

Psychology, as always, was a major force for war. In Congress, War Hawks like Henry Clay, Richard Johnson, Felix Grundy, George Troup, and Peter Porter were a zealous, outspoken minority that eventually stampeded America into war. The War Hawks were young impassioned men who had never served in the military and wanted to equal the generations of their fathers and grandfathers who had fought valiantly in America's War for Independence. Andrew Jackson exemplified this zealotry when he declared: 'We are going to fight for the reestablishment of our national character, misunderstood and vilified at home and abroad.'[13]

What became known as the War Congress convened on November 4, 1811, following the 1810 election. Republicans outnumbered Federalists by 108 to 36 in the House, and 30 to 6 in the Senate. War Hawks dominated the Republican Party. In January, Congress voted to expand the army to 35,603 officers and men by the year's end. To entice recruits, Congress raised the enlistment bonus from $12 to $31, and offered 160 acres of land to those who completed their service. Anti-British feeling soared higher when Madison informed Congress on March 8, 1812, that British secret agents were trying to get the New England states to secede from the United States.[14] In April, Congress authorized the president to raise an additional 15,000 troops for 18-month enlistments and muster 80,000 militiamen. What the Republicans refused to do on each step they took toward war was to raise taxes to pay for their vast military expansion. The government instead would borrow the money and heap the debt on future generations.

Madison finally caved to the War Hawk pressure and sent a war declaration bill to Congress on June 1. The House of Representative voted 79 to 49 on June 4, and the Senate by 17 to 13 on June 17. The president signed the bill the following day, June 18, 1812. The War Hawks, that era's neoconservatives, had stampeded Americans to war with two related drumbeats, patriotism to defend the nation's honor and interests against a threatening enemy, and greed to grab all the spoils along the way. In doing so, they drowned out sober minded Cassandras who warned that the war was a terrible mistake that would most likely lead to military and economic disaster. Tragically that prediction came true.

Whitehall responded to America's military build-up with concessions. In May, the British actually offered to share trading licenses for Europe with American merchants. Then, on June 16, Whitehall announced its intention to suspend the Orders in Council, thus eliminating the Republican Party's most important excuse for going to war. The actual suspension came a week later. Trenchant observer George, Lord Aberdeen noted: 'The American war has excited a great sensation and is doubtless a most calamitous thing; people imagine everything will be right when the Americans hear of the repeal of the orders in Council, I scarcely think this will be the case.'[15] Aberdeen was prescient.

After receiving word of this concession in August, President Madison and Congress did not use it as a face-saving excuse to declare victory and call off the war. When word arrived that the president and congress did not stand down, Whitehall had no choice but to figure out what to do. The first obvious steps were to begin blockading American ports and sending reinforcements to Canada. Any thought of actually invading some vulnerable, vital American region could only proceed after a major build-up of troops and supplies on that front. So, by necessity, the British had to rest on the defensive, waiting for the Americans to take the initiative, and only thereafter, figure out a counter-offensive.[16]

By virtually every measure of power, Britain surpassed America. Britain's 10 million people were a quarter larger than America's 7.5 million people. Britain was the world's greatest industrial, financial, commercial, and naval power. The only silver lining for Americans was that most of Britain's army and navy were committed elsewhere around the world, and little could initially be siphoned to North America.

The American army was an oxymoron. In June 1812, the army numbered only 6,744 officers and men in regular regiments, a sliver of the authorized 36,000-men strength, and about 5,000 in volunteer regiments with 18-month enlistments. The quality was even more pathetic than the numbers. In his memoirs, General Winfield Scott recalled an army in which 'the old officers had ... sunk into either sloth, ignorance, or habits of intemperate drinking.'[17] This pretty much summed up the typical soldier as well. During the war, the Madison administration tried to alleviate the dismal quality of recruits by raising the enlistment bonus from \$31 to \$124, and the mustering out reward from 120 to 360 acres of land. But these efforts could not possibly resolve the conundrum of amateur officers trying to transform civilians into professional soldiers. Exacerbating this core problem were perennial shortages of arms, munitions, provisions, uniforms, blankets, tents, draft animals, and wagons.

As for militia, the United States had plenty of them. An 1802 survey of state militias found 525,000 men enrolled, not including those of Maryland, Delaware, and Tennessee that did not send Washington their numbers. The trouble was that the militia was militarily all but worthless. There were only 249,000 firearms among them or less than one for every two men. Historically, with a few exceptions at the battles of Concord, Bunker Hill, and Bennington, militia tended to cut and run at the first shots fired their way. During the 1812 War, the militiamen would repeatedly defy orders to invade Canada, arguing they were only required to defend the United States.[18]

For War Hawks, Canada was the great prize, although few publicly admitted it. As Henry Clay put it, 'Canada was not the end but the means ... the object of the War being the redress of injuries, and Canada being the instrument by which that redress was to be obtained.'[19] The War Hawks insisted that Canadians would greet the American armies as liberators from British oppression and happily join the United States. The Madison administration devised a strategy that they believed would lead to Canada's rapid conquest and the war's end. Three armies would simultaneously invade Canada, with their respective objectives Montreal, York, and Amherstburg.[20]

Certainly Canada appeared to be an easy picking. With 500,000 people, Canada's population was 15 times smaller than America's, and its economy a fraction as dynamic. To defend Canada, the British had about 5,600 regulars and 86,000 militiamen. Most of these men were in heavily populated Quebec province. There were only about 4,500 redcoats scattered in small detachments in forts along the Saint Lawrence River valley and Great Lake basin. Indian allies bolstered British power along the frontier. General George Prevost was Canada's governor general and commander-in-chief.[21]

On the Upper Great Lakes, three leaders were crucial for defeating a likely American conquest. General Isaac Brock was Upper Canada's military commander headquartered at Fort George on the Niagara River. Colonel Henry Proctor commanded Fort Malden at Amherstsburg, Britain's sole stronghold on Lake Erie. Finally, brilliant Shawnee chief Tecumseh led most Indian warriors. After learning on June 24 that Congress had declared war against Britain, Brock wrote Proctor to ready his men for action and promised that he would arrive with reinforcements as soon as possible.

Proctor had around 300 regulars and 300 militiamen, backed by Tecumseh, lesser chiefs, and 600 warriors. Not content to await the American invasion, Proctor organized and dispatched an expedition of 45 regulars, 180 militia, and 400 Indians to take Fort Mackinac. Only 61 men defended Fort Mackinac; their captain agreed to surrender shortly after viewing the horde before him on July 16. With word of Fort Mackinac's capture, Proctor and Tecumseh could concentrate on eliminating the swelling threat just across the Detroit River.[22]

Governing Michigan Territory was General William Hull, a Revolutionary War veteran long past his prime, befuddled and so gout-ridden that he could mount his horse only with assistance. Nonetheless, after reaching Detroit on July 5, Hull initially acted boldly. On July 15, he led 450 troops and 1,400 militiamen across the Detroit River to occupy Sandwich, Canada. But then Hull just encamped his men there instead of rapidly marching them toward Fort Malden, 15 miles south.

Tecumseh transformed the campaign on August 3, by leading his warriors across the river and attacking supply trains on the road leading north to Detroit. News that his supply line was cut spooked Hull into withdrawing back across the river and holing up in Detroit. Upon learning that Fort Mackinac had fallen, Hull ordered Fort Dearborn's commander on Lake Michigan's southwest shore to abandon his post to avoid the same fate. Potawatomi and Winnebago Indians massacred 53 of the 90 troops and civilians who fled on August 15.[23] Of the three forts guarding America's Upper Great Lakes frontier, only Detroit remained. This would soon change.

A flotilla packed with supplies, reinforcements, and Brock reached Fort Malden on August 13. Brock had Proctor erect a battery of cannons and mortars on the river's east bank directly opposite Detroit. On August 16, Brock led 330 regulars, 400 militia, 5 cannons, and 600 Indians across the river 3 miles below Detroit and marched north. Hull deployed his men across the road leading to Detroit, but they did not stay long. Terrified by Indian war whoops, Hull ordered a hasty retreat into the fort. Brock then sent his chilling message to Hull: 'It is far from my intention to join in a war of extermination, but you must be aware that the numerous body of Indians who have attached themselves to my troops, will be beyond control the moment the contest begins.'[24] Hull promptly rendered into British hands Detroit, 582 troops, 1,606 militia, 5,000lb of gunpowder, and the brig *Adams*. Hull would later be court-martialed, sentenced to death, and pardoned for his cowardice.[25]

With Detroit's capture, the front line of America's northwest frontier fell south a hundred miles to Fort Wayne on the watershed between the Wabash and Maumee Rivers. Brock followed up his victory by sending his Indians against Fort Wayne, which they attacked but failed to take on September 5. Further west, on the Mississippi River, British and Indians captured Prairie du Chien, at the Wisconsin River mouth, then canoed downstream to besiege Fort Madison, which was abandoned a year later on September 3, 1813.

Meanwhile, Brock hurried back to the Niagara frontier, where an American army was preparing to invade Canada. The Niagara River flows 35 miles north from Lake Erie to Lake Ontario, dividing the United States eastward from Canada westward. On the American side, the forts and larger towns along the river included Buffalo, Black Rock, Fort Schlosser, Lewiston, Fort Grey, Youngstown, and Fort Niagara; from his Lewiston headquarters, General Stephen van Rensselaer commanded that front's 2,300 troops and 4,000 militiamen. On the Canadian side, Fort Erie, Fort Chippewa, Queenstown, Fort George, and Newark; from his Fort George headquarters, Brock commanded that front's 1,200 troops, 800 militiamen, and 300 Indians.[26]

Van Rensselaer planned a two-pronged invasion; under the cover of an artillery barrage, he would cross from Lewistown to attack Queenstown, while General Alexander Smyth crossed a half-dozen miles downriver from Youngstown to attack Fort George. Two flaws fouled an otherwise sound strategy. Van Rensselaer had only 35 boats which together could carry only about 600 men; ferrying his entire army would take most of a day. Then there was Smyth, as inept as he was jealous of Van Rensselaer; Smyth found excuses for not crossing.

Colonel Solomon Van Rensselaer, the commander's younger and militarily experienced brother, led the initial landing on October 13. As the Americans struggled up Queenstown Heights, six bullets struck down Van Rensselaer. General Van Rensselaer sent over Lieutenant Colonel Winfield Scott to take command. Scott rallied the troops and led them to capture Queenstown Heights. Brock was at Fort George when he heard cannon fire upriver at Queenston. Before galloping to Queenston, he ordered General Roger Scheaffe to muster 1,000 troops and quick-march to the sound of the guns. Brock reached the Heights just as Scott's troops were routing the redcoats. A bullet killed Brock. Scott sent a plea across the river for reinforcements. Van Rensselaer ordered the Ohio militiamen into the boats, but they, cowed by witnessing the carnage on the river's far side, bulked, claiming that they were only required to serve on American soil. Only 350 troops joined Scott atop the Heights. Scheaffe and his troops reached Queenston, rallied the remnants of the British forces, and surrounded the Americans. With his men's ammunition expended and no hope of reinforcements, Scott had no choice but to surrender his 958 surviving troops, having suffered 120 dead and 150 wounded. The British lost only 14 killed, 77 wounded, and 21 missing, and the Indians 5 killed and 7 wounded.[27] The battle likely would have ended in an American rather than British victory had Smyth crossed downriver and diverted Scheaffe by threatening Fort George.

Disheartened by this disastrous defeat atop all the frustrating months that led to it, Van Rensselaer resigned. When Smyth assumed command on October 16, his army counted 4,000 regulars and several thousand militiamen. He conceived a plan of attacking Fort Erie but promptly scrubbed it when Pennsylvania's militia refused to go along. The White House cashiered Smyth and replaced him with General Morgan Lewis.

The third and most important of the planned invasions of Canada never took place. General Henry Dearborn was, like William Hull, an overweight, bumbling, timid shadow of the man who had fought in America's War for Independence. He reached Albany on May 3, 1812, with orders to organize an army. After Congress declared war, Dearborn was assigned the campaign to capture Montreal. By November 1812, he had massed 3,000 regulars and 3,000 militiamen at Plattsburgh just as ice and snow began to bury Lake Champlain and the road north toward Montreal. He led his army to the frontier, but, on November 20, when the militiamen refused to cross, he turned tail for winter quarters in Plattsburgh.

In all, the war's first seven months were as stunning a success for the British as they were disastrous for the Americans. The British captured large American forces at Detroit and Queenstown, and contingents at Forts Mackinac and Dearborn. Their grip on the upper Great Lakes seemed as unshakeable as their threat to carry the war deep into the United States seemed imminent.

General William Henry Harrison, the Northwest Territory's governor, spent most of 1812 trying to train and equip an army capable of squaring off with the British, Canadians, and Indians. In early January, he dispatched General James Winchester with 884 troops to protect the American settlement of Frenchtown on the Raison River that flows into Lake Erie. Learning of the advance, Colonel Proctor mustered 334 British, 212 militiamen, and several hundred Indians to attack Winchester's army on January 21, 1813. While Proctor lost 24 killed and 161 wounded, the Americans suffered 292 dead before Winchester surrendered the 592 survivors. The Indian massacre of about 30 captive Americans later inspired the war cry, 'Remember the River Raison.'[28]

In spring 1813, Harrison marched with 500 troops and 500 militiamen down the Maumee River and established Fort Meigs just half a dozen miles upstream of Lake Erie. He dispatched a force to erect Fort Stephenson on the Sandusky River a few miles upstream of Lake Erie. As he massed troops and supplies for a campaign against Detroit, the British beat him to the punch.

Proctor, recently promoted to general, marched south with 500 troops, 450 militia, and 1,200 Indians in late April, and deployed around Fort Meigs on May 1.[29] He had a battery of 2 24-pounder cannons erected on the north bank directly across from the fort, and another battery of 6-pounders erected on the south bank. He split his regulars and militia to guard each battery, while most of the Indians scattered in clusters on the south bank to snipe at the fort. The batteries opened fire later this day and their bombardment continued for days thereafter, but could not breach the walls. Proctor expressed his frustration that: 'The Enemy had during our Approach so completely entrenched and covered himself as to render unavailing every Effort of our Artillery.'[30] Nonetheless, Proctor believed that his siege would eventually starve out the defenders.

A courier slipped from Fort Meigs through the British and Indian lines on May 2. The message was from Harrison to General Green Clay, who led 1,200 Kentucky militiamen encamped up the Maumee River. Clay and his men were to descend the river and attack the battery on the north bank, at which point part of the garrison would surge out to attack the south battery. On May 5, the Kentuckians landed near the battery, overran it, and spiked the guns. But then Clay made a fatal mistake. Rather than hold this position, he led his exuberant men after the fleeing British and Indians. Proctor threw in his regulars which halted the Kentuckians with several volleys, then routed them with a bayonet charge. The Indians surged after and slaughtered the fleeing men. Meanwhile, Harrison sent out a regiment that briefly captured the British battery and scattered the Indians, before withdrawing after Tecumseh rallied his men and counter-attacked. The British scored their latest lopsided victory, inflicting on the Americans 135 killed, 188 wounded, and 630 prisoners, at the cost of only 14 dead, 47 wounded, and 41 prisoners; Indian losses were unrecorded.[31] This stunning victory satiated most Indians, who drifted away with their scalps, captives, and loot over the next few days. Meanwhile, the Canadian militiamen pestered Proctor to release them for spring planting. Proctor finally abandoned the siege on May 9.

For the next two months, Proctor resupplied his troops and the Indians. He and 400 troops, 100 militia, and 1,000 Indians reappeared before Fort Meigs on July 20. Once again the British artillery bombardment failed to breach the fort's walls. Eight days later, Proctor broke off the siege, but instead of returning to Detroit, led his men east to Fort Stephenson on the Sandusky River. Fearing that the fort was indefensible, Harrison sent instructions to Major George Croghan to withdraw with his 160 men east to Cleveland. Croghan disobeyed the order and vowed to die fighting the invaders. On August 2, the Americans 'kept up such a destructive fire that the enemy … broke and fled in the wildest confusion.'[32] Proctor suffered 29 killed, 44 wounded, and 28 missing to American losses of only one killed and seven wounded. The repulse so disheartened the Indians that they told Proctor that they would head home. Without Indians, the British regulars and militia would be outnumbered if Harrison marched against them. Proctor had no choice but to withdraw to Detroit.[33]

The Madison administration understood that a victory on that front was unlikely unless the Americans commanded Lake Erie. The White House assigned Lieutenant Jesse Elliott the task of building a fleet. In October 1812, Elliott arrived at Black Rock on the Niagara River, where two schooners were anchored. Elliott reasoned that he could acquire a fleet faster by stealing than building it. Anchored across the river beneath Fort Erie's guns were two sloops, the *Detroit* and *Caledonia*. On the night of October 8, Elliott and 50 men rowed in 2 barges with muffled oars to the vessels, swarmed aboard, overwhelmed the defenders, then cut the cables. The raiders aboard the *Detroit* burned it after it ground ashore on an island. Those on the *Caledonia* steered it to Black Rock. In the fighting the Americans killed or captured around 70 British and liberated 40 American prisoners held aboard the vessels.

Black Rock's vulnerability to British attack caused the White House to order Elliott to shift his naval base to Presque Isle, a peninsula that curled about a half mile into Lake Erie and sheltered a deep bay. From the nearby forest, oaks supplied the skeleton and planks, and pines the masts, yardarms, and pitch to caulk seams. All the tools, munitions, cannons, and provisions had to be hauled by wagon to Buffalo then sailed 100 miles southwest to the shipyard. Troops eventually widened trails into roads from Presque Isle eastward 200 miles to Harrisburg and southward 130 miles to Pittsburgh. When Elliott appeared to make little progress, Madison superseded him with Captain Oliver Hazard Perry.

Perry arrived with 150 sailors and shipwrights aboard 4 warships from Black Rock in June 1813.[34] By early September, Perry's fleet included his flagship, the 20-gun *Lawrence*, the 20-gun *Niagara* commanded by Elliott, and seven smaller warships. The Americans faced both a formidable enemy commander and fleet. Captain Robert Barclay was a veteran of Nelson's navy and had lost an arm at Trafalgar. At Fort Malden, he had massed a fleet of 6 warships, including the 21-gun *Detroit*, 18-gun *Queen Charlotte*, 13-gun *Lady Prevost*, 10-gun *General Hunter*, 2-gun *Little Belt*, and 1-gun *Chippewa*.

Perry sailed his fleet to Put-in-Bay in the Bass Islands a dozen or so miles off Lake Erie's south shore and directly across from Amherstsburg on the north shore. Learning of Perry's presence, Barclay ordered his captains to weigh anchor on September 10. The fleets closed for action by midday. At first the British appeared likely to prevail. Their guns pounded the *Lawrence* so badly that Perry had himself and his flag rowed to the *Niagara*. After the *Detroit* and *Queen Charlotte* became entangled, Perry sailed the *Niagara* directly beside them and opened fire. A bullet struck down Barclay. Carnage spread across each fleet, with 41 British killed and 94 wounded, and 27 Americans killed and 96 wounded. The Americans eventually forced all six British warships to strike their colors. Perry triumphantly reported to the White House that 'We have met the enemy and they are ours.'[35]

With American warships commanding Lake Erie, Harrison was now free to march north from Fort Meigs without worrying about the British landing an army on his rear. Perry packed 4,500 troops and militia aboard his fleet and landed them at the Detroit River mouth on September 27. At word of the landing, Proctor ordered Fort Detroit and Fort Malden burned, then withdrew northeastward with his troops. This may have been prudent but it appeared cowardly in Indian eyes. Tecumseh openly sneered at Proctor, reminding him that British officials:

> ... always told us that you would never draw your foot off British ground; but now, Father, we see you are drawing back.... without seeing the enemy. We must compare our Father's conduct to a fat animal that carries his tail upon its back, but when afrightened ... drops it between his legs and runs off.[36]

This was not the first time the Indians had witnessed such behavior. The British had previously abandoned them to their fate at the end of America's independence war.

Harrison's 3,500 men caught up to Proctor's 800 troops and 500 Indians a mile south of Moraviantown on the Thames River's west bank on October 5. The Americans overwhelmed the British and Indians, killed at least 31 Indians, and killed 18, wounded 25, and captured 591 redcoats, while losing 7 killed and 22 wounded. Tecumseh was among the dead. Only 269 British and several hundred warriors escaped eastward. Total British losses during the campaign came to 634 officers and men.[37]

Although Harrison captured the British artillery and supply train, he did not follow up his victory with a march 100 miles east to Burlington on Lake Ontario. Had he done so, the American position at the lake's west end and Niagara valley would have been virtually impregnable. In spring 1814, an American army could have marched around Lake Ontario's north shore, capturing York and Kingston before joining forces with an army from Sackets Bay then, with overwhelming numbers, descend the Saint Lawrence to Montreal itself. This advance would have forced the British to scrub their operations in Chesapeake Bay and sail to the rescue. What then happened in Canada is impossible to know. What is certain is that the British would not have captured and burned Washington City in August or launched the New Orleans campaign in December, and they probably would have agreed to peace much sooner.

Instead an uneasy power balance prevailed on Lake Ontario. On the northwest shore, York, Upper Canada's capital, was a town of about a thousand people and several hundred houses and buildings. On the northeast shore, Kingston crowned a promontory where the lake poured past into the Saint Lawrence River. Three American forts guarded Lake Ontario's southern shore, with Fort Niagara at the Niagara River mouth on the west, Fort Oswego at the Oswego River mouth in the center, and Sackets Harbor on the east. There was rough naval parity as, by spring 1813, British Captain James Yeo had 6 warships and American Captain Isaac Chauncey had the 26-gun *General Pike*, 3 brigs, and 9 schooners. The Americans and British were locked in a warship-building race.

The Madison administration ordered General Dearborn and Captain Chauncey to work together to capture Kingston in April 1813, then march westward along Lake Ontario's shore to seize York and Fort George. After receiving false reports that bloated the 2,000 redcoats in Kingston to 7,000, Dearborn and Chauncey decided to sail to York instead. General Zebulon Pike led 1,700 troops ashore there on April 27. In defending York, General Scheaffe and his 700 men suffered 62 killed, 94 wounded, and 290 captured, but inflicted 320 casualties on the Americans before they fled toward Kingston. The worst carnage happened when the British detonated the fort's gunpowder magazine; Pike was among the dead. After carrying away most provisions and munitions, the Americans burned York's public buildings. The British would cite this arson to excuse their torching of Washington in August 1814.[38]

General John Vincent commanded 1,100 troops and militiamen at Fort George and Newark, and 750 troops deployed at Fort Erie and other positions along the Niagara River. He faced a mounting threat just across the Niagara River. By late May, General Morgan Lewis massed 4,500 troops around Lewiston. He assigned Colonel Winfield Scott and Captain Oliver Hazard Perry the task of carefully planning and leading an attack across the river. The American artillery opened fire on May 24. Three days later Chauncey's fleet arrived and its warships bombarded Newark and Fort George. Later on May 27, Scott led 3,000 troops packed in 180 boats across the river to land west of Fort George, then quick-marched them to the fort's rear to sever the enemy's retreat. Vincent sent 600 troops out to attack. Scott's men held steady and poured volleys into the redcoats, who fled with Vincent and the rest of the garrison to Burlington Heights. Scott was about to pursue when Lewis appeared and ordered him to secure Fort George instead. The British suffered 52 killed, 44 wounded, and 262 captured to American losses of 39 killed and 111 wounded.[39] The loss of Fort George forced the British garrisons at Queenston, Fort Chippewa, and Fort Erie to march away to avoid being cut off and forced to surrender as well. The Americans now controlled the entire Niagara River valley and as far inland as Stoney Creek, 7 miles from Burlington Heights. The ineptness of America's generals guaranteed that this dominant position would not last long.

Chauncey, with Scott and 250 troops aboard, sailed to Burlington Heights, but did not close for action before the overwhelming numbers of British cannons and troops. Reasoning that the British had marched most of their troops from nearby York, the Americans headed for Upper Canada's capital at York. Once again they faced light resistance, burned supplies, then reembarked and sailed back to the Niagara River mouth.

Vincent dispatched Colonel John Harvey with 700 troops for a dawn attack on the Americans at Stoney Creek on June 5. The hand-to-hand fighting was savage with a New York private shuddering at memories of 'Indians yelling, arms clashing, begging, groaning, dying, swearing, and fighting … our men and the British commingled, some holding each other fighting, stabbing and cutting; others with clubbed muskets thrashing the enemy down with butts.'[40] The British overran the camp, killing 55 and capturing Generals William Winder and John Chandler along with 111 Americans, while suffering 23 killed, 136 wounded, and 55 captured.[41] The Americans fled to Fort George. As the British pursued, General Dearborn, who now commanded the army, panicked and ordered all positions evacuated on Canada's side of the river except Fort George.

At Fort George, Dearborn ordered Colonel Charles Boerstler to advance with 550 troops against Beaver Dam, the most advanced British position. A force of only 46 British commanded by Lieutenant James Fitz Gibbon and 350 Indians ambushed and cut off Boerstler. During a lull in the fighting, Fitz Gibbon demanded that Boerstler give up while he could still restrain his Indians. Boerstler surrendered his 462 surviving men and 2 cannons, having suffered 30 dead and 70 wounded to Indian losses of perhaps 20 dead and 30 wounded.[42]

Meanwhile, General Prevost and Captain Yeo decided to sail from Kingston against Sackets Harbor, which they believed was lightly defended, rather than against Chauncey's fleet. Colonel Edward Baynes led 750 troops ashore on May 29. General Jacob Brown commanded 400 troops and 500 militiamen. The redcoats scattered the militiamen but broke against the volleys of the American regulars. The British fled back to the flotilla, having lost 47 dead, 154 wounded, and 16 captured to American losses of 22 killed, 85 wounded, and 154 captured. Unfortunately, an American naval officer panicked and ordered his men to burn a warehouse packed with half a million dollars' worth of supplies.[43]

Yeo then sailed around the lake's northern shore. He first ensured that Kingston was safe, dropped anchor briefly before York's smoldering ruins and then before Burlington, and finally, on August 7, reached the Niagara River mouth where Chauncey's fleet was still moored. Chauncey ordered his captains to lift anchors, unfurl sails, and man guns for battle. The disparity in their respective types of cannons determined each captain's tactics. With twice as many long-range 24-pounders, Chauncey sought to sail parallel to the British fleet and pound it from a distance. With twice as many snub-nosed 32-pounder carronades, Yeo sought to close for short-range broadsides then boarding. They maneuvered for three days as each tacked to get upwind of the other, a strategy the capricious winds frustrated. Three American schooners, top-heavy with cannons, capsized and sank on August 8. Yeo's warships caught up and captured two more schooners on the night of August 10. Chauncey finally reached Sackets Harbor's safety on August 11.

Word of Perry's crushing victory inspired Chauncey to try to do the same. On September 28, he sailed with his fleet to find and hopefully destroy Yeo's fleet. The American spotted the British and gave chase. Although Yeo escaped with most of his ships to shelter at Burlington Heights, Chauncey and his sailors did capture five schooners.

After a lull of several months, fighting on the Niagara River front erupted in December 1813. Word of a British offensive caused General George McClure on December 10, to order Fort George's garrison to abandon the fort, burn Newark and Queenston, and withdraw to the American side. General Gordon Drummond, who now commanded British forces on the Niagara front, sent 562 troops led by Colonel John Murray across the river against Fort Niagara on the night of December 18. Using the password extracted from a captured sentry, the redcoats surged into the fort, slaughtered 65 Americans and captured 344, while suffering a mere 6 killed and 5 wounded. The British held Fort Niagara for the war's duration. This same night General Phineas Riall led 500 troops and 500 Indians over to burn Lewiston, Manchester, Youngstown, and Fort Schlosser, then withdrew to Canada.

For these humiliating defeats, General Morgan Lewis became the latest American commander on the Niagara front to be cashiered and replaced by someone just as incompetent. On December 31, 1813, General Amos Hall, Lewis's replacement, marched with 2,000 militia against 1,000 British troops and 400 Indians led by Riall that crossed over to capture Black Rock. The British and Indians routed the Americans then chased them beyond

Buffalo, which they burned before returning to Canada. Hall lost 30 killed, 40 wounded, 69 captured, and eventually his post, while Riall suffered 112 casualties.[44]

The latest display of inept American leadership came after the White House tried to harness on campaign two enemies, Generals James Wilkinson and Wade Hampton, with the latter subordinate to the former. From different jump-off points, Wilkinson at Sackets Bay and Hampton at Burlington, Vermont, they were supposed to join forces and capture Montreal. A nasty competition for men and supplies rather than cooperation marred their relationship.

Hampton opened his campaign in early September, when he led 4,000 infantry, 200 dragoons, and 1,000 militiamen from Burlington across Lake Champlain to Plattsburgh, then westward to the Chateaugay River that flows into the Saint Lawrence upstream of Montreal. Although the militiamen refused to step foot into Canada on legal grounds, the presence of around 800 French Canadian militiamen led by Lieutenant Colonel Charles de Salaberry at the town of Chateaugay may have been a greater deterrent. Rather than outflank the enemy, Hampton hurled his troops directly against the Canadian breastworks on October 16. The Canadians repelled the attack, killing or wounding about 50 Americans. This was enough for Hampton, who gave up and withdrew to winter quarters at Four Corners.

It was not until October 17 that Wilkinson and 7,000 troops and militia packed into 300 boats, protected by a dozen gunboats, and began rowing north from Sackets Harbor. Wilkinson avoided Kingston and descended the Saint Lawrence River. During the night of November 6, the army ran past Fort Wellington's guns at Prescott just across from Ogdensburg, then ground ashore several miles below on the north bank. Wilkinson disembarked the brigades of Generals Alexander Macomb and Jacob Brown with the mission to clear the shore of enemy batteries ahead of the bateaux fleet. The Americans captured Fort Matilda at the river's narrowest passage on November 10. The rest of the army came ashore there, leaving most of the supplies in the boats.

Shadowing the Americans downriver were 800 redcoats led by Colonel Joseph Morrison. On November 11, Wilkinson turned his army at Crysler's Farm to attack Morrison. Stoned on laudanum, Wilkinson turned over the battle to General John Boyd and retired to his tent. The British repulsed the American assault, then counter-attacked and routed them, killing 102, wounding 237, and capturing 100, while suffering 22 killed, 148 wounded, and 9 missing.[45]

Wilkinson led his army to Cornwall, crossed the river, and marched south to winter at French Mills. Three months later, he led 4,000 north only to find his route blocked by 180 troops at Lacolle Mill on March 30, 1814. Rather than leave a covering force to starve out the defenders, Wilkinson ordered an attack which the British repulsed, inflicting 150 casualties while losing 60 dead and wounded. Wilkinson ordered his army to retreat back to French Mills. Only then did the Madison administration remove Wilkinson from command.

Britain's shipbuilding campaign surpassed that of the Americans in 1814. In May 1814, Yeo sailed with 1,000 troops led by General Gordon Drummond. Their objective was Fort Oswego, where they disembarked just beyond cannon-range on May 5. Facing overwhelming odds, the Americans abandoned the fort. The British carried away or burned 1,000 barrels of provisions, destroyed the fort, then sailed away. The raid cost the British 18 dead and 73 wounded.[46] Yeo then headed toward Sackets Harbor. Along the way on May 20, lookouts spotted 19 bateaux rowing up the Big Sandy River. Yeo packed 200 troops led by Captain Stephen Popham into longboats to pursue and destroy that supply convoy. The Americans opened fire on the British, cut them off, killed 19, wounded 28, and captured 141, at the cost of 2 men killed.[47]

The Madison administration finally picked a competent general to command the Niagara front. Jacob Brown was a militia brigadier general whose valiant defense of Sackets Harbor earned him a regular army major general's commission. He made the most of this authority. Winfield Scott was promoted to brigadier general and served as Brown's second-in-command. The campaign's first objective was Fort Erie. On July 3, Scott led his brigade across the Niagara River to deploy around the fort. The British commander surrendered with his 150 men that evening.

After learning of Scott's invasion, General Riall led 1,400 troops, 200 militiamen, and 300 Indians from Fort George to Fort Chippewa. Brown reacted to word of Riall's advance by ordering Scott to march his brigade against him, with General Peter Porter's brigade following. As the American army deployed south of the Chippewa River on July 5, the British army crossed the bridge, fanned out, and attacked. Scott expertly maneuvered his troops into line and ordered volleys that decimated the British attack. 'Those are regulars, by God!' Riall reputedly shouted in amazement.[48] The British lost 148 dead, 221 wounded, and 46 captured to Scott's 44 killed and 224 wounded, and Porter's 54 casualties.[49]

Brown had Scott spearhead the pursuit. Scott's brigade paused at Queenston. Riall rallied his troops at Fort George; reinforcements led by General Drummond swelled British ranks to 3,000 men. Scott asked Brown for permission to march around Riall's right flank. Brown, however, worried that the British army would soon outnumber his own, withdrew to Chippewa on July 24. Then, after hearing a false report that Drummond had crossed to America's side of the Niagara, Brown sent Scott forward to probe toward Queenston.

Actually Drummond had advanced with 1,600 troops on July 28, to Lundy's Lane just 7 miles from Chippewa. Scott sent a courier galloping back to Brown requesting reinforcements to support his attack. Scott tried to turn the British left flank, but the redcoats drove him back. Brown arrived with Porter's brigade and quickly assessed the situation with Scott. Brown launched an attack on the battery in the enemy line's center. After the Americans captured those cannons, Drummond advanced his flanks to catch them in a crossfire. The Americans stood their ground. The redcoats attacked. Bullets wounded Brown and Scott; Brown relinquished command to General Eleazar Ripley, who ordered the army to retreat. The British lost 84 killed, 559 wounded, and 193 missing, while the Americans suffered 173 dead, 571 wounded, and 117 missing.[50]

With Drummond hard on his heels, Ripley withdrew to Fort Erie. As Drummond deployed most of his men around Fort Erie, he had Lieutenant Colonel John Tucker lead 600 troops across the river to attack Black Rock on August 3; an American force half their size repulsed the invaders at Conjocta Creek. After two days of bombarding Fort Erie, Drummond launched an assault by three columns of troops on August 15. The Americans were ready and poured a devastating fire into the redcoats. Two columns fell back with heavy losses, while the third swarmed over a bastion and tried to turn its cannons on the defenders. Sparks ignited several gunpowder barrels and the explosion killed or wounded a hundred redcoats and scattered the rest. In all, the assault cost the British 366 dead and wounded, and 549 captured, or 1 of every 3 men, while the Americans suffered 84 casualties. Drummond resorted to trying to bombard the fort into submission. On the night of September 17, American troops sortied, overran two batteries, and spiked the guns. The British and Americans suffered 607 and 511 casualties, respectively. Drummond withdrew his shattered army to Fort George.[51] General George Izard took command from General Brown. On November 5, 1814, he ordered Fort Erie blown up and the garrison withdrawn to America's side of the border. The guns finally fell silent on the Niagara front.

America's most important victory of 1814 occurred on Lake Champlain. The British massed an army and navy at the lake's north end that appeared invincible. General George Prevost's 10,000 troops outgunned by 5 to 1 General Alexander Macomb's 1,500 regulars and 700 militiamen at Plattsburgh, while Captain George Downie's 4 warships and 12 gunboats mounted 92 cannons to the 86 cannons of Captain Thomas Macdonough's 4 warships and 10 gunboats anchored bow to stern across Plattsburgh's bay. As Prevost advanced, Macomb withdrew from Plattsburgh south beyond the Saranac River, On September 6, Prevost's army marched into Plattsburgh and there awaited Downie's fleet to appear and attack Macdonough's fleet.

To Prevost's worsening anger, this did not happen until September 11. The American vessels pounded the British warships and gunboats as they approached; although the British gunboats escaped, all four warships surrendered. The Americans suffered 52 killed and 58 wounded, and the British 57 killed, 72 wounded, and 300 captured; Downie was among the dead.[52]

Prevost, meanwhile, ordered attacks across the two Saranac River bridges, while a third column crossed a ford a mile upstream. The Americans succeeded in blunting each assault. The British suffered 37 killed, 150 wounded, and 55 captured, to American casualties of 38 killed and 64 wounded, and 20 missing. Upon learning that all four British warships had struck their colors, Prevost ordered his army to retreat to Canada, fearing that otherwise Macdonough would sail against his supply line. In his haste to get away, Prevost left behind huge amounts of provisions and munitions, while over 300 of his men deserted to the Americans.[53] Whitehall recalled Prevost to London for court martial for his failure, but he died of an apparent heart attack before he was brought to trial.

Chapter 17

High and Shallow Seas, 1812–15

Sir: As the Chesapeake appears now ready for sea, I request that you will do me the favor to meet the Shannon with her, ship to ship, to try the fortune of our respective flags.

Captain Philip Broke

I am an undone man. I am the first British naval officer that has struck his flag to an American.

Captain John Carden

There is more boasting about the defeat of one American frigate than there used to be about the defeat of whole fleets. This is no small compliment to the Americans.

William Cobbett

When President Madison and Congress started the 1812 War, America's navy numbered only seven frigates, three sloops, and seven brigs. However miniscule these numbers, they could have been far worse. If President Jefferson had had his way, he would have eliminated the entire blue-water fleet. Just as Jefferson believed in relying on militia to defend American territory, he just as zealously believed that gunboats in harbors best protected America's shores. In 1812, there were 176 gunboats rotting at anchor; they would prove to be militarily useless and thus an utter waste of the $1½ million expended to build, equip, arm, and man them.[1]

The War Hawks squared the United States off against the world's greatest naval power, whose fleet then boasted 584 warships, including 102 ships-of-the-line, 124 frigates, and 358 smaller warships. Of course, most of these warships were deployed far from North America. The British initially had only 1 ship-of-the-line, 9 frigates, and 27 smaller warships in Canadian waters, mostly at the fleet's headquarters at Halifax, Nova Scotia. The Admiralty would steadily reinforce these forces over the next two-and-a-half years.[2]

Nonetheless, in this David versus Goliath naval war, the Americans won two of three battles by capturing or sinking 17 British warships, while losing 10 warships. Three related reasons explain this – American warships were better made, manned, and armed than comparable British warships. In all, the war at sea at once inspired American jubilation and British despair.[3]

Madison enormously expanded American naval power when he signed into law the Act Concerning Letters of Marque on June 26, 1812. Indeed, American privateers actually damaged Britain strategically and economically far more than the navy. In the war's first half year, privateers captured 450 prizes while the navy took only 50. During the entire war, Lloyd's of London recorded that American privateers took over 1,175 vessels, of which 802 were either brought back to a prize court or destroyed, and 375 recaptured by British warships. These depredations forced the Admiralty to divert ever more warships from blockade to convoy duty. Trans-Atlantic insurance rates soared by 30 percent from 1812 to 1814 even though merchant ships were required to sail in huge, slow-moving convoys protected by warships.[4]

The 1812 War's first cannon shots thundered at sea. Anchored in New York's harbor was a 5-warship flotilla commanded by Commodore John Rodgers that included his flagship the 44-gun *President*, 56-gun *United States*, 38-gun *Congress*, 18-gun *Hornet*, and 16-gun *Argus*. His squadron put to sea on June 23, and chased the 38-gun *Belvidera* away from New York Bay then eastward. The *Belvidera* finally escaped when the captain ordered all extra equipment and water casks dumped overboard to lighten the load and quicken the speed. The Americans would rarely enjoy such overwhelming naval power again. Rodgers then led his squadron in search of British merchant vessels.

In mounting indignation, Admiral Herbert Sawyer, the Royal Navy's North America commander, listened to the *Belvidera*'s captain recount the chase after he brought his battered vessel to Halifax. With Rodgers' squadron at sea, Sawyer could not implement his plan of blockading each large American port. He assigned Captain Philip Broke to command a ship-of-the-line and four frigates, including the *Belvidera*, and ordered him to find Rodgers' squadron and smite the upstart Americans a very stern lesson in naval power and national superiority. After his warships captured the 14-gun *Nautilus* off Sandy Hook at New York Bay's entrance, Broke deployed them along the coast from northern New Jersey to New York Bay, with Captain James Dacres's 38-gun *Guerriere*, the southernmost.[5]

Captain Isaac Hull's 54-gun *Constitution* was sailing north from Annapolis when lookouts spotted *Guerriere* on July 12. Hull closed for action then abruptly veered eastward when the rest of Broke's squadron sailed to support the *Guerriere*. The chase lasted a week as Hull led his pursuers to Boston, where he safely anchored. Most of Broke's squadron returned to blockade New York Bay, but the *Guerriere* continued northward to protect Saint Lawrence Bay against the *Constitution* and other American warships.

Hull swiftly resupplied the *Constitution* and sailed from Boston on August 2. He steered toward Saint Lawrence Bay hoping that he and his crew would reap a fortune ravaging British merchant ships. Lookouts on the *Constitution* and *Guerriere* spotted each other on August 19, and each captain sailed directly against the other. In less than 30 minutes, the *Constitution*'s broadsides bashed the *Guerriere* to the verge of sinking. Dacres struck his colors. Hull removed the *Guerriere*'s crew before torching it.

The next epic frigate duel erupted on October 25, 1812, when Captain Stephen Decatur's 56-gun *United States* blasted Captain John Carden's 49-gun *Macedonia* into surrender. Once again superior seamanship and gunnery decided the battle. The *United States* fired over 70 broadsides to the *Macedonia*'s 30. The British crew suffered 6 killed and 72 wounded to the America crew's 7 killed and 5 wounded. This victory was especially symbolic for American propagandists since Carden had a reputation for cruelty and anti-Americanism. Being defeated by the upstart Americans enraged and shamed Carden. In delivering his sword to Decatur, Carden expressed his anguish that 'I am an undone man. I am the first British naval officer that has struck his flag to an American.' Decatur hastened to reassure him: 'You are mistaken, sir; your *Guerriere* has been taken by us, and the flag of a frigate was struck before yours.'[6]

The Americans racked up more victories, with the 18-gun *Wasp* capturing the 16-gun *Frolic* in October 1812; the 18-gun *Hornet*, the 18-gun *Peacock* in February 1813; the 46-gun *Essex*, the 20-gun *Alert* and a transport with 197 redcoats in July 1813; the 16-gun *Enterprise*, the 14-gun *Boxer* in September 1813; the 32-gun *Peacock*, the 18-gun *Epervier* in April 1814; the 32-gun *Wasp*, the 18-gun *Reindeer* in May 1814; and the *Wasp*, the 18-gun *Avon* in September 1814. Yet, the British won their share, although almost always when their warships spread far more canvas and manned far more cannons than the Americans, such as the capture of the 12-gun *Viper* by the 32-gun *Narcissus* in November 1812, the 10-gun *Argus* by the 11-gun *Pelican* in August 1813, and the 14-gun *Vixen* by the 38-gun *Belvidera* in December 1813. British expeditions destroyed some American warships in their lairs, like the 44-gun *Columbia* and 22-gun *Argus* at Washington's navy yard, and the 28-gun *Adams* at Castine, Maine. The Royal Navy, supplemented by British privateers, devastated American shipping. In all, the British captured 714 merchant ships and burned 200 or so more. They also captured or destroyed at least 93 American privateers.[7]

Captain Lawrence commanded the ill-fated 50-gun *Chesapeake*, the frigate that suffered the unprovoked British attack in 1807. In May 1813, Lawrence and his crew longed for the open sea and prize money reaped from capturing British vessels, but two frigates blocked Boston. One frigate was the 52-gun *Shannon*. Captain Philip Broke had commanded the *Shannon* for seven years, and had honed his gunners to fire rapid and deadly broadsides. On May 31, Broke issued a letter to Lawrence with these fighting words: 'Sir: As the *Chesapeake* appears now ready for sea, I request that you will do me the favor to meet the *Shannon* with her, ship to ship, to try the fortune of our respective flags.'[8] He promised that the other frigate, the 38-gun *Tenedos*, would not join the combat no matter what. Honor demanded no other course for Lawrence than to accept this challenge. On June 1, the *Chesapeake* sailed forth flying a banner reading 'Free Trade and Sailor's Rights.' The frigates closed for combat. Just 13 minutes after the first exchange of broadsides, the *Chesapeake* struck its colors. British gunners had devastated the *Chesapeake* with 362 shots, killing 48 and wounding 99, while the *Shannon* suffered 23 killed and 58 wounded while enduring 158 shots. Lawrence was among the dying, his last words: 'Don't give up the ship.'[9] News of the *Shannon*'s triumph sparked jubilation among war-weary Britons. In his Political Register, William Cobbett reported that there was 'more boasting about the defeat of one American frigate than there used to be about the defeat of whole fleets. This is no small compliment to the Americans.'[10]

America's frigate captains ventured ever further toward the ends of the earth. Captain Hull's *Constitution* encountered Captain Henry Lambert's *Java* off Brazil's coast on December 29, 1813. The *Constitution*'s broadsides so badly bashed the *Java* that, after she struck her colors, Hull ordered her sunk rather than towed to a port.

The era's most distant naval battles took place in the South Pacific. Captain David Porter commanded the 32-gun *Essex*, which, during the first half of 1813, ravaged British shipping in the South Atlantic. In June, he sailed into the Pacific, captured a dozen whalers, and converted one into the *Essex Junior*. On March 26, 1814, the two American warships were anchored at Valparaiso, Chile, when the Royal Navy's 46-gun *Phoebe* and 26-gun *Cherub* appeared. The enemy captains and crews glared at each other and waited for the others to sail from the neutral port. A storm broke the stalemate on March 28. Unsportingly, the British captains sailed against the two American warships when the *Essex* was disabled. British broadsides killed 58 and wounded 65, while only 5 British sailors were killed and 10 were wounded.[11]

Initially Whitehall was reluctant to blockade the United States.[12] Doing so would exacerbate the problems that British manufacturers suffered from their loss of European markets because of Napoleon's Continental System. The Admiralty finally derived a compromise between British strategic and economic interests. Trade would continue with New England, the largest market and a mostly anti-war region. The navy would blockade the rest of the Atlantic and Gulf coasts. Even this less comprehensive blockade took a long time to implement as ever more warships were diverted from distant seas to American waters. By February 1813, the blockade included 15 ships-of-the-line, 15 frigates, and 50 smaller warships.[13] With the reopening of Europe's markets after Napoleon's empire collapsed, the Admiralty extended the blockade to New England's coast on April 2, 1814.

The blockade devastated America's economy. Foreign trade plummeted and, with it, government revenues. Most Americans got poorer as they paid higher prices for goods. Only military contractors reaped fortunes by providing often shoddy equipment, weapons, uniforms, munitions, and provisions to the army and navy.

The Madison administration exacerbated this when, in December 1813, Congress passed a bill that prevented any American ships from leaving port, forbade any British imports, and allowed trade only in licensed neutral vessels. From 1811 to 1814, the tonnage of American ships involved in foreign trade shriveled from 948,000 to 60,000, and tariff revenues from $13.3 million to $6 million.[14] This forced the White House to perform its latest flip-flop by getting Congress to revoke the embargo in March 1813, just four months after implementing it. To fight its war, the Madison administration was forced increasingly to rely on loans at higher interest and discount rates.

As if the blockade were not damaging and humiliating enough, the British launched coastal raids to devastate American communities. During spring 1813, Admiral George Cockburn's flotilla systematically looted and burned, and occasionally raped and murdered its way around Chesapeake Bay, leaving behind smoldering ruins at Frenchtown, Havre de Grace, Georgetown, Fredericktown, Principio, and Hampton.[15] Cockburn boasted that his men 'soon became experts at the art of burning Yankee property.'[16] Lieutenant Charles Napier was among the few Britons ashamed of these crimes against humanity, with 'every horror … committed with impunity, rape, murder, pillage; and not a man was punished.'[17] Yet, typically, the Americans were their own worst enemies. All along, Jefferson's much vaunted militiamen and gunboat crews could only helplessly watch the destruction of their communities from a safe distance when they did not flee beyond the horizon.

Duels between American and British warships dwindled as the blockade tightened. By early 1813, the Royal Navy had 10 ships-of-the-line, 38 frigates, and 52 smaller warships in American waters, now under Admiral John Warren's command.[18] The British bottled up more American warships in their ports until by late 1814 almost none were at sea. Of America's frigates, the Royal Navy plugged the *Constitution* at Boston, the *Constellation* at Norfolk, the *Adams* at Alexandria, the *President* at Newport, and the *United States* at New London.

Victories in the war's last naval battles spilt one to two between Britain and America. On January 14, 1815, 3 British frigates, the 40-gun *Endymion*, 38-gun *Pomone*, and 38-gun *Tenedos* caught up to Captain Stephen Decatur's 52-gun *President* and pounded him into striking his colors. On February 20, 1815, the *Constitution*, now commanded by Captain Charles Stewart, squared off against the 34-gun *Cyrene* and 20-gun *Levant* near Madeira, and battered them both into surrendering. On March 23, the 20-gun *Hornet* captured the 19-gun *Penguin* after a running fight.

Overall, the naval war between Britain and America was far more important psychologically than strategically. The two to one ratio of victories at sea over the British diverted Americans from the mostly dismal news from the frontier. Of course, this same news had the opposite effect on Britain's politicians and public.

The absurdity of fighting the United States struck ever more Britons. Opposition members of Parliament pointed out that the war cost £10 million a year, five times the Royal Navy's £2 million payroll. Simply by tripling wages, the Royal Navy could solve its recruitment problem and thus no longer need to press American sailors. This policy would simultaneously end the reason for the war and save money. Conservatives blasted this proposal. Britain was fighting America for more important reasons than mere money – the nation's sacred honor was at stake. The war would continue until Britain had satisfied its honor.[19]

Chapter 18

Spain, 1812

It appears certain that Marmont will not risk an action unless he should have an advantage; and I shall certainly not risk an action unless I should have an advantage.

Wellington

The People ... are absolutely mad for joy. They look up to Lord Wellington as a God and call him the Saviour of their Country.

Major Alexander Gordon

The year 1812 was the turning point in the wars against Napoleon. At Europe's far eastern end, the emperor launched his disastrous invasion of Russia, while at the other end, Wellington finally gained the upper hand over Iberia. To bolster his Russian invasion forces, Napoleon reduced his forces in the Peninsula from the peak of 350,000 in 1811 to 230,000 by mid-1812. As intelligence reports of French withdrawals reached him, Wellington became increasingly optimistic about allied prospects: 'Strong as the enemy are at present ... they are weaker than they have ever been during the war ... We have a better chance of success now ... than we have ever had.'[1]

Wellington's 45,000 troops reached and surrounded Cuidad Rodrigo on January 8, 1812. The walled town was on a low rise on the Agueda River's north bank and within cannon range of surrounding low hills. Wellington's batteries opened fire on January 13 and by January 19 had battered four breaches around the wall. The garrison refused to surrender.

Wellington ordered an assault that night, with a column charging each breach. The fighting was as surreal as it was bloody:

A tremendous fire was opened upon us, and, as our column was entering the ditch, [a] ... magazine on the ramparts blew up ... the night was brilliantly illuminated for some moments, and everything was made visible. Then as suddenly came utter darkness, except for flashes from cannon and muskets which threw a momentary glare.[2]

As the redcoats fought through the breaches and spread out through the town, eventually 1,937 defenders threw down their muskets and surrendered. The British suffered 568 casualties in the assault and around 1,100 during the entire short siege, while 530 French were killed or wounded; among the dead was General Robert Craufurd, the Light Division's commander.[3]

The violence did not end with the surrender. To the shame of many British troops, their comrades:

> ... more eager for plunder than their duty, broke and ran in defiance of their officers ... and committed shameful excesses disgraceful to the whole army ... The dead were scarcely cold when they were inhumanely stripped ... Some men were so drunk that they fired promiscuously in the streets and killed many of their comrades.[4]

Countless paused to guzzle wine then, 'having drunk sufficiently ... again sallied out in quest of more plunder; others got so intoxicated that they lay in a helpless state in different parts of the town, and lost what they had previously gained.'[5] It took three days before the officers restored their men to order.

British newspapers trumpeted only Cuidad Rodrigo's capture, not the horrors that followed. Most of the war-weary public was ecstatic at the clear-cut victory. The government elevated Wellington from viscount to earl, and doubled his bonus to £4,000.

For nearly five weeks Wellington rested his army, replenishing its ranks and supplies. He then sent General Rowland Hill with 14,000 troops east to Merida to blunt any advance by Marshal Auguste Marmont's 22,000-men army at Salamanca. Leaving a strong force at Cuidad Rodrigo, he marched south with most of the army toward Badajoz on March 6. Ten days later they arrived and encircled the city just beyond cannon shot.

Badajoz was a far tougher fortress to besiege than Ciudad Rodrigo. It crowned a mesa on the Guadiana River's south bank. A bridge led across the river to Fort San Cristobal. General Armand Phillipon and 4,000 French troops defended Badajoz. The land spreading from the mesa was hard, rocky, mostly flat earth. The best place for siege guns was a low rise southeast of the city. By the rainy night of March 19, the British had spent several exhausting days constructing a battery there. The French sallied against the battery, bayoneted or routed the defenders, spiked the guns, and retired with as many tools as they could carry. The French and British suffered 180 and 150 casualties, respectively.[6] The British repaired the damage and from there forked four parallel lines closer to Badajoz. A 28–gun battery was emplaced by March 25 and opened fire. Three smaller batteries were completed over the next five days. By March 30, 38 cannons were steadily blasting portions of the wall to rubble.

Hill and his division rejoined Wellington with intelligence, later found to be false, that the armies of Massena and Soult were preparing to march to Badajoz's relief. This prompted Wellington to order a night assault against three breaches on April 6. The fighting was hellish. Sergeant William Lawrence:

> … was one of the ladder party … On our arriving at … the wall … a shower of shot, canister, and grape … was hurled … amongst us … I received two small … shots in my left knee and a musket shot in my side … Still I stuck to my ladder … Numbers had by this time fallen but … we hastened to the breach. There … we found a cheval de fries had been fixed … Vain efforts were made to remove this fearful obstacle, during which my left hand was fearfully cut by one of the blades … We were forced to retire … My wounds were still bleeding … My comrades persuaded me to the rear, but this proved a task of great difficulty for on arriving at the ladders I found them filled with the dead and wounding hanging … just as they had fallen … so I crawled on my hands and knees till I got out of the reach of the enemy's musketry.[7]

Private John Donaldson recalled that the French:

> … threw fire balls in every direction' to illuminate the attackers 'and they opened a fire of round and grape shot which raked through them, killing and wounding whole sections … We … got down into the ditch … When the ladders were placed, each eager to mount [the troops] crowded them in such a way that many of them broke, and the poor fellows who had nearly reached the top were precipitated a height of thirty to forty feet and impaled on the bayonets of their comrades below … while [troops] who got to the top without accident were shot on reaching the parapet, and, tumbling headlong, brought down those beneath them.[8]

The French repulsed the first wave of assaults. Wellington ordered a second wave. This time the British broke through and spread out through the maze of streets. Phillipon ordered his surviving men to lay down their arms. The siege of Badajoz cost the British 4,670 casualties, with 3,713 killed and wounded during the assault.[9]

The sack of Badajoz was even more vicious than that of Cuidad Rodrigo, with mass murders and mass rapes accompanying systematic looting. Robert Blakeney, a young subaltern of the 28th Regiment, was appalled that the 'infuriated soldiery resembled ... a pack of hell-hounds vomited up from the infernal regions for the extirpation of mankind than ... a well organized, brave, disciplined, and obedient British army.' Officers were powerless to stop their men and sometimes joined in:

> There was no safety for women even in the churches, and any who interfered or offered resistance were sure to get shot. Every house presented a scene of plunder, debauchery, and bloodshed committed with wanton cruelty ... by our soldiery, and in many instances I saw the savages tear the rings from the ears of beautiful women ... when the savages came to a door which had been locked or barricaded, they applied ... the muzzles of a dozen firelocks ... fired off together ... Men, women, and children were shot ... for no other ... reason than pastime.[10]

Wellington left Hill with his division to guard Badajoz's devastated ruins while he hurried with the rest of his army back to Cuidad Rodrigo. After arriving there on April 22, he spent a month repairing the fortress and massing supplies. He then sent Hill orders to destroy the bridge at Almaraz on the Tagus and thus sever the road linking Salamanca and Seville. Leaving half his division at Badajoz, Hill quick-marched 7,000 troops to Almaraz, routed a 360-man French garrison, blew up the bridge on May 18, then withdrew to Badajoz. Couriers now had to gallop messages between Marmont and Soult twice as far via the bridge over the Tagus at Toledo.

Wellington devised a grand allied strategy designed to liberate Spain's western half from French domination. Wellington would march directly toward Marmont's 49,000 troops at Salamanca. Hill's 19,000 troops would drive off General Jean Baptiste Drouet, count d'Erlon's 12,000 troops near Merida. Antonio Ballesteros's 18,000 troops would threaten Marshal Nicholas Soult's 25,000 deployed around Seville. Admiral Home Popham would land several thousand soldiers and marines to join General Gabriel Mendizabal in operations against General Jean Dorsenne's scattered army of 35,000 troops along a swath of northern Spain. General Jose Santocildes would take Astorga and the surrounding region. Portuguese General Francisco

Silveira would take Zamora on the Douro River. General Thomas Maitland would land 11,000 British, Sicilian, and Spanish troops someplace along Spain's Catalonian coast to threaten Marshal Louis Suchet's 25,000-man army around Valencia and General Charles Decaen's 15,000 troops around Barcelona.

The allied campaigns in the southwest and north failed to inflict major defeats on the French. A division of Soult's army routed Ballesteros before Hill reached him, forcing Hill to withdraw north before superior French forces. Mendizabal and Popham captured Santander then Bilbao. General Marie Caffarelli, who replaced Dorsenne, recaptured Bilbao after two days of hard fighting. Mendizabal and Popham retreated to and held Santander, which would serve as a crucial forward supply base for Wellington's 1813 campaign. Spanish troops eventually besieged Astorga, Toro, and Zamora, but failed to take those fortress cities. Maitland landed near Alicante but was forced to withdraw after learning that one of Suchet's divisions had routed Jose O'Donnell's 12,000 men. All these operations were sideshows to Wellington and his army in the center ring.

With his divisions split among three columns, Wellington led his army toward Salamanca on June 13, and four days later they marched unopposed into the city. Marmont withdrew northward beyond cavalry screening the horizon. Left behind were 800 French garrisoning a complex of 3 fortified convents on the city's south edge overlooking the Tormes River. Wellington detached Henry Clinton's division to take that fort while he deployed the rest of his men along a line of low hills and ridges centered on San Christobal village north of Salamanca.

Marmont advanced within sight on June 20, but kept most of his men beyond cannon shot as small detachments of cavalry and light infantry probed the enemy lines. Over the next two days skirmishes cost each side a couple hundred casualties. Wellington observed that 'It appears to me that they are as determined as me not to fight.'[11] Hoping that Wellington would follow, Marmont withdrew to Huerta on the Tormes River during the night of June 22. Meanwhile on June 26, after several days of bombardment, Clinton's troops stormed the fortified convents and killed or captured the 800-man garrison while suffering 430 casualties.[12]

For a month Marmont waited in worsening impatience for Wellington to take the bait. Wellington meanwhile hoped that the enemy would come to him, explaining that: 'It appears certain that Marmont will not risk an action unless he should have an advantage; and I shall certainly not risk an action unless I should have an advantage; and matters therefore do not appear likely to be brought to that criterion very soon.'[13]

Marmont lost patience first. On July 21, he marched his army south across the Tormes River upstream of Salamanca then arced around to threaten Wellington's supply line. Wellington led most of his army south of the river to parallel the enemy's march. Major Gordon noted that it 'was beautiful to see two armies making together 100,000 men maneuvering so near one another.'[14] Numerically the armies were nearly dead even. Wellington's 48,569 troops were split among 6 line divisions led by Generals Henry Campbell, Edward Pakenham, Lowry Cole, James Leith, Henry Clinton, and John Hope, the Light Division by Charles Alten, and the cavalry brigade by Stapleton Cotton. The infantry and cavalry numbered 25,577 and 3,543 British, and 17,421 and 482 Portuguese, respectively. Finally, there were 54 British cannons with 1,186 gunners, and a 6-cannon, 114-man Portuguese battery. Marmont's army was slightly larger, 49,999 troops including 41,575 infantry in 8 divisions, 3,390 cavalry, and 5,034 gunners manning 78 cannons.[15]

On July 22, most of Wellington's troops were deployed on the reverse slopes of low hills and ridges known as Los Arapiles a half-dozen miles southeast of Salamanca. Famously Wellington was munching a chicken leg and scanning the French divisions strung out across 4 miles of the plains beyond, when he exclaimed: 'By God, that will do!' He mounted his horse, cantered to General Pakenham nearby, and ordered him immediately to lead his division against the French before him. He then sent couriers galloping to his other infantry, cavalry, and artillery commanders with the same message.[16]

Psychologically the footsore French were unready for battle. They assumed that Wellington would continue to shadow them until they found an opportunity to attack. So the sudden appearance and dash of Wellington's divisions down the slopes unnerved them. The French generals ordered their troops to face the onslaught, load, and prepare to fire. The battle lasted only a few hours as one British division after another shattered the French division before it. British General William Gomm recalled that 'the spirit of our people rose … when they reached the enemy's solid columns' and they 'opened a fire like a volcano upon them, there was … a general shout of exultation … The enemy wavered … till … complete rout ensured.'[17]

As the sun set Wellington did something he later regretted. Most of the French were retreating southeast toward Alba, which he thought Spanish troops still held, but they had evacuated the town two days earlier. So he ordered his troops to march toward Huerta, assuming that Marmont would try to escape that way: 'When I lost sight of them in the dark, I marched upon Huerta … and they went by Alba. If I had known there had been no garrison in Alba, I should have marched there, and should probably have had the whole.'[18]

Nonetheless, Wellington scored a decisive victory, as his troops inflicted 12,000 casualties on the French, and captured 2,500 troops, 12 cannons, and 2 imperial eagles, while suffering 5,214 casualties, including 3,176 British and 2,038 Portuguese.[19] Marmont was among those grievously wounded. Wellington nearly was; a bullet ricocheted off his saddle holster and grazed his thigh. French General Maximilien Foy later gallantry paid tribute to Wellington:

> The battle of Salamanca is the most masterly … [and] raises Lord Wellington's reputation almost to the level of Marlborough. Hitherto we had been aware of his prudence, his eye for choosing a position, and his skill in utilizing it. At Salamanca he has shown himself a great and able master of maneuvers. He kept his dispositions concealed for almost the whole day. He waited till we were committed to our movements before he developed his own … He fought in the oblique order – it was a battle in the style of Frederick the Great.[20]

For a few days Wellington pursued the French army's remnants, now commanded by General Bertrand Clausel, as they fled northeastward. The heaviest fighting erupted on July 23, when British cavalry charged the French army's rear guard near Garcia Hernandez, broke several squares, and inflicted 1,400 casualties. Wellington's troops marched unopposed into Valladolid on July 29, and captured 17 cannons and 800 convalescing French troops.

The word that King Joseph was marching with 17,000 troops to join Clausel prompted Wellington to reconsider his strategy. If the report was true, then only a few thousand French troops now guarded the capital and its huge supply depot. If Wellington captured Madrid, France's grip on Spain would suffer a massive military and political blow. On August 6, he detached General Clinton with 18,000 troops to join Spanish General Santocildes's army and together tail Clausel, while he led the rest of his army east toward Madrid via Segovia.

The word that Joseph was heading north to join Clausel was wrong. Actually, he was heading in the opposite direction. Typically, he panicked at word of Salamanca and Wellington's pursuit of Claudel. He ordered Soult to abandon the siege of Cádiz and mass his forces. But, rather than order Soult to march north, join forces with d'Erlon, and advance against Wellington's rear, Joseph urged him to withdraw eastward toward Valencia. Joseph, his chief of staff Marshal Jean Baptiste Jourdan, 18,000 troops, 15,000 civilians, and 2,000 wagons left Madrid on August 10 and hurried to join Soult and d'Erlon at Valencia on September 16.[21]

Wellington's march to Madrid became a triumphal procession. Major Gordon recalled the 'universal joy of the inhabitant in every place we pass through, and their detestation of the French is certainly as great as it ever was.'[22] On August 12, Wellington led his army into Madrid, where they reveled in being 'feted by the People' who 'are absolutely mad for joy. They look up to Lord Wellington as a God and call him the Saviour of their Country; thousands of people when he is public come to embrace him, and are too happy to kiss his hands, knees or the hem of his garment.'[23] The 2,500 French troops garrisoning the Retiro, a castle at Madrid's edge, surrendered 2 days later.

Wellington's 1812 campaign did not end with Madrid's occupation, but entered its latest critical phase. His army was lodged between Soult's 60,000 troops southward and Clausel's 40,000 troops northward that was marching against Santocildes and Clinton. Hill's army of 19,000 British and Portuguese, and 4,000 Spanish troops was at Toledo.

Wellington decided to head north and trap Clausel against Clinton, leaving Hill to protect his rear. Strategically this plan was superior to awaiting Soult in Madrid or marching south against him. Indeed Spain's capital was indefensible, as Major Gordon remarked: 'Madrid from its situation can never be made a point of stand, and must always be abandoned when the circumstances require it.'[24] By concentrating British forces at Burgos in northern Spain and linking with Popham and the Royal Navy at Santander, Wellington threatened to sever France's communication line that stretched from Bayonne then branched out across Spain. If he did so, then most French forces would have only the tenuous communication line leading from Perpignan at the Pyrenees Mountains' east end. In the spring, Wellington could either march into France at Bayonne or toward Barcelona.

Wellington led his men north on August 31. Learning of Wellington's advance, Clausel hurried his army to Burgos, garrisoned the citadel with 2,200 troops, and withdrew to Vitoria. Wellington's army reached Burgos on September 18, but, with their largest guns 3 18-pounders, could not mount a proper siege. The following day, he launched an assault that the French repulsed, inflicting 421 casualties while suffering 198. Wellington reckoned that if his troops could not batter down the walls they could undermine them. His troops inched siege lines and tunnels toward the citadel. On September 29, engineers detonated a mine beneath the west wall but it failed to open a breach. On October 4, a mine detonated and blasted open a small gap, but the French repelled the subsequent assault with heavy losses. On October 18, a third mine was detonated and assault mounted with an even bloodier failure:

> A most tremendous fire opened upon us from … front and rear … They poured down fresh men, and ours kept falling into the ditch, dragging and knocking down others. We were so close that they fairly put their muskets into our faces, and we pulled one of their men through an enclosure … We had hardly any men left on the top, and at last we gave way. How we got over the palisade I know not … the fire was tremendous: shot, shell, grape, musketry, large stones, hand grenades … were used against us.[25]

So far the siege had cost Wellington 2,059 casualties, while 1,400 French remained defiant in the citadel, having suffered 623 killed and wounded.[26]

Despite the stalemate at Burgos, the Peninsula's center of strategic gravity had shifted decisively over the past few months. Allied armies had pushed French armies back from the Portuguese frontier and the toehold of Cádiz to Spain's eastern half. Soult with 60,000 troops was reported halfway between Valencia and Madrid. General Joseph Souham, who replaced Clausel, commanded about 42,000 troops at Victoria. General Marie Caffarelli had 11,000 troops at Bilbao. Marshal Louis Suchet's 20,000 troops held the region around Valencia, and General Decean's 15,000 troops deployed in Catalonia's cities. At Burgos, Wellington's 34,000 troops were roughly equal parts British, Portuguese, and Spanish. Hill and 36,000 troops, including 28,000 British and Portuguese, and 8,000 Spaniards, were deployed in the region around Madrid. Popham and 1,500 marines held Santander. Spanish forces had reestablished control over much of western and central Spain. In the southwest, the French abandoned their siege of Cádiz on August 24; General Ballesteros with 16,000 troops and General John Skerrett with 5,500 redcoats marched forth, entered Seville unopposed on August 27, and took possession of vast amounts of supplies and 500 cannons. Skerrett then marched to join Hill. Wellington and Hill occupied Spain's strategic center and could join to march with a superior force against Souham or Soult.

Nonetheless, Wellington saw more dangers than opportunities as he mulled the strategic situation. Intelligence reports claimed that Soult was marching against Hill at Madrid while Caffarelli and Souham had joined forces and were fast approaching him at Burgos. His worst worry was that the Spaniards typically would snatch defeat from victory's jaws: 'Everything in which the Spaniards are concerned is going as badly as possible, and I really believe there is not a man in the country ... capable of comprehending, much less of conducting, any great concern.'[27] Captain William Swabey echoed this prevailing fear:

> The fundamental cause of our giving up Madrid I attribute to the total abandonment of the slightest hope that the Spaniards will ever do anything to help themselves. The trial was fairly made during our possession of Madrid. The imbecility of their government, but more than all their national vanity, blinded them to the necessity of active and efficient measures and rendered the opportunity useless. The moment of action whilst the country was in possession of their government was lost.[28]

After sending orders for Hill to meet him at Salamanca, Wellington broke off the siege of Burgos and led his army westward on October 21. Two days later, 6,000 French cavalry caught up and charged 1,300 British cavalry guarding Wellington's rear; the fight cost the French 300 and the British 230 casualties. Wellington picked up his retreat's pace; his army marched 26 days over mostly flat ground the next day. Souham quickened his own army's pace. The allied rear and French advance guards clashed almost daily.[29] After Hill joined Wellington at Salamanca on November 8, the army numbered 52,000 British and Portuguese, and 18,000 Spaniards. Soult and Souham were fast converging and when they did would number 95,000 troops.

Wellington ordered his army to withdraw on November 15. The winter rains turned the roads into quagmires 'nearly knee-deep in a stiff mud into which no man could thrust his foot with the certainty of having a shoe at the end of it when he pulled it out again.'[30] Wood was so soaked that it was nearly impossible to ignite for cooking and warmth. The draft animals died from lack of fodder. In the diminishing army's wake were scores of spiked cannons, blown up caissons, and burned supply wagons, and 3,000 stragglers that either died or surrendered to the French. That was not all: 'Many peasants lay dead by the roadside, murdered ... The old trade was going on, killing ... and capturing our daily bread.'[31] Wellington's army was mostly a mob when he called a halt at Cuidad Rodrigo on November 19. Wellington blamed the Spanish for his army's plight: 'My plan was to bring Ballesteros upon the left flank of Soult's march ... If this game had been well played, it would have answered my purpose.'[32] Scapegoating the Spaniards for his own failure was unfair. That said, Ballesteros did react to news of Wellington's appointment as commander-in-chief by declaring he would never obey him.

Wellington's retreat from Burgos dismally ended an otherwise dazzling year of victories. In all, his forces captured over 20,000 French troops and killed or wounded another 10,000, while incurring about 12,000 casualties. His triumph at Salamanca revealed that he was as brilliant at launching attacks as he was at defending well-chosen positions. It took him only 12 days to capture Cuidad Rodrigo and 20 days to capture Badajoz. His only defeats were at the siege of Burgos, where he suffered 2,000 casualties, and the retreat from Salamanca to Cuidad Rodrigo where he lost 3,000 troops to death or capture.

As importantly, Wellington revealed himself to be as outstanding a strategist as he was a tactician. The Peninsula's strategic fulcrum had shifted decisively eastward from western to central Spain. Although Wellington withdrew his army to Cuidad Rodrigo, allied forces liberated Spain's northwest and southwest. Popham's force continued to hold Santander midway along the north coast. An allied force captured Alicante on the east coast. The westernmost French forces were now at Salamanca. The French retook Madrid without a fight, but they would render it just as easily the next year.

Upon learning of his stunning victory against Marmont near Salamanca, Parliament voted Wellington £100,000 while Prince Regent George titled him a marquess. Wellington received a Spanish gift that he at once welcomed and cursed – the Cortes decreed on September 22, that Wellington was henceforth the generalissimo or commander-in-chief of the Spanish army. He did not immediately accept the command, but said he first needed Whitehall's approval. That came on November 22. Wellington viewed the title as far more trouble than it was worth. He feared that no one would obey him while everyone would blame him for whatever went wrong

Wellington's initial dark pessimism lightened early in 1813. News of Napoleon's devastating defeat in Russia inspired joyous celebrations. Reinforcements and supplies steadily replenished his army. In late January Wellington successfully concluded a week of negotiating his powers as generalissimo with Spain's government in Cádiz. Major Gordon observed that:

Lord Wellington returned here two days ago, and has succeeded in everything he wished with the Regency and Cortes. He has the entire command of their Armies and nomination of their officers. In short he has the military power and resources of the Country so completely in his hands, that … he is in hope of being able to make something of their Armies.[33] Unfortunately, the performance of Spain's politicians, generals, merchants, and soldiers would fall far short of the promises.

Chapter 19

Spain, 1813

I am certain that I shall never be stronger ... or more efficient than I am now; and the enemy will never be weaker. I cannot have a better opportunity for trying the fate of battle, which, if the enemy should be unsuccessful, must oblige him to withdraw entirely.

Wellington

Napoleon's 1812 Russian campaign cost him over half a million troops, several hundred thousand horses, a thousand cannons, and his reputation for invincibility. While no one believed that peace was imminent, hope awakened among Napoleon's enemies that the war's end hovered just beyond history's horizon either through diplomacy or his destruction by allied armies. As for the Russian campaign's impact on the Peninsular War, Prime Minister Robert Jenkinson, Earl of Liverpool wrote Wellington a reasonable but wrong prediction: 'The most formidable army ever collected by Bonaparte has been substantially destroyed ... Under these circumstances the question naturally occurs whether he will leave the French army in Spain? ... Whatever it may cost Bonaparte to abandon Spain, I think he will prefer that alternative to the loss of Germany.'[1]

Napoleon was deadset to cling to both, and in doing so accelerated his ultimate demise. In early 1813, around 150,000 French troops remained in Spain. The two largest clusters included Marshal Louis Suchet with 40,000 troops along the northeast coast from Valencia to Gerona, and General Bertrand Clausel with 60,000 troops across western central Spain. About half of Clausel's men were scattered in detachments and the rest split among three corps defending Salamanca led by Generals Honore Gazan, Jean Baptiste Drouet, comte d'Erlon, and Honore Reille, each with about 12,000 troops. Contingents of French troops garrisoned cities and fortresses along routes leading eventually either to Bayonne or Perpignan in France at opposite ends of the Pyrenees Mountains. King Joseph abandoned Madrid on March 17, and headed north to establish his capital at Vitoria, within a few days' carriage ride of France.

Wellington designed his 1813 campaign plan to drive the French from the Peninsula. Each allied army was to mass and march against the largest French force in the region. He had good reason to be highly confident of success: 'I am certain that I shall never be stronger ... or more efficient than I am now; and the enemy will never be weaker. I cannot have a better opportunity for trying the fate of battle, which, if the enemy should be unsuccessful, must oblige him to withdraw entirely.'[2]

Wellington immediately commanded 81,000 British and Portuguese troops, and 21,000 Spanish troops. Elsewhere, there were about 12,000 Spanish and British troops threatening French-held cities in northern Spain, Jose O'Donnell's 14,000 men poised to march on Madrid, and 50,000 Spanish troops deployed either near Marshal Suchet around Valencia or General Charles Decaen near Barcelona. General John Murray was poised to land his 8,000 troops near Alicante and link with Spanish troops.

Shoe-leather rather than gunpowder was crucial for winning the 1813 campaign's first phase. Wellington ensured that each man started the campaign with three pairs of shoes along with a new uniform. He ordered the men to discard their winter coats and carry only one blanket; for warmth and shelter, the men could huddle within large tents borne by mules. Tin pots replaced cast-iron pots. With these changes, he at once raised his men's morale, lightened their loads, and strengthened their health. Francis Seymour Larpent, Wellington's advocate general, explained:

Last year the mules per company allowed by government were employed in carrying the heavy iron camp-kettles, and our men had no tents: though they were allowed them, they could not be carried. This year, Lord Wellington has light tin kettles made, one for every six men ... to be carried by one of the men ... This plan sets the mules free, and thus three tents have been carried for every company, and ... this now ... contributes much to the health of the army.'[3] Wellington honed his men's skills and further bolstered their moral with daily hours of close order drill and target practice. One soldier recalled: 'We were very busy with parades and drills and field days ... [Wellington] never came near us without a cheer from the men that made the wood ring.[4]

Wellington launched his campaign on May 22. He split his army in two and cantered between them to coordinate their movements. While General Rowland Hill with 30,000 troops in 2 divisions marched straight toward

Salamanca, General Thomas Graham looped 50,000 troops in 6 divisions north of the Douro River to sever Clausel's retreat. The French fled the twin juggernauts. Hill's army marched unopposed into Salamanca on May 26, Graham's army into Zamora on June 2, and the two forces joined at Toro on June 3. The French withdrew so swiftly that the advanced allied guard fought few skirmishes and collected many stranglers. For virtually all the soldiers:

> ... our march for the first two or three hundred miles was like a party of pleasure in comparison to others ... We passed through a most delightful level country, abounding in all the verdant beauties of nature ... Everything and every countenance now wore ... joy, the men singing and telling their jocose stories.[5]

Wellington's shift of his base of operations from Lisbon to Santander further propelled the campaign. The army did not have to drag heavy siege guns all the way from Portugal, but instead united with them in northern Spain. This freed more draft animals and wagons to carry supplies, which, in turn, kept the soldiers fitter, fleeter, and less inclined to plunder farm houses along the way.

After withdrawing his forces in northern and central Spain east to Vitoria, Joseph counted 66,000 troops, including 49,000 infantry, 11,300 cavalry, and 5,700 gunners manning 138 cannons. Wellington immediately commanded 79,062 troops: 61,741 infantry – 27,273 British, 27,560 Portuguese, and 6,800 Spaniards; 8,317 cavalry – 7,244 British and 893 Portuguese; and 3,300 gunners manning 78 British and 12 Portuguese cannons. Heading the line divisions were Generals Kenneth Howard, William Stewart, Thomas Picton, Lowry Cole, John Oswald, and George Dalhousie, while Charles Alten led the Light Division and General Stapleton Cotton the cavalry division; there was a Portuguese division and two independent Portuguese brigades.[6]

Taking full advantage of his overwhelming strength, Wellington split his army into four columns, sent two directly at Joseph's troops deployed around Vitoria, and each other column to arc around and hit the enemy in the flank or, ideally, rear. What Wellington aimed at on June 21, 1813, was that holy grail for generals, the double envelopment. He nearly pulled it off. General Robert Long recalled that during the battle the French 'behaved very ill. Their position was very strong and with ... spirit their defense might have been brilliant. But their infantry did not stand as I expected they would, their cavalry could be of no use from the nature of the ground, and when they saw themselves turned a panic seized the whole.'[7] The 82nd regiment's experience, as related by Subaltern George Wood, typified the fighting that day: 'Our front was exposed to … a French regiment on the right of the battery, but after … a few sharp volleys, which we … returned, they … retreated into a thicket. Toward this we advanced firing, and drove them furiously before us till they were completely routed.'[8] The French did not give way so easily everywhere. Cavalryman William Hay's regiment:

> soon came in sight of the French cavalry … Our trumpet sounded the charge when … their flanks were thrown back, and there stood, formed in squares, about 3,000 infantry. These opened such a close and well-directed fire on our advance squadrons that, not only were we brought to a standstill, but the … leading squadrons went about, and order was not restored till a troop of horse artillery arrived on our flank and … opened such a fire of grape that … I saw men fall like a pack of cards.[9]

The allies inflicted on the French 7,999 casualties, including 756 killed, 4,414 wounded, and 2,829 captured or missing, while suffering 5,148 casualties, including 3,675 British, 921 Portuguese, and 552 Spaniards.[10] Although Joseph escaped with most of his troops, he lost all but 2 of his cannons, over 500 caissons, his entire supply train, and 5 million francs. Wellington was incensed when he learned that some generals and soldiers alike had spoiled an even more decisive victory. His double envelopment might have completely blocked the French retreat had Graham fulfilled his orders to loop around from the north, sever the road to Bayonne, and march into Vitoria. Instead, he let his men get bogged down in a fight for the village of Gamarra Mayor, where he should have left a covering force and pushed on to his objectives.

The allied army would certainly have taken far more prisoners had not so many troops stopped to loot the French supply train. The looting moved to Vitoria where for days 'houses, shops, and government officers are burgled … The inhabitants of the pueblos round about are hesitant about coming into town with the result that trade has fallen off and food run short.'[11] The turmoil in the allied rear endangered their diligent comrades who trailed the French. Captain Thomas Browne was chasing the enemy with the 18th Hussars when:

... we overtook a line of carriages and baggage, which offered so much temptation to many of the soldiers ... that they could not resist falling to ... plunder, whilst others with their officers continued in pursuit. The squadron was thus considerably weakened in number ... The French rearguard ... suddenly detached a body of cavalry ... which, falling on the few of the Eighteenth who were in advance, killed some, wounded others, and took some prisoners. In this last lot I was myself included, my horse having been killed, and my head cut longitudinally with a sabre so as to knock me over.[12]

Wellington complained that the victory:

... annihilated all order and discipline. The soldiers ... have got among them about a million sterling in money ... The night of the battle, instead of being passed in getting rest and food to prepare for the pursuit of the following day, was spent by the soldiers ... in plunder. The consequence was that they were incapable of marching in pursuit of the enemy.[13]

Yet Wellington needed only a day or so to restore order and vigorously pursue the French army's remnants that had disintegrated into a mob without cannons, munitions, or supplies. Indeed he could have advanced to the French frontier, mopping up thousands of enemy troops along the way. But prudence kept him from turning a decisive into a devastating victory. Wellington's caution after Victoria contrasted with Napoleon's ruthless annihilation of most of the remaining Prussian army after his army won the twin battles of Jena and Auerstadt in 1806.

Wellington had a good if not unassailable reply to this criticism:

After having driven the French from the frontiers of Portugal ... to the frontiers of France, it is generally expected that we shall invade France, and some even expect that we shall be at Paris in a month. None appear to have taken a correct view of our situation ... An army which has ... fought such battles ... has much deteriorated ... The equipment ... ammunition, the soldiers' shoes require renewal; the magazines for the new operations require to be collected ... then observe that this new operation is the invasion of France, in which country everybody is a soldier, where the whole population is armed and organized ... the majority of them ... have served somewhere.[14]

Yet, looking back much later, Wellington conceded that his post-Vitoria strategy of getting bogged down in northern Spain rather than relentlessly pursuing the beaten French army back into its homeland was 'one of the greatest faults he committed during the war.'[15]

What Wellington did instead was mass forces to besiege the last major French-held fortresses in northern Spain, San Sebastian and Pamplona. This should have been a job for the Spanish army, while he dashed with his British and Portuguese troops toward Bayonne. Allied troops approached Pamplona on June 25. The only large battle immediately following Vitoria was at Tolosa on June 27, when Graham's 26,000 troops routed General Maximilien Foy's 16,000. Graham did not pursue Foy but instead veered north to San Sebastian, arriving on June 29.

San Sebastian lay on a headland surrounded on three sides by water, with the sea on the west and north sides, and the Urumea River flowing past on the east side; a narrow isthmus connected San Sebastian to the mainland. Concentric walls protected the town and a citadel crowned the headland's heights. General Louis Rey commanded the 2,996-man garrison.[16] Beginning on July 7, Graham's engineers supervised the digging of trenches and mines ever closer to the town. Batteries of 24-pounders systematically demolished the walls and buildings: 'The guns have each fired upwards of 300 rounds ... daily between daybreak and sunset ... Great part of the town is ruin by our fire. The crashing of houses and roaring of guns make a horrible din.'[17] Although the guns breached the wall on July 22, Graham hesitated to order an assault. When he finally did so on July 25, the French were ready. Graham's plan was for one column to charge up the isthmus while another crossed the river at low tide. The French slaughtered the redcoats struggling through the water or rumble:

> ... beams and timber, shells, hand grenades and every missile that could ... destroy life were hurled from the ramparts on the heads of the men ... Those who scrambled onto the breach found it was wide and sufficient enough at the bottom, but at the top ... from hence to the street was at least twenty feet [drop] ... On the beach were left by the tide more [men] than would have loaded a wagon of fish, killed in the water by the shot of the garrison ... And it not being sufficiently low at the time of the attack those who fell wounded and might have recovered were swept away by the current which runs here very rapid. Nor was it an easy matter for any man to keep his feet as the stones were so slippery.[18]

The senseless attack cost 571 casualties and savaged British morale, exacerbated when the word spread that Wellington unfairly blamed the troops for failing in an impossible mission. They condemned Graham and other officers for treating the troops like cannon fodder 'with as much sang froid as they do upon the supply of ammunition necessary to bring down the wall.'[19]

Pamplona sprawled across a broad mesa and was enclosed by thick walls studded with bastions and heavy cannons. Given its height, Pamplona could not be systematically besieged by inching parallels closer to the city. It could only be blockaded with ample numbers of troops and starved out. Wellington assigned Hill's corps this mission. Hill deployed some of his troops around Pamplona, and on July 4, attacked the advanced guard of General d'Erlon's corps in the nearby foothills and drove them up the road zigzagging up the Pyrenees to the fortress of Saint Jean Pied de Port at a pass. Anyone who believed that this was a last-gasp French offensive would soon be disillusioned.

The British campaign in eastern Spain was indecisive. Despite enjoying superior troop numbers, Britain and Spain lacked good generals. In early April, General John Murray landed with 8,000 British and Sicilian troops near Alicante, and experienced enormous frustrations trying to coordinate joint operations with the region's Spanish Generals Francisco Elio and Lorenzo Del Parque, who each commanded about 15,000 troops. With 12,000 troops, Suchet beat Elio at Yecla on April 11, but was repelled by Murray at Castalla on April 13. Leaving Elio and Del Parque to pursue Suchet, Murray embarked his men on transports that sailed up the coast to within 8 miles of Tarragona, where they disembarked. There Murray was joined by General Francisco Copons and 8,000 Spanish troops. Learning of the landing, Suchet and Decaen detached forces to converge on the enemy.

General William Bentinck arrived to take command from Murray on June 17, extracted the force, and sailed back to Alicante. Murray was later court-martialed but only lightly punished for his failures. General Jean Harispe with 14,000 troops routed Del Parque as his army neared Valencia. Bentinck's advance eventually pressured Suchet to abandon Tarragona and withdraw up the coast. At Ordal on September 13, Suchet launched his 12,000 troops at Bentinck's army whose British contingent was commanded by Colonel Frederic Adam. The French routed the allies, inflicting 600 casualties on the British alone including Adam, who was shot dead. This ended the British campaign on that front.

Upon learning of Vitoria, Napoleon recalled his hapless brother Joseph to Paris, and assigned Marshal Nicolas Soult to rebuild the shattered French army and drive Wellington from France's back door. After reaching Bayonne on July 12, Soult replenished the surviving regiments' ranks, and massed reinforcements and supplies. Wellington aided his efforts by calling off his pursuit and instead tying up his army by besieging San Sebastian and Pamplona. By late July, Soult's army numbered 88,811, including 72,664 infantry, 7,147 cavalry, and 9,000 gunners manning 140 cannons.[20]

Soult began his campaign on July 25, with his army split into three. While General Eugene Villatte with 20,000 troops defended the frontier along the Bidassoa River, Soult launched twin attacks against allied forces guarding passes over the Pyrenees. After heavy fighting on July 26, the corps of Generals Clausel with 17,218 troops and Reille with 17,235 troops captured Roncesvalles pass, and d'Erlon's corps with 20,957 troops Maya pass.[21] The victorious French columns then snaked down the valleys on Spain's side of the mountains to converge on Pamplona. They never got there.

Wellington was at San Sebastian overseeing the siege when he learned of the French offensive. Within hours he and his staff were cantering to the front. Wellington massed allied forces in the valleys and foothills blocking the roads descending from the two passes. He assigned Hill to lead the Maya front, while he commanded the Roncesvalles front which Soult and most French troops threatened and was closer to Pamplona.

Wellington deployed his troops in two lines to block two adjacent narrow valleys and the ridge between them, with Cole's division in front and those of Picton, O'Donnell, and Pablo Morillo behind. Clausel and Reille marched down the valleys and attacked on July 28. The battle of Sorauren was named after the village in the western valley where some of the fiercest fighting took place. Captain Thomas Browne, one of Wellington's staff officers, recalled the sheer awesomeness of the French attack:

At daybreak the French columns were observed, formed in columns ... and ready for battle. These columns were very deep and ... moved steadily onwards in the most imposing mass I ever beheld ... The enemy's grenadiers in their bear skin caps with red feathers and blue frock coats appeared the most warlike body of troops possible. As they moved on they threw out their skirmishers, which were met by the British light troops, and thus the work of this bloody day began.[22]

Sergeant William Lawrence of the 40th just as vividly described the fighting:

> Orders had been issued by our officers not to fire till we could do good work, but this soon came to pass, for the French quickly sallied up, and fired first, and we returned it … I never saw a single volley do so much execution … almost every man of their first two ranks falling, and then we instantly charged and chased them down the mountain, doing … more fearful havoc.[23]

Soult ordered new attacks on the allies with the same blood-soaked results until he ran out of reserves. The British and Portuguese troops repelled this series of attacks, inflicting over 4,000 casualties while incurring 2,650, including 1,358 British, 1,102 Portuguese, and 192 Spanish.[24]

Soult ordered Clausel and Reille to resume their attack at Sorauren on July 30, while d'Erlon attacked Hill south of Lizaso. The troops under Wellington's immediate command drove off the French, but d'Erlon's corps routed Hill's. Wellington rushed troops to shore up his army's crumbling western flank. The allies eventually repelled d'Erlon the next day. Having suffered 12,563 casualties, including 1,308 killed, 8,545 wounded, and 2,710 captured, or one-quarter of his 53,000 men that actually fought, Soult ordered his battered army to withdraw back over the mountains on August 1. Wellington's men had won the series of clashes known as the battle of the Pyrenees with 7,100 casualties, including 4,708 British, 1,732 Portuguese, and about 1,000 Spaniards, of 40,000 allied troops.[25] Wellington reported that 'I never saw such fighting … it began on the 25th and, excepting the 29th, … we had it every day till the 2nd. The battle of the 28th was fair bludgeon work.'[26]

Wellington ordered advances up each road to the passes and there posted forces powerful enough to resist another assault. He then returned to San Sebastian to oversee its siege, while allied forces tightened their grip around Pamplona. At San Sebastian, Wellington had stockpiles of ammunition and heavy guns bought to the front. On August 26, 63 cannons opened fire and pounded the town and fortress day and night until 11 o'clock on the morning of September 3, when they abruptly ceased. Although the bombardment transformed most walls and buildings into piles of blasted stone and charred wood, the surviving French troops reemerged to devastate twin allied assaults up the isthmus and across the river. One soldier described hellish scenes of:

> … legs and arms sticking up, some their clothes in flames, and number not dead but so jammed as not to be able to extricate themselves …
> I gained the trench which was … filled with the dead and dying …

One was making the best of his way minus an arm, another his face so disfigured ... as to leave to trace of the features of a human being; others creeping along with the leg dangling to a piece of skin; and ... some endeavoring to keep in the bowels.[27]

The first assault failed. Graham ordered a second which captured the town, while the French withdrew into the citadel. The surviving attackers vented their rage in a vicious sack of the town:

As the fighting began to ... faint, the horrors of plunder and rapine succeeded. Fortunately there were few females in the place, but the fate of the few which were there I cannot even now think without a shudder. The houses were everywhere ransacked, the furniture wantonly broken, the churches profaned, the images dashed to pieces, wind and spirit cellars were broken open, and the troops heated already with angry passions, became absolutely made by intoxication. All good order and discipline were abandoned. The officers no longer had the slightest control over their men, who ... controlled the officers, [of whom some were murdered] when they vainly attempted to bring them back to a state of subordination.[28]

Wellington at once condemned and justified the sack of San Sebastian. He wrote that his investigation revealed 'that the inhabitants ... co-operated with the enemy in the defense of the town, and actually fired upon the Allies.'[29] General Rey did not surrender until September 8. San Sebastian's capture cost the allies 2 months and 3,700 casualties, with the last assault alone costing 2,376 killed and wounded; only 1,234 defenders marched into captivity, while another 450 were hospitalized.[30]

Wellington was not at San Sebastian during the horrific assault and sack, but was at San Marcial with mostly Spanish troops along the River Bidassoa, where Soult launched attacks there and at Vera on August 31. The Spaniards eventually drove off the French, inflicting around 2,500 casualties, while suffering 1,700 at San Marcial, and 1,300 to 850 casualties at Vera.[31] During the battle, Wellington revealed the complex thinking, sensitivity, and steadfastness behind his military brilliance:

I had placed the Spanish troops in a position known ... for its strength ... As I was sitting on a rock watching what was going on ... one of their officers ... said ... twas impossible they could hold out any longer, and requested [that] I ... send my troops in to assist them. I looked through my glass, and I observed that the French were already in a movement to retreat ... 'Well, then,' I said, 'had not you better keep your position a little longer and gain the honour of the day rather than give up the post to our troops?' They did so, and now I see ... that they claimed this as one of their greatest victories.[32]

Wellington felt his army was unprepared to invade France, but was increasingly pressured by British allies, politicians, and the public to do so:

I see that, as usual, the newspapers on all sides are raising the public expectations and that the Allies are anxious that we should enter France, and that our government have promised that we should as soon as the enemy should be finally expelled from Spain ... I think I ... will bend a little to the views of the Allies, if it can done with safety to the army, notwithstanding that I should prefer to turn my attention to Catalonia, as soon as I have secured this frontier.

Still, he wielded every excuse not to invade: 'I feel a great disinclination to enter the French territory under the existing circumstances. The superiority of numbers which I can take into France will consist in about 25,000 Spaniards, neither paid nor fed, and who will plunder, and will set the whole country against us.'[33] Wellington eventually found ways to trump these potential problems.

Chapter 20

France, 1813–14

These fellows think themselves invulnerable, but I will beat them out and with great ease.

Wellington

I have not come to France to pillage; I have not had thousands of officers and soldiers killed and wounded for the remainder to plunder the French.

Wellington

Despite his losses during the week-long battle of the Pyrenees, Marshal Nicolas Soult's army still numbered 68,231 troops, including 57,243 infantry, 6,788 cavalry, and 4,200 gunners manning 97 cannons. Yet Soult faced two formidable challenges. First, Wellington's army numbered 88,816 troops, including 63,143 British and Portuguese and 25,673 Spaniards, and thus outgunned his own by 20,000 men.[1] Second, Soult's army was stretched thin along a 23-mile front running from Maya pass and along the Pyrenees foothills then behind the Bidassoa River until it flowed into the Atlantic Ocean. This front was split into three sectors, with General Honore Charles Reille's two division corps defending the lower, General Bertrand Clausel's three division corps the middle centered at Vera, and General Jean Baptiste Drouet d'Erlon's three division corps the upper with most of his troops guarding Maya pass. General Maximilien Sebastian Foy's three divisions were camped in reserve around Saint Jean Pied de Port.

With overwhelming numbers of troops at his command, Wellington confidently anticipated shattering the French line: 'These fellows think themselves invulnerable, but I will beat them out and with great ease ... It appears difficult, but the enemy have not men to man the works and lines they occupy ... I can pour a greater force on certain points than they can concentrate to resist me.'[2] And that is exactly what happened. Wellington's army triumphantly invaded France in a three-pronged attack on October 7, 1813. While General Rowland Hill feinted at Maya to distract the enemy,

General John Hope's 24,000 waded across the Bidassoa at low tide near Hendaye and General William Beresford's 33,000 crossed upstream at Vera. The crossing at Hendaye began:

> ... about five in the morning and in a short time infantry, cavalry, and artillery found themselves on French ground. The stream at this point was nearly four feet deep, and had Soult been aware of what we were about, we should have found the passage a very arduous undertaking. Three miles above we discovered the French army and ere long came under fire ... The French army, not long after we began to return their fire, was in full retreat.[3]

The allies won the passage at a fairly low cost, suffering 400 casualties and inflicting 450 at Hendaye, and suffering 800 and inflicting 1,250 at Vera and Maya.[4]

Soult withdrew to the Nivelle River which runs from the Pyrenees into the ocean just past Saint Jean de Luz. As Wellington readied his army for its latest offensive, a worse psychological than strategic burden lifted from his mind when he learned that Pamplona's 3,000-man garrison surrendered on October 31. He had now completely cleared the swath of Spain under his command of French forces. He was no longer Janus-faced at enemy forces before and behind him, but from now could focus on defeating the French in their home country.

Wellington's strategy at the Nivelle River on November 10, essentially repeated what he had done at the Bidassoa, with one corps crossing at low tide near the mouth, another crossing upstream, and a third attacking the enemy's left flank anchored in the mountains. This time the main thrust came with Beresford's corps in the center, while the corps of Hope and Hill feinted against Soult's right and left, respectively. Eventually all 3 corps punched through the French lines, inflicting 4,350 casualties and capturing 59 cannons, while suffering 2,450 casualties.[5]

Soult fell back to the Nive River, a far stronger position with his right anchored at the fortress of Bayonne a few miles from the ocean, and his left in the steep Pyrenees foothills. The Nive flows through Bayonne and into the Adour River that drains into the ocean 3 miles beyond. Wellington would have to attack this position with far fewer troops than in previous battles. His immediate army numbered 63,000 troops, including 36,000 British, 23,000 Portuguese, and a single 4,000-man division of the best Spanish troops. He returned 40,000 other Spanish soldiers to their own country.[6]

He had good reasons for doing so, noting grimly that: 'I have not come to France to pillage; I have not had thousands of officers and soldiers killed and wounded for the remainder to plunder the French.'[7] After entering France, he faced a worsening dilemma: 'Our success and everything depends upon our moderation and justice, and upon the good conduct and discipline of our troops ... Hitherto, these have behaved well, and there appears a new spirit among the officers ... to keep their troops in order.' He feared the consequences of Spanish atrocities, while understanding the vengeance and desperation behind them:

> I despair of the Spaniards. They are in so miserable a state that it is hardly fair to expect that they will refrain from plundering a beautiful country into which they enter as conquerors; particularly adverting to the miseries which their own country has suffered from its invaders. I cannot, therefore, venture to bring them ... into France unless I can feed and pay them ... Without pay and food, they must plunder; and if they plunder, they will ruin us all.[8]

Even shorn of his Spanish troops, Wellington's army still outgunned Soult by 63,000 to 60,000 troops. Wellington's three corps simultaneously attacked on December 9. Hope's troops cleared the coast road of enemy forces and approached within a few miles of Bayonne. Beresford's engineers erected a pontoon bridge across the Nive at Ustaritz, and two of his four divisions marched over to fan out in a bridgehead. Hill's troops waded the Nive at Combo and secured a cluster of villages.

Soult reacted the next day with a series of counter-attacks that threatened to turn Wellington's left flank. Reille's corps slammed into and scattered Hope's advanced regiments; Hope withdrew his corps to Barrouillet. After harsh fighting, Clausel's corps forced the Light Division to withdraw from Arcangues. Foy's division reinforced Clausel's corps. Wellington threw in reinforcements that pushed back Reille's corps. The fighting ended inconclusively, with respective French and allied losses of about 1,200 and 1,500. Then, this night, 1,500 German troops deserted Soult after learning of Napoleon's overwhelming defeat at Leipzig.[9]

Rather than withdraw, Soult boldly thinned his center and sent his wing troops under Reille and d'Erlon against Hope and Hill, respectively, early the next morning of December 11. Wellington did not push Beresford's other two divisions across the Nive for a massive assault against the French that might have broken through and relieved the pressure on Hope and Hill. Instead, he had Beresford withdraw his two divisions already across and attack the left flank of the French forces attacking Hope. Meanwhile, Hill led a counter-attack that pushed back d'Erlon. The 3-day battle ended in a bloody draw, with total French losses of around 3,300 and allied of around 1,775.[10]

That was the most serious fighting for the next three months. Wellington was in no hurry to attack the latest French position. The Joyeuse River flows north into the Ardour River about a dozen miles upstream of the sea. Soult deployed 55,000 troops in nearly equal parts behind those rivers. The Ardour ran deep, wide, swift, and unfordable between the Joyeuse and the sea. The Joyeuse had numerous fords between its junction with the Ardour and the Pyrenees foothills. Soult prepared a fall-back position behind the Bidouse River that flowed parallel a few miles behind the Joyeuse River. Anchoring Soult's right flank was the fortress city of Bayonne, on the Ardour River's south side, 3 miles from the sea. General Pierre Thouvenot commanded the 8,033-man garrison.

Weather was as much a French ally as the rivers. It was a monotonously wet and cold winter that kept troops huddled within tents or around smoky fires and turned roads into quagmires. During the interlude, Wellington massed supplies and filled his depleted regiments with new recruits. He assigned Hope's corps the mission of besieging Bayonne, while the corps of Beresford and Hill deployed along the Ardour and Joyeuse, respectively.

The first break in the dismal rainy winter weather came in early February 1814. Wellington eagerly sought to take advantage of the blue skies and dry roads. On February 14, Hill's corps attacked across each Joyeuse River ford, routed the French regiments before them, hurried across the Bidouse River, then prepared for French counter-attacks that never came. Stretched to the breaking point, Soult could not mass enough troops for an attack. Instead, he withdrew his army east to Orthez on the Gave du Pau River that joins the Ardour River where it ascends from the northeast.

Leaving Hope's corps of 18,000 British and Portuguese, and 16,000 Spanish troops to carry on Bayonne's siege, Wellington led the rest of the army after Soult.[11] As Beresford's corps directly hounded Soult, Hill's corps quick-marched to outflank it from the south. By splashing across the shallow upstream waters of first the Saison then Gave d'Oloron Rivers, Hill prevented Soult from blunting Beresford's advance at deeper waters downstream.

Meanwhile, Hope launched his siege's second phase on the night of February 23. His engineers constructed a pontoon bridge across the Ardour River's mouth as British warships bombarded French troops on the north bank. With the bridge finished on February 26, Hill marched two divisions across the river then arced them around the citadel at Saint Étienne guarding the bridge leading to Bayonne. Within days, Hope had batteries of heavy cannons emplaced on the Ardour's north bank to join the bombardment of Bayonne from the east, south, and west sides, and the Saint Étienne citadel on the north bank. Bayonne's defenders now numbered 17,000 troops.

Wellington's army caught up to the French at Orthez, where Soult deployed most of his 36,000 infantry, 3,000 cavalry, and 48 cannons on a ridgeline overlooking the town and the Gave du Pau River. Wellington commanded 44,042 men, including 39,157 infantry, 3,373 cavalry, and 42 cannons manned by 1,512 gunners. On February 27, he sent Hill's corps directly across the river at Orthez to assault the enemy left flank, while Beresford's corps crossed downstream at Lahonton and attacked the right and center. By late afternoon, the allies drove the French from the field, inflicting 4,000 casualties while sustaining 2,164, including Wellington whose hip was badly bruised by a musket ball that glanced off his scabbard.[12]

As Wellington lay in bed recovering, he received a startling message. The mayor of Bordeaux informed him that royalists had seized the city and requested British troops to help them hold it. Wellington marched Hill in pursuit of Soult and sent Beresford north to secure Bordeaux, whose port on the Gironde River would make an excellent supply base for his army's campaign deep into southern France. Much of the population cheered Beresford and his men as saviors when they paraded into Bordeaux on March 12. Leaving a division of troops behind, Beresford hurried to join Wellington's army which had advanced to Aire.

Wellington launched his latest offensive on March 18, when he led the army south and east of Aire. Soult fell back through Tarbes, where his rear guard fought off Wellington's advanced guard on March 20, then fled to Toulouse, which he reached on March 24. Toulouse sprawled along the eastern and northern bank of the Garonne River where it sharply flows from south to west; a bridge runs from Toulouse to the suburb of Saint Cyprien squeezed in the angle on the west bank. Walls surrounded the land sides of both Toulouse and Saint Cyprien, and along the top of a ridge running north to south a mile east of the city. With reinforcements Soult's army now numbered 42,000 troops to Wellington's 46,573, including 40,706 infantry, 3,617 cavalry, and 2,250 gunners manning 46 cannons.[13]

Wellington's first step in capturing Toulouse was somehow to cross the river. On March 27, he sent Beresford to a ford upstream but the French blunted his advance. On April 4, he marched Hill to a ford further upstream, but the French also thwarted this crossing. He then led his army down to

Toulouse, deployed Hill at Saint Cyprien and sent Beresford several miles downstream to construct a pontoon bridge and cross the Garonne. This time the crossing succeeded and Beresford deployed his troops in an arc north and east of Toulouse.

Wellington ordered his army to attack on April 11. Hill's troops fought their way into Saint Cyrien. The French repulsed Beresford's attack, then counter-attacked, which the allies fought off. This time Wellington's army suffered more casualties than Soult's – 4,568 to 3,236 – but won their latest victory when Soult withdrew his army south to Carcassonne.[14] Hoping to avoid further death and destruction, Toulouse's government opened the city to the invaders the following day.

Then came the electrifying news on April 12 that the allies had captured Paris on March 31; Foreign Minister Charles Maurice Talleyrand-Perigord had convinced the Senate to depose Napoleon on April 3; and Napoleon had abdicated and the Senate offered Louis XVIII the throne of France on April 6. A few days later word arrived that on April 11, the allies had signed the Treaty of Fontainebleau that granted Napoleon the right to rule the small island of Elba off Tuscany's coast and annually receive a French subsidy of 1 million francs.[15]

The elation that the war was finally over was darkened by knowing that the death and destruction at Toulouse was for naught. Tragically, the killing and maiming were not yet done. At Bayonne, General Thouvenot remained defiant despite knowing of Napoleon's abdication. On the night of April 14, he launched a sortie from the citadel at Saint Étienne that overran the allied lines and inflicted 843 casualties while suffering 891; General Hope was among the wounded. Thouvenot held out at Bayonne until April 26, when he grudgingly agreed to surrender.

Wellington and his staff rode off to Paris on April 30 and arrived on May 4. During the next two weeks, Wellington joined the celebrations and discussions with allied leaders over the fate of post-Napoleonic Europe. On May 17, he and his staff headed back to his army. Meanwhile, determined to put the war behind them, the allies granted France a generous peace with the Treaty of Paris, signed on May 20, 1814. France's frontiers reverted to those of 1792, a clear gain over those of 1789. France would suffer neither an indemnity nor foreign occupation. The Bourbons would once again rule France, this time with Louis XVIII on the throne.[16] Wellington issued his last General Order to his army and bid farewell on June 14, 1814. He could never have imagined that exactly a year later, he would be commanding an allied army against Napoleon's last campaign.

Chapter 21

Washington and Baltimore, 1814

Destroy and lay waste such towns and cities upon the coast as may be found assailable ... and ... spare merely the lives of the armed inhabitants of the United States.

Admiral Alexander Cochrane

Never was nectar more grateful to the palates of the gods, than the crystal goblet of Madeira and water I quaffed at Mr. Madison's expense.

Captain James Scott

You may thank old Madison for this. It is he who got you in this scrape.

Admiral George Cockburn

Admiral Alexander Cochrane utterly hated America and Americans, who he scorned as cowards, ingrates, and traitors for breaking with Britain's enlightened Empire.[1] Word that the Americans had sacked and burned the town of York, Upper Canada's capital, gave him the excuse to instruct his subordinates 'to destroy and lay waste such towns and cities upon the coast as may be found assailable ... and ... spare merely the lives of the unarmed inhabitants of the United States.'[2] In doing so, Cochrane merely echoed Secretary at War Henry, Earl Bathurst, who authorized British commanders 'in any descent ... to threaten the inhabitants with the destruction of their property' and 'levy upon them contributions in return for your forbearance.'[3] No one fulfilled this order more gleefully than Admiral Alexander Cockburn, Cochrane's second-in-command.[4] From their unassailable base on Tangier Island in Chesapeake Bay's heart, British naval commanders sailed their warships in all directions, anchored off one town after another, and either extracted protection money or disgorged marines and sailors to loot and burn property, and often rape women and murder anyone who resisted.

Transports packed with 3,400 Peninsular War veterans reached Tangier Island on August 15, 1814. These reinforcements brought General Robert Ross's troops to over 4,500 men. Cochrane and Ross quickly decided what to do with them.[5] On August 18, the armada sailed to the Patuxent River mouth guarded by Captain Joshua Barney's 17 gunboats. As Barney prudently led his flotilla upriver, Ross disembarked his troops at Benedict, then, with Cockburn riding alongside, marched them along the river's west bank. On August 22, Barney ordered his gunboats burned before hurrying with his 400 sailors and marines to join the army.

After learning of the British expedition, General William Winder massed around 6,300 men, nearly all militia, at Bladensburg, just 5 miles east of Washington City. The British army was nearing Bladensburg on the evening of August 23, when Ross received a letter from Cochrane recalling the army to the fleet's safety. Cockburn talked Ross into disobeying the order and instead marching onward. On August 24, the British attacked and routed the Americans at Bladensburg, killing 26 and capturing 51 Americans, while suffering 64 dead and 185 wounded.[6] The American militiamen did not stop running when they reached Washington, but left the nation's capital in their dust. In doing so they simply emulated their nation's leaders. President James Madison and his administration had fled as soon as they learned of Bladensburg.

A few American troops lingered to fire scattered shots then vanish as the British marched into Washington City. Captain James Scott recalled that we:

> ... descended the Capitol Hill ... and entered the heart of the city, by the Pennsylvania Avenue. This was a fine and spacious causeway ... with a row of trees ... The President's palace, a handsome stone building, so lately the headquarters of the enemy, stood at the extremity of the avenue, and was evacuated by the guard of soldiers, with their two field pieces, only a few minutes before we made ourselves masters of the place.[7]

What they discovered in the Executive Mansion was richly appropriate, as Scott recalled:

> We found the cloth laid for the expected victorious generals, and ... a feast worthy of the resolute champions of republican freedom. A large store of super-excellent Madeira and other costly wines stood cooling in ice ... Fagged nearly to death, dusty, feverish and thirty ... I absolutely blessed them for their erring provident. Never was nectar more grateful to the palates of the gods, than the crystal goblet of Madeira and water I quaffed at Mr. Madison's expense.[8]

Having satiated their hunger and thirst, those British officers and 'gentlemen' then proceeded to loot the Executive Mansion.

Even then, Ross, Cockburn, and their officers were not done. Their final act was to order the Executive Mansion burned along with Congress, the Library of Congress, the Naval Yard, the War, State, and Treasury Departments, and the bridge across the Potomac. To a group of ladies who pleaded with him to stop the destruction, Cockburn scornfully replied: 'You may thank old Madison for this. It is he who got you in this scrape.'[9]

Not everyone gloated at the looting and burning of America's capital. Captain Harry Smith 'had no objection to burn arsenals, dockyards, frigates building, store, barracks, etc., but ... we were horrified at the order to burn the elegant House of Parliament and the President's house.'[10] Lieutenant George Gleig also reacted with shame rather than glee at the atrocities committed by his countrymen: 'To destroy the flotilla was the sole object of the disembarkation; and but for the instigations of Admiral Cockburn, who accompanied the army, the capital of America would probably have escaped its visitation. It was he, who ... suggested the attack upon Washington.'[11] This may have been true, but Ross enthusiastically embraced Cockburn's exhortation to destroy Washington City.

Meanwhile, a British squadron of two frigates and five smaller warships commanded by Captain James Gordon sailed up the Potomac River and paused just beyond cannon shot of Fort Washington, 10 miles below the capital. The garrison's commander panicked and fled with his men. After learning that the fort was empty, Gordon ordered his flotilla to proceed 4 miles further to Alexandria, where he captured 21 vessels filled with 16,000 flour barrels, 1,000 tobacco hogsheads, 150 cotton bales, and enormous amounts of other goods.[12] The flotilla sailed back down the Potomac and rejoined the British fleet in the Chesapeake.

The British spent 24 hours devastating Washington before Ross and Cockburn led their troops back to the fleet. After reembarking with their loot, the armada sailed north toward Baltimore. Cochrane boasted to Bathurst that he intended Baltimore to suffer Washington's fate: 'Baltimore may be destroyed or laid under a severe contribution.'[13]

Unlike Washington, forts and entrenchments guarded Baltimore. On September 12, Ross led his army ashore at North Point then toward the city. Halfway there, General John Stricker and 3,200 militiamen barred their passage. Ross hurried his artillery up to bombard the Americans, then ordered his troops to fix bayonets and advance. Midshipman John Bluett recalled how the redcoats 'saluted them with a general discharge of small arms and artillery, and charging under cover of the smoke, came suddenly upon them, and routed them with great slaughter, so that finding it impossible to stand against us, they threw down their arms and ran like hares.' Before fleeing, the militiamen fired several rounds that killed 46 and wounded 295 British, while suffering 25 killed, 139 wounded, and 50 captured.[14] Bluett shuddered recollecting 'the custom of the Yankeys to conceal them[selves] in trees and being excellent marksmen, they picked off a good many of our stragglers.'[15] One of those marksmen killed General Ross.

Colonel Arthur Brooke took command and led the British army toward Baltimore as the fleet slowly sailed west up the bay. They halted several miles short of Baltimore on September 13. Fort McHenry guarded the south shore and the Lazaretto battery the north shore. Cochrane ordered his warships to bombard Fort McHenry. Midshipman Robert Barrett was in the thick of the action:

> Our squadron ... anchored in a line of battle, about one mile and three-quarters distant from the heavy batteries which defended the entrance of ... Baltimore harbor ... and immediately commenced a heavy fire of shells and rockets upon the forts ... The hissing rockets and the fiery shells glittered in the air ... whilst ... the rain fell in torrents – the thunder broke in mighty peals after each successive flash of lightning, that for a moment illuminated the surrounding darkness. This was the period ... approaching midnight, selected for the boats of the squadron to make a diversion in favour of our army, by feigning an attack on the fortifications ... Musket flashes and continuous cheers along the flotilla added excitement and interest to a scene already imposing.[16]

During 25 hours, the British fired against Fort McHenry over 1,500 rounds, of which 400 hit the target. Yet Fort McHenry was so well-built that the Americans suffered only 4 men killed and 24 wounded. The Americans repulsed an attack by 1,200 troops in longboats against a beach a half mile from the fort.

Fort McHenry's defiance atop Ross's death disheartened the British commanders. Cochrane and Brooke decided to return the armada to their Tangier Island lair. Their campaign inflicted enormous economic and even worse psychological damage on the United States. Baltimore's stalwart defense could not relieve the American humiliation at being routed at Bladensburg then having their capital looted and burned. In all, Britain's Chesapeake campaign worsened rather than broke the deadlocked war.

Chapter 22

New Orleans, 1814–15

I have it much at heart to give them a complete drubbing before peace is made.

Admiral Alexander Cochrane

I owe to Britain a debt of retaliatory vengeance ... should our forces meet.

Andrew Jackson

There never was a more complete failure.

Captain Edward Codrington

In mulling his Chesapeake campaign, Admiral Alexander Cochrane gloated at routing the Americans at Bladensburg and destroying Washington, but winced at being repulsed before Baltimore. He was deadset to decisively crush the Americans: 'I have it much at heart to give them a complete drubbing before peace is made.'[1] He reckoned the best place for this was New Orleans as the first step in conquering the Mississippi River valley from the United States. Cochrane could not have anticipated that leading the resistance against the invaders would be one of the fiercest enemies Britain ever faced in its history.[2]

Andrew Jackson hated Britain. Unlike Cochrane, he had a good reason to hate. His mother, two brothers, and numerous cousins died during America's War for Independence; he was constantly reminded of British cruelty by the scar across his hand and forehead where a redcoat captain had slashed him for defiantly refusing to blacken his boots. He was a natural warrior and leader, brilliant at sizing up an enemy, devising a plan, and inspiring his men frenzily and mercilessly to pulverize that enemy.

Yet, the first time that Jackson actually led troops to war was in late 1813 against the Creek Indians. The Creek tribe sprawled in villages across most of today's Alabama. Like every tribe, the Creeks were bitterly split between those who fatalistically accepted and those who resisted American imperialism. The Red Stick faction was determined to die fighting the

Americans. During the war that followed, most fulfilled this vow. The war erupted on July 27, 1813, when militia attacked a group of Red Sticks who were returning to their villages with a load of arms and munitions they got from British agents at Pensacola. The Red Sticks retaliated by overrunning Fort Mims on August 30, and massacring nearly 250 soldiers and civilians. The surrounding states of Tennessee, Georgia, and Mississipi organized militia expeditions to crush the Red Sticks. Only one, led by Jackson, penetrated and devastated the Red Stick heartland.

Jackson's troops built a chain of forts from Tennessee south into Creek country and defeated the Red Sticks in a series of battles, Tallushatchee on November 3, Talladega on November 9, 1813, Emuckfau on January 22, Enotachopco Creek on January 24, and, decisively, Horseshoe Bend on March 28, 1814. In all, the Americans slaughtered a couple thousand Red Sticks while suffering several hundred dead and wounded. On August 9, 1814, Jackson gathered all the Creek chiefs, Red Sticks and collaborators alike, and forced them to sign the Treaty of Fort Jackson, whereby they surrendered 23 million acres or half their land to the United States. The timing of the war's end was fortuitous for America. Jackson and his battle-hardened troops could now turn their guns against British redcoats. Jackson swore that 'I owe to Britain a debt of retaliatory vengeance ... should our forces meet.'[3]

Whitehall began organizing an expedition to invade America's Gulf region in August 1814. The object, as Secretary at War Henry, Earl Bathurst explained, was 'to occupy some important and valuable possession, by the restoration of which the conditions of peace might be improved, or which we might be entitled to exact the cession of, as the price of peace.'[4] No potential jewel in this campaign's crown glistened more brightly than New Orleans. Bathurst had first tapped General Robert Ross to command this expedition. After Ross was killed at Baltimore, he chose General Edward Pakenham, Wellington's brother-in-law and a distinguished Peninsular War veteran. From August to November, the armada's naval and army contingents gathered at Negril Bay, Jamaica.

Meanwhile, the British launched some spoiling operations to deplete and divert the Americans. On August 14, Major Edward Nicolls led 100 troops ashore at Pensacola, where he worked with Spanish officials and officers to strengthen the port's defenses. His next step was to capture Fort Bowyer that guarded Mobile Bay's entrance. On September 12, Nicolls landed nearby with 225 marines and Indians, and assaulted the fort. The 160-man garrison repelled the attack, killing 32 and wounding 37 redcoats, and destroyed the

22-gun *Hermes* that ran aground within range of the fort's guns, while losing 4 men killed and 5 wounded. Bullets struck Nicolls in his eye and leg; he and his men hastily reembarked and sailed back to Pensacola.[5]

Now it was Jackson's turn. In an exchange of increasingly heated letters, Florida Governor Manteo Manrique rejected Jackson's demands that the Spanish expel the British and stop aiding the Indians. On October 23, Jackson led 2,138 troops east from Mobile to Pensacola. In doing so, he violated orders not invade Spanish territory for fear of provoking them to war against the United States. The American army appeared before Pensacola on November 6. When Manrique remained defiant, Jackson launched an attack the next day that routed the defenders. Manrique surrendered. Nicolls withdrew with his men to Fort Barrancas guarding the bay, then had it destroyed as he and his men sailed away. With Pensacola now as secure as Mobile, Jackson reckoned the British would next target New Orleans. He led his army into New Orleans on December 1.[6]

The British armada packed with 7,500 troops sailed from Negril Bay on November 27. An invader had three choices to reach New Orleans. The longest and best defended was the 120 miles from the Gulf of Mexico up the Mississippi River, with Fort Saint Philippe guarding mile 50, the English Turn battery mile 92, and, finally, Fort Saint Leon mile 95. Or he could avoid this gauntlet by sailing to the west end of Lake Borgne, actually a bay, transfer troops, cannons, and supplies to bateaux, then row through the bayous half a dozen miles and emerge 8 miles south of the city. Finally, he could sail northwest from Lake Borgne into Lake Pontchartrain, land on its south shore, capture Fort Saint John, then march overland 5 miles to New Orleans.

Pakenham and Cochrane sailed for Lake Borgne, dropping anchor off Cat Island on December 8. The only Americans defending these waters were 182 men packed into 5 gunboats. Cochrane sent 1,200 troops in 40 longboats against them on December 14. In the attack, the British killed 6 Americans, wounded 35, and captured the rest along with their vessels, while suffering 17 killed, 77 wounded, and 2 sunken boats.[7] Cochrane then sailed the armada to Pea Island, where the troops disembarked to camp while their commanders debated the next move. It was a miserable, marshy place, freezing and rain-lashed. The troops huddled soaked and listless for days without tents or fires before their commanders finally chose a route.[8]

After obtaining guides, General John Keane and the first brigade slowly advanced by longboat westward through the bayou maze on December 22, as the second and third brigades embarked and followed. Keane and his men emerged 8 miles south of New Orleans on December 23. After suffering so much over the preceding weeks, the British army's morale soared knowing that New Orleans was just a half-day's march away. Lieutenant George Gleig found from:

> ... the General down to the youngest drum-boy a confident anticipation of success [that] seemed to pervade all ranks, and in the hope of an ample reward in store for them, the toils and grievances ... were forgotten ... Several Americans had already deserted, who ... assured us that there were not present 5,000 soldiers in the State; that the principal inhabitants had long ago left the place, that such as remained were ready to join us as soon as we should appear among them, and that ... we might lay our account with a speedy and bloodless campaign.[9]

Jackson swiftly disabused the British that New Orleans was some easy picking. Shortly after learning that redcoats had appeared below the city, he convened his officers and ordered them to prepare for an attack that night. After dark, two schooners, the *Carolina* and *Louisiana*, drifted with the current to anchor opposite the British camp. Gleig recalled the *Carolina*'s ghostly appearance:

> ... which seemed to be stealing up the river till she came opposite to our camp, where her anchor was dropped, and her sails leisurely furled ... Several musket shots were ... fired at her ... of which no notice was taken, till at length, having fastened all her sails, and swung her broadside towards us, we could distinctly hear one cry out in a commanding voice, 'Give them this for the honour of America.' The words were instantly followed by the flashes of her guns, and a deadly shower of grape swept down numbers in the camp.[10]

The schooners fired several broadsides then abruptly ceased. This signaled Jackson's men to attack. The fighting was desperate as 'all discipline was lost. Each officer, as he was able to collect twenty or thirty men round him, advanced into the middle of the enemy, when it was fought hand to hand, bayonet to bayonet, and sword to sword.'[11] The British suffered 46 killed, 167 wounded, and 64 missing, and the Americans 24 killed, 115 wounded, and 74 missing.[12] While believing that his army would ultimately triumph, British Captain John Cooke generously lauded the enemy commander: 'General Jackson had shown himself a general of the first class both in attack and defense, since his first surprise. And although so far the Americans possessed the most consummate and able tactician, still the British general commanded the best troops … from discipline and brilliant deeds in the field their conduct will not be surpassed.'[13]

Had the British attacked the next day, they might have routed the Americans and captured New Orleans. Keane then had 4,700 men to Jackson's 1,800, whose camp was not fortified. Instead, Keane sat tight with his men. Over the next couple of days more British troops and supplies appeared, with General Pakenham arriving to take command from Keane on Christmas day.

Meanwhile, Jackson pulled his army behind the quarter mile long Rodriquez Canal that linked the river and a swamp, and was sited 5 miles from the city. As reinforcements swelled his army, he had the troops build an earthen wall studded with redoubts for artillery batteries. Manning this line were around 5,000 men of the most diverse army in American history, including regulars, volunteers from several states, French- and Spanish-speaking militia companies, free black militia companies, Choctaw Indians, and pirates manning many of the cannons. He posted 700 troops across the river and had them construct breastworks and batteries. Finally, behind each front line on either bank he had two fall-back defense lines constructed, just in case.

Pakenham viewed Jackson's defenses as near impregnable. He scapegoated Keane for mishandling the campaign: 'I regret the defeat of our forces due to the error made on the 23rd of December. Our troops should have advanced to New Orleans immediately.' When Pakenham talked of withdrawing and attacking from another direction, Cochrane exploded in wrath: 'We are not defeated and there is nothing wrong with our position. If the army shrinks from the attack here, I will bring up my sailors and marines from the fleet. We will storm the American lines and march into the city. Then the soldiers can bring up the baggage.'[14]

Stung by Cochrane's words, Pakenham launched a limited attack on December 27. The Americans slaughtered the redcoats, killing or wounding 151, while suffering only 7 dead and 10 wounded.[15] Gleig recalled that:

… the Americans are excellent shots, as well with artillery as with rifles … all striking full into the midst of our ranks, occasioned terrible havoc. The shrieks of the wounded … the crash of firelocks, and the … killed, caused … confusion, and what added to the panic, was that from the houses beside which we stood, bright flames suddenly burst out. The Americans expecting this attack filled them with combustibles …

and directing one or two guns against them, loaded with red hot shot, in an instant set them on fire.[16]

The only British success was sinking the *Carolina* with cannon fire.

The latest British debacle, a devastating artillery duel, occurred on New Year's Day, 1815. Once again the losses were lopsided, with the British suffering 44 dead and 55 wounded to the American 11 dead and 23 wounded, of whom most were foolish civilian spectators from New Orleans.[17] British Captain Edward Codrington recalled that:

> ... we had our batteries, by severe labour, ready ... to destroy and silence the opposing batteries, and give opportunity for a well directed storm. But instead of doing so, not a gun of the enemy appeared to suffer ... our firing too high was not made out until we had expended too much of our ... ammunition to push the matter further ... We have by this allowed the enemy to increase our difficulties and gain spirits, and the harassing job of withdrawing the guns half buried in the mud, occasioned by the pouring rain of that night, wore down the whole army.[18]

Pakenham and his officers finally agreed on a massive assault. Shortly after dawn on January 8, Pakenham hurled 5,300 troops against Jackson's main line, while Colonel William Thornton led 600 picked troops across the river to attack 700 Louisiana and Kentucky militia commanded by General David Morgan. Pakenham's redcoats marched into a devastating storm of first cannon balls, then canister, rifle shots, and finally musket volleys. Sergeant John Cooper recalled: 'At the word "Forward!" the two lines approached the ditch under a murderous discharge of musketry; but crossing the ditch and scaling the parapet were found impossible without ladders. These had been prepared, but the regiment that should have carried them left them behind, and thereby caused, in few minutes, a dreadful loss of men and officers.'[19] Codrington recalled that we 'had but to retreat ... leaving the ground in front of the enemy's line covered with killed and wounded. There never was a more complete failure.'[20] Meanwhile, Thornton's attack scattered the Americans and spiked the guns, but withdrew after observing their comrades routed on the opposite shore.

During the battle, the British suffered 2,037 casualties, including 291 killed, 1,262 wounded, and 484 missing or captured; Pakenham was among the dead.[21] The losses would have been far worse had not so many redcoats preferred discretion to valor. Jackson contemptuously quipped that he:

> ... never had so grand and awful an idea of the resurrection on that day. After the smoke ... had cleared ... I saw in the distance more than five hundred Britons merging from the heaps of their dead comrades ... coming forward and surrendering ... They had fallen at our first fire ... without having received so much as a scratch, and lay prostrate as if dead until the close of the action.[22]

The Americans suffered only 13 killed, 39 wounded, and 19 missing or captured, or 71 casualties. Jackson and his men triumphed in one of the most lopsided victories in military history. During the entire campaign, the British lost over 2,450 men compared with around 350 Americans.[23]

General John Lambert, the new commander, and his officers were trapped in a dilemma which for ten days they debated how to escape. They could not overrun Jackson and would be overrun if they tried to retreat. The only chance was if Cochrane sailed his fleet up the Mississippi and rescued them by pounding the enemy with broadsides. Meanwhile, they evacuated the wounded by boat through the bayous to transports in Lake Borgne. When word arrived that Fort Saint Philippe had repelled Cochrane's flotilla, Lambert gave orders to quietly withdraw during the night of January 18. The next morning the Americans were astonished to see the empty British camp.

Lambert and his officers were determined to dilute their humiliating and devastating defeat with some small victory. They decided to make a final stab at Fort Bowyer and this time took it at the cost of 13 dead and 18 wounded. The American garrison surrendered on February 12. The British did not stay long. Two days later, word arrived that on Christmas Eve 1814, American and British diplomats signed the Treaty of Ghent that ended the war.[24]

Britain's Gulf campaign had been an enormous and needless sacrifice of lives and treasure. On a vastly more appalling scale, this was also true for the war itself. The 1812 War's results are clearer than its causes. The British and Americans each suffered more than 10,000 dead from battle or disease; many times that number injured; millions of dollars heaped on their national debts; and millions of dollars in destroyed property, although here the

British outdid the Americans culminating with their burning of Washington City. And for all this the belligerents fought each other to a standstill, with neither capable of a decisive victory. By the war's end, the Americans and British clung to mere toeholds in the other's territory. The British held Fort Niagara and a 50-mile stretch of Maine's coast. The Americans controlled the Detroit River valley. Under the Treaty of Ghent, each side would withdraw its troops to restore the status quo ante bellum or what each had before the war. Commissions would address any lingering disputes over freedom of the seas or territory. In the end, only contractors and a perverse sense of honor won the 1812 War; by any other measure Britain and America lost terribly.

It was actually Wellington who broke the diplomatic deadlock. Whitehall asked him to command the British army in Canada. He reluctantly consented but only if the Cabinet agreed not 'to demand any concession of territory from America ... You have not been able to carry it into the enemy's territory, notwithstanding your military success and now undoubted military superiority, and have not even cleared your own territory.'[25] Only if the Americans rejected turning back the territorial clock to before the war, would Wellington sail to Canada. Fortunately for Britain and the United States alike, the American diplomats seized this face-saving concession to end the war. The history of each country and the world would read far differently had Wellington been fighting in North America rather than Flanders in early summer 1815.

Chapter 23

Waterloo, 1815

Napoleon has humbugged me, by God! He has gained twenty-four hours' march on me.

Wellington

Old Blucher has had a damned good hiding, and has gone back to Wavre, eighteen miles to the rear. We must do the same. I suppose they'll say in England that we have been licked; well I can't help that.

Wellington

Just because you have been beaten by Wellington, you regard him as a great general. I tell you that Wellington is a bad general and the English are bad troops and this battle will be a picnic ... We will sleep this night in Brussels.

Napoleon

It has been ... the nearest run thing you ever saw in your life ... By God! I don't think it would have done if I had not been there.

Wellington

Nothing except a battle lost can be half so melancholy as a battle won ... I hope to God I have fought my last battle.

Wellington

Prince Clemens von Metternich, Austria's chancellor, was enjoying a deep sleep on the night of March 5, 1815, when an aide awakened him and handed him a letter. Metternich nodded wearily, tossed the letter aside, and fell back asleep. He did not break the letter's seal until well after dawn the next morning. What Metternich read horrified him. Napoleon had escaped from Elba and his whereabouts were unknown. Metternich sent messages to representatives of the other Great Powers, Russia, Prussia, and Britain, to gather and decide what to do. Arthur Wellesley, Duke of Wellington represented Britain.

Napoleon got increasingly edgy shortly after stepping foot on the small island of Elba, off Tuscany's coast, on May 4, 1814. He presided over a tiny court, 1,000 soldiers, and 13,700 subjects. Typically, he embarked on a frenzy of administrative, legal, and economic reforms to modernize Elba, but soon ran out of things to do because he ran out of money. The island's economy could not generate enough revenue to realize his ambitions and Louis XVIII refused to send him the 1 million francs promised under the Treaty of Fontainebleau. Atop these fiscal problems came rumors that the Congress of Vienna was planning to depose and exile him to a remote island. Other rumors insisted that ever more French people resented the Bourbons and longed for Napoleon to return to lead them. Finally, the allies not only kept his wife and son from joining him, but Empress Marie Louise and dashing Austrian General Adam von Neipperg were said to be lovers.[1]

Late on the afternoon of February 26, 1815, Napoleon, his staff, and 1,026 troops squeezed aboard 3 small ships and sailed for France. They set foot on French soil near Antibes on March 1. From there Napoleon led his men due north over the mountains. Louis XVIII ordered his commanders to find and destroy Napoleon. The turning point came in a mountain pass half a day's march from Grenoble on March 7. There 5,000 French troops barred the way. Napoleon deployed his own men then strode alone toward the other line. 'Soldiers!' he called out, 'I am your Emperor. If there is any soldier among you who wishes to kill his Emperor, here I am.' The soldiers cried 'Vive l'Empereur!' and surged joyfully around him.[2]

From there Napoleon's march was a triumphal procession. Louis XVIII and his entourage packed into carriages and clattered away to their latest exile on March 19. They did not stop running until they reached Liège, close enough to several ports to sail to a more secure site overseas if need be. Napoleon entered Paris on March 20, and immediately began reorganizing his realm's administration, finances, and military. He received no direct reply to his pleas to the Great Powers for recognition of his rule and peace. However, what they did do convinced him that he had no choice but to prepare France for war.[3]

At Vienna, the great and lesser powers took little time deciding what to do after hearing the stunning news that Napoleon had escaped. Even before learning where he was, representatives of Britain, Russia, Austria, Prussia, Spain, Sweden, Portugal, and Bourbon France declared him an outlaw on March 13. The declaration's wording was curious:

In breaking the Convention which established him on the Isle of Elba, Bonaparte is destroying the sole legal title to which his existence is attached. In reappearing in France with projects of confusion and disorder, he has placed himself beyond the protection of the law ... The Powers declare that Napoleon Bonaparte is placed outside civil and social relations, and that as an enemy and disturber of the peace ... has rendered himself subject to public prosecution.[4]

After learning that Louis had fled and Napoleon had retaken France's throne, Britain, Russia, Austria, and Prussia reactivated their alliance on March 25. Each would muster at least 150,000 troops to march against Napoleon, a campaign partly underwritten with £5 million of British gold. This would be the seventh and final coalition since 1793 that Britain had entered, helped fund, and tried to lead against France. Castlereagh instructed Wellington that for the alliance to succeed 'it must be done upon the largest scale ... you must inundate France with force in all directions.'[5] The strategy was for five armies to invade France and crush Napoleon by mid-summer. Two armies would march from the Low Countries, with Arthur Wellesley, Duke of Wellington commanding a mixed force of British, Dutch, Flemish, and German troops, and Gebhard von Blücher a Prussian army. In Germany Karl von Schwarzenberg and Michel Barclay de Tolly their respective Austrian and Russian armies for the long march to Paris. Meanwhile, an Austrian army led by Johan von Frimont would invade southeastern France from western Italy.

Wellington wrapped up the diplomacy and planning, and departed Vienna on March 29. Upon reaching Brussels on April 4, he immediately began mobilizing and organizing all available troops and supplies, and receiving reinforcements from Britain. He spent days reconnoitering various paths of advance that Napoleon might take and defensible positions along those ways. He studied Marlborough's campaigns in the region. King William I named Wellington the commander-in-chief of all Dutch troops on May 3. The same day, Wellington met Blücher at Tirlemont, midway between Brussels and Liège, their respective headquarters. The generals vowed to protect each other's flank no matter how fierce Napoleon's inevitable onslaught. If so, they would prevail with their overwhelming numbers of troops, nearly twice as many as the French army beyond the frontier; if not, Napoleon would likely defeat them separately.

Wellington's planning was limited by the lack of concrete intelligence on the disposition of Napoleon's corps and thus his probable intentions. He expressed his frustration at:

... the situation in which we are placed at present neither at war nor at peace, unable ... to patrol up to the enemy and ascertain his position ... All we can do is to put our troops in such a situation, as, in case of a sudden attack by the enemy, to render it easy to assemble, and to provide against the chance of being cut off from the rest.[6]

He recalled that Napoleon:

... took a position in which his numbers, his movements, and his designs could be concealed, protected, and supported by his formidable fortresses on the frontier up to the last moment previous to their being carried into execution. The Allied generals could not attack this position without being prepared to attack a superior army so posted. They could not therefore have the initiative of the operations in the way of attack....The initiative, then, rested with the enemy, and the course to be pursued by the Allied Generals ... was to be prepared in all directions, to wait till it should be seen in what direction the attack should be made, and then to assemble the armies as quickly as possible to resist the attack, or to attack the enemy with the largest force that could be collected.[7]

The best that Wellington could do was spread his corps across his stretch of the front at strategic junctions so that they could unite rapidly against an attack. He was well aware of Napoleon's history of launching strategic envelopments. Anticipating that Napoleon might try to hook around his right flank and cut his army off from Antwerp and other seaport supply centers, Wellington deployed Rowland Hill's corps from Menin nearly to Mons, where William, Prince of Orange's corps took over and spread nearly to Nivelle. Regiments of the cavalry corps were deployed behind those two front corps, while the reserve corps was quartered in Brussels.

Napoleon, meanwhile, spent two-and-a-half months massing supplies, conscripting troops, and directing regiments to one of eight corps along the frontiers or four corps in the interior. The most important cluster of corps was on the border where Wellington and Blücher were massing their own armies. This was the closest launch pad for an invasion of France. Somehow Napoleon had to destroy Wellington and Blücher before Schwarzenberg and Barclay de Tolly invaded France. If not, the campaign would resemble that of 1814 and end with his overthrow. He designated the five corps on this front the Army of the North and shut the border so that no one could carry word of his troop dispositions to the enemy.

Napoleon left Paris on the night of June 12 and arrived at Beaumont, his initial headquarters, the next afternoon.[8] His plan was simple. He would lead his army north in two wings, shatter the hinge between the armies of Wellington and Blücher, then destroy each separately. Doing so was a long-shot at best. He was severely outgunned.

On the campaign's eve, Napoleon's Army of the North numbered 122,652 troops to the combined armies of Wellington and Blücher that numbered 222,555 men. Napoleon's army included the corps of Jean Baptiste Drouet d'Erlon's 20,950-man 1st Corps; Honore Reille's 25,100-man 2nd Corps; Dominique Vandamme's 17,150-man 3rd Corps; Maurice Gerard's 15,700-man 4th Corps; George Lobau Mouton's 10,300-man 6th Corps; the Imperial Guard's 20,200 troops; and 21,652 cavalry in 4 corps or attached to each infantry corps.[9] Wellington had 92,309 troops, including 68,829 infantry and 14,474 cavalry split among 3 infantry corps and a cavalry corps. William, Prince of Orange, commanded the 1st Corps with 25,233 troops, General Rowland Hill the 2nd Corps with 24,033 troops, Wellington himself headed the Reserve Corps with 20,563 infantry and 912 cavalry, and General John Paget, Earl of Uxbridge the cavalry corps with 10,155 men. Fewer than 1 in 3 of Wellington's soldiers were British, 28,000 redcoats to 65,000 Dutch, Flemish, and German troops. As in Spain, he grouped British and foreign regiments in the same brigades to ensure balance between his hardened veterans and the mostly green and less reliable foreigners. Blücher's army numbered 130,246 troops and 304 cannons, with General Hans Joachim von Ziethen's 32,692-man 1st Corps, General Georg von Pirch's 32,704-man 2nd Corps, General Johann von Thielemann's 24,456-man 3rd Corps, and General Graf Bülow von Dennewitz's 31,102-man 4th corps.[10]

Napoleon launched his campaign early on the morning of June 14. Marshal Michel Ney commanded the left wing corps of d'Erlon and Reille, and Marshal Emmanuel de Grouchy the right wing corps of Vandamme, Gerard, and Lobau. Ney's orders were to quick-march due north and pulverize any of Wellington's forces along the road to Brussels, while Grouchy drove the Prussians eastward away from Wellington. Napoleon and his Imperial Guard would initially advance with Grouchy.

Wellington certainly did not expect Napoleon to attack as soon as he did. He first learned of the French invasion mid-afternoon on June 15. He fired off a flurry of orders to his commanders to converge on Quatre Bras, a strategic crossroads midway between the frontier and Brussels. Then, that evening he famously attended the ball of Charlotte, Duchess of Richmond and her husband Charles Lennox, the duke.[11] In doing so, he kept a promise that he had made weeks earlier to her. When Charlotte asked him whether she should hold her ball, he replied, 'Duchess, you may give your ball with the greatest safety, without fear of interruption.'[12]

Throughout the ball couriers arrived with the latest information. Wellington eventually:

> ... said to the Duke of Richmond, 'I think it is time for me to go to bed likewise,' and then, while wishing him good night, whispered to ask him if he had a good map in his house. The Duke of Richmond said he had, and took him into this dressing-room. The Duke shut the door and said, 'Napoleon has humbugged me, by God! He has gained twenty-four hours' march on me.' The Duke of Richmond said, 'What do you intend doing?' The Duke of Wellington replied, 'I have ordered the army to concentrate at Quatre Bras; but we shall not stop him there, and if so, I must fight him here,' at the same time pressing his thumb-nail over the position of Waterloo. He then said adieu, and left the house by another way out.[13]

Wellington left Brussels at dawn on June 16, and reached his troops at Quatre Bras around 10 o'clock that morning. To his surprise, there were no French in sight. He cantered 3 hours to join Blücher at Sombreffe near Ligny. What he witnessed appalled him. Blücher had deployed his troops on front slopes facing the French, who were then deploying, and would be exposed to relentless pounding by French artillery and skirmishers. He whispered to Sir Henry Hardinge, the British liaison with Blücher, that the Prussians would be 'damnably mauled' if Blücher did not redraw his troops to relative safety behind the slopes. When Hardinge gently passed on this observation, General August von Gneisenau, Blücher's chief of staff, was not grateful for the advice, snapping, 'That is true, but our men like to see their enemy.'[14] Wellington returned swiftly to his own army.

The battle of Ligny unfolded exactly as Wellington had feared. Napoleon unleashed an artillery bombardment that devastated the 84,000 Prussians, then marched most of his 68,000 troops at the remnants. Blücher withdrew his battered army that evening, having suffered 18,772 casualties to Napoleon's 13,721.[15] He made a crucial decision to head north to Wavre with three of his four corps, while sending Ziethen's corps northeast to cover his supply depot at Liège. He was deadset to keep his promise to support Wellington at all costs.

Meanwhile, Wellington reached Quatre Bras just in time to direct the battle. The usually impetuous Ney hesitated from attacking. He was well aware of Wellington's tactical brilliance, having fought and lost several battles against him in the Peninsula. He assumed that Wellington had concealed overwhelming numbers of troops in the woods and fields around Quatre Bras. In mid-afternoon, Ney launched Reille's corps in a series of piecemeal attacks that Wellington parried with fresh regiments marching up. In early evening, Wellington counter-attacked with most of his 36,000 troops and 70 cannons that drove back Ney's 47,000 troops. The duke's men held their ground at a higher cost of 4,600 casualties than the 4,100 French casualties.[16]

The battles of either Ligny or Quatre Bras and thus the campaign would have turned out sharply different had not Napoleon and Ney unwittingly got in a tug-of-war over d'Erlon's corps on the road between them. D'Erlon could have smashed either into Blücher's right flank or Wellington's left flank, thus turning Ligny from a limited into a decisive victory or Quatre Bras from a defeat into a victory. Instead, d'Erlon and his men spent the day marching back and forth between the battles without ever firing a shot as he followed the latest order from Napoleon or Ney. Napoleon later insisted that had Ney 'attacked the English with all his troops, he would have crushed them ... And if after having committed that first error he had not made his second blunder, by preventing the Comte d'Erlon from joining me ... Blucher's entire army would have been captured or destroyed.'[17]

Around 7 in the morning of June 17, Wellington read a report of the battle of Ligny. To his staff, he explained: 'Old Blucher has had a damned good hiding, and has gone back to Wavre, eighteen miles to the rear. We must do the same. I suppose they'll say in England that we have been licked; well I can't help that.'[18] With his cavalry and light infantry protecting his rear, Wellington withdrew his army 10 miles and deployed most of it along the low ridge a mile south of Waterloo, while posting contingents in two strongholds in the shallow valley below, a walled chateau named Hougoumont that guarded his right and a walled farm complex called La Haye Saint before his center. Although his left flank lacked a similar defense, this did not matter as long as Blücher arrived there on time. All along Wellington ensured that 'the two armies communicated throughout the night' of June 17 and throughout the next day.[19]

Napoleon ordered Grouchy to pursue Blücher with the corps of Gerard and Vandamme, while he led Lobau's corps to join Ney at Quatre Bras.

When Napoleon arrived the next morning, he was enraged to learn that Wellington's army had disappeared north and Ney's men were still at the crossroads rather than in hot pursuit. Napoleon ordered Ney to set his men in motion. But a heavy rain began and slowed the pursuit to a muddy slog. He later learned that Grouchy had mistakenly followed Ziethen rather than Blücher, thus leaving Blücher free to join Wellington at Waterloo on June 18.

The armies at Waterloo were evenly matched in numbers if not quality, with Wellington fielding about 73,200 troops and Napoleon about 77,500 troops, although the French had 246 cannons to 157 for the British; man for man, the French army was superior to Wellington's mongrel army of British, Dutch, Flemish, and German troops in experience and discipline.[20]

Wellington enjoyed four advantages over Napoleon. First, the rain slowed Napoleon's advance to a crawl on June 17 and soaked the earth and roads so thoroughly that he could not deploy his troops and begin the battle until around noon on June 18. Second, Napoleon's stomach was troubling him so that he let Ney handle much of the battle and only issued a half-dozen general orders all day. Third, Blücher was marching his army to the rescue, and Bülow's corps would assault the French right flank in late afternoon. Finally, Wellington asserted every dimension of his tactical genius at Waterloo, later recalling that 'I never gave myself so much trouble as I did that day to place the Troops; I went & chose the ground for every Corps myself.'[21]

A quarter mile from Wellington's ridge was another low ridge along which Napoleon deployed his troops and cannons. In late morning, the French began cheering and shouting 'Vive l'Empereur!' as Napoleon rode among them. A British artillery officer called out to Wellington, 'There's Bonaparte, Sire, I think I can reach him, may I fire?' The Duke was aghast. 'No, Generals commanding armies have something else to do than to shoot at one another.'[22]

Around the same time, Napoleon had less chivalrous words for his opponent. Marshal Soult, his chief of staff, cautioned him about Wellington's prowess. This enraged Napoleon, who snarled: 'Just because you have been beaten by Wellington, you regard him as a great general. I tell you that Wellington is a bad general and the English are bad troops and this battle will be a picnic … We will sleep this night in Brussels.'[23]

Just before noon, the 84 French cannons in place opened fire. Wellington immediately withdrew his troops behind the ridge. Most balls plopped harmlessly into the sodden earth rather than bounced to wreak havoc through any troops in their path as they would have on dry earth.

Napoleon had Reille send Jerome Bonaparte's division to capture Hougoumont, a chateau anchoring the right flank. The battle there raged throughout the day. As Jerome's attacks failed, Reille committed his other divisions to the struggle. Wellington was pleased that Napoleon took this bait. He had carefully placed regiments in and around the chateau, screened by batteries to devastate any attack. He would not have been greatly concerned even if the French captured the chateau because 'they could not have held it long, as our howitzers completely commanded it.'[24]

The French guns ceased fire abruptly around 2 o'clock. Napoleon, believing that the British were retreating, ordered d'Erlon to attack. D'Erlon marched his 19,000 men forward in 2 huge columns down into the valley to the right of La Haye Saint and up the ridge. Wellington hurried his regiments back into line as his gunners blasted the vast targets moving slowly, steadily toward them. As the depleted French columns struggled up the ridge, the defenders decimated them with volleys of musket fire. Wellington then delivered the *coup de grâce* with a cavalry charge that routed d'Erlon's corps. Napoleon ordered some of his own cavalry regiments to charge. They drove back the British cavalry, then withdrew. A stretch of the valley from ridge to ridge was strewn with heaps of mostly dead and wounded French troops.

A brief lull ensued as the only sound of heavy firing came from Hougoumont. Napoleon ordered several regiments forward to attack La Haye Saint, a walled farm complex a couple of hundred yards before the ridge. Someone pointed out a mass of troops far to the east. The hope that those were Grouchy's corps was soon dispelled when Prussian flags were clearly seen. Blücher's advance guard had arrived. Napoleon ordered Lobau to attack with his corps and drive them back. It was then that Napoleon withdrew to the yard of an inn called La Belle Alliance and largely observed, while Ney took over the battle.

As the French artillery reopened fire, Wellington again withdrew his troops behind the ridge. Believing that Wellington was retreating, Ney ordered a cavalry charge. Wellington had his regiments form squares. Captain Rees Gronow observed Wellington enter one of the squares, 'accompanied by one aide-de-camp; all the rest of the staff being either killed or wounded. Our Commander-in-Chief … appeared perfectly composed, but looked very thoughtful and pale.'[25] For Gronow, the:

… charges of cavalry were in appearance very formidable, but in reality a great relief, as the artillery could no longer fire on us; the very earth shook under the enormous mass of men and horses. I shall never forget the strange noise our bullets made against the breastplates of the cuirassiers … who attacked us in great fury.[26]

Ensign Cready recalled that the French cavalry's:

first charge was magnificent. As soon as they quickened their trot into a gallop, the Cuirassiers bent their heads so the peak of their helmets looked like visors and they seemed cased in armour … Not a shot was fired till they were within thirty yards when the word – and our men fired away at them. The effect was magical – thro' the smoke we could see helmets falling … horses plunging and rearing in the agonies of fright and pain and crowds of soldiery dismounted.

The French cavalry charged repeatedly. 'There was no difficulty in repulsing them but our ammunition decreased alarmingly – at length our artillery wagon galloped up [and] emptied two or three casks of cartridges into the square.'[27] For about 15 minutes there was a tense standoff as 'our People would not throw away their fire till the Cuirassiers charged, & they would not charge until we had thrown away our fire.'[28] When General Colin Halkett sent a courier racing to Wellington with a plea to retreat, the Iron Duke replied: 'Tell him that what he asks is impossible. He and I and every Englishman on the field must die on the spot which we occupy.'[29]

Although the French did finally capture La Haye Saint, the Prussians pushed back Lobau and overran Plancenoit, a village on the French right flank. Napoleon ordered his Young Guard to attack Plancenoit; those elite troops captured the village after vicious fighting. Blücher threw in fresh troops that pushed out the Young Guard. The Prussians were now poised to roll up the French right. Ney pleaded with Napoleon to order his Old Guard to attack Wellington's center, arguing that the enemy was near the breaking point. Napoleon finally agreed. The Old Guard marched across the valley and up the slope. Wellington lined up his regiments and ordered them to open fire. The Old Guard faltered. Wellington ordered his troops to charge with lowered bayonets. The Old Guard broke and fled.

The allied armies converged, routing the French before them. Toward dusk Wellington and Blücher rode forward to joyfully shake hands at La Belle Alliance. Their armies had shattered the French army, inflicting 46,656 casualties, while Wellington's men suffered 17,000 and Blücher's 7,000 dead, wounded, and missing.[30]

   Napoleon the general did not impress Wellington. During the battle, the Duke quipped, 'D–n the fellow, he is a mere pounder after all.'[31] Later he explained that 'Napoleon did not manoeuvre at all: he just moved forward in the old style in columns, and was driven off in the old style.'[32] Nonetheless, he admitted that 'I never took so much trouble about any Battle & never was so near being beat.'[33] He generously acknowledged the aid he received from his ally: 'I should not do justice to my own feelings, or to Marshall Blucher and the Prussian army, if I did not attribute the successful result of this arduous day to the cordial and timely assistance I received from them. The operation of General Bulow upon the enemy's flank was a most decisive one.'[34] Yet Wellington found in himself the crucial element for the allied victory: 'I don't think it would have done if I had not been there.'[35]

Chapter 24

Requiem

I have given myself up to the English; but I would not have done so to any other of the allied powers. In surrendering to any of them, I should be subject to the caprice and will of an individual – in submitting to the English, I place myself at the mercy of a nation. Adieu.

Napoleon Bonaparte

I look upon Salamanca, Vitoria, and Waterloo as my three best battles – those which had great and permanent consequences. Salamanca relieved the whole south of Spain, changed all the prospects of the war, and was felt even in Prussia. Vitoria freed the Peninsula altogether, broke off the armistice at Dresden and thus led to Leipzig and the deliverance of Europe; and Waterloo did more than any other battle I know towards the true object of all battles – the peace of the world.

Arthur, Duke of Wellington

Stunning news on June 28 broke the tedium of a month-long blockade of the neighboring ports of Rochefort and La Rochelle by Captain Frederick Maitland and his crew of the 74-gun *Bellerophon* and the men aboard two accompanying frigates.[1] Wellington and Blücher had crushed Napoleon at the battle of Waterloo and the upstart had abandoned his army's remnants and fled to Paris. Maitland soon learned from informants on the mainland that the day after Napoleon reached Paris on June 21, the Senate and National Assembly, emboldened by his devastating defeat, voted jointly to depose him. Napoleon erupted with rage but could do nothing but abdicate. He lingered a few days at Malmaison, the palace near Paris that he had shared many happy years with Josephine before giving it to her with their divorce; she had died the previous year and he now had only melancholy memories and regrets. Meanwhile, couriers brought word that the allied armies were approaching Paris and that Blücher had dispatched his light cavalry to range far across the French countryside to hunt Napoleon down and kill him. On June 25, Napoleon fled Paris in hope of reaching a port and boarding a vessel that could evade the blockade and sail him to exile overseas.

Word reached Maitland on July 11 that a prominent man had arrived on the nearby Île d'Aix and had offered local boat captains a large sum of money to convey him and several followers past the British warships and across the Atlantic. No one took his money. Then, on July 13, Maitland and his men rejoiced when lookouts with spyglasses reported that unseen hands had replaced the tricolor flags flying above towns on the mainland and the Île d'Aix with white Bourbon flags. The following dawn a schooner flying a white flag sailed toward the *Bellerophon*. Aboard were Emmanuel de Las Cases and General Charles Lallemand, who identified themselves as Napoleon's aides. Las Cases explained that the 'Emperor is so anxious to spare the further effusion of human blood that he will proceed to America in any way the British government chooses to sanction ... even in a British ship of war.'[2]

Maitland explained that he could only promise British justice and insist on Napoleon's unconditional surrender. Napoleon submitted the following day, July 15. He boarded the *Bellerophon* with a letter to Prince Regent George that read: 'I come to take my place before the hearth of the British people. I place myself under the protection of their laws, which I now claim of Your Royal Highness, as that of the most powerful, most consistent, and most generous of my enemies.'[3]

They sailed to Portsmouth but Napoleon's sojourn in Britain was brief. As he awaited his fate confined to the *Bellerophon*, Liverpool, Castlereagh, and the rest of the Cabinet debated what to do with him. On July 28, they finally decided to exile Napoleon to the remote island of Saint Helena in the southern Atlantic Ocean. Napoleon was transferred to the 74-gun *Northumberland*, which sailed on August 7.

Meanwhile, the French government agreed to an armistice on July 3. Wellington and Blücher led their troops into Paris on July 7. Louis XVIII reached Paris the following day, once again arriving with a foreign army's baggage train. The war was finally over. This time the peace for France was harsh. Under the Treaty of Paris, signed, on November 20, 1815, France would be reduced to her 1789 boundaries, pay an indemnity of 700 million francs, and be occupied by foreign troops for five years.

The person ultimately responsible for all this stepped ashore on Saint Helena on October 15. He would spend the rest of his life there dictating his memoirs, bickering with Governor Hudson Lowe, and mulling a lifetime of triumphs and disasters. Napoleon Bonaparte died on May 5, 1821, but the era named after him essentially ended at Waterloo.

And for that one man above all was responsible. Waterloo was the appropriate climax to the career of Arthur Wellesley, the Duke of Wellington, who had mastered the art of military power on land. Wellington candidly assessed his own impact on the war:

> I look upon Salamanca, Vitoria, and Waterloo as my three best battles – those which had great and permanent consequences. Salamanca relieved the whole south of Spain, changed all the prospects of the war, and was felt even in Prussia. Vitoria freed the Peninsula altogether, broke off the armistice at Dresden and thus led to Leipzig and the deliverance of Europe; and Waterloo did more than any other battle I know towards the true object of all battles – the peace of the world.[4]

Wellington's victories, however, depended on those of someone who achieved epic fame before him. During this era, only one other Briton matched Wellington's prowess at war. Horatio Nelson mastered the art of military power at sea, and achieved immortality for his victories at the Nile, Copenhagen, and, above all, Trafalgar that devastated France's naval power.

The victories of Wellington and Nelson obscure the harsh reality that Britain's military record during the Age of Revolution and Napoleon was mixed. On land, no general came close to displaying Wellington's sustained brilliance in India, the Peninsula, and Flanders. A few generals did lead notable campaigns against formidable enemy forces like Ralph Abercromby in Egypt in March 1801, John Stuart in Calabria in July 1806, Isaac Brock at Detroit in August 1812 and Queenstown Heights in October 1812; and above all Rowland Hill in an array of campaigns. However, most generals were mediocrities at best, elevated to critical commands by political connections rather than merit. British forces suffered humiliating debacles while led by William Beresford at Buenos Aires in August 1806; John Whitelocke at Buenos Aires in August 1807; Frederick Augustus, Duke of York at Walcheren in October 1807; John Moore in Spain from October 1808 to January 1809; and Edward Pakenham at New Orleans from December 1813 to January 1814.

The Royal Navy, in contrast, was far more consistent than the army in racking up victories. Although no one matched Nelson's three decisive sea battles, admirals that devastated enemy fleets included Samuel Hood at

Toulon in December 1793, Richard Howe in the north Atlantic in June 1794, John Jervis off Cape Saint Vincent in February 1797, and Adam Duncan off Camperdown in October 1797. Although they never commanded fleets during this war, captains like Edward Pellew, Thomas Cochrane, William Sidney Smith, and Cuthbert Collingwood won their own battle laurels. While there were no truly inept admirals, a few restrained their captains from converting minor into major victories such as Henry Hotham over Nelson near Hyères in March and June 1795, and James Gambier over Cochrane at Basque Roads in April 1809.

The Royal Navy's war record did vary with its enemies. The imbalance in fighting skills between the British and French navies was stunning. For instance, from 1793 to 1815, the British captured or sank 229 French frigates, while the French captured or sank merely 17 British frigates, of which the British recaptured 9![5] During this era, only the Americans bested the Royal Navy. During the 1812 War, American captains captured 17 British warships, while losing 10 warships. America's greatest naval victory took place at the battle of Put-in-Bay on Lake Erie in September 1813, when Captain Oliver Perry's flotilla battered Captain Robert Barclay's entire flotilla of six warships to strike its colors.

Battles can only be understood within the opposing strategies of the campaigns in which they erupt. If tactics are what leaders pursue in battle, strategy involves getting to or from battles. The strategies of Britain's civilian and military leaders were as controversial as the battle tactics of its generals and admirals on campaign.

The prime minister and his Cabinet determined Britain's grand strategy against its enemies. After the war opened in February 1793, Prime Minister William Pitt and the ministers debated which of two opposing strategies to pursue. Foreign Secretary William Grenville called for a 'continental' strategy whereby Britain built up a huge army with which to invade France and march to Paris in a broad offensive with allied European armies; the goal was to destroy the enemy regime and reimpose Bourbon family rule. War Secretary Henry Dundas called for a 'maritime' strategy whereby the Royal Navy systematically destroyed enemy fleets, blockaded enemy ports, and captured enemy colonies around the world; the goal was the British Empire's aggrandizement at the expense of the French Empire and its allies. Each strategy aimed at defeating France, the continental strategy by one massive blow, the maritime strategy by steadily destroying France's economy and thus its ability to finance its war. The continental strategy emphasized building and underwriting a winning coalition of armies against France. The maritime strategy emphasized expanding Britain's already superior naval, merchant, colonial, financial, and industrial power while sweeping the seas of French naval and merchant ships.

The ministers only agreed that Britain could afford to follow either strategy but not both. Initially Whitehall tried to resolve the tug-of-war between the Continental and Maritime camps by stretching the rope either way, often to the snapping point. From 1793 to 1795, York led an army expedition in the Low Countries in rough coordination with Dutch, Austrian, and Prussian armies, while the Royal Navy blockaded French ports, swept the seas of French naval and merchant vessels, and captured French colonies. The French eventually defeated one by one the enemy armies in the Low Countries and along the Rhine, Italian, and Spanish frontiers.

The maritime strategy then prevailed for 13 years after the humiliating return of York's expedition in 1795. During this time, the navy systematically destroyed French naval power and conquered France's colonial empire, culminating with the battle of Trafalgar in October 1805. This left Britain with unchallenged naval and commercial power, but did little to check French conquests in Europe, especially after Napoleon Bonaparte took over the government in 1799.

The shift to the continental strategy began symbolically with Wellesley's brief campaign that liberated Portugal from French occupation in 1808, then substantively in 1809 when Wellesley returned to command the British, Portuguese, and, eventually, Spanish armies against France's for mastery over the Iberian Peninsula. Although Lisbon was a long way from Paris, a consensus gradually coalesced in Whitehall that British-led armies in the Peninsula were as crucial in undermining France's domination of the continent as were Austrian, Russian, and Prussian armies in central Europe. Even then the diplomacy of coalition warfare often led to compromises that actually hindered the war against France. For instance, in 1809, Whitehall dispatched a massive expedition to Holland to divert French attention from its war against Austria. Wellesley was enraged that all those troops and supplies were not reinforcing his own army; he protested that: 'You cannot maintain military operations in the Peninsula and in Holland with British troops; you must give up either the one or the other.' The reason was simple. Britain simply was not economically or militarily powerful enough to maintain 'two armies in the field.'[6]

Nonetheless, it was the continental strategy that eventually destroyed Napoleon's rule twice, in 1814 and then 1815. By late 1813, the army of

Wellesley, now Duke of Wellington, had driven the French from nearly all of the Peninsula and invaded southwest France. In April 1814, by the time Napoleon abdicated in the face of overwhelming allied armies that had captured Paris, Wellington's army had fought all the way to Toulouse deep in southern France. Then, after Napoleon retook power in March 1815, Wellington was the obvious choice to command a British, Dutch, Flemish, and German army in the Low Countries in coalition with a nearby Prussian army and distant Austrian and Russian armies marching toward France. Napoleon's ultimate defeats would not have been possible without the 1812 Russian campaign and the six-year Peninsular War. Of the two, Napoleon later reckoned his 'Spanish ulcer' the most destructive: 'All ... my disasters are connected with that fatal knot.'[7] Napoleon lost perhaps a quarter of a million troops there that might have overwhelmed Russia in 1812 had they joined Napoleon's half-million troops who eventually perished there.

Although France could only be decisively defeated in Europe, ultimately by capturing Paris, deposing Napoleon, and imposing Louis XVIII, the maritime strategy was crucial in preparing the way for the continental strategy. Wellington could not fight his way across the Peninsula and into France from 1808 to 1814 unless the Royal Navy obliterated the French navy, a reality that the duke readily acknowledged: 'If anyone wishes to know the history of this war, I will tell them that it is our maritime superiority which gives me the power of maintaining my army, while the enemy are unable to do so.'[8]

As an island realm, every overseas land campaign was necessarily a joint navy-army operation. In this, Britain's army and navy eventually excelled. Captain Edward Brenton of the Royal Navy explained this vital reason for Britain's ultimate triumph: 'All our failures in former wars may be attributed to the irresponsibility of our chiefs, to councils of war, and to the jealousies existing between the army and the navy. In this respect our service had wonderfully improved.'[9] Those 'jealousies' did not disappear but army and navy leaders reduced them to near the vanishing point during 22 years of nearly constant war.

Total war, or a state's mobilization of all available human and material resources against the enemy, was another dimension of strategy that British leaders took years to understand let alone implement. They eventually mastered the art of total war because they had little choice in doing so. France's revolutionaries initiated and Napoleon perfected the art of total war. Indeed the masses of troops that Napoleon mobilized and the intensity and pace with which he wielded them against his enemies was unprecedented. No other country was capable of matching the sheer numbers of men and materiel that Napoleon mobilized; only a coalition could do so.

A people's or guerrilla war of civilians and soldiers fighting enemies in their midst is the ultimate stage of total war. The French and nearly all other states which suffered invasion abstained from a people's war. Only in Calabria, Tyrolea, Russia, and, above all, Spain, did guerrillas join regular troops in fighting a war without mercy against the invaders. In doing so they terrorized the French either into holing up in their strongholds or dispatching huge forces to guard supply trains and even couriers. In the Peninsula Major Edward Cocks, an intelligence officer, noted the importance of Spain's people's war for British operations: 'The Spanish guerillas have annoyed the enemy very much; they are very useful because they oblige the enemy to form so many detachments in order to secure his communications and command in some measure the resources of the country.'[10] Wellington made good use of the guerrilla war that the Spanish were waging against the French, explaining: 'Independent small bodies operating upon the enemy may be extremely useful when these operations are connected and carried on in concert with in concert with ... a large body of troops which ... occupy the whole of the enemy's attention.'[11] The Peninsula's terrain favored guerrilla warfare. Much of the Peninsula was sparsely populated or outright wilderness, with mountains and forests in which guerrillas could hide, observe, and strike with overwhelming force. Numerous ports and deep-water coves along the Peninsula's coasts also aided the guerrillas. British naval superiority let ships drop anchor and send ashore munitions and supplies to local guerrilla bands.

Whitehall made plenty of critical strategic decisions from 1793 to 1815 that seemed like the best at the time but proved to be disastrous. For instance, the British obsession with the Low Countries was understandable if misplaced. Each of the four campaigns that Whitehall launched there in 1793–5, 1799, 1807, and 1814 literally and figuratively bogged down and was extracted only after immense losses of men and money. Only in 1815, was a campaign there decisive and only because Wellington commanded it.

Likewise, the West Indian strategy made perfect sense when Whitehall implemented it. The strategy was straightforward and dictated by circumstances – seize the enemy's colonies before he seized yours. French Marine Minister Admiral Denis Decrès explained the relationship between colonial and naval power: 'There's no point in a navy without colonies; there is no point in colonies without a powerful navy.'[12] Yet Britain's systematic conquest of France's West Indian empire involved a terrible dilemma – the greater one's success in capturing islands, the heavier the cost in lives and cash. 'Victory' in the Caribbean was pyrrhic, given the 100,000 British soldiers and sailors who died there during the era, nearly all from disease. The West Indies were literally the graveyard of military careers. Of the 88,969 regular troops who served there from 1793 to 1801, 43,750 died. The worst charnel house was Saint Domingue, where one of three soldiers died. Atop this carnage, another 8,600 men were discharged for bad health, while 3,000 more discharged themselves by deserting. This brings the total loss to British army to seven of every ten soldiers sent there. The loss in the army's soft power was just as enormous but is impossible to measure. Many of these troops were either hardened veterans of the Flanders campaign or elite flank companies detached from their regiments in Britain. As for the navy, the statistics are much less precise, but about one in five men died while serving in these waters. Battle deaths accounted for only about one of every hundred men.[13] Then there was the financial cost. By one estimate, Whitehall may have paid as much as £30 million for its West Indian campaigns from 1793 to 1801, compared with £35.7 million for its European and Mediterranean campaigns, £13.4 million for its armies, and £22.4 million in subsidies to its allies.[14]

Were the gains for Britain and subsequent losses for France and its allies worth so many deaths? In retrospect, perhaps not, but for Pitt and the Cabinet the maritime strategy of conquering the colonies of its enemies made perfect strategic and economic sense. Michael Duffy, who wrote the classic study of Britain's West Indian campaigns from 1793 to 1801, goes so far as to argue that Abercromby's expedition of 1795–6 'saved the war.' The reason was that Whitehall needed to secure its hold on the Caribbean and rake in diplomatic bargaining chips to trade for a favorable peace treaty. Britain also gained economically from 1793 to 1801, as its share of the international sugar trade expanded from one-third to two-thirds, and the share of West Indian trade in Britain's total trade rose from one-fifth to one-fourth.[15]

Yet Britain could have achieved more at a lower cost of lives and money in the West Indies simply by blockading enemy colonies rather than trying to capture them. Naval operations could have paid for themselves with all the seizures of expensive cargos being shipped back and forth across the Atlantic basin. With the Royal Navy supreme in the West Indies, the British could have thwarted invasions and crushed slave revolts with relatively small garrisons of acclimated troops. This was largely France's strategy. Paris committed only enough ships and troops to the West Indies to stave off the inevitable conquest as long as possible at as high an enemy cost as possible. Napoleon foolishly changed this strategy by trying to conquer the West Indies. He reckoned his loss of 20,000 troops largely in Saint Domingue from 1801 to 1804 among his worst mistakes.

Upon concluding a treaty whereby Haitian General Toussaint Louverture promised, among other things, not to attack the British as they withdrew from Saint Domingue, Lieutenant Colonel Thomas Maitland was exuberant: 'Thank God I have at length got Great Britain rid of the whole of the encumbrance of this island.'[16] That pretty much sums up the entire British experience in the Caribbean during the era.

So, how would the war have changed had the 89,000 troops Whitehall sent to the Caribbean instead been landed somewhere in Europe? Would the subsequent campaigns in the Low Countries have been victories rather than humiliating defeats? Certainly, the more troops that Whitehall committed to any European front would have forced Paris to divert more troops and supplies from other fronts to counter it, thus spreading their power ever thinner.

Overall, Britain's leaders mastered the art of not just military power but national power during the Age of Revolution and Napoleon. And that ultimately was grounded in overwhelming economic power – financial, commercial, agrarian, and industrial. Entrepreneurs, financiers, and inventors made Britain's economy the world's most dynamic. The Bank of England and sophisticated money-changers let Britain's government raise enough money not just to build and maintain a navy with more than twice as many warships as the two second largest navies combined, but underwrite seven coalitions that eventually crushed France. Britain emerged from these wars to become and remain the global superpower for the next century.[17]

List of Abbreviations

Addington Correspondence	George Pellew, ed., *The Life and Correspondence of the Right Hon. Henry Addington, 1st Viscount Sidmouth*, 3 vols (London: John Murray, 1897).
Archives Parlementaires	*Archives Parlementaire de 1787 à 1860: Recueil complet des débats législatifs et politiques des chambres Françaises*, 127 vols (Paris: Bibliothèque Nationale de France, 1879–1913).
ASPFR	*American State Papers, Foreign Relations.*
Auckland Correspondence	Bishop of Bath and Wells, ed., *The Journal and Correspondence of William, Lord Auckland*, 4 vols (London: R. Bentley, 1861–2).
BL	British Library
British Diplomacy	C.K. Webster, ed., *British Diplomacy: Select Documents dealing with the Reconstruction of Europe, 1813–15* (London: G. Bell, 1921).
British Foreign Policy	Harold Temperley and Lillian Penson, eds, *The Foundations of British Foreign Policy* (London: Frank Cass and Company, 1966).
British Statistics	B.R. Mitchell and Phyllis Deane, *Abstract of British Historical Statistics* (Cambridge: Cambridge University Press, 1962).
Castlereagh Correspondence	Charles William Vane, Marquis of Londonderry, ed., *The Correspondence, Despatches, and Other Papers of Viscount Castlereagh, Second Marquis of Londonderry*, 12 vols (London: John Murray, 1848–53).
Cornwallis Correspondence	Charles Ross, ed., *The Correspondence of Charles, First Marquis, Cornwallis*, 3 vols (London: John Murray, 1859).
Creevey Papers	John Gore, ed., *The Thomas Creevey Papers* (New York: Macmillan, 1904).
Croker Papers	Louis J. Jennings, ed., *The Croker Papers: The Correspondence and Diaries of John Wilson Croker, Secretary to the Admiralty from 1809 to 1830*, 3 vols (London: John Murray, 1885).
Farington Diary	James Greig, ed., *The Farington Diary*, 8 vols (London: Hutchinson, 1922).
Fortescue Manuscripts	*Report on the Manuscripts of J.B. Fortescue, esq., preserved at Dropmore*, vols 1–10 (London: Historical Manuscripts Commission, 1892–1927).

FO	Foreign Office.
HO	Home Office.
George III Correspondence	Arthur Aspinall, ed., *The Later Correspondence of George III*, 5 vols (Cambridge: Cambridge University Press, 1962–70).
George, Prince Correspondence	Arthur Aspinall, ed., *The Correspondence of George Prince of Wales, 1770–1812*, 8 vols (London: Cassell, 1963–71).
George IV Letters	Arthur Aspinall, ed., *The Letters of George IV, 1812–30* (Cambridge: Cambridge University Press, 1938).
Gordon Letters	Rory Muir, ed., *The Letters of Lieutenant Colonel Alexander Gordon, 1808–1815* (London: Sutton, 2003).
Leeds Political Memoranda	Oscar Browning, ed., *The Political Memoranda of Francis Fifth Duke of Leeds* (London: Nicolas and Sons, 1884).
Malmesbury Correspondence	James Harris, Earl Malmesbury, *The Diaries and Correspondence of James Harris, the First Earl of Malmesbury*, 4 vols (London: Richard Bentley, 1845),
Memoirs of the Courts	Duke of Buckingham and Chandos, ed., *Memoirs of the Courts and Cabinets of George the Third*, 2 vols (London: Hurst & Blackett, 1853–5).
Napoléon Correspondance	Thierry Lentz et al., eds, *Napoléon Bonaparte Correspondance Générale*, Vols 1–15 (Paris: Fayard, 2004–18).
Nelson Dispatches	Nicolas Harris, ed., *The Dispatches and Letters of Vice-Admiral Lord Viscount Nelson*, 7 vols (Cambridge: Cambridge University Press, 2011).
NYPL	New York Public Library.
Parliamentary Debates	William Cobbett, ed., *Parliamentary Debates*, 22 vols (London: R. Bagshaw, 1804–12).
Parliamentary Debates from 1803	T.C. Hansard, ed., *The Parliamentary Debates from the Year 1803* (London: T.C. Hansard, 1812).
Parliamentary History	William Cobbett, ed., *The Parliamentary History of England from the Earliest Times to 1803*, 36 vols (London: R. Bagshaw, 1806–20).
Parliamentary Register	John Debrett, ed., *The Parliamentary Register, or, History of the Proceedings and Debates of the House of Commons*, 2nd ser. 45 vols (London: R. Spottiswoode, 1781–96); 3rd ser. 18 vols (London: R. Spottiswoode, 1797–1802).
Pitt-Rutland Correspondence	Charles Rutland, Duke of, *Correspondence between the Right Hon. William Pitt and Charles, Duke of Rutland* (London: R. Spottiswoode, 1842).
Pitt Speeches	*The Speeches of the Right Hon. William Pitt in the House of Commons*, 3 vols (London: Longman, Hurst, and Orne, 1817).
Pitt War Speeches	Richard Copeland, ed., *The War Speeches of William Pitt the Younger* (Oxford: Clarendon, 1918).

PRO	Public Record Office (The National Archives).
Rose Correspondence	L.V. Harcourt, ed., *The Diaries and Correspondence of the Right Hon. George Rose* (London: Richard Bentley, 1860).
Smith Correspondence	J. Barrow, ed., *The Life and Correspondence of Admiral Sir William Sidney Smith*, 2 vols (London: Richard Bentley, 1848).
Stanhope Conversations	Philip Henry, Fifth Earl of Stanhope, *Notes of Conversations with the Duke of Wellington, 1831–1851* (London: John Murray, 1885).
Stanhope Miscellanies	Philip Henry, First Earl of Stanhope, *Miscellanies: Collected and Edited by Earl Stanhope* (London: John Murray, 1872).
WO	War Office.
Wellesley-Pole Letters	Charles Webster, ed., *Some Letters of the Duke of Wellington to his Brother, William Wellesley Pole* (Camden Miscellany, Royal Historical Society, Vol. 18, 1948).
Wellington Conversations	Gerald Wellington, ed., *The Conversations of the First Duke of Wellington with George William Chad* (Cambridge: St Nicholas Press, 1956).
Wellington Dispatches	Colonel Gurwood, ed., *The Dispatches of Field Marshall the Duke of Wellington*, 8 vols (London: Park, Furnivall, and Parker, 1944).
Wellington Reminiscences	Alice, Countess of Strafford, ed., *Personal Reminiscences of the Duke of Wellington by Francis, the First Earl of Ellesmere* (New York: E.F. Dutton, 1903).
Wellington Supplements	Duke of Wellington, *The Supplementary Despatches, Correspondence, and Memoranda of Field Marshall Arthur, Duke of Wellington*, 15 vols (London: John Murray, 1858–72).
Wraxall Memoir	Nathaniel Wraxall, ed., *The Historical and Posthumous Memoirs of Sir Nathaniel William Wraxall, 1772–1784* (London: Bickers & Sons, 1884).

Notes

Introduction

1. For the only comprehensive and systematic overview of the related economic, military, population, technological, cultural, leadership, and thus political forces shaping British foreign policy from 1789 to 1815, see: William R. Nester, *Titan: The Art of British Power during the Age of Revolution and Napoleon* (Norman: University of Oklahoma Press, 2016).

   For an overview of Whitehall's efforts to organize the war effort, see: Roger Knight, *Britain against Napoleon: The Organization of Victory, 1793–1815* (Norman: University of Oklahoma Press, 2013). For the classic study of how Britain financed the seven coalitions against Revolutionary France then Napoleon, see: John W. Sherwig, *Guineas and Gunpowder: British Foreign Aid in the Wars with France, 1793–1815* (Cambridge, Mass.: Harvard University Press, 1969). For an excellent analysis of the assertion of Britain's financial power during an earlier era that puts the latter in perspective, see: John Brewer, *The Sinews of Power: War, Money, and the English State, 1688–1783* (New York: Alfred A. Knopf, 1988).

   For British strategies against Napoleon, see: Richard Glover, *Britain at Bay: Defense against Bonaparte, 1803–14* (London: Allen and Unwin, 1973); Christopher D. Hall, *British Strategy in the Napoleonic War, 1803–1815* (Manchester: Manchester University Press, 1992); Rory Muir, *Britain and the Defeat of Napoleon, 1807–1815* (New Haven: Yale University Press, 1996). For the prequel, see: Brendan Simms, *Three Victories and a Defeat: The Rise and Fall of the British Empire* (New York: Basic Books, 2009).

   For the British state's origins and development, see: Brewer, *The Sinews of Power*; M.J. Braddick, *The Nerves of State: Taxation and the Financing of the English State, 1558–1714* (Manchester: Manchester University Press, 1996); Tony Claydon and Ian McBride, eds, *Protestantism and National Identity: Britain and Ireland, 1650–1850* (Cambridge: Cambridge University Press, 1998); J.C.D. Clark, *English Society, 1688–1832: Ideology, Social Structure, and Political Practice during the Ancient Regime* (Cambridge: Cambridge University Press, 2000); Michael J. Turner, *The Age of Unease: Government and Reform in Britain, 1782–1832* (London: Longman, 2000); Philip Harling, *The Modern British State: An Historical Introduction* (Oxford: Clarendon, 2001); Eric J. Evans, *The Forging of the Modern State: Early Industrial Britain, 1783–1870* (New York: Pearson, 2001); H.T. Dickinson, ed., *A Companion to Eighteenth Century Britain* (Oxford: Blackwell, 2002); H.T. Dickinson, ed., *A Companion to Eighteenth Century Britain* (Oxford: Blackwell Publishing, 2006).

   For British foreign policy during straddling, or leading to this era, see: Paul Langford, *Modern British Foreign Policy: The Eighteenth Century, 1688–1815* (New York: Vintage, 1976); Derek McKay and Hamish K. Scott, *The Rise of the Great Powers, 1648–1815* (London: Longman, 1982); Ian R. Christie, *Wars and Revolutions: Britain, 1760–1815* (Cambridge, Mass.: Harvard University Press, 1982); Jeremy Black, *Natural and Necessary Enemies: Anglo-French Relations in the Eighteenth Century* (Athens: University of Georgia Press, 1986); Jeremy Black, ed., *Knight Errant and True Englishmen: British Foreign Policy, 1660–1800* (Edinburgh: University of Edinburgh Press, 1989); C.A. Bayly, *Imperial Meridian: The British Empire and the World, 1780–1830* (London: Longman, 1989); John Clarke, *British Diplomacy and Foreign Policy, 1782–1865: The National Interest* (Boston: Unwin, Hymen, 1989); H.M. Scott, *British Foreign Policy in the Age of the American Revolution* (Oxford: Oxford University Press,1990); Jeremy Black, *A System of Ambition: British Foreign Policy, 1660–1793* (New York: Longmans, 1993); Jeremy Black, *British Foreign Policy in an Age of Revolution, 1783–1793* (Cambridge: Cambridge University Press, 1994); Wilfrid Prest, *Albion Ascendant: English History, 1660–1815* (Oxford: Oxford University Press, 1998); Jeremy Black, *A System of Ambition?: British Foreign Policy, 1660–1793* (London: Longman, 2000); Linda Colley, *Captives: Britain, Europe, and the World, 1600–1850* (London: Pantheon, 2002); Niall Ferguson, *Empire: How Britain Made the Modern World* (New York: Basic Book, 2004); Simms, *Three Victories and a Defeat*; Boyd Hilton, *A Mad, Bad, & Dangerous People?: England, 1783–1846* (New York: Oxford University Press, 2008); Linda Colley, *Britons: Forging the Nation, 1707–1837* (New Haven: Yale University Press, 2009); Adolphus Ward and George Gooch, eds, *The Cambridge History of British Foreign Policy, 1783–1919* (New York: Cambridge University Press, 2011).

2. For developments in early modern warfare before this era, see: Andre Corvisier, *Armies and Society in Europe, 1494–1789* (Bloomington: University of Indiana Press, 1976); John Childs, *Armies and Warfare in Europe, 1648–1789* (Manchester: Manchester University Press, 1982); C.B.A. Behrens, *Society, Government, and the Enlightenment: The Experiences of Eighteenth Century France and Prussia* (London: Harper and Row, 1985); Christopher Duffy, *The Military Experience in the Age of Reason, 1715–1789* (New York: Barnes and Noble, 1987); Brent Nosworthy, *The Anatomy of Victory: Battle Tactics, 1689–1763* (New York: Hippocrene Books, 1992).

For war's continuities and changes during both eras, see: Azar Gat, *The Origins of Military Thought from the Enlightenment to Clausewitz* (New York: Oxford University Press, 1989); Russell F. Weigley, *The Age of Battles: The Quest for Decisive Warfare from Brietenfeld to Waterloo* (Bloomington: Indiana University Press, 1991); Roger Chickering and Stig Forster, eds, *War in an Age of Revolution, 1775–1815* (New York: Cambridge University Press, 2010).

For the French revolutionary wars, see: Samuel F. Scott, *The Response of the Royal Army in the French Revolution: The Role and Development of the Line Army, 1787–1793* (Oxford: Oxford University Press, 1978); Steven T. Ross, *Quest for Victory: French Military Strategy, 1792–1799* (New York: Barnes and Company, 1978); John A. Lynn, *The Bayonets of the Republic: Motivation and Tactics in the Army of Revolutionary France, 1791–1794* (Urbana: University of Illinois Press, 1984); Howard G. Brown, *War, Revolution, and the Bureaucratic States: Politics and Army Administration in France, 1791–1799* (New York: Oxford University Press, 1995); Paddy Griffith, *The Art of War of Revolutionary France, 1789–1802* (Mechanicsburg, Pa.: Stackpole Books, 1998).

For Napoleon's wars, see: Baron Henri de Jomini, *The Art of War* (Westport: Greenwood Press, 1862); David Chandler, *The Campaigns of Napoleon: The Mind and Method of History's Greatest Soldier* (New York: Macmillan, 1966); Gunther Rothenberg, *The Art of War in the Age of Napoleon* (Bloomington: Indiana University Press, 1981); David Chandler, *On the Napoleonic Wars* (London: Greenhill Books, 1991); Geoffrey Parker, *The Military Revolution: Military Innovation and the Rise of the West, 1500–1800* (New York: Cambridge University Press, 1996); Brent Nosworthy, *With Musket, Cannon, and Sword: Battle Tactics of Napoleon and His Enemies* (New York: Da Capo Press, 1996);

David Gates, *The Napoleonic Wars, 1803–1815* (New York: Arnold Press, 1997); John R. Elting, *Swords around a Throne: Napoleon's Grande Armée* (New York: Da Capo, 1997); Carl von Clausewitz, *On War* (New York: Wadsworth Classic, 1999); Digby Smith, *The Greenhill Napoleonic Wars Data Book: Actions and Losses in Personnel, Colours, Standards, and Artillery, 1792–1815* (London: Greenhill Books, 1998); Vincent J. Esposito and John R. Elting, *A Military History and Atlas of the Napoleonic Wars* (London: Greenhill Books, 1999); Owen Connelly, *Blundering to Victory: Napoleon's Military Campaigns* (New York: Rowan and Littlefield, 2006); Robert Harvey, *War of Wars: The Great European Conflict, 1793–1815* (New York: Carol and Graf, 2006); Jonathan Riley, *Napoleon as a General* (London: Hambledon Continuum, 2007); Charles Esdaile, *Napoleon's Wars: An International History, 1803–1815* (New York: Viking, 2007); David Bell, *The First Total War* (New York: Houghton Mifflin, 2007); Christy Pichichiore, *The Military Enlightenment: War and Culture in the French Empire, From Louis XIV to Napoleon* (Ithaca: Cornell University Press, 2017).

For armies, uniforms and arms, see: Philip Haythornthwaite, *The Napoleonic Source Book* (London: Arms and Armour, 1990); Anthony D. Darling, *Red Coat and Brown Bess* (Bloomfield: Museum Restoration Service, 1993); Philip Haythornthwaite and Michael Chappell, *Uniforms of the Peninsular War, 1807–1814* (London: Arms and Armour, 1995); Philip Haythornthwaite and Christopher Warner, *Uniforms of the French Revolutionary Wars* (London: Arms and Armour, 1997).

3. Books on Britain's early modern political economic development could fill a small library.

For a theoretical view, see: John Hatcher and Mark Bailey, *Modelling the Middle Ages: The History and Theory of England's Economic Development* (New York: Oxford University Press, 2001).

For the government's role, see: Julian Hoppit, *Britain's Political Economies: Parliament and Economic Life, 1660–1800* (New York: Cambridge University Press, 2017).

For agrarian power, see: Mark Overton, *Agricultural Revolution in England: The Transformation of the Agrarian Economy, 1500–1850* (Cambridge: Cambridge University Press, 1996); G.E. Mingay, *Parliamentary Enclosure in England: An Introduction to Its Causes, Incidence, and Improvements, 1750–1850* (London: Longman, 1997).

For financial power, see: Ralph Willard Hidy, *The House of Baring in American Trade and Finance: English Merchant Bankers at Work, 1763–1861* (Cambridge, Mass.: Harvard University Press, 1949); L.S. Pressnell, *Country Banking in the Industrial Revolution* (Oxford: Oxford University Press, 1956); Patrick K. O'Brien, 'The Political Economy of British Taxation, 1660–1815,' *Economic History Review*, Vol. 41 (1988), 1–32; Patrick O'Brien and Philip A. Hunt, 'The Rise of a Fiscal State in England, 1485–1815,' *Historical Research*, Vol. 96 (1993), 129–76; Patrick O'Brien, *Power with Profit: The State and Economy, 1688–1815* (London: Weidenfeld & Nicolson, 1991); Lawrence Stone, ed., *An Imperial State at War: Britain from 1689 to 1815* (London: Routledge, 1994); M.J. Braddick, *The Nerves of State: Taxation and the Financing of the English State, 1558–1714* (Manchester: Manchester University Press, 1996); Niall Ferguson, *The World's Banker: The History of the House of Rothschild* (London: Weidenfeld & Nicolson, 1998).

For entrepreneural, cultural, and social power, see: Sidney Pollack, *The Genesis of Modern Management: A Study of the Industrial Revolution in Great Britain* (New York: Penguin, 1965); Neil McKendrick, John Brewer, and J.H. Plumb, *The Birth of a Consumer Society: The Commercialization of Eighteenth Century England* (Bloomington: University of Indiana Press, 1982); Julian Hoppit, *The Rise and Failures of English Business, 1700–1800* (Cambridge: Cambridge University Press, 1987); Janet Wolfe and John Seed, eds, *The Culture of Capital: Art, Power, and the Nineteenth Century Middle Class* (Manchester:

Manchester University Press, 1988); Peter Earle, *The Making of the English Middle Class: Business, Society, and Family Life in London, 1660–1730* (Berkeley: University of California Press, 1989); Peter Langford, *A Polite and Commercial People: England, 1727– 1783* (Oxford: Oxford University Press, 1989); Alan J. Kidd and David Nicolls, eds, *The Making of the British Middle Class?: Studies of Regional and Cultural Diversity since the Eighteenth Century* (Stroud: Sutton, 1998); Penelope J. Corfield, *Power and the Professions in Britain, 1700–1850* (New York: Routledge, 2000); F.M.L. Thompson, *Gentrification and the Enterprise Culture: Britain, 1780–1980* (Oxford: Oxford University Press, 2001).

For urbanization power, see: M.D. George, *London Life in the Eighteenth Century* (Harmondsworth: Penguin, 1966), 319; Penelope J. Corfield, *The Impact of English Towns, 1700–1800* (Oxford: Oxford University Press, 1982); Jan de Vries, *European Urbanization, 1500–1800* (Cambridge, Mass.: Harvard University Press, 1984), table 3.6; Peter Borsay, *The English Urban Renaissance: Culture and Society in the Provincial Town, 1660–1770* (Oxford: Oxford University Press, 1989); Jeffrey G. Williamson, *Coping with City Growth during the British Industrial Revolution* (New York: Cambridge University Press, 1990); Peter Clark, ed., *The Cambridge Urban History of Britain, 1540–1840* (New York: Cambridge University Press, 2000).

For transportation power, see: J.R. Ward, *The Finance of Canal Building in Eighteenth Century England* (London: Oxford University Press 1974); E. Pawson, *Transport and Economy: The Turnpike Roads of Eighteenth Century Britain* (New York: Academic Press, 1977).

For related trade and industrial power, see: C.N. Parkinson, *The Trade Winds: A Study of British Overseas Trade during the French Wars, 1793–1815* (London: Allen and Unwin, 1948); Bernard Semmel, *The Rise of Free Trade Imperialism: Classical Political Economy, the Empire of Free Trade, and Imperialism, 1750–1850* (Cambridge: Cambridge University Press, 1970); Judith Blow Williams, *British Commercial Policy and Trade Expansion, 1750– 1850* (Oxford: Oxford University Press, 1972); Ralph Davis, *The Industrial Revolution and British Overseas Trade* (Leicester: Leicester University Press, 1979); Eric Hobsbawm, *Industry and Empire: The Economic History of Britain since 1750* (New York: W.W. Norton, 1999); William J. Ashworth, *Customs and Excise: Trade, Production, and Consumption in England, 1640–1845* (Oxford: Oxford University Press, 2003).

For industrial power, see: A.E. Munsen, and Eric Robinson, *Science and Technology in the Industrial Revolution* (Manchester: University of Manchester Press, 1969); G.N. Tunzelman, *Steam Power and British Industrialization to 1860* (Oxford: Oxford University Press, 1978); Maxine Berg, *The Age of Manufacturers: Industry, Innovation, and Work in Britain, 1700–1820* (Oxford: Oxford University Press, 1985); François Crouzet, *The First Industrialists: The Problem of Origins* (Cambridge: Cambridge University Press, 1985); François Crouzet, *Britain Ascendant: Comparative Studies in Franco-British Economic History* (New York: University of Cambridge Press, 1985); N.F.R. Crafts, *British Economic Growth during the Industrial Revolution* (Oxford: Oxford University Press, 1985); L.A. Clarkson, *Proto-Industrialization: The First Phase of Industrialization?* (London: Macmillan, 1985); E.A. Wrighley, *Continuity, Chance, and Change: The Character of the Industrial Revolution in England* (Cambridge: Cambridge University Press, 1988); Pat Hudson, ed., *Regions and Industries: A Perspective on the Industrial Revolution in Britain* (Cambridge: Cambridge University Press, 1989); Pat Hudson, *The Industrial Revolution* (London: Macmillan, 1992); Peter Mathias, *The First Industrial Nation: An Economic History of Britain, 1700–1914* (New York: Routledge, 2001); Eric J. Evans, *The Forging of the Modern State: Early Industrial Britain, 1783– 1870* (New York: Pearson, 2001); Roderick Floud and Paul Johnson, eds, *The Cambridge*

Economic History of Modern Britain: Industrialization, 1700–1860 (New York: Cambridge University Press, 2004); Kenneth Morgan, *The Birth of Industrial Britain: Social Change, 1750–1859* (New York: Pearson, 2004); Joel Mokyr, *The Enlightened Economy: Britain and the Industrial Revolution, 1700–1850* (New York: Penguin, 2011); Barrie Trinder, *Britain's Industrial Revolution: The Making of a Manufacturing People* (New York: Carnegie Publishing, 2014).

For the British empire, see: Vincent T. Harlow, *The Founding of the Second British Empire, 1763–1793* (London: Longman, 1964); P.J. Cain and A.G. Hopkins, *British Imperialism: Innovation and Expansion, 1688–1914* (New York: Longman, 1993); Lawrence James, *The Rise and Fall of the British Empire* (New York: St Martin's Griffith Press, 1994); P.I. Marshall, ed., *The Oxford History of the British Empire: The Eighteenth Century* (Oxford: Oxford University Press, 1998); David Armitage, *The Ideological Origins of the British Empire* (Cambridge: Cambridge University Press, 2000).

4. For the early modern relationship between Britain's naval and national power, see: William James, *Naval History of Great Britain, 1793–1820*, 5 vols (London: Richard Bentley, 1822–4); R.G. Albion, *Forests and Sea Power* (Cambridge, Mass.: Harvard University Press, 1926); Michael Lewis, *A Social History of the Navy, 1783–1815* (London: Allen and Unwin, 1960); Otto von Pivka, *Navies of the Napoleon Era* (London: D. & C. Newton Abbot, 1980); N.A.M. Rodger, *The Wooden World: An Anatomy of the Georgian Navy* (New York: W.W. Norton, 1986); J. Coad, *The Royal Dockyards, 1690–1815: Architecture and Engineering Works of the Sailing Navy* (Aldershot: Scolar Press, 1989); Richard Harding, *The Evolution of the Sailing Navy, 1509–1815* (Basingstoke: Palgrave Macmillan, 1995); Jeremy Black and Philip Woodfine, eds, *The British Navy and the Use of Naval Power in the Eighteenth Century* (Leicester: Leicester University Press, 1998); Richard Harding, *Seapower and Naval Warfare, 1650–1830* (Annapolis: Naval University Press, 1999); Margarette Lincoln, *Representing the Royal Navy: British Sea Power, 1750–1815* (Burlington: Ashgate, 2002); Peter Padfield, *Maritime Power and the Struggle for Freedom: Naval Campaigns that Shaped the Modern World, 1788–1851* (London: John Murray, 2003); Clive Wilkinson, *The British Navy and the State in the Eighteenth Century* (London: Boydell Press, 2004); N.A.M. Rodger, *The Command of the Ocean: A Naval History of Britain, 1649–1815* (New York: W.W. Norton, 2006).

5. *Britain's Rise to Global Superpower* is a 'battles and leaders' and 'strategies and tactics' account of Britain during the Age of Revolution and Napoleon. It presents the era's twenty-two most important British land and sea military campaigns. Each chapter's 'methodology' involves simply explaining what major events happened, why they happened, and the results. The prominent scholarly books for each campaign are presented in one or more endnotes for that chapter. The Art of Power and Requiem chapters provide comprehensive and systematic analyses for understanding the reasons for and results of the campaigns in the context of the entire era.

Astonishingly, no one has ever done this before. Of the twenty-two campaigns presented in *Britain's Rise to Global Superpower*, only two were decisive, Trafalgar at sea and Waterloo on land. And, yes, the brilliant leadership of Nelson and Wellington was the most important reason why Trafalgar and Waterloo were decisive British victories. Different leaders might well have resulted in those battles either being lost or not fought. The notion that leadership – good, bad, and mediocre – can be the decisive force that determines what happens in a conflict will undoubtedly startle and even anger some 'scholars' schooled in the neo-marxist belief that only grand forces like 'capitalism,' 'class,' or 'the people' matter. But, the critical importance of leadership is as historically correct even as some believe it to be ideologically or politically incorrect.

Chapter 1

1. John Sturgis, ed., *A Boy in the Peninsular War: The Services, Adventures, and Experiences of Robert Blakeney, Subaltern in the 28th Regiment* (London: John Murray, 1899), 12.

2. For British reactions to the French Revolution, see: Alfred Cobban, ed., *The Debate on the French Revolution* (London: N. Kaye, 1950); F. O'Gorman, *The Whig Party and the French Revolution* (Basingstoke: Macmillan, 1967); Albert Goodwin, *The Friends of Liberty: The English Democratic Movement in the Age of the French Revolution* (Cambridge, Mass.: Harvard University Press, 1979); J.E. Cookson, *The Friends of Peace: Anti-War Liberalism in England, 1793–1815* (Cambridge: Cambridge University Press, 1982); F. Kennedy, *The Jacobin Clubs in the French Revolution: The First Years* (Princeton: Princeton University Press, 1982); Robert Dozier, *For King, Constitution, and Country: The English Loyalists and the French Revolution* (Lexington: University of Kentucky Press, 1983); Colin Jones, ed., *Britain and Revolutionary France: Conflict, Subversion, and Propaganda* (Exeter: University of Exeter Press, 1983); Marilyn Butler, ed., *Burke, Paine, Godwin, and the Revolution Controversy* (Cambridge: Cambridge University Press, 1984); H.T. Dickinson, *British Radicalism and the French Revolution, 1789–1815* (Oxford: Oxford University Press, 1985); Seamus Deane, *The French Revolution and Enlightenment in England, 1789–1832* (Cambridge, Mass.: Harvard University Press, 1988); Gwyn A. Williams, *Artisans and Sans Culottes: Popular Movements in France and Britain during the French Revolution* (London: Edward Arnold, 1989); H.T. Dickinson, *Britain and the French Revolution* (Basingstoke: Macmillan, 1989); Derek Jarrett, *Three Faces of Revolution: Paris, London, New York in 1789* (London: G. Philip, 1989); Mark Philp, ed., *The French Revolution and British Popular Politics* (Cambridge: Cambridge University Press, 1991); Marilyn Morris, *The British Monarchy and the French Revolution* (New Haven: Yale University Press, 1998).

3. *Archives Parlementaires*, 15:510.

4. William Pitt speech, February 17, 1792, *Parliamentary History*, 29:826.

5. For nineteenth-century accounts by people who either themselves or their descendants knew Pitt, see: George Tomline Pretyman, *Memoirs of the Life of the Right Hon. William Pitt*, 3 vols (London: John Murray, 1821); Philip Henry, Lord Stanhope, *Life of the Right Honorable William Pitt*, 4 vols (London: John Murray, 1867).

   For the most detailed and wordy biography, see the trilogy: John Ehrman, *The Younger Pitt: The Years of Acclaim* (Stanford: Stanford University Press, 1969); John Ehrman, *The Younger Pitt: The Reluctant Transition* (Stanford: Stanford University Press, 1983); John Ehrman, *The Younger Pitt: The Consuming Struggle* (Stanford: Stanford University Press, 1996). For good one-volume biographies, see Robin Reilly, *William Pitt the Younger: A Biography* (New York: G.P. Putnam's Sons, 1978); Eric Evans, *William Pitt the Younger* (New York: Routledge, 1999); William Hague, *William Pitt the Young* (New York: Harper Perennial, 2004). For Pitt and the French Revolution, see: Jennifer Mori, *William Pitt and the French Revolution, 1785–1795* (New York: St Martin's Press, 1997).

6. For the French Revolution, see: Will and Ariel Durant, *Rousseau and Revolution* (New York: Simon and Schuster, 1967); William Doyle, *The Oxford History of the French Revolution* (New York: Oxford University Press, 1989); Simon Schama, *Citizens: A Chronicle of the French Revolution* (New York: Alfred A. Knopf, 1989; Jeremy Popkin, *A Short History of the French Revolution* (New York: Routledge, 2014); Lynn Hunt and Jack Censer, *The French Revolution and Napoleon: Crucible of the Modern World* (New York: Bloomsbury, 2017); Ian Davidson, *The French Revolution: From Enlightenment to Tyranny* (New York: Pegasus, 2017); Timothy Tackett, *The Coming of the French Revolution* (Cambridge, Mass.: Harvard University Press, 2017).

7. Schama, *Citizens*, 640.

8. Charles François Doumouriez, *La Vie et les Mémoires du Général Dumouriez, Avec des notes et éclairissements historiques par M. M. Berville et Barière*, 4 vols (Paris: Baudoins Frères, 1822–3), 1:405–6.

9. For overviews of British policy during the first years of war, see: Ehrman, *The Younger Pitt: The Reluctant Transition.*

10. Peter Jupp, *Lord Grenville, 1759–1834* (New York: Oxford University Press, 1985); Holden Furber, *Henry Dundas, First Viscount Melville, 1741–1811: Political Manager of Scotland, Statesman, Administrator of British India* (Oxford: Oxford University Press, 1931); Cyril Matheson, *The Life of Henry Dundas, First Viscount Melville, 1742–1811* (London: Constable and Company, 1933).

11. King George III to William Pitt, September 14, 1793, Ehrman, *Younger Pitt*, 1:318.

12. For the best books, see note 2 above.

13. *Archives Parlementaires*, 10:472–4.

14. *Archives Parlementaires*, 10:520–2.

15. *Archives Parlementaires*, 10:674.

16. For British military organization, policies, and power, see: Richard Glover, *Peninsular Preparation: The Reform of the British Army, 1795–1809* (Cambridge: Cambridge University Press, 1988; J.A. Houlding, *Fit for Service: The Training of the British Army, 1715–1795* (Oxford: Oxford University Press, 1981); Alan James Guy, *The Road to Waterloo: The British Army and the Struggle against Revolutionary and Napoleonic France* (London: National Army Museum, 1990); Philip J. Haythornthwaite, *The Armies of Wellington* (London: Brockhampton Press, 1996); J.E. Cookson, *The British Armed Nation, 1793–1815* (Oxford: Oxford University Press, 1997); Jeremy Black, *Britain as a Military Power, 1688–1815* (London: Routledge, 1999); Edward J. Coss, *All the King's Shilling: The British Soldier under Wellington, 1808–1814* (Norman: University of Oklahoma Press, 2010); Andrew Bamford, *Sickness, Suffering, and the Sword: The British Regiment on Campaign, 1808–1815* (Norman: University of Oklahoma Press, 2013).

17. Wellington to Liverpool, January 2, 1810, *Wellington Dispatches*, 5:404.

18. Haythornthwaite, *Armies of Wellington*, 17–18.

19. Haythornthwaite, *Armies of Wellington*, 23.

20. Charles J. Esdaile, *Fighting Napoleon: Guerrillas, Bandits, and Adventurers in Spain, 1808–1814* (New Haven: Yale University Press, 2004), 78.

21. Haythornthwaite, *Armies of Wellington*, 28.

22. Haythornthwaite, *Armies of Wellington*, 32.

23. Philip Haythornthwaite, *Wellington: The Iron Duke* (Washington DC: Potomac Books, 2007), 42.

24. William Grattan, *Adventure with the Connaught Rangers, 1809–1814* (London: Henry Colburn, 1847), 50.

25. For British cavalry, see: Bryan Fosten, *Wellington's Heavy Cavalry* (London: Osprey Books, 1982); Bryan Fosten, *Wellington's Light Cavalry* (London: Osprey Books, 1982); Philip Hayhornthwaite, *British Cavalrymen, 1792–1815* (London: Osprey Books, 1994); Ian Fletcher, *Galloping at Everything: The British Cavalry in the Peninsular War and at Waterloo, 1808–15* (Mechanicsburg: Stackpole Books, 1999).

26. August Schaumann, *On the Road with Wellington: The Diary of a War Commissary in the Peninsular Campaign* (London: Naval and Military Press, 2009), 219.

27. Fletcher, *Galloping at Everything*, 19.

28. Haythornthwaite, *Armies of Wellington*, 114.

29. Haythornthwaite, *Armies of Wellington*, 48.

30. Haythornthwaite, *Armies of Wellington*, 21.
31. Haythornthwaite, *Armies of Wellington*, 44.
32. Haythornthwaite, *Armies of Wellington*, 43.
33. John R. Western, *The English Militia in the Eighteenth Century: The Story of a Political Issue, 1660–1802* (London: Routledge, 1965).
34. Haythornthwaite, *Armies of Wellington*, 183.
35. J.E. Cookson, *The British Armed Nation, 1793–1815* (Oxford: Oxford University Press, 1997); Austin Gee, *The British Volunteer Movement, 1794–1814* (Oxford: Oxford University Press, 2003).
36. Haythornthwaite, *Armies of Wellington*, 145, 150.
37. Haythornthwaite, *Armies of Wellington*, 148.
38. Otto von Pivka, *The Black Brunswickers* (London: Osprey Publishing, 1973).
39. *Stanhope Conversations*, 14. For analyses of the British army during this era, see: Haythornthwaite, *Armies of Wellington*; Edward J. Coss, *All the King's Shilling: The British Soldier under Wellington, 1808–1814* (Norman: University of Oklahoma Press, 2010); Andrew Bamford, *Sickness, Suffering, and the Sword: The British Regiment on Campaign, 1808–1815* (Norman: University of Oklahoma Press, 2013).
40. Eileen Hathaway, ed., *Benjamin Harris: A Dorset Rifleman* (London: Shinglepicker Press, 1995), 92.
41. Cobbett's Weekly Political Register, June 13, 1812, 741–2, NYPL.
42. Schaumann, *Diary*, 269.
43. Haythornthwaite, *Armies of Wellington*, 88.
44. Wellington to Rowland Hill, June 18, 1812, *Wellington Dispatches*, 9: 238.
45. David Gates, *The Spanish Ulcer: A History of the Peninsular War* (New York: Da Capo Press, 1986), 23.
46. For the overview of British naval strategy and operations during this era, see: William James, *Naval History of Great Britain, 1793–1820*, 5 vols (London: Richard Bentley, 1822–4); G.J. Marcus, *The Age of Nelson* (London: Allen and Unwin, 1971); C. Northcote Parkinson, *Britannia Rules: The Classic Age of Naval History, 1793–1815* (London: Alan Sutton Publishing, 1994); James Henderson, *The Frigates: An Account of the Lighter Warships of the Napoleonic Wars, 1793–1815* (London: Leo Cooper, 1994); Robert Woodman, *The Victory of Sea Power: Winning the Napoleonic War, 1806–1814* (London: Chatham Publishing, 1998); Peter Padfield, *Maritime Power and the Struggle for Freedom: Naval Campaigns that Shaped the Modern World, 1788–1851* (London: John Murray, 2003); Richard Harding, *British Admirals of the Napoleonic Wars: The Contemporaries of Nelson* (London: Chatham, 2005); Roy Adkins and Lesley Adkins, *The War for all the Oceans: From Nelson at the Nile to Napoleon at Waterloo* (New York: Viking, 2006); Noel Mostert, *The Line Upon a Wind: The Great War at Sea, 1793–1815* (New York: W.W. Norton, 2007); Sam Willis, *In the Hour of Victory: The Royal Navy at War in the Age of Nelson* (New York: W.W. Norton, 2014).

For naval shipbuilding and resources, see: R.G. Albion, *Forests and Sea Power* (Cambridge, Mass.: Harvard University Press, 1926); Roger Morriss, *The Royal Dockyards during the Revolutionary and Napoleonic Wars* (Leicester: Leicester University Press, 1983); J. Coad, *The Royal Dockyards, 1690–1815: Architecture and Engineering Works of the Sailing Navy* (Aldershot: Scolar Press, 1989).

For naval administration, manpower, and ship-life, see: Michael Lewis, *A Social History of the Navy, 1783–1815* (London: Allen and Unwin, 1960); N.A.M. Rodger, *The Wooden World: An Anatomy of the Georgian Navy* (New York: W.W. Norton, 1986); Brian Lavery, *Nelson's Navy: The Ships, Men, and Organization, 1793–1815* (Annapolis: Naval Institute Press,1989).

For overviews of the French navy, see: Martine Acerra and Jean Meyer, *Marine et Revolution* (Rennes: Edition Ouest France, 1988); J. Martray, *La Destruction de la marine Française par la Révolution* (Paris: France Empire, 1988); Patrick Crowhurst, *The French War on Trade: Privateering, 1793–1815* (London: Scolar Press, 1989); William S. Cormack, *Revolution and Political Conflict in the French Navy, 1789–1793* (Cambridge: Cambridge University Press, 1995); Michel Verge Franceschi, *La Marine Française au XVIIIe Siècle* (Paris: Sede, 1996); J.M. Humbert and B. Ponsonnet, *Napoléon et la Mer: Un Rêve d'Empire* (Paris: Seuil, 2004); J.J. Ségéric, *Napoléon Face à la Royal Navy* (Paris: Marine Editions, 2008); Jean-Claude Gillet, *La Marine impériale: Le Grand Rêve de Napoléon* (Paris: Bernard Giovanangeli Editeur, 2010).

47. Horatio Nelson to William Nelson, February 8, 1782, *Nelson Dispatches*, 1:57.

48. Rodger, *Wooden World*, 256.

49. Edward Brenton, ed., *The Life and Correspondence of John, Earl of St. Vincent* (1838, repr. London: Elibron Classics, 2005), 1:432.

50. Brenton, ed., *St. Vincent Correspondence*, 1:455.

51. Mostert, *Line Upon a Wind*, 36–43.

52. Mostert, *Line Upon a Wind*, 132–3.

53. Geoffrey Bennett, *Nelson the Commander* (New York: Scribners' Sons, 1972), 84.

54. Bennett, *Nelson*, 69.

55. Mostert, *Line Upon a Wind*, 64.

56. For the classic work on the dilemma, see Albion, *Forests and Sea Power*.

57. Mostert, *Line Upon a Wind*, 64.

58. Gillet, *La Marine impériale*, 68.

59. David Sobel, *Longitude: The True Story of a Lone Genius Who Solved the Greatest Scientific Problem of His Time* (New York: Penguin, 2006).

60. Parkinson, *Britannia Rules*, 9.

61. Gillet, *La Marine Impériale*, 17

62. G.F. Mainwaring, and Bonamy Dobree, *Mutiny: The Floating Republic* (London: Pen & Sword, 2004); Ann Veronica Coats and Philip Macdonald, *The Naval Mutinies of 1797: Unity and Perseverance* (London: Boydell Press, 2011).

63. Parkinson, *Britannia Rules*, 10.

64. Rodger, *Wooden World*, 205–51.

65. Voltaire, *Candide* (New York: Dover Publications, 1991), 64.

66. Anonymous, *The Proceedings of the Court Martial of Admiral Byng* (London: Gale, 2012).

67. Bennett, *Nelson*, 66.

68. For the best biographies, see: Elizabeth Longford, *Wellington: Years of the Sword* (New York: Harper and Row, 1969); Arthur Bryant, *The Great Duke or the Invincible General* (New York: William Morrow and Company, 1972); Jac Weller, *Wellington in the Peninsula* (Mechanicsburg: Stackpole Books, 1992); Christopher Hibbert, *Wellington: A Personal History* (Reading, Mass.: Perseus Books, 1997); Michael Glover, *Wellington as Military Commander* (New York: Penguin, 2001); John Severn, *Architects of Empire: The Duke of Wellington and His Brothers* (Norman: University of Oklahoma Press, 2007); Huw J. Davies, *Wellington's Wars: The Making of a Military Genius* (New Haven: Yale University Press, 2012); Rory Muir, *Wellington: The Path to Victory* (New Haven: Yale University Press, 2014).

69. George Robert Gleig, *The Life of Arthur, Duke of Wellington* (London: Longman Green, 1889), 4.

70. Gleig, *Wellington*, 1:6.

71. *Stanhope Conversations*, 182.

72. For the best biographies, see: Bennett, *Nelson* ; Terry Coleman, *The Nelson Touch: The Life and Legend of Horatio Nelson* (New York: Oxford University Press, 2002); Oliver Warner, *Nelson's Battles* (London: Pen & Sword Books, 2003); David Cannadine, ed., *Admiral Lord Nelson: Context and Legacy* (Houndmills: Palgrave Macmillan, 2005).
73. Brenton, ed., *St. Vincent Correspondence*, 2:42.
74. Horatio Nelson to Emma Hamilton, 16, 1801, Thomas Pettigrew, ed., *Memoirs of the Life of Vice-Admiral Lord Viscount Nelson*, 2 vols (London: T and W. Boone, 1849), 1:444.
75. Horatio Nelson to George Rose, October 6, 1805, *Nelson Dispatches*, 7:80.
76. John Jervis to Gilbert Elliot, August 22, 1796, Brenton, ed., *St. Vincent Correspondence*, 1:213.

Chapter 2

1. For the allied takeover and siege of Toulon, see: Robert Forczyk, *Toulon 1793: Napoleon's First Great Victory* (London: Osprey Books, 2005); Bernard Ireland, *The Fall of Toulon: The Last Opportunity to Defeat the French Revolution* (London: Cassell Military Paperbacks, 2005); Charles James Fox, *Napoleon Bonaparte and the Siege of Toulon: The First Victory of a Future Emperor of France, 1793* (London: Leonaur, 2010).
2. Ireland, *Fall of Toulon*, 143.
3. Horatio Nelson to Fanny Nelson, August 4, 1793, *Nelson Dispatches*, 1:316.
4. For the Terror, see: R.R. Palmer, *Twelve Who Ruled: The Year of Terror in the French Revolution* (Princeton, NJ: Princeton University Press, 1941); David Andress, *The Terror: The Merciless War for Freedom in Revolutionary France* (New York: Farrar, Straus, and Giroux, 2006).
5. Horatio Nelson to Fanny Nelson, September 11, 1793, *Nelson Dispatches*, 1:324.
6. Bonaparte to Committee of Public Safety, October 25, 1793, *Napoléon Correspondance*, 1:139.
7. For Bonaparte's initial plan, see Bonaparte to Committee of Public Safety, October 25, 1793,
    Napoléon Correspondance, 1:139; For his extensive plan, see Bonaparte to Bouchotte, November 14, 1793, *Napoléon Correspondance*, 1:142–7. For other revealing letters of Napoleon Bonaparte's activities during the siege, see: Bonaparte to Gassendi, September 18, 1793; Bonaparte to Carteaux, October [n.d.], 1793; Napoleon Bonaparte to Chauvet, October [n.d.], 1793; Napoleon Bonaparte to Government Representatives, October 16, 1793; Bonaparte to unknown, October [n.d.], 1793; Bonaparte to Gassendi, October 18, 1793; Bonaparte to Government Representatives, October 22, 1793; Bonaparte to unknown, October 24,1793; Bonaparte to Sucy, November 3, 1793; Bonaparte to Gassendi, November 4, 1793;
    Bonaparte to Dupin, November 30, 1793; Bonaparte to Gassendi, December 7, 1793; Bonaparte to Dupin, December 24, 1793; *Napoléon Correspondance*, 1:129; 131–2;132–3; 133–4; 134–5; 136; 137; 138; 140; 140–1; 148–9; 149; 154.
8. Sidney Smith to William, Lord Auckland, *Auckland Correspondence*, 3:157.
9. Ireland, *Fall of Toulon*, 232–3.
10. Ireland, *Fall of Toulon*, 210.
11. Bonaparte to Dupin, November 30, 1793, *Napoléon Correspondance*, 1:148–9.
12. Ireland, *Fall of Toulon*, 251.
13. Ireland, *Fall of Toulon*, 261–2, 249.
14. Bonaparte to Dupin, December 24, 1793, *Napoléon Correspondance*, 1:154.
15. Jean-Claude Gillet, *La Marine impériale: Le Grand Rêve de Napoléon* (Paris: Bernard Giovanangeli Editeur, 2010), 8.
16. Bonaparte to Dupin, December 24, 1793, *Napoléon Correspondance*, 1:154.

Chapter 3

1. For the Low Countries, see: E.H. Kossman, *The Low Countries, 1780–1940* (New York: Oxford University Press, 1978); J.H.C. Bloom and E. Lamberts, eds, *History of the Low Countries* (New York: Berghahn Books, 2006); Paul Arblaster, *A History of the Low Countries* (New York: Palgrave Macmillan, 2012).

   For Holland's rise and decline as a great power, see: Simon Schama, *The Embarrassment of Riches: An Interpretation of Dutch Culture in the Golden Age* (New York: Knopf, 1987); C.R. Boxer, *The Dutch Seaborne Empire, 1600–1800* (New York: Penguin, 1991); Jonathan Israel, *The Dutch Republic: Its Rise, Greatness, and Fall, 1477–1806* (New York: Oxford University Press, 1995); Wim Klooster, *The Dutch Moment: War, Trade, and Settlement in the Seventeenth Century Atlantic World* (Ithaca: Cornell University Press, 2016).

   For the seventeenth-century Anglo-Dutch wars, see: D.R. Hainsworth, *The Anglo-Dutch Wars, 1652–1674* (London: Sutton, 1998); J.R. Jones, *The Anglo-Dutch Wars of the Seventeenth Century* (New York: Routledge, 2015).

   For overviews of the French Revolutionary Wars of which most are fought in the Low Countries, see: Steven T. Ross, *The Quest for Victory: French Military Strategy, 1792–1799* (New York: Barnes and Company, 1978); T.C.W. Blanning, *The French Revolutionary Wars, 1787–1802* (London: Arnold, 1996); Paddy Griffith, *The Art of War of Revolutionary France, 1789–1802* (Mechanicsburg: Stackpole Books, 1998).

   For an excellent overview of British operations in the Low Countries during this era, see: Andrew Limm, *Walcheren to Waterloo: The British Army in the Low Countries during the French Revolutionary and Napoleonic Wars, 1793–1815* (London: Pen & Sword, 2018).
2. Ehrman, *Younger Pitt*, 1:269.
3. Ross, *Quest for Victory*, 45.
4. Alfred H. Burne, *The Noble Duke of York: The Military Life of Frederick Duke of York and Albany* (London: Staples Press, 1948).
5. Unless otherwise noted, all force strength and casualty statistics for this chapter were culled from Digby Smith, *The Greenhill Napoleonic Wars Data Book: Actions and Losses in Personnel, Colours, Standards, and Artillery, 1792–1815* (London: Greenhill Books, 1998).
6. Burne, *Noble Duke of York*, 46.
7. Charles Crauford to William, lord Auckland, September 23, 1794, *Auckland Correspondence*, 3:243.
8. Charles Crauford to William, lord Auckland, May 9, 1794, *Auckland Correspondence*, 3:210–12.
9. Charles Crauford to William, lord Auckland, August 8, 1794, *Auckland Correspondence*, 3:224–6.
10. Charles Crauford to William, lord Auckland, August 8, 1794, *Auckland Correspondence*, 3:226–7.
11. Charles Crauford to William, lord Auckland, September 26, 1794, *Auckland Correspondence*, 3:245–6.
12. *Wellington Reminiscences*, 161.
13. *Stanhope Conversations*, 182.
14. Horatio Nelson to Fanny Nelson, February 25, 1795, *Nelson Dispatches*, 2:8.

Chapter 4

1. For overviews of naval warfare, see: Alfred Thayer Mahan, *The Influence of Sea Power Upon History: The French Revolution and Empire, 1793–1812*, 2 vols (Boston: Little, Brown, 1892); Roger Morriss, *The Royal Dockyards during the Revolutionary and Napoleonic Wars*

(Leicester: Leicester University Press, 1983); Martine Acerra and Jean Meyer, *Marines et Révolution* (Rennes: Ouest France, 1988); C. Northcote Parkinson, *Britannia Rules: The Classic Age of Naval History, 1793–1815* (London: Alan Sutton Publishing, 1994); Peter Padfield, *Maritime Power and the Struggle for Freedom: Naval Campaigns that Shaped the Modern World, 1788–1851* (Woodstock: Overlook Press, 2003); Roy Adkins and Lesley Adkins, *The War for all the Oceans: From Nelson at the Nile to Napoleon at Waterloo* (New York: Viking, 2006); Noel Mostert, *The Line Upon a Wind: The Great War at Sea, 1793–1815* (New York: W.W. Norton, 2007); Sam Willis, *In the Hour of Victory: The Royal Navy at War in the Age of Nelson* (New York: W.W. Norton, 2014).

For French naval power and strategy, see: Acerra and Meyer, *Marines et Révolution*; J. Martray, *La Destruction de la marine Française par la Révolution* (Paris: France Empire, 1988); Patrick Crowhurst, *The French War on Trade: Privateering, 1793–1815* (London: Scolar Press, 1989); William S. Cormack, *Revolution and Political Conflict in the French Navy, 1789–1793* (Cambridge: Cambridge University Press, 1995); Michel Verge Franceschi, *La Marine Française au XVIIIe Siècle* (Paris: Sede, 1996); J.M. Humbert and B. Ponsonnet, *Napoléon et la Mer: Un Rêve d'Empire* (Paris: Seuil, 2004); J.J. Ségéric, *Napoléon Face à la Royal Navy* (Paris: Marine Editions, 2008); Jean-Claude Gillet, *La Marine impériale: Le Grand Rêve de Napoléon* (Paris: Bernard Giovanangeli, 2010).

For the classic work on the West Indies and British strategy during this era, see: Michael Duffy, *Soldiers, Sugar, and Seapower: The British Expeditions to the West Indies and the War against Revolutionary France* (Oxford: Clarendon Press, 1987). See also: Frances Armytage, *The Free Port System in the British West Indies* (London: Longmans, 1953); E.L. Cox, *The Free Coloreds in the Slave Societies of St. Kitts and Grenada, 1763–1833* (Knoxville: University of Tennessee, 1984); Martin Howard, *Death Before Glory: The British Soldier in the West Indies in the French Revolutionary and Napoleonic Wars, 1793–1815* (London: Pen & Sword, 2015).

For the Mediterranean, see: Gareth Glover, *The Forgotten War against Napoleon: Conflict in the Mediterranean* (London: Pen & Sword, 2017).

2. Henri Lémery, *La Révolution française à la Martinique* (Paris: Larose, 1936); T.O. Ott, *The Haitian Revolution, 1789–1801* (Knoxville: University of Tennessee Press, 1973); Jeremy Popkin, *A Concise History of the Haitian Revolution* (New York: Wiley-Blackwell, 2011).

3. D. Geggus, 'The British Government and the Saint Domingue Slave Revolt, 1791–1793,' *English Historical Review*, Vol. 96 (1981), 285–305; 'Digest of the Proceedings in the … Home Department with respect to the West Indies from December 1792 to December 1793,' BL add. mss 59239.

4. Edward Brenton, ed., *The Life and Correspondence of John, Earl of St. Vincent* (1838, repr. London: Elibron Classics, 2005), 1:93–4.

5. Duffy, *Soldiers, Sugar, and Seapower*, 88.

6. Duffy, *Soldiers, Sugar, and Seapower*, 94–5, 100; Brenton, ed., *St. Vincent Correspondence*, 1:116.

7. Duffy, *Soldiers, Sugar, and Seapower*, 103–4.

8. Duffy, *Soldiers, Sugar, and Seapower*, 124.

9. For the Glorious First of June, see: Michael Duffy, ed., *The Glorious First of June, 1794: A Naval Battle and Its Aftermath* (Liverpool: Liverpool University Press, 2001). See also: David Syrett, *Admiral Lord Howe: A Biography* (Annapolis: Naval Institute Press, 2005).

10. Pasquale Paoli to George III, September 1, 1793, PRO FO 79/9. See also: Peter Thrasher, *Pasquale Paoli: An Enlightenment Hero* (New York: Anchon books, 1970).

11. Horatio Nelson to Fanny Nelson, April 1, 1795, *Nelson Letters*, 2:26.

12. Horatio Nelson to George Keith, June 6, 1800, *Nelson Dispatches*, 4:248.
13. Horatio Nelson to Dixon Hoste, December 12, 1795, *Nelson Dispatches*, 2:116.
14. Horatio Nelson to Gilbert Elliot, December 4, 1795, *Nelson Dispatches*, 2:113.
15. Gillet, *La Marine impériale*, 61.
16. James Davidson, *Admiral Lord St. Vincent – Saint or Tyrant?: The Life of Sir John Jervis, Nelson's Patron* (London: Pen & Sword, 2006).
17. Mostert, *Line Upon a Wind*, 175.
18. Bernton, ed., *St. Vincent Correspondence*, 1:137–40.
19. For Napoleon's first Italian campaign, see: Martin Boycott-Brown, *The Road to Rivoli: Napoleon's First Campaign* (London: Cassell, 2001). See also: Carl von Clauswitz, *Napoleon's 1796 Campaign* (Lawrence: University Press of Kansas, 2018). For Bonaparte's account, see: Napoleon Bonaparte, *Mémoires de Napoléon: La Campagne d'Italie* (Paris: Tallandier, 2010).
20. Henry Dundas to George Spencer, September 16, 1796, *Spencer Papers*, 1:321–2.
21. Cuthbert Collingwood to Blackett, December 5, 1796, Brenton, ed., *St. Vincent Correspondence*, 1:264–5.
22. John Jervis to Gilbert Elliot, August 22, 1796, Brenton, ed., *St. Vincent Correspondence*, 1:213.
23. Carole Divall, *General Sir Ralph Abercromby and the French Revolutionary Wars, 1792–1801* (London: Pen & Sword, 2019).
24. Duffy, *Sugar, Soldiers, and Seapower*, 196, 203, 206, 211, 215.
25. Duffy, *Sugar, Soldiers, and Seapower*, 218, 219, 221–2.
26. Duffy, *Sugar, Soldiers, and Seapower*, 235–6.
27. Phillippe Girard, *Toussaint Louverture: A Revolutionary Life* (New York: Basic Books, 2016).
28. Duffy, *Sugar, Soldiers, and Seapower*, 258.
29. Duffy, *Sugar, Soldiers, and Seapower*, 288–90.
30. James, Lord Dunfermline, *Lieutenant-General Sir Ralph Abercromby, 1793–1801: A Memoir by his Son* (London: Naval & Military Press, 1861), 58–9.
31. For the battle of St Vincent, see: John Jervis official account, February 16, 1797, Brenton, ed., *St. Vincent Correspondence*, 1:315–18; Christopher Lloyd, *St. Vincent and Camperdown* (London: Macmillan, 1963).
32. Mostert, *Line Upon a Wind*, 194.
33. G.F. Mainwaring, and Bonamy Dobree, *Mutiny: The Floating Republic* (London: Pen & Sword, 2004); Ann Veronica Coats and Philip Macdonald, *The Naval Mutinies of 1797: Unity and Perseverance* (London: Boydell Press, 2011).
34. Parkinson, *Britannia Rules*, 44.
35. John Jervis to William Parker, September 4, 1797, Brenton, ed., *St. Vincent Correspondence*, 1:369.
36. Brenton, ed., *St. Vincent Correspondence*, 1:376–9, 390–2.
37. Lloyd, *St. Vincent and Camperdown*.
38. Horatio Nelson to John Jervis, July 27, 1797, *Nelson Dispatches*, 2:130.
39. Henry Dundas to William Grenville, March 31, 1799, *Fortescue Manuscripts*, 4:513.
40. Duffy, *Sugar, Soldiers, and Seapower*, 302; Mary Beacock Frye and Christopher Dracott, *John Graves Simcoe, 1752–1806: A Biography* (London: Dundern, 1998).

Chapter 5

1. For the classic study of the 1798 rebellion and invasion, see: Thomas Pakenham, *The Year of Liberty: The Story of the Great Irish Rebellion of 1798* (London: Hodder and Stoughton, 1969).

For Ireland, see: Edith M. Johnston, *Ireland in the Eighteenth Century* (Dublin: Gill and Macmillan, 1974); M.R. O'Connell, *Irish Politics and Social Conflict in the Age of the American Revolution* (Westport: Greenwood, 1976); R.B. McDowell, *Ireland in the Age of Imperialism and Revolution, 1760–1801* (Oxford: Clarendon Press, 1979); T.W. Moody and W.E. Vaughan, *A New History of Ireland: Eighteenth Century Ireland, 1691–1800* (Oxford: Oxford University Press, 1986); Gerard O'Brien, *Anglo-Irish Politics in the Age of Grattan and Pitt* (Dublin: Irish Academic Press, 1987); Thomas Bartlett, *The Fall and Rise of the Irish Nation: The Catholic Question, 1691–1830* (New York: Barnes and Noble Books, 1992); James Kelly, *Prelude to Union: Anglo-Irish Politics in the 1780s* (Cork: Cork University Press, 1992).

2. Cornwallis to William Pitt, October 17, 1798, *Cornwallis Correspondence*, 2:418.
3. Marianne Elliot, *Wolfe Tone: The Prophet of Irish Independence* (New Haven: Yale University Press, 1990). For the United Irishmen and the revolutionary movement, see: Richard Madden, *The United Irishmen: Their Lives and Times*, 4 vols (Dublin: J. Madden and Company, 1857–60); Marianne Elliot, *Partners in Revolution: The United Irishmen and France* (New Haven: Yale University Press, 1982); Hugh Gough and David Dickson, eds, *Ireland and the French Revolution* (Dublin: Irish Academic Press, 1990); Jim Smyth, *The Men of No Property: Irish Radicals and Popular Politics in the Late Eighteenth Century* (Basingstoke: Palgrave Macmillan, 1992); A.T.Q. Stewart, *A Deeper Silence: The Hidden Origins of the United Irishmen* (Belfast: Blackstaff Press, 1993); David Dickson, Daire Keogh, and Kevin Whelan, eds, *The United Irishmen: Republicanism, Radicalism, and Rebellion* (Dublin: Irish Academic Press, 1993); Daire Keogh, *The French Disease: The Catholic Church and Irish Radicalism, 1790–1800* (Dublin: Irish Academic Press, 1993); Nancy J. Curtain, *The United Irishmen: Popular Politics in Ulster and Dublin, 1791–1798* (Oxford: Oxford University Press, 1994).
4. E.H. Stuart Jones, *An Invasion that Failed: The French Expedition to Ireland, 1796* (Oxford: Oxford University Press, 1950).
5. Stephen Taylor, *Commander: The Life and Exploits of Britain's Greatest Frigate Commander* (New York: W.W. Norton, 2012).
6. Chaim Rosenberg, *Losing America, Conquering America: Lord Cornwallis and the Remaking of the British Empire* (Jefferson: McFarland, 2017).
7. G.A. Hayes-McCoy, *Irish Battles: A Military History of Ireland* (New York: Barnes and Noble, 1969), 274, 276.
8. General Order, February 26, 1798, James, Lord Dunfermline, *Lieutenant-General Sir Ralph Abercromby, 1793–1801: A Memoir by His Son* (London: Naval & Military Press, 1861), 93–4.
9. Proclamation [1798], *Auckland Correspondence*, 3:420.
10. Pakenham, *Year of Liberty*, 84.
11. Cornwallis to Portland, July 8, 1798, *Cornwallis Correspondence*, 2:356.
12. Cornwallis to Portland, July 8, 1798, *Cornwallis Correspondence*, 2:356-57.
13. Cornwallis to Portland, July 8, 1798, *Cornwallis Correspondence*, 2:357.
14. John Fitzgibbon, Earl Clare to William, lord Auckland, May 21, 1798, *Auckland Correspondence*, 3:422–3.
15. John Beresford to William, lord Auckland, May 30, 1798, *Auckland Correspondence*, 3:433.
16. Cornwallis to Portland, June 28, 1798, *Cornwallis Correspondence*, 2:355.
17. John Fitzgibbon, Earl Clare to William, lord Auckland, [June 1798], *Auckland Correspondence*, 3:436.
18. For a vivid account of Edward's capture, see John Beresford to William, lord Auckland, May 20, 1798, *Auckland Correspondence*, 3:413–17.

19. Cornwallis to Portland, June 28, 1798, *Cornwallis Correspondence*, 2:358.
20. Cornwallis to Portland, September 16, 1798, *Cornwallis Correspondence*, 2:405.
21. Cornwallis to Portland, June 28, 1798, *Cornwallis Correspondence*, 2:355.
22. Pakenham, *Year of Liberty*, 314.
23. Pakenham, *Year of Liberty*, 292–3, 342–3.

Chapter 6
1. A.B. Rodger, *The War of the Second Coalition, 1798 to 1801: A Strategic Commentary* (Oxford: Oxford University Press, 1964); Piers Mackesy, *The Strategy of Overthrow, 1798–1799* (London: Longman, 1974); Piers Mackesy, *War without Victory: The Downfall of Pitt, 1799–1802* (Oxford: Oxford University Press, 1984); For the Mediterranean, see: Gareth Glover, *The Forgotten War against Napoleon: Conflict in the Mediterranean* (London: Pen & Sword, 2017).
2. George Spencer to John Jervis, May 19, 1798, *Nelson's Dispatches*, 3:24.
3. George Spencer to John Jervis, May 19, 1798, *Nelson's Dispatches*, 3:24.
4. Horatio Nelson to George Spencer, June 15, 1798, *Nelson's Dispatches*, 3:31.
5. For the Egyptian campaign, see: Jean-Joël Brégeon, *L'Egypte Française au Jour le Jour* (Paris: Perrin, 1991); Henry Laurens, *Les Origines Intellectuelles de l'Expédition d'Egypte: L'Orientalisme Islamisant en France, 1698–1798* (Paris: Editions Isis, 1987); Patrice Bret, *L'Egypte: Au Temps de l'Expédition Bonaparte, 1798–1801* (Paris: Hachette, 1998); Henry Laurens et al., *L'Expédition d'Egypte, 1798–1801* (Paris: A. Collins, 1989); Jean-Jacques Luthi, *Regards sur l'Egypte au Temps de Bonaparte* (Paris: Harmattan, 1999); J. Christopher Herold, *Bonaparte in Egypt* (New York: Pen & Sword, 2005); Juan Cole, *Napoleon's Egypt: Invading the Middle East* (New York: Palgrave Macmillan, 2008); Nina Burleigh, *Mirage: Napoleon's Scientists and the Unveiling of Egypt* (New York: Harper, 2008); Paul Strathern, *Napoleon in Egypt* (New York: Bantam, 2009).
6. Bregeon, *L'Egypte Française*, 97; Jean-Claude Gillet, *La Marine impériale: Le Grand Rêve de Napoléon* (Paris: Bernard Giovanangeli Editeur, 2010), 99–103.
7. Laurens, *Les Origines Intellectuelles de l'Expédition d'Egypte*; Bret, *L'Egypte: Au Temps de l'Expédition Bonaparte, 1798–1801* (Paris: Hachette, 1998) ; Luthi, *Regards sur l'Egypte au Temps de Bonaparte.*
8. Gillet, *La Marine impériale*, 105.
9. Napoleon Bonaparte to Jean Baptiste Perree, July 5, 1798, Napoleon Bonaparte to the Directory, July 6, 1798, Napoleon Bonaparte to Paul Brueys, July 27, 30 (2 letters), 1798, Napoleon Bonaparte to Honore Ganteaume, August 15 (2 letters), 1798, *Napoléon Correspondance*, 2:173, 175–7, 207–8, 216, 217, 277–8, 278.
10. For Nelson's campaign that climaxed with the battle of the Nile, see: Brian Lavery, *Nelson and the Nile: The Naval War against Napoleon Bonaparte, 1798* (London: Caxton Editions, 2003); Gregory Fremont-Barnes and Howard Gerrard, *Nile 1778: Nelson's First Great Victory* (London: Osprey, 2011).
11. Horatio Nelson to John Jervis, July 20, 1798, *Nelson Dispatches*, 3:45.
12. Michèle Battesti, *La Bataille d'Aboukir* (Paris: Economica, 1998).
13. Horatio Nelson to William Wyndham, August 21, 1798, *Nelson Dispatches*, 3:109.
14. Kate Williams, *England's Mistress: The Infamous Life of Emma Hamilton* (New York: Ballantine Books, 2006); Quintin Colville, *Emma Hamilton: Seduction and Celebrity* (London: Thames and Hudson, 2016).
15. Terry Coleman, *The Nelson Touch: The Life and Legend of Horatio Nelson* (New York: Oxford University Press, 2002), 179.

16. Kevin McCranie, *Admiral Lord Keith and the Naval War against Napoleon* (Tallahassee: University Press of Florida, 2006).
17. Norman E. Saul, *Russia, and the Mediterranean, 1797–1807* (Chicago: University of Chicago Press, 1964).
18. For Paul, see: Hugh Ragsdale, *Paul I: A Reassessment of His Life and Reign* (Pittsburgh: University of Pittsburgh Press, 1979); Hugh Ragsdale, *Tsar Paul and the Question of Madness: An Essay in History and Psychology* (New York: Praeger, 1988); Roderick Macgrew, *Paul I of Russia, 1754–1801* (New York: Oxford University Press, 1992); Angelo Rappoport, *The Curse of the Romanovs: A Study of the Lives and Reigns of Two Tsars, Paul I and Alexander I of Russia* (New York: Forgotten Books, 2012).
19. Stanford Shaw, *Between Old and New: The Ottoman Empire under Selim III, 1789–1806* (Cambridge, Mass.: Harvard University Press, 1971); Tuncay Zorlu, *Innovation and Empire in Turkey: Sultan Selim III and the Modernisation of the Ottoman Navy* (London: I.B. Tauris, 2008).
20. Horatio Nelson to Spencer Smith, October 7, 1798, *Nelson Dispatches*, 3:145–6.
21. Noel Mostert, *The Line Upon a Wind: The Great War at Sea, 1793–1815* (New York: W.W. Norton, 2007), 333.
22. Napoleon Bonaparte to Ahmed Djezzar, August 22, 1798; September 12, 1798; November 19, 1798, *Napoléon Correspondance*, 2:311–12; 414; 647.
23. Tom Pocock, *A Thirst for Glory: The Life of Admiral Sir Sidney Smith* (London: Thistle, 2013).
24. Edward Brenton, ed., *The Life and Correspondence of John, Earl of St. Vincent* (1838, repr. London: Elibron Classics, 2005), 1:461–2.
25. *Smith Correspondence*, 1:293–4.
26. Roy Adkins and Lesley Adkins, *The War for all the Oceans: From Nelson at the Nile to Napoleon at Waterloo* (New York: Viking, 2006), 62.
27. Adkins and Adkins, *War for all the Oceans*, 63.
28. Philip Henry, Lord Stanhope, *Life of the Right Honorable William Pitt*, 4 vols (London: John Murray, 1867), 3:498.

Chapter 7
1. A.B. Rodger, *The War of the Second Coalition, 1798 to 1801: A Strategic Commentary* (Oxford: Oxford University Press, 1964); Piers Mackesy, *Statesmen at War: The Strategy of Overthrow, 1798–1799* (London: Longman, 1974); Piers Mackesy, *War without Victory: The Downfall of Pitt, 1799–1802* (Oxford: Oxford University Press, 1984).
2. Philip Ball, *A Waste of Blood and Treasure: The 1799 Anglo-Russian Invasion of the Netherlands* (New York: Pen & Sword, 2017).
3. Henry Dundas to William Grenville, July 31, 1799, *Fortescue Manuscripts*, 5:215.
4. *The Annual Register or a View of the History, Politics, and Literature for the Year 1799* (London: Dodsley's Annual Register, 1801), 213–15.
5. E. Walsh, *A Narrative of the Expedition to Holland in the Autumn of the Year 1799* (London: B. Hamilton, 1800).
6. Unless otherwise indicated, all battle statistics for this chapter come from Digby Smith, *The Greenhill Napoleonic Wars Data Book: Actions and Losses in Personnel, Colours, Standards, and Artillery, 1792–1815* (London: Greenhill Books, 1998).
7. Captain Herbert Taylor to York, September 20, 1799, *Fortescue Manuscripts*, 5:418.
8. Smith, *Greenhill Napoleonic Wars Data Book*, 166.
9. York to Dundas, September 20, 1799, *Fortescue Manuscripts*, 5:416.
10. Henry Dundas to William Grenville, November 24, 1799, *Fortescue Manuscripts*, 6:36–7.

11. Smith, *Greenhill Napoleonic Wars Data Book*, 170–1.
12. Steven T. Ross, *Quest for Victory: French Military Strategy, 1792–1799* (New York: A.S. Barnes and Company, 1978), 281.
13. Grenville to Mulgrave, October 29, 1799, *Fortescue Manuscripts*, 5:505.
14. Philip Ziegler, *Addington: A Life of Henry Addington, First Viscount Sidmouth* (New York: John Day Company, 1965); Charles John Fedorak, *Henry Addington, Prime Minister, 1801–1804: Peace, War, and Parliamentary Politics* (Akron: Akron University Press, 2002).
15. Dudley Pope, *The Great Gamble: Nelson at Copenhagen* (New York: Simon and Schuster, 1972); Gareth Glover, *The Two Battles of Copenhagen, 1801 and 1807: Britain and Denmark in the Napoleonic Wars* (London: Pen & Sword, 2018).
16. Noel Mostert, *Line Upon a Wind: The Great War at Sea, 1793–1815* (New York: W.W. Norton, 2007), 384.
17. Horatio Nelson to Hyde Parker, March 24, 1801, Francis John Higginson, *Naval Battles of the Century* (London: W.W. Chambers, 1903), 11.
18. Mostert, *Line Upon a Wind*, 389.
19. Mostert, *Line Upon a Wind*, 390.
20. Mostert, *Line Upon a Wind*, 390.
21. Mostert, *Line Upon a Wind*, 396.
22. The story first appeared in print five years later in the first biography of Nelson, and was related to the author by the *Elephant*'s surgeon, who was below tending wounded at the time but apparently heard Nelson's quips after the battle: James Harrison, *The Life of Horatio Lord Viscount Nelson*, 2 vols (London: Ranelagh Press, 1806), 2:295. The spyglass to the eye version first appeared in James Clarke and John McArthur, *The Life of Admiral Lord Nelson*, 2 vols (London: T. Cadell and W. Davies, 1809), 2:266–7. The quote comes from Robert Southey, *The Life of Nelson* (London: Longman Green, 1813), 227.
23. Geoffrey Bennett, *Nelson the Commander* (New York: Scribner's Sons, 1972), 198.
24. Horatio Nelson to Hyde Parker, April 2, 1801; Horatio Nelson to Henry Addington, May 8, 1801, *Nelson's Dispatches*, 4:250–8; 272–4.
25. Horatio Nelson to Pahlen, May 9, 1801; Horatio Nelson to Vansittart, May 12, 1801; Colonel Stewart's Narrative, *Nelson Dispatches*, 4:274; 274–5; 276–7.
26. Mostert, *Line Upon a Wind*, 366.
27. William Smith to George Spencer, March 13, 1800, *Smith Correspondence*, 2:28–9.
28. Smith, *Greenhill Napoleonic Wars Data Book*, 178.
29. For the best account, see: Piers MacKesy, *British Victory in Egypt: The End of Napoleon's Conquest* (New York: Tauris Parke Paperbacks, 2010).
30. Carole Divall, *General Sir Ralph Abercromby and the French Revolutionary Wars, 1792–1801* (London: Pen & Sword, 2019); Kevin McCranie, *Admiral Lord Keith and the Naval War against Napoleon* (Tallahassee: University Press of Florida, 2006).
31. Mackesy, *British Victory in Egypt*, 49.
32. Mackesy, *British Victory in Egypt*, 43, 44.
33. Mackesy, *British Victory in Egypt*, 49, 70–1; James, Lord Dunfermline, *Lieutenant-General Sir Ralph Abercromby, 1793–1801: A Memoir by his Son* (London: Naval & Military Press, 1861), 273.
34. Mackesy, *British Victory in Egypt*, 56.
35. This is the best estimate of several, Mackesy, *British Victory in Egypt*, 62.
36. Mackesy, *British Victory in Egypt*, 75.
37. Thomas Grenville to Grenville, May 9, 1801, *Fortescue Manuscripts*, 7:17.
38. Mackesy, *British Victory in Egypt*, 101–2.

39. Mackesy, *British Victory in Egypt*, 99.
40. Mackesy, *British Victory in Egypt*, 132–3, 137.
41. Egyptian News, communicated by Mr. Addington [May 1801], *Fortescue Manuscripts*, 7:18.
42. Mackesy, *British Victory in Egypt*, 202.
43. Mackesy, *British Victory in Egypt*, 224.
44. Mackesy, *British Victory in Egypt*, 227.
45. Sketch of a Plan for Peace, settled at the Cabinet at the Time of the Discussions with Otto, [n.d.] 1800, *Addington Correspondence*, 1:257–60.
46. John D. Grainger, *The Amiens Truce: Britain and Bonaparte, 1801–1803* (Rochester: Boydell Press, 2004).
47. Mostert, *Line Upon a Wind*, 421.

Chapter 8

1. For overviews of British India and the campaigns of this era, see: P.J. Marshall, ed., *The Problems of Empire: Britain and India, 1757–1813* (London: Allen and Unwin, 1968); M.E. Yapp, *Strategies of British India: Britain, Iran, and Afghanistan, 1798–1850* (Oxford: Oxford University Press, 1980); Edward Ingram, *Commitment to Empire: Prophecies of the Great Game for Asia, 1797–1800* (Oxford: Oxford University Press, 1981); C.A. Bayly, *Empire and Information: Intelligence Gathering and Social Communications in India, 1780–1880* (Cambridge: Cambridge University Press, 1996); Rupali Mishra, *A Business of State: Commerce, Politics, and the Birth of the East India Company* (Cambridge, Mass.: Harvard University Press, 2018).
2. Steven T. Ross, *Quest for Victory: French Military Strategy, 1792–1799* (New York: A.S. Barnes and Company, 1978), 152.
3. Mornington to Court of Directors, August 3, 1799, Lieutenant Colonel Gurwood, ed., *The Dispatches of Field Marshall the Duke of Wellington during His Various Campaigns in India, Denmark, Portugal, Spain, the Low Countries, and France, 1799–1818*, 12 vols (London: John Murray, 1838), 2:2:88–9.
4. John Fortescue, *A History of the British Army* (London: Macmillan, 1910), 4:939.
5. For the Wellesley brothers, see: John Severn, *Architects of Empire: The Duke of Wellington and His Brothers* (Norman: University of Oklahoma Press, 2007). For Wellington, see: Jac Weller, *Wellington in India* (London: Frontline Books, 2013).
6. Mornington to Dundas, June 7, 1799, Gurwood, ed., *Wellesley India Dispatches*, 2:38.
7. Weller, *Wellington in India*, 44–5.
8. Arthur Wellesley to Mornington, May 8, 1799, *Wellington Supplements*, 1:212–17.
9. Arthur Wellesley to John Collins, *Wellington Supplements*, 4:123; Weller, *Wellington in India*, 82, 85.
10. Elizabeth Longford, *Wellington: Years of the Sword* (New York: Harper and Row, 1969), 67.
11. *Croker Papers*, 2:102–3.
12. David Baird, *The life of General the Right Honorable Sir David Baird*, 2 vols (London: Richard Bentley, 1832), 1:226.
13. Richard Wellesley to Arthur Wellesley, December 1, 1800, *Wellington Dispatches*, 1:37.
14. Richard Wellesley to Henry Addington, October 9, 1800, *Addington Correspondence*, 1:268.
15. Weller, *Wellington in India*, 88–100.
16. Arthur Wellesley to Adjutant General, September 10, 1800, *Wellington Dispatches*, 1:75–7.
17. Mornington to Court of Directors, December 24, 1802, Gurwood, ed., *Wellesley India Dispatches*, 3:3–12.

18. Weller, *Wellington in India*, 140–52.

19. Weller, *Wellington in India*, 157.

20. *Croker Papers*, 2:99.

21. Weller, *Wellington in India*, 195–232.

22. Weller, *Wellington in India*, 200, 214, 240–8.

23. Arthur Wellesley to Thomas Munro, August 20, 1800, *Wellington Dispatches*, 1:64–6.

24. Arthur Wellesley to Lieutenant Colonel Barry Close, January 22, 1804, *Wellington Dispatches*, 2:69.

25. Quoted in Severn, *Architects of Empire*, 159.

26. Arthur Wellesley, Memorandum upon Operations in the Maratha Territory, December 1800 and January 1801, *Wellington Dispatches*, 1:357–65.

27. Arthur Wellesley to Colonel James Stevenson, August 17, 1803, Gurwood, ed., *Wellesley India Dispatches*, 2:210.

Chapter 9

1. John D. Grainger, *The Amiens Truce: Britain and Bonaparte, 1801–1803* (Rochester: Boydell Press, 2004).

2. Noel Mostert, *The Line Upon a Wind: The Great War at Sea, 1793–1815* (New York: W.W. Norton, 2007), 433.

3. Napoleon to Dejean, July 26, 1804; Napoleon Bonaparte to Eustache Bruix, August 22, 1803; Napoleon Bonaparte to Denis Decrès, August 22, 1803; Napoleon Bonaparte to Louis Berthier, August 23, 1803, *Napoléon Correspondance*, 4:231–2; 282–4; 284–5; 286.

4. Napoleon to Latouche-Treville, July 2, 1804, *Napoléon Correspondance*, 4:756.

5. Thierry Lentz, *Nouvelle Histoire du Premier Empire: Napoléon et la Conquête de l'Europe, 1804–1810* (Paris: Fayard, 2002), 149. For a vivid account by Napoleon's valet, see: Louis Constant, *Mémoires Intimes de Napoléon Ie par Constant, son valet de chambre*, 2 vols (Paris: Mercure de France, 1967), 245–52. For Napoleon reaction, see: Napoleon to Josephine, 21, 1804, *Napoléon Correspondance*, 4:775.

6. For the Trafalgar campaign, see Alan Schom, *Trafalgar: Countdown to Battle, 1803–1805* (New York: Oxford University Press, 1990); Robert Gardiner, *The Campaign of Trafalgar, 1803–05* (London: Chatham Publishing, 1997); Michelle Battisti, *Trafalgar: Les Aleas de la Strategie Navale* (Paris: Editions Napoléon Ie, 2004); M. Monarque, *Trafalgar* (Paris: Tallandier, 2005); Mark Adkin, *The Trafalgar Companion: The Complete Guide to History's Most Famous Sea Battle and the Life of Lord Nelson* (London: Arum Press, 2005); Roy Adkins, *Nelson's Trafalgar* (New York: Penguin, 2006); Adam Nicolson, *Seize the Fire: Heroism, Duty, and Nelson's Battle of Trafalgar* (New York: Harper Perennial, 2006); Richard Harding, *A Great and Glorious Victory: New Perspectives on the Battle of Trafalgar* (London: Seaforth, 2008).

7. Napoleon to Decrès, September 29 (5 letters), *Napoléon Correspondance*, 4:896–02.

8. Schom, *Trafalgar*, 176–7; Roy Adkins and Lesley Adkins, *The War for all the Oceans: From Nelson at the Nile to Napoleon at Waterloo* (New York: Viking, 2006); C. Northcote Parkinson, *Britannia Rules: The Classic Age of Naval History, 1793–1815* (London: Alan Sutton Publishing, 1994), 96.

9. Parkinson, *Britannia Rules*, 97.

10. Napoleon to Decrès, August 14, 1805, *Napoléon Correspondance*, 5:570.

11. Napoleon to Ganteaume, September 6, 1804, Napoleon to Villeneuve, December 12, 1804; Napoleon to Decrès, December 14, 1804, Napoleon to Missiessy, December 23, 1804, *Napoléon Correspondance*, 4:857–8; 971–4; 975–6; 984–6.

12. Napoleon to Villeneuve, May 8, 1805, *Napoléon's Correspondance*, 5:283–6.

13. Napoleon to Allemand, June 9, 1805, *Napoléeon Correspondance*, 5:395–6.
14. Napoleon to Villeneuve, August 13, 1805, *Napoléeon's Correspondance*, 5:568.
15. Napoleon to Eugene, July 27, 1805; Napoleon to Talleyrand, August 3, 4, 7, 10, 11, 12, 13, 16, 18, 19, 22, 23 (2 letters) 1805, Napoleon to Decrès, August 13 (2 letters); 14, Napoleon to Berthier, August 24, 26, 29, 1805, *Napoléon Correspondance*, 5:518; 529, 539, 534, 548, 554, 560–1, 565–667, 579, 583, 589, 598–600, 607–8, 608–9 ; 561–2, 562–3; 612–13, 624–6; 642–4.
16. Napoleon to Villeneuve, September 14, 1805; Napoleon to Decrès, September 15, 1805, *Napoléon Correspondance*, 5:690; 693.
17. Parkinson, *Britannia Rules*, 106.
18. Schom, *Trafalgar*, 304–54.
19. Jean-Claude Gillet, *La Marine impériale: La Grand Rêve de Napoléon* (Paris: Bernard Giovanangeli Edieur, 2010), 274–5.
20. Terry Coleman, *The Nelson Touch: The Life and Legend of Horatio Nelson* (New York: Oxford University Press, 2002s), 322.

Chapter 10
1. Roy Adkins and Lesley Adkins, *The War for all the Oceans: From Nelson at the Nile to Napoleon at Waterloo* (New York: Viking, 2006), 173.
2. Thomas Fernyhough, *The Military Memoirs of Four Brothers engaged in the Service of their Country* (London: William Sams, 1829), 75–6.
3. Adkins and Adkins, *War for all the Oceans*, 188.
4. William W. Kaufman, *British Policy and the Independence of Latin America, 1804–1814* (New Haven: Yale University Press, 1951); Klaus Gallo, *Great Britain and Argentina: From Invasion to Recognition, 1806–1826* (London: Palgrave, 2001); Ian Fletcher, *The Waters of Oblivion: The British Invasion of the Rio de Plata, 1806–07* (London: Spellmount, 2006).
5. Fernyhough, *Military Memoirs*, 89–90.
6. Richard Hopton, *The Battle of Maida, 1806* (London: Pen & Sword, 2008).
7. Digby Smith, *The Greenhill Napoleonic Wars Data Book: Actions and Loses in Personnel, Colours, Standards, and Artillery, 1792–1815* (London: Greenhill Books, 1998), 221.
8. Roy Adkins and Lesley Adkins, *The War for all the Oceans: From Nelson at the Nile to Napoleon at Waterloo* (New York: Viking, 2006), 202.
9. For an overview, see: Thomas Munch-Petersen, *Defying Napoleon: How Britain Bombarded Copenhagen and Seized the Danish Fleet in 1807* (London: Sutton Publishing, 2007); Gareth Glover, *The Two Battles of Copenhagen, 1801 and 1807: Britain and Denmark in the Napoleonic Wars* (London: Pen & Sword, 2018).
10. Traité de Tilsit avec la Russe, 7 Juillet 1807, Michel Kerautret, ed., *Les Grand Traités de l'Empire (1804–1810): Documents Diplomatiques du Consulat et de l'Empire*, Tome 2 (Paris: Nouveau Monde Editions/Fondation Napoléon, 2004), 277–90.
11. Traité de Tilsit avec la Prusse, 9 Juillet 1807, Kerautret, ed., *Grand Traités*, Tome 2, 290–300. See also the supplementary: Convention de Konigsberg avec la Prusse, 12 Juillet, 1807, Kerautret, ed., *Grand Traités*, Tome 2, 301–3.
12. Munch-Petersen, *Defying Napoleon*, 77, 79,
13. Munch-Petersen, *Defying Napoleon*, 61–81, 83–96, 97–116, 117–38.
14. Munch-Petersen, *Defying Napoleon*, 139.
15. Munch-Petersen, *Defying Napoleon*, 152.
16. Munch-Petersen, *Defying Napoleon*, 174–5.
17. Smith, *Greenhill Napoleonic Wars Data Book*, 254.
18. *Wellington Reminiscences*, 61.

19. Munch-Petersen, *Defying Napoleon*, 202.
20. W.G. Perrin, ed., 'The Journal of Surgeon Charles Chambers of H.M. Fireship Prometheus,' in *Naval Miscellany* (London: Navy Records Society, 1928), 3:393–5.
21. John Sturgis, ed., *A Boy in the Peninsular War: The Services, Adventures, and Experiences of Robert Blakeney, Subaltern in the 28th Regiment* (London: John Murray, 1899), 12.
22. Munch-Petersen, *Defying Napoleon*, 215–16.
23. Henry Ross-Lewin, *With the Thirty-Second in the Peninsula and other Campaigns* (Dublin: Hodges, Figgis, and Company, 1904), 80–1.
24. Arthur Wellesley to William Wellesley Pole, September 15, 1807, *Wellesley-Pole Letters*, 1–4.
25. Quoted in Munch-Petersen, *Defying Napoleon*, 245.
26. Napoleon to Denis Decrès, January 8, 10, 27, 1809; Napoleon to Jean Baptiste Willaumez, January 9, 1809; Napoleon to Henri Clarke, January 10, 1809, *Napoléon Correspondance*, 8:1,427, 1,445–6, 1,537; 1439; 1,442.
27. Napoleon to Denis Decrès, March 5, 1809, *Napoléon Correspondance*, 9:160.
28. C. Northcote Parkinson, *Britannia Rules: The Classic Age of Naval History, 1793-1815* (London: Alan Sutton Publishing, 1994), 134.
29. Thomas Dundonald, tenth Earl Cochrane, *The Autobiography of a Seaman*, 2 vols (London: Mclaren, 1861), 342.
30. Robert Hervey, *The Life and Exploits of a Fighting Captain* (New York: Da Capo, 2001); Donald Thomas, *Cochrane: Britannia's Sea Wolf* (London: Cassells, 2001); David Cordingly, *Cochrane the Dauntless: The Life and Adventures of Admiral Thomas Cochrane, 1775–1860* (New York: Bloomsbury, 2008).
31. Noel Mostert, *The Line Upon a Wind: The Great War at Sea, 1793–1815* (New York: W.W. Norton), 575.
32. Parkinson, *Britannia Rules*, 136.

Chapter 11
1. For English-Portuguese relations, see: L.M.E. Shaw, *The Anglo-Portuguese Alliance and the English Merchants in Portugal, 1654–1810* (London: Ashgate, 1998); Martin Robson, *Britain, Portugal, and South America in the Napoleonic Wars: Alliances and Diplomacy in Economic Maritime Conflict* (London: I.B. Tauris, 2011); Jorge Canizares-Esguerra, *Entangled Empires: The Anglo-Iberian Atlantic, 1500–1830* (College Station: University of Pennsylvania Press, 2018).

For Portugal's rise and decline as a great power, see: A.R. Disney, *A History of Portugal and the Portuguese Empire: From the Beginnings to 1807*, 2 vols (New York: Cambridge University Press, 2009); A.J.R. Russell-Wood, *The Portuguese Empire, 1415–1808: A World on the Move* (Baltimore: Johns Hopkins University Press, 1998); Roger Crowley, *Conquerors: How Portugal Forged the First Global Empire* (New York: Random House, 2015).
2. Otto von Pivka, *The Portuguese Army of the Napoleonic War* (London: Osprey, 1977).
3. Traité Franco-Espagnol de Fontainebleau, October 27, 1807, Michel Kerautret, ed., *Les Grand Traités de l'Empire (1804–1810): Documents Diplomatiques du Consulat et de l'Empire*, Tome 2 (Paris: Nouveau Monde Editions/Fondation Napoléon, 2004), 320–5.
4. For the British rescue, see: Laurentino Gomes, *1808: The Flight of the Emperor: How A Weak Prince, A Mad Queen, and the British Navy Tricked Napoleon and Changed the New World* (New York: Lyons Press, 2013).
5. Hew Dalrymple, *Memoirs written by Sir Hew Dalrymple, Bart., of his Proceeding as connected with the affairs of Spain and the Commencement of the Peninsular War* (London: Thomas and William Boone, 1830).

6. Arthur Wellesley to William Wellesley Pole, August 19, 1808, *Wellesley-Pole Letters*, 5.

7. Arthur Wellesley to Castlereagh, August 1, 1808, *Wellington Dispatches*, 4:55.

8. *Coker Papers*, 1:12–13.

9. Arthur Wellesley to Castlereagh, July 21, 1808, *Wellesley Dispatches*, 4:39.

10. Arthur Wellesley to Nicolas Trant, August 13, 1808, *Wellesley Dispatches*, 4:87–8.

11. Jac Weller, *Wellington in the Peninsula* (Mechanicsburg: Stackpole Books, 1992), 41.

12. Stephen Morley, *Memoirs of a Sergeant of the Fifth Regiment of Food, containing an Account of his Services in Hanover, South America, and the Peninsula* (Ashford: Ken Trotman, 1842), 45–6.

13. Weller, *Wellington in the Peninsula*, 39.

14. Arthur Wellesley to William Wellesley Pole, August 19, 1808, *Wellesley-Pole Letters*, 5.

15. David Gates, *The Spanish Ulcer: A History of the Peninsular War* (New York: Da Capo, 2001), 89.

16. Christopher Hibbert, ed., *Recollections of Rifleman Harris* (London: Cassell Military, 1985), 23.

17. John Fortescue, *History of the British Army* (London: Macmillan, 1910), 6:231.

18. Arthur Wellesley to William Wellesley Pole, August 22, 1808, *Wellesley-Pole Letters*, 5–6.

19. Arthur Wellesley to William Wellesley Pole, August 24, 1808, *Wellesley-Pole Letters*, 6.

20. Weller, *Wellington in the Peninsula*, 57.

21. Arthur Wellesley to William Wellesley-Pole, August 24, quoted in Huw J. Davies, *Wellington's Wars: The Making of a Military Genius* (New Haven: Yale University Press, 2012), 95.

22. John Leach, *Rough Sketches of the Life of an Old Soldier* (London: John Murray, 1831), 55–6.

23. Arthur Wellesley to William Wellesley Pole, August 24, 1808, *Wellesley-Pole Letters*, 6–8.

24. Arthur Wellesley to William Wellesley Pole, September 16, 1808, *Wellesley-Pole Letters*, 11.

25. Arthur Wellesley to Castlereagh, August 23, 1808, *Wellington Supplements*, 6:123–4.

26. Gates, *Spanish Ulcer*, 92.

Chapter 12

1. Traité de Bayonne avec Charles IV, 5 Mai, 1808; Traité entre Napoléon et Ferdinand, 10 Mai, 1808, Michel Kerautret, ed., *Les Grand Traités de l'Empire (1804–1810): Documents Diplomatiques du Consulat et de l'Empire*, Tome 2 (Paris: Nouveau Monde Editions/Fondation Napoléon, 2004), 365–9; 370–2.

2. For the Peninsular War, see: David Gates, *The Spanish Ulcer: A History of the Peninsular War* (New York: Da Capo, 2001); Charles Esdaile, *The Peninsular War: A New History* (New York: Palgrave Macmillan, 2003); Charles J. Esdaile, *Fighting Napoleon: Guerrillas, Bandits, and Adventurers in Spain, 1808–1814* (New Haven: Yale University Press, 2004); Charles Esdaile, *Peninsular Witnesses: The Experience of War in Spain and Portugal, 1808–1811* (London: Pen & Sword, 2009); Ian Robertson, *An Atlas of the Peninsular War* (New Haven: Yale University Press, 2010).

3. Esdaile, *Peninsular War*, 82.

4. Theodore Hook, *The Life of Sir David Baird* (London: R. Bentley, 1832).

5. Alexander Gordon to Aberdeen, December 4, 17, 1808, *Gordon Letters*, 18, 24.

6. Alexander Gordon to Aberdeen, December 18, 1808, *Gordon Letters*, 26.

7. Alexander Gordon to Aberdeen, November 17, 1808, *Gordon Letters*, 8.

8. Alexander Gordon to Aberdeen, November 23, 1808, *Gordon Letters*, 11–12.

9. Alexander Gordon to Aberdeen, December 9, 1808, *Gordon Letters*, 19–20.

10. Alexander Gordon to Aberdeen, December 17, 22, 1808, *Gordon Letters*, 24, 28–9.
11. Weller, *Wellington in the Peninsula*, 62.
12. Alexander Gordon to Aberdeen, December 24, 1808, *Gordon Letters*, 30.
13. Alexander Gordon to Aberdeen, November 17, 1808, *Gordon Letters*, 9.
14. James Moore, *A Narrative of the Campaign of the British Army in Spain Commanded by His Excellency Lieut. General Sir John Moore* (London: Joseph Johnson, 1809), 177.
15. Ian Fletcher, *Galloping at Everything: The British Cavalry in the Peninsular War and at Waterloo, 1808–15* (Mechanicsburg: Stackpole Books, 1999), 95.
16. Henry Curling, ed., *Recollections of Rifleman Harris* (London: Peter Davies, 1928), 126–7.
17. Esdaile, *Peninsular War*, 153.
18. August Schaumann, *On the Road with Wellington: The Diary of a War Commissary in the Peninsular Campaign* (London: Naval and Military Press, 2009), 127–8.
19. Alexander Gordon to Aberdeen, January 14, 1809, *Gordon Letters*, 34.
20. Thomas Howell, *Journal of a Soldier of the Seventy-First Regiment from 1806 to 1815, Memorials of the Late War*, Vol. 1 (Edinburgh: Balfour and Clarke, 1828), 66.
21. Gates, *Spanish Ulcer*, 114.
22. John Sturgis, ed., *A Boy in the Peninsular War: The Services, Adventures, and Experiences of Robert Blakeney, Subaltern in the 28th Regiment* (London: John Murray, 1899), 124–5.
23. Alexander Gordon to Aberdeen, January 14, 1809, *Gordon Letters*, 35.
24. Alexander Gordon to Melville, November 29, 1808, *Gordon Letters*, 16.

Chapter 13
1. Robert Asprey, *The Reign of Napoleon* (New York: Basic Books, 2001), 217.
2. Arthur Griffiths, *The Wellington Memorial, His Comrades and Contemporaries* (London: G. Allen, 1897), 308.
3. Arthur Wellesley, Memorandum on the Defense of Portugal, March 7, 1809, *Wellington Dispatches*, 5:261–3.
4. Castlereagh to Arthur Wellesley, April 2, 1809, *Castlereagh Correspondence*, 7:47.
5. Jac Weller, *Wellington in the Peninsula* (Mechanicsburg: Stackpole Books, 1992), 83–5; Ian Fletcher, *Galloping at Everything: The British Cavalry in the Peninsular War and at Waterloo, 1808–15* (Mechanicsburg: Stackpole Books, 1999), 101.
6. Arthur Wellesley to Castlereagh, May 18, 1809, *Wellington Dispatches*, 4:317.
7. Arthur Wellesley to John Villiers, May 31, 1809, *Wellington Dispatches*, 3:262.
8. George Robert Gleig, *The Life of Arthur, Duke of Wellington* (London: Longman Green, 1889), 430–1.
9. Weller, *Wellington in the Peninsula*, 74, 79.
10. Elizabeth Longford, *Wellington: Years of the Sword* (New York: Harper and Row, 1969), 183.
11. Arthur Wellesley to William Huskinsson, May 5, 1809; Arthur Wellesley to John Villiers, May 31 and June 1, 1809; Arthur Wellesley to Castlereagh, June 11, 1809; *Wellington Dispatches*, 4:302; 374 and 382–3; 413–14; Castlereagh to Arthur Wellesley, July 11, 1809, *Castlereagh Correspondence*, 7:95–6.
12. Arthur Wellesley to Benardino Freire, July 24, 1809, *Wellington Dispatches*, 4:526–7.
13. Arthur Wellesley to Castlereagh, July 24, 1809, *Wellington Dispatches*, 4:527–9.
14. For Wellesley's frustrating efforts just to get Cuesta into a secure position, see: *Wellington Conversations*, 1.
15. Weller, *Wellington in the Peninsula*, 105–7.
16. Charles Esdaile, *The Peninsular War: A New History* (New York: Palgrave Macmillan, 2003), 206.

17. Weller, *Wellington in the Peninsula*, 104.

18. Arthur Wellesley to William Wellesley-Pole, August 1, 8, 1809, *Wellesley-Pole Letters*, 17–18.

19. David Gates, *The Spanish Ulcer: A History of the Peninsular War* (New York: Da Capo, 2001), 181.

20. Arthur Wellesley to William Wellesley Pole, August 1, 8, 1809, *Wellesley-Pole Letters*, 19.

21. Esdaile, *Peninsular War*, 213.

22. Esdaile, *Peninsular War*, 213.

23. Arthur Wellesley to Richard Wellesley, September 1, 1809, *Wellington Dispatches*, 3:467.

Chapter 14

1. For the Walcheren campaign, see: Théo Fleishman, *L'Expédition Anglaise sur le Continent en 1809* (Brussels: La Renaissance du Livre, 1973); Gordon C. Bond, *The Grand Expedition: the British Invasion of Holland in 1809* (Athens: University of Georgia Press, 1979); Andrew Limm, *Walcheren to Waterloo: The British Army in the Low Countries during the French Revolutionary and Napoleonic Wars, 1793–1815* (London: Pen & Sword, 2018).

   For analyses of Walcheren Fever, see: T.H. McGuffie, 'The Walcheren Expedition and the Walcheren Fever,' *English Historical Review*, Vol. 62, 1947, 191–202; Robert M. Feibel, 'What Happened at Walcheren: The Primary Sources,' *Bulletin of the History of Medicine*, Vol. 42, 1968, 62–79; Kate Elizabeth Crowe, 'The Walcheren Expedition and the New Army Medical Board: A Reconsideration,' *English Historical Review*, Vol. 88, 1973, 770–885.

2. For key documents and accounts of the Walcheren expedition's planning and execution, see: 'Testimony of Dundas,' February 5, 1810, *Parliamentary Debates*, Vol. 15, appendix col. 86; 'Testimony of Castlereagh,' March 1, 1810, *Parliamentary Debates*, March 1, 1810, *Parliamentary Debates*, Vol. 15, appendix col. 522; 'Memorandum upon the supposed practicality of Destroying the French Ships and Vessels I the Scheldt and in the Arsenals at Antwerp,' May 31, 1809, 'Memorandum relative to the projected Expedition against Walcheren,' June 1, 1808, *Castlereagh Correspondence*, 5:257–61, 261–5; 'Memorandum Relative to the projected Expedition to the Scheldt,' June 3, 1809, *Parliamentary Debates*, Vol. 15, Appendix, cols 154–6.

3. 'Testimony of Castlereagh,' March 1, 1810, *Parliamentary Debates*, March 1, 1810, *Parliamentary Debates*, Vol. 15, appendix col. 522.

4. Bond, *Grand Expedition*, 17.

5. Home Popham to Castlereagh, June 13, 1809, *Castlereagh Correspondence*, 6:274.

6. Capt. Graham Moore to Thomas Creevey, September 19, 1809, *Creevey Papers*, 95; C. Northcote Parkinson, *Britannia Rules: The Classic Age of Naval History, 1793–1815* (London: Alan Sutton Publishing, 1994), 141.

7. C.G. Gardyne, *The Life of a Regiment: The History of the Gordon Highlanders from its formation in 1794 to 1816* (London: Medici Society, 1929), 172.

8. Lindell Hart, ed., *The Letters of Private Wheeler* (New York: Houghton Mifflin, 1952), 24–5.

9. Castlereagh to George III, July 15, 1809, *Castlereagh Correspondence*, 6:283; 'Return, showing the effective strength of the army which embarked for serve in the Scheldt in the month of July 1809,' February 12, 1809, *Parliamentary Debates*, 7:59.

10. Thomas Howell, *Journal of a Soldier in the Seventy-First Regiment from 1806 to 1815* (Edinburgh: Balfour and Clarke, 1828), 71–2.

11. Roy Adkins and Lesley Adkins, *The War for all the Oceans: From Nelson at the Nile to Napoleon at Waterloo* (New York: Viking, 2006), 290.

12. Bond, *Grand Expedition*, 106; Adkins and Adkins, *War for all the Oceans*, 300.
13. Bond, *Grand Expedition*, 115.
14. For analyses of Walcheren Fever, see: McGuffie, 'The Walcheren Expedition and the Walcheren Fever,' 191–202; Feibel, 'What Happened at Walcheren,' 62–79; Crowe, 'The Walcheren Expedition and the New Army Medical Board: A Reconsideration,' 770–885.
15. Philip J. Haythornthwaite, *The Armies of Wellington* (London: Brockhampton Press, 1996), 236.
16. *The Times*, April 5, 1810, NYPL.
17. Barry E. O'Meara, *Napoleon in Exile, or a Voice from St. Helena: The Opinions and Reflections of Napoleon on the Most Important Events of His Life and Government in His Own Words* (New York: Worthington, 1890), 1:157.

Chapter 15
1. Jac Weller, *Wellington in the Peninsula* (Mechanicsburg: Stackpole Books, 1992), 119.
2. Arthur Wellesley to John Villiers, January 1, 1810, *Wellington Dispatches*, 5:126.
3. Arthur Wellesley to Liverpool, April 2, 1810, *Wellington Dispatches*, 6:2.
4. Alexander Gordon to Aberdeen, December 13, 1809, *Gordon Letters*, 75.
5. Memorandum to Lieut. Colonel Fletcher Commanding Royal Engineers, October 29, 1809, *Wellington Dispatches*, 5:317; Weller, *Wellington in the Peninsula*, 144–5.
6. Weller, *Wellington in the Peninsula*, 137–9.
7. Wellington to Wellesley-Pole, September 5, 1810, *Wellington Supplements*, 6:588.
8. Liverpool to Wellington, March 13, 1810, BL add. ms 38325.
9. Wellington to Liverpool, April 2, 1810, *Wellington Dispatches*, 6:5.
10. Wellington to Liverpool, April 6, 1810, *Wellington Dispatches*, 6:6.
11. Wellington to Liverpool, July 14, 1810, PRO WO 1/245, ff. 92–3.
12. Digby Smith, *The Greenhill Napoleonic Wars Data Book: Actions and Losses in Personnel, Colours, Standards, and Artillery, 1792–1815* (London: Greenhill Books, 1998), 344.
13. John Leach, *Rough Sketches of an Old Soldier* (London: John Murray, 1833), 166.
14. August Schaumann, *On the Road with Wellington: The Diary of a War Commissary in the Peninsular Campaign* (London: Naval and Military Press, 2009), 249.
15. Weller, *Wellington in the Peninsula*, 140.
16. Wellington to Liverpool, November 3, 1810, *Wellington Dispatches*, 6:583.
17. Wellington to Liverpool, December 21, 1810, *Wellington Dispatches*, 7:54.
18. Weller, *Wellington in the Peninsula*, 153.
19. David Gates, *Spanish Ulcer: A History of the Peninsular War* (New York: Da Capo, 2001), 225, 241.
20. Alexander Gordon to Aberdeen, December 22, 1810, *Gordon Letters*, 140.
21. Smith, *Greenhill Napoleonic Wars Data Book*, 353–5.
22. Esdaile, *The Peninsular War: A New History* (New York: Palgrave Macmillan, 2003), 338.
23. Gates, *Spanish Ulcer*, 249–52.
24. Weller, *Wellington in the Peninsula*, 168–70, 158.
25. Esdaile, *Peninsular War*, 354.
26. Schaumann, *Diary*, 303.
27. Wellington to William Wellesley, July 2, 1811, *Wellington Supplements*, 7:177.
28. Weller, *Wellington in the Peninsula*, 183–5
29. Weller, *Wellington in the Peninsula*, 183–5.
30. George Bankes, ed., *The Autobiography of Sergeant William Laurence, a Hero of the Peninsula and Waterloo Campaign* (London: Sampson Low and Company, 1886), 93–4.
31. Alexander Gordon to Aberdeen, August 8, 1811, *Gordon Letters*, 240.

32. *Stanhope Conversations*, 90.
33. Wellington to Wellesley-Pole, July 2, 1811, PRO, RP ms A/43.
34. Lindell Hart, ed., *The Letters of Private Wheeler* (New York: Houghton Mifflin, 1952), 61.
35. John Donaldson, *Recollections of the Eventful Life of a Soldier* (London: Naval and Military Press, 2009), 142–3.
36. Weller, *Wellington in the Peninsula*, 192.
37. Richard Wellesley to Spencer Percival, October 9, 1810, *Wellesley Papers*, BL, add. mss. 37295.
38. Alexander Gordon to Aberdeen, December 12, 1811, *Gordon Letters*, 272.

Chapter 16

1. For the diplomacy leading up to and accompanying the 1812 War, see: Bradford Perkins, *Prologue to War: England and the United States, 1805–1812* (Berkeley: University of California, 1963); Bradford Perkins, *Castlereagh and Adams: England and the United States, 1812–1823* (Berkeley: University of California Press, 1964).
   For the best overview of the 1812 War, see: Donald R. Hickey, *The War of 1812: A Forgotten Conflict* (Urbana: University of Illinois Press, 1990). Other very good accounts include: Harry L. Coles, *The War of 1812* (Chicago: University of Chicago Press, 1965); Reginald Horsman, *The War of 1812* (London: Eyre and Spottiswoode, 1969); John R. Elting, *Amateurs to Arms!: A Military History of the War of 1812* (New York: Da Capo Press, 1995); J. Mackay Hitsman, *The Incredible War of 1812: A Military History* (Toronto: Robin Brass Studio, 1996); John C. Fredricksen, *The War of 1812 Eyewitness Accounts: an Annotated Bibliography* (Westport: Greenwood Press, 1997); Walter R. Borneman, *1812: The War that Founded a Nation* (New York: Harper, 2004); John Latimer, *1812: War with America* (Cambridge, Mass.: Harvard University Press, 2009). For an excellent literature review, see: Donald R. Hickey, 'The War of 1812: Still a Forgotten Conflict?', *Journal of Military History*, Vol. 65, No. 3 (July 2001), 741–69.
2. Alexander de Conde, *The Quasi-War: The Politics and Diplomacy of the Undeclared War with France, 1797-1801* (New York: Charles Scribner's Sons, 1966); Howard Nash, *The Forgotten Wars: The U.S. Navy in the Quasi-War with France and the Barbary Pirates, 1789–1805* (New York: Barnes Company, 1968); William Stinchcombe, *The XYZ Affair* (New York: Praeger, 1980).
3. Ian W. Toll, *Six Frigates: The Epic History of the Founding of the U.S. Navy* (New York: W.W. Norton, 2006), 271.
   For a complete study, see: James F. Zimmerman, *The Impressment of American Seamen* (New York: Columbia University Press, 1925).
4. Edward Brenton, ed., *The Life and Correspondence of John, Earl of St. Vincent* (1838, repr. London: Elibron Classics, 2005), 1:288.
5. For the Continental System, see: Eli Hecksher, *The Continental System, an Economic Interpretation* (Oxford: Clarendon Press, 1922); Frank Melvin, *Napoleon's Navigation System: A Study of Trade Control during the Continental Blockade* (New York: Nabu Press, 2010); K. Aalestadl and J. Joos, *Revisiting Napoleon's Continental System: Local, Regional, and European Experiences* (New York: Palgrave Macmillan, 2014).
6. Hickey, *War of 1812*, 18.
7. G.L.N. Collingwood, *A Selection from the Public and Private Correspondence of Vice Admiral Lord Collingwood Interspersed with Memoirs of His Life* (London: John Murray, 1829), 317.

8. William R. Nester, *The Jeffersonian Vision, 1800–1815* (Washington DC: Potomac Books, 2012).

9. Donald R. Hickey, 'The Monroe-Pinkney Treaty of 1806: A Reappraisal,' *William and Mary Quarterly*, Vol. 44, No. 1, January 1987, 65–88.

10. Curtis P. Nettels, *The Emergence of a National Economy, 1775–1815* (New York: Harper and Row, 1969), 396.

11. W.F. Galpin, 'The American Grain Trade to the Spanish Peninsula, 1810–1814,' *American History Review*, Vol. 28 (October 1922), 25.

12. Thomas Jefferson to William Duane, August 4, 1812, Andrew A. Lipscomb, ed., *The Writings of Thomas Jefferson*, 20 vols (Washington DC: Thomas Jefferson Memorial Association of the United States, 1905), 11:265.

13. Andrew Jackson Proclamation, March 12, 1812, John Spencer Bassett, ed., *The Correspondence of Andrew Jackson*, 6 vols (Washington DC: Carnegie Institute, 1926–33), 1:122–3.

14. James Madison Speech before Congress, March 9, 1812, *Annals of the Congress of the United States*, 1st sess., 1162.

15. Aberdeen to Alexander Gordon, August 8, 1812, *Gordon Letters*, 308–9.

16. Wesley B. Turner, *British Generals in the War of 1812: High Command in the Canadas* (Montreal: McGill University Press, 1999).

17. Winfield Scott, *The Memoirs of Lieut.-General Scott, L.L.D., Written by Himself*, 2 vols (New York: Sheldon, 1864), 1:31.

18. Elting, *Amateurs to Arms!*, 7–8.

19. Henry Clay to Thomas Bodley, December 18, 1812, James Hopkins and Mary Hargreaves, eds, *The Papers of Henry Clay*, 10 vols (Lexington: University of Kentucky Press, 1959–88), 1:842.

20. For the Great Lake and St Lawrence fronts, see: Alec R. Gilpin, *The War of 1812 in the Old Northwest* (East Lansing: Michigan State University Press, 1958); Richard Dillon, *We Have Met the Enemy: Oliver Hazard Perry: Wilderness Commodore* (New York: Harper and Row, 1965); Pierre Berton, *The Invasion of Canada, 1812–1813* (Toronto: McClelland and Stewart, 1980); Pierre Berton, *Flames Across the Border: The Canadian-American Tragedy, 1813–1814* (Boston: Little, Brown, 1981); William Welsh and David Skaggs, eds, *The War on the Great Lakes: Essays Commemorating the 175th Anniversary of the Battle of Lake Erie* (Kent: Kent State University Press, 1991); Gerard Altoff, *Deep Water Sailors, Shallow Water Soldiers* (Put-in-Bay: Perry Group, 1993); David Skagg, and Gerard Altoff, *A Signal Victory: The Lake Erie Campaign, 1812–1813* (Annapolis: Naval Institute Press, 1997); Robert Malcomson, *The Lords of the Lake: The Naval War on Lake Ontario* (Annapolis: Naval Institute Press, 1998).

21. Hitsman, *Incredible War*, 31–2.

22. R. David Edmunds, *Tecumseh and the Quest for Indian Leadership* (New York: Little, Brown, 1984); John Sugden, *Tecumseh: A Life* (New York: Henry Holt, 1998).

23. Latimer, *1812*, 69.

24. Earnest A. Cruikshank, ed., *Documents Relating to the Invasion of Canada and the Surrender of Detroit* (Manchester: Ayer Company, 1979), 192.

25. Latimer, *1812*, 68.

26. Latimer, *1812*, 76.

27. John S.D. Eisenhower, *Agent of Destiny: The Life and Times of General Winfield Scott* (New York: Free Press, 1997), 41.

28. Glen G. Clift, *Remember the Raisin! Kentucky and Kentuckians in the Battles and Massacres at Frenchtown, Michigan Territory, in the War of 1812* (Frankfort: Historical Society, 1961).

29. E. Hallaman, *The British Invasion of Ohio – 1813* (Columbus: Ohio Historical Society, 1958).
30. Henry Proctor to George Prevost, May 14, 1813, *British Documents*, 2:34.
31. Larry L. Nelson, *Men of Patriotism, Courage, and Enterprise! Fort Meigs and the War of 1812* (Westminster, Mary. Heritage Books, 2003).
32. John C. Fredericksen, 'The Pittsburgh Blues and the War of 1812: The Memoir of Private Nathaniel Vernon,' *Pennsylvania History*, Vol. 56 (July 1989), 206.
33. David D. Anderson, 'The Battle of Fort Stephenson: The Beginning of the End of the War of 1812 in the Northwest,' *Northwest Ohio Quarterly*, Vol. 33 (Spring 1961), 81–90.
34. Dillon, *We Have Met the Enemy*; Welsh and Skaggs, eds, *The War on the Great Lakes*; Altoff, *Deep Water Sailors, Shallow Water Soldiers*; Skagg and Altoff, *A Signal Victory*.
35. Douglas E. Clanin, ed., 'The Correspondence of William Henry Harrison and Oliver Hazard Perry, July 5, 1813–July 21, 1813,' *Northwest Ohio Quarterly*, Vol. 60 (Autumn 1988), 153–80.
36. Tecumseh speech, September 18, 1813, Niles Register Number 5, November 6, 1813, NYPL.
37. Latimer, *1812*, 169.
38. Elting, *Amateurs to Arms!*, 118.
39. Elting, *Amateurs to Arms!*, 124.
40. Elihu H. Shepard, *The Autobiography of Elihu H. Shepard, Formerly Professor of Languages in St. Louis College* (St Louis: George Knapp, 1869), 56.
41. Elting, *Amateurs to Arms!*, 126.
42. Donald Dewar, and Paul Hutchinson, *The Battle of Beaverdams: The Story of Thorold's Battle in the War of 1812* (St Catherines: Slabtown Press, 1996).
43. Latimer, *1812*, 143.
44. Elting, *Amateurs to Arms!*, 154–5.
45. Latimer, *1812*, 214.
46. Elting, *Amateurs to Arms!*, 101.
47. Richard Palmer, 'Lake Ontario Battles: Part 3; The Battle of Sandy Creek,' *Inland Seas*, Vol. 53 (1997), 282–91.
48. Borneman, *1812*, 188.
49. Elting, *Amateurs to Arms!*, 187.
50. Latimer, *1812*, 297.
51. Elting, *Amateurs to Arms!*, 249, 252.
52. Borneman, *1812*, 212–13.
53. Latimer, *1812*, 358–9.

Chapter 17
1. Ian Toll, *Six Frigates: The Epic History of the Founding of the U.S. Navy* (New York: W.W. Norton, 2006), 287.
2. To place the 1812 naval war in context and for excellent statistics, see: Brian Tunstall, *Naval Warfare in the Age of Sail: The Evolution of Fighting Tactics, 1650–1815* (Annapolis: Naval Institute Press, 1990); Jean-Claude Gillet, *La Marine impériale: Le Grand Rêve de Napoléon* (Paris: Bernard Giovanangeli Editeur, 2010), 17; Toll, *Six Frigates*, 332.
3. C. Northcote Parkinson, *Britannia Rules: The Classic Age of Naval History, 1793–1815* (London: Alan Sutton Publishing, 1994), 149.
   For the naval war, see: Alfred T. Mahan, *Sea Power in Its Relations to the War of 1812* (Boston: Little, Brown, 1905); C.S. Forrester, *The Naval War of 1812* (London: Landsborough Publications, 1958); Robert Gardiner, ed., *The Naval War of 1812* (London: Caxton Publishing, 2001); Toll, *Six Frigates*.

For the privateering war, see: John Philips Cranwell and William Bowers Crane, *Men of Marque: A History of Private Armed Vessels out of Baltimore during the War of 1812* (New York: W.W. Norton, 1940); Jerome R. Garitee, *The Republic's Private Navy: The American Privateering Business as Practiced by Baltimore during the War of 1812* (Middletown: Wesleyan University Press, 1977); Donald A. Pettrie, *The Prize Game: Lawful Looting on the High Seas in the Days of Fighting Sail* (Annapolis: Naval Institute Press, 1999).

For published documents, see: William S. Dudley and Michael J. Crawford, eds, *The Naval War of War: A Documentary History*, 3 vols (Annapolis: Naval Institute Press, 1985, 1992, 2004).

4. *Parliamentary Debates from 1803*, 29:649–50; Donald R. Hickey, *The War of 1812: A Forgotten Conflict* (Urbana: University of Illinois Press, 1990), 96–7. For the privateering war, see: Cranwell and Crane, *Men of Marque*; Garitee, *The Republic's Private Navy*; Pettrie, *The Prize Game.*

5. John G. Brighton, ed., *Admiral Sir P.V.B. Broke: A Memoir* (London: Sampson Low, 1866); Peter Padfield, *Broke and the Shannon* (London: Hodder and Stoughton, 1968).

6. Samuel Leech, *Thirty Years from Home: or A Voice from the Main Deck, Being Six Years in a Man-of-War* (Boston: J.M. Whittemore, 1847), 50.

7. Julian Gwyn, *Frigates and Foremasts: The North American Squadron in Nova Scotia Waters, 1745–1815* (Vancouver: University of British Columbia Press, 2003), 128–49; John Boileau, *Half-Hearted Enemies: Nova Scotia, New England, and the War of 1812* (Halifax: Formac, 2005), 29–30.

8. Toll, *Six Frigates*, 406.

9. Toll, *Six Frigates*, 405–17; H.F. Pullen, *The Shannon and the Chesapeake* (Toronto: McClelland and Stewart, 1970).

10. Quoted in John Latimer, *1812: War with America* (Cambridge, Mass.: Harvard University Press, 2009), 168.

11. Gerard S. Graham, and R.A. Humphreys, eds, *The Navy and South America, 1783–1820* (London: Navy Records Society, 1962), 132–4, 141–2.

12. For the best overview, see: Wade G. Dudley, *Splintering the Wooden Wall: The British Blockade of the United States, 1812–1815* (Annapolis: Naval Institute Press, 2003). See also: Joseph A. Goldenberg, 'The Royal Navy's Blockade in New England Waters, 1812–1815,' *International History Review*, Vol. 6 (1984), 424–7.

13. Toll, *Six Frigates*, 385.

14. Curtis P. Nettels, *The Emergence of a National Economy, 1775–1815* (New York: Harper and Row, 1969), 385, 396, 399.

15. For Cockburn, see: A.J. Pack, *The Man Who Burned the White House: Admiral Sir George Cockburn, 1772–1853* (Emsworth: Kenneth Mason, 1987); Roger Morriss, *Cockburn and the British Navy in Transition: Admiral Sir George Cockburn, 1772–1852* (Exeter: University of Exeter Press, 1997).

16. Latimer, *1812*, 161.

17. William F.P. Napier, *The Life and Opinions of General Sir Charles James Napier*, 4 vols (London: John Murray, 1858), 1:221.

18. Walter R. Borneman, *1812: The War that Founded a Nation* (New York: Harper, 2004), 174.

19. Toll, *Six Frigates*, 428–9.

Chapter 18

1. Wellington to Liverpool, May 26, 1812, *Wellington Dispatches*, 9:177.
2. William Verner, ed., *A British Rifleman: The Journals and Correspondence of George Simmons during the Peninsular War and Campaign of Waterloo* (London: A.C. and Black, 1899), 221.
3. Jac Weller, *Wellington in the Peninsula* (Mechanicsburg: Stackpole Books, 1992), 197.
4. F.A. Whinyates, ed., *Diary of the Campaigns in the Peninsula for the Years 1811, 12, and 13* (London: Royal Artillery Institute, 1984), 70–1.
5. William Grattan, *The Adventures of a Connaught Ranger from 1808 to 1814* (London: Henry Colburn, 1847), 1:207–8.
6. Weller, *Wellington in the Peninsula*, 200.
7. George Bankes, ed., *The Autobiography of Sergeant William Lawrence, a Hero of the Peninsular War and Waterloo Campaign* (London: Sampson Low and Company, 1886), 111–13.
8. John Donaldson, *Recollections of the Eventful Life of a Soldier* (London: Naval and Military Press, 2009).
9. Weller, *Wellington in the Peninsula*, 204.
10. John Sturgis, ed., *A Boy in the Peninsular War: The Services, Adventures, and Experiences of Robert Blakeney, Subaltern in the Twenty-Eighth Regiment* (London: John Murray, 1899), 273–4.
11. Wellington to Edward Pellew, July 1, 1812, *Wellington Dispatches*, 9:269.
12. Weller, *Wellington in the Peninsula*, 210.
13. Wellington to Thomas Graham, July 3, 1812, *Wellington Dispatches*, 9:270.
14. Alexander Gordon to Aberdeen, July 25, 1812, *Gordon Letters*, 299.
15. Weller, *Wellington in the Peninsula*, 227–30.
16. Charles Greville, *The Greville Memoirs: A Journal of the Reigns of King George IV and William IV and Queen Victoria*, ed. H. Reeve, 8 vols (London: Longmans, 1888), 4:141.
17. Francis Carr-Gomm, ed., *The Letters and Journals of Field Marshal Sir William Gomm, 1799–1815* (London: John Murray, 1881).
18. Wellington to Thomas Graham, July 25, 1812, *Wellington Dispatches*, 9:310.
19. Weller, *Wellington in the Peninsula*, 230.
20. Weller, *Wellington in the Peninsula*, 226.
21. Charles Esdaile, *The Peninsular War: A New History* (New York: Palgrave Macmillan, 2003), 400.
22. Alexander Gordon to Aberdeen, July 28, 1812, *Gordon Letters*, 304.
23. Alexander Gordon to Aberdeen, August 16, 1812, *Gordon Letters*, 312–13.
24. Alexander Gordon to Aberdeen, August 30, 1812, *Gordon Letters*, 316.
25. Ian Fletcher, ed., *In the Service of the King: The Letters of William Thornton Keep* (Staplehurst: Spellmount, 1997), 143.
26. Weller, *Wellington in the Peninsula*, 235–7.
27. Esdaile, *Peninsular War*, 403.
28. F.A. Whinyates, ed., *William Swabey, Diary of the Campaigns in the Peninsula for the Years 1811, 12, and 13* (London: Ken Trotman, 1984), 157–8.
29. Weller, *Wellington in the Peninsula*, 239.
30. John Kincaid, *Adventures in the Rifle Brigade* (London: Richard Drew Publishing, 1909), 92.
31. George Bell, *Rough Notes of an Old Soldier during Fifty Years Service* (London: Day and Son, 1867), 53.
32. Wellington to William Cooke, November 25, 1812, Esdaile, *Peninsular War*, 420.
33. Alexander Gordon to Aberdeen, January 27, 1813, *Gordon Letters*, 363.

Chapter 19

1. Liverpool to Wellington, December 22, 1812, *Wellington Supplements*, 7:502.
2. Wellington to Bathurst, May 11, 1813, *Wellington Dispatches*, 10:372.
3. George Larpent, ed., *The Private Journal of Judge Advocate F.S. Larpent, attached to lord Wellington's Headquarters, 1812–14* (London: Richard Bentley, 1853), 1:226.
4. George Bell, *Rough Notes of an Old Soldier during Fifty Years Service* (London: Day and Son, 1867), 64, 63.
5. George Wood, *The Subaltern Officer: A Narrative* (London: Septimus Prowett, 1825), 180–1.
6. Jac Weller, *Wellington in the Peninsula* (Mechanicsburg: Stackpole Books, 1992), 266–8.
7. Thomas McGuffie, ed., *Peninsula Cavalry General: The Correspondence of Lieutenant General Robert Ballard Long* (London: Harrap, 1951), 275.
8. Wood, *Subaltern Officer*, 183–4.
9. Sarah Wood, ed., *William Hay: Reminiscences under Wellington, 1808–1815* (London: Simpkin, Marshall, Hamilton, Kent, and Company, 1901), 113.
10. Weller, *Wellington in the Peninsula*, 269.
11. Bell, *Rough Notes of an Old Soldier*, 71.
12. Robert Buckley, ed., *The Napoleonic War Journal of Captain Thomas Henry Browne* (London: Bodley Head, 1987), 214.
13. Wellington to Bathurst, June 29, 1813, *Wellington Dispatches*, 10:473.
14. Wellington to Bathurst, August 8, 1813, *Wellington Dispatches*, 6:663-64.
15. Sir Herbert Maxwell, *The Life of Wellington*, 2 vols (London: Sampson, Low, Marston, 1899), 1:331.
16. Ian C. Robertson, *Wellington Invades France: The Final Phase of the Peninsular War, 1813–14* (London: Greenhill Books, 2003), 101.
17. Edward Sabine, ed., *The Letters of Lieutenant Colonel Sir Augustus Simon Frazer, K.C.B., Commanding the Royal Horse Artillery in the Army under the Duke of Wellington Written During the Peninsular War and Waterloo Campaign* (London: John Murray, 1858), 197–8.
18. Stanley Monick, ed., *Douglas's Tale of the Peninsula and Waterloo, 1808–14* (London: Pen & Sword, 1997), 79–80.
19. Francis Carr-Gomm, ed., *The Letters and Journals of Field Marshal Sir William Gomm, 1799–1815* (London: John Murray, 1881), 312.
20. Weller, *Wellington in the Peninsula*, 302.
21. Weller, *Wellington in the Peninsula*, 302.
22. Robert Buckley, ed., *The Napoleonic War Journal of Captain Thomas Henry Browne* (London: Bodley Head, 1987), 229–30.
23. George Bankes, *The Autobiography of Sergeant William Lawrence* (London: Sampson Low and Company, 1886), 147–8.
24. Weller, *Wellington in the Peninsula*, 296.
25. Robertson, *Wellington Invades France*, 96.
26. Wellington to William Bentinck, August 5, 1813, *Wellington Dispatches*, 10:602.
27. Stanley Monick, *Douglas's Tale of the Peninsula and Waterloo* (London: Pen & Sword, 1997), 82–3.
28. George Robert Gleig, *The Subaltern* (London: John Murray, 1825), 56.
29. Wellington to Henry Wellesley, October 23, 1813, Charles Esdaile, *The Peninsular War: A New History* (New York: Palgrave Macmillan, 2003), 469.
30. Weller, *Wellington in the Peninsula*, 307–8; Robertson, *Wellington Invades France*, 110–11.
31. Weller, *Wellington in the Peninsula*, 310, 311.
32. *Stanhope Conversations*, 106–7.
33. Wellington to Bathurst, September 19, 1813, *Wellington Dispatches*, 7:10.

Chapter 20

1. Jac Weller, *Wellington in the Peninsula* (Mechanicsburg: Stackpole Books, 1992), 338–41.
2. G.C.M. Smith, ed., *The Autobiography of Sir Harry Smith*, 2 vols (London: John Murray, 1902), 1:142.
3. Nicolas Bentley, ed., *Selections from the Reminiscences of Captain Gronow* (London: Folio Society, 1977), 13.
4. Weller, *Wellington in the Peninsula*, 314, 317.
5. Ian C. Robertson, *Wellington Invades France: The Final Phase of the Peninsular War, 1813–14* (London: Greenhill Books, 2003), 157.
6. Weller, *Wellington in the Peninsula*, 327.
7. Wellington to General Manuel Freyre, November 14, 1813, *Wellington Dispatches*, 11:287.
8. Wellington to Bathurst, November 27, 1813, *Wellington Dispatches*, 11:306–7.
9. David Gates, *The Spanish Ulcer: A History of the Peninsular War* (New York: Da Capo, 2001), 446–7.
10. Weller, *Wellington in the Peninsula*, 336.
11. Weller, *Wellington in the Peninsula*, 361.
12. Weller, *Wellington in the Peninsula*, 362, 349.
13. Weller, *Wellington in the Peninsula*, 362.
14. Weller, *Wellington in the Peninsula*, 359.
15. Traité de Fontainebleau, 11 avril, 1814 ; Declaration du Gouvernment Provisiore, 11 avril, 1814; Ratification par l'Empereur Napoléon, 12 avril, 1813 ; Declaration faite au nom de Louis XVIII, Michel Kerautret, ed., *Les Grand Traités de L'Empire, 1810–1815: Documents diplomatiques du Consulat et de L'Empire*, Tome 3 (Paris: Nouveau Monde Editions, 2004), 3:126–7; 127; 128; 133.
16. Traité de Paix du 30 Mai 1814, Kerautret, ed., *Grand Traités*, Tome 3, 3:145–58.

Chapter 21

1. Alexander Cochrane, *The Fighting Cochranes: A Scottish Clan over Six Hundred Years of Naval and Military History* (London: Quiller Press, 1983).
2. Noel Mostert, *The Line Upon a Wind: The Great War at Sea, 1793–1815* (New York: W.W. Norton, 2007), 670.
3. Mostert, *Line Upon a Wind*, 671.
4. A.J. Pack, *The Man Who Burned the White House: Admiral Sir George Cockburn, 1772–1853* (Emsworth: Kenneth Mason, 1987); Roger Morriss, *Cockburn and the British Navy in Transition: Admiral Sir George Cockburn, 1772–1852* (Exeter: University of Exeter Press, 1997).
5. W.M. Marine, *The British Invasion of Maryland, 1812–1815* (Hatboro: Tradition Press, 1965); Anthony S. Pitch, *The Burning of Washington: The British Invasion of 1814* (Annapolis: Naval Institute Press, 1998); Christopher T. George, *Terror on the Chesapeake: The War of 1812 on the Bay* (Shippensburg: White Mane Books, 2000).
6. John Latimer, *1812: War with America* (Cambridge, Mass.: Harvard University Press, 2009), 315.
7. James Scott, *Recollections of Naval Life* (London: Richard Bentley, 1834), 303.
8. Scott, *Recollections*, 303–4.
9. George Dangerfield, *The Awakening of American Nationalism, 1815–1828* (New York: Harper and Row, 1965), 5.
10. G.C.M. Smith, ed., *The Autobiography of Sir Harry Smith, 1787–1819* (London: John Murray, 1902), 200.

11. George Robert Gleig, *A Narrative of the Campaigns of the British Army at Washington and New Orleans under Generals Ross, Pakenham, and Lambert, in the Years 1814 and 1815* (London: John Murray, 1826), 148.

12. Walter R. Borneman, *1812: The War that Founded a Nation* (New York: Harper, 2004), 233.

13. Alexander Cochrane to Henry Earl Bathurst, August 28, 1814, PRO WO, 1/141.

14. Latimer, *1812*, 328.

15. Roy Adkins and Lesley Adkins, *The War for all the Oceans: From Nelson at the Nile to Napoleon at Waterloo* (New York: Viking, 2006), 422.

16. Robert Barrett, 'Naval Recollections of the Late American War,' *United Services Journal and Naval and Military Magazine*, No. 1, 462–3.

Chapter 22

1. Noel Mostert, *The Line Upon a Wind: The Great War at Sea, 1793–1815* (New York: W.W. Norton, 2007), 670.

2. For the Creek, Gulf, and New Orleans campaigns, see: Robin Reilly, *The British at the Gates: The New Orleans Campaign in the War of 1812* (New York: G.P. Putnam's Sons, 1974); Frank Lawrence Owsley, *The Struggle for the Gulf Borderlands: The Creek War and the Battle of New Orleans, 1812–1815* (Gainesville: University of Florida Press, 1981); David S. Heidler and Jeanne T. Heidler, *Old Hickory's War: Andrew Jackson and the Quest for Empire* (Mechanicsburg: Stackpole Books, 1996); Robert Remini, *The Battle of New Orleans: Andrew Jackson and America's First Military Victory* (New York: Penguin Books, 1999); Brian Kilmeade and Don Yaeger, *Andrew Jackson and the Miracle of New Orleans: The Battle That Shaped America's Destiny* (New York: Sentinel, 2017).

3. Remini, *Battle of New Orleans*, 15.

4. Donald R. Hickey, *The War of 1812: A Forgotten Conflict* (Urbana: University of Illinois Press, 1990), 205.

5. John R. Elting, *Amateurs to Arms!: A Military History of the War of 1812* (New York: Da Capo Press, 1995), 287.

6. Heidler and Heidler, *Old Hickory's War*, 44–6.

7. John Latimer, *1812: War with America* (Cambridge, Mass.: Harvard University Press, 2009), 376.

8. George Robert Gleig, *A Narrative of the Campaigns of the British Army at Washington and New Orleans under Generals Ross, Pakenham, and Lambert, in the Years 1814 and 1815* (London: John Murray, 1826), 260.

9. Gleig, *Narrative*, 262–3.

10. Gleig, *Narrative*, 285.

11. Gleig, *Narrative*, 286–7.

12. Latimer, *1812*, 378.

13. Captain John J. Cooke, *A Narrative of Events in the South of France and of the Attack on New York, in 1814 and 1815* (London: T. and W. Boone, 1835), 212, 214.

14. Cooke, *Narrative*, 203.

15. Remini, *Battle of New Orleans*, 96–7.

16. Gleig, *Narrative*, 309–10.

17. Remini, *Battle of New Orleans*, 114–15.

18. Lady Bourchier, ed., *Memoir of the Life of Admiral Sir Edward Codrington*, 2 vols (London: Longman, Green, 1873), 2:334.

19. John Cooper, *Rough Notes of Seven Campaigns in Portugal, Spain, France, and America, during the Years 1809–10–11–12–13–14–15* (Carlisle: G. and T. Coward, 1914), 130.

20. Bourchier, ed., *Memoir of Codrington*, 335–6.

21. Remini, *Battle of New Orleans*, 167.

22. Remini, *Battle of New Orleans*, 156.

23. Elting, *Amateurs to Arms!*, 308; Hickey, *War of 1812*, 212.

24. For the diplomacy that ended the war, see: Fred L. Engelman, *The Peace of Christmas Eve* (New York: Harcourt, Brace, 1962); Bradford Perkins, *Castlereagh and Adams: England and the United States, 1812–1823* (Berkeley: University of California Press, 1964); Frank A. Updyke, *The Diplomacy of the War of 1812* (Gloucester, Mass.: P. Smith, 1965).

25. Wellington to Liverpool, November 7, 1814, *Wellington Dispatches*, 9:422.

Chapter 23

1. For the best first-person account of Napoleon's Elba sojourn, see that of Britain's commissioner to this throne, Neil Campbell, *Napoleon at Fontainebleau and Elba* (London: John Murray, 1869).

2. Alan Schom, *Napoleon Bonaparte* (New York: HarperCollins, 1997), 712–13.

3. For the best overview of Napoleon's three months in power culminating with Waterloo, see: Alan Schom, *One Hundred Days: Napoleon's Road to Waterloo* (New York: Oxford University Press, 1992).

4. *Le Moniteur*, 13 avril, 1815, NYPL.

5. Castlereagh to Wellington, March 26, 1815, *Castlereagh Correspondence*, 10:285–6.

6. Wellington to Prince of Orange, May 11, 1815, *Wellington Dispatches*, 12:375.

7. *Wellington Reminiscences*, 218–19.

8. For the Waterloo Campaign, see: Scott Bowden, *The Armies at Waterloo: A Detailed Analysis of the Armies that Fought History's Greatest Battles* (Arlington, Texas: Empire Games Press, 1983); Mark Adkin, *The Waterloo Companion: The Complete Guide to History's Most Famous Battle* (Mechanicsburg: Stackpole Books, 2001); Andrew Roberts, *Napoleon and Wellington: The Battle of Waterloo and the Great Commanders Who Fought It* (New York: Simon and Schuster, 2001); Geoffrey Wootten, *Waterloo 1815: The Birth of Modern Europe* (London: Osprey, 2005); Gareth Glover, *Waterloo: Myth and Reality* (London: Pen & Sword Press, 2014); Gordon Corrigan, *Waterloo: A New History, Wellington, Napoleon, and the Battle that Saved Europe* (New York: Pegasus Books, 2014); Gregory Fremont-Barnes, *Waterloo 1815: The British Army's Day of Destiny* (London: History Press, 2015); Brendan Simms, *The Longest Afternoon: The 400 Men Who Decided the Battle of Waterloo* (New York: Basic Books, 2015); Nigel Sale, *The Lie at the Heart of Waterloo: The Battle's Last Half Hour* (London: History Press, 2015).

9. David Chandler, *The Campaigns of Napoleon: The Mind and Method of History's Greatest Soldier* (New York: Macmillan, 1966), 115–17.

10. Adkin, *Waterloo Companion*, 38–50, 66–72.

11. Creevey Journal, June 16, 1815, *Creevey Papers*, 223.

12. Elizabeth Longford, *Wellington: Years of the Sword* (New York: Harper and Row, 1969), 416.

13. *Malmesbury Correspondence*, 2:445–6.

14. *Stanhope Conversations*, 109; *Wellington Conversations*, 5.

15. Scott Bowden, *The Armies at Waterloo: A Detailed Analysis of the Armies that Fought History's Greatest Battles* (Arlington: Empire Games Press, 1983), 372.

16. Adkin, *Waterloo Companion*, 74.

17. Edouard Fleury de Chaboulon, *Les Cent-Jours: Mémoires pour servir à l'histoire de la vie privée, du retour et du règne de Napoléon en 1815*, 2 vols (Paris: Rouveyre, 1952), 2 :134.

18. Sir Herbert Maxwell, *The Life of Wellington*, 2 vols (London: Sampson, Low, Marston, 1899), 2:37–8.
19. *Wellington Reminiscences*, 231.
20. Adkin, *Waterloo Companion*, 37, 51.
21. *Wellington Conversations*, 7.
22. George Robert Gleig, *The Life of Arthur Duke of Wellington* (London: Longman Green, 1889), 267.
23. Christopher Hibbert, *Wellington: A Personal History* (Reading, Mass.: Perseus Books, 1997), 177–8.
24. *Wellington Reminiscences*, 182.
25. John Raymond, ed., *The Reminiscences and Recollections of Captain Gronow*, 2 vols (London: Bodley Head, 1964), 1:69–70.
26. Raymond, *Gronow*, 1:190–1.
27. Quoted in Huw J. Davies, *Wellington's Wars: The Making of a Military Genius* (New Haven: Yale University Press, 2012), 238–9.
28. *Wellington Conversations*, 5.
29. Arthur Bryant, *The Great Duke: A Brilliant Biographical Narrative of Wellington the Soldier* (New York: William Morrow and Company, 1975), 443.
30. Adkin, *Waterloo Companion*, 74.
31. *Wellington Reminiscences*, 179.
32. Wellington to Beresford, July 2, 1815, *Wellington Dispatches*, 12:529.
33. Hibbert, *Wellington*, 185.
34. Wellington to Bathurst, June 19, 1815, *Wellington Dispatches*, 12:484.
35. *Creevey Papers*, 236–7.

Chapter 24
1. The following information is cleared from Sir Frederick Lewis Maitland, *The Surrender of Napoleon* (London: H. Colbum, 1826).
2. Maitland, *Surrender of Napoleon*.
3. Louis Marchand, *Mémoires de Marchand, Premier Valet de Chambre et Exécuteur testamentaire de l'Empereur*, 2 vols (Paris: Plon, 1952–5), 1:205.
4. *Croker Papers*, 2:235.
5. Ian W. Toll, *Six Frigates: The Epic History of the Founding of the U.S. Navy* (New York: W.W. Norton, 2006), 7.
6. Wellington to Bathurst, December 21, 1813, *Wellington Dispatches*, 11:384–7.
7. Emmanuel Auguste Dieudonne Las Cases, *Memoirs of the Life, Exile, and Conversations with the Emperor* (New York: Worthington Company, 1890), 1:135.
8. Wellington to Thomas Martin, September 16, 1813, Sir Richard Vessey Hamilton, ed., *The Letters and Papers of Admiral of the Fleet Sir Thomas Byam Martin*, 3 vols (London: Navy Records Society, 1903), 2:393.
9. Edward Brenton, ed., *The Life and Correspondence of John, Earl of St. Vincent* (1838, repr. London: Elibron Classics, 2005), 1:348.
10. John Page, ed., *Intelligence Officer in the Peninsula: The Letters and Diaries of Major the Honourable Edward Charles Cocks, 1786–1812* (London: Hippocrene Books, 1986), 134–5.
11. Wellington to John Villiers, November 20, 1809, PRO WO 1/242, ff. 420–2.
12. Jean-Claude Gillet, *La Marine impériale: Le Grande Rêve de Napoléon* (Paris: Bernard Giovanangeli Editeur, 2010), 93.

13. Michael Duffy, *Soldiers, Sugar, and Seapower: The British Expeditions to the West Indies and the War against Revolutionary France* (Oxford: Clarendon Press, 1987), 326–93.
14. Duffy, *Soldiers, Sugar, and Seapower*, 372.
15. Duffy, *Soldiers, Sugar, and Seapower*, 371, 377, 380.
16. Duffy, *Soldiers, Sugar, and Seapower*, 309.
17. For the most comprehensive exploration, see: William Nester, *Titan: The Art of British Power in the Age of Revolution and Napoleon* (Norman: University of Oklahoma Press, 2016).

Select Bibliography

Primary Sources

Anonymous, *The Proceedings of the Court Martial of Admiral Byng*, London: Gale, 2012.

Aspinall, Arthur, ed., *The Letters of George IV, 1812–30*, Cambridge: Cambridge University Press, 1938.

Aspinall, Arthur, ed., *The Later Correspondence of George III*, 5 vols, Cambridge: Cambridge University Press, 1962–70.

Aspinall, Arthur, ed., *The Correspondence of George Prince of Wales, 1770–1812*, 8 vols, London: Cassell, 1963–71.

Bankes, George, ed., *The Autobiography of Sergeant William Lawrence, a Hero of the Peninsular War and Waterloo Campaign*, London: Sampson Low and Company, 1886.

Barrett, Robert, 'Naval Recollections of the Late American War,' *United Services Journal and Naval and Military Magazine*, number one, 462–3.

Barrow, J., ed., The Life and Correspondence of Admiral Sir William Sidney Smith, 2 vols, London: Richard Bentley, 1848.

Bell, George, *Rough Notes of an Old Soldier during Fifty Years Service*, London: Day and Son, 1867.

Bentley, Nicolas, ed., *Selections from the Reminiscences of Captain Gronow*, London: Folio Society, 1977.

Bishop of Bath and Wells, ed., *The Journal and Correspondence of William, Lord Auckland*, 4 vols, London: R. Bentley, 1861–2.

Bourchier, Lady, ed., *Memoir of the Life of Admiral Sir Edward Codrington*, 2 vols, London: Longman, Green, 1873.

Brighton, John G., ed., *Admiral Sir P.V.B. Broke: A Memoir*, London: Sampson Low, 1866.

Browning, Oscar, ed., *The Political Memoranda of Francis Fifth Duke of Leeds*, London: Nicolas and Sons, 1884.

Buckingham and Chandos, Duke of, ed., *Memoirs of the Courts and Cabinets of George the Third*, 2 vols, London: Hurst & Blackett, 1853–5.

Buckley, Robert, ed., *The Napoleonic War Journal of Captain Thomas Henry Browne*, London: Bodley Head, 1987.

Campbell, Neil, *Napoleon at Fontainebleau and Elba*, London: John Murray, 1869.

Carr-Gomm, Francis, ed., *The Letters and Journals of Field Marshal Sir William Gomm, 1799–1815*, London: John Murray, 1881.

Chaboulon, Edouard Fleury de, *Les Cent-Jours: Mémoires pour servir à l'histoire de la vie privée, du retour et du règne de Napoléon en 1815*, 2 vols, Paris: Rouveyre, 1952.

Clanin, Douglas E., ed., 'The Correspondence of William Henry Harrison and Oliver Hazard Perry, July 5, 1813–July 21, 1813,' *Northwest Ohio Quarterly*, Vol. 60 (Autumn 1988), 153–80.

Cobbett, William, ed., *Parliamentary Debates*, 22 vols, London: R. Bagshaw, 1804–12.

Cobbett, William, ed., *The Parliamentary History of England from the Earliest Times to 1803*, 36 vols, London: R. Bagshaw, 1806–20.

Cochrane, Dundonald, Thomas, tenth Earl, *The Autobiography of a Seaman*, 2 vols, London: Mclaren, 1861.

Collingwood, G.L.N., ed., *A Selection from the Public and Private Correspondence of Vice Admiral Lord Collingwood Interspersed with Memoirs of His Life*, London: John Murray, 1829.

Constant, Louis, *Mémoires Intimes de Napoléon Ie par Constant, son valet de chambre*, 2 vols, Paris: Mercure de France, 1967.

Cooke, Captain John J., *A Narrative of Events in the South of France and of the Attack on New York, in 1814 and 1815*, London: T. and W. Boone, 1835.

Cooper, John, *Rough Notes of Seven Campaigns in Portugal, Spain, France, and America, during the Years 1809–10–11–12–13–14–15*, Carlisle: G. and T. Coward, 1914.

Copeland, Richard, ed., *The War Speeches of William Pitt the Younger*, Oxford: Clarendon, 1918.

Cruikshank, Earnest A., ed., *Documents Relating to the Invasion of Canada and the Surrender of Detroit*, Manchester, N.H.: Ayer Company, 1979.

Curling, Henry, ed., *Recollections of Rifleman Harris*, London: Peter Davies, 1928.

Dalrymple, Hew, *Memoirs written by Sir Hew Dalrymple, Bart., of his Proceeding as connected with the affairs of Spain and the Commencement of the Peninsular War*, London: Thomas and William Boone, 1830.

Dangerfield, George, *The Awakening of American Nationalism, 1815–1828*, New York: Harper and Row, 1965.

Debrett, John, ed., *The Parliamentary Register, or, History of the Proceedings and Debates of the House of Commons*, 2nd Ser. 45 vols, London: R. Spottiswoode, 1781–96; 3rd Ser. 18 vols, London: R. Spottiswoode, 1797–1802.

Donaldson, John, *Recollections of the Eventful Life of a Soldier*, London: Naval and Military Press, 2009.

Dudley, William S., and Michael J. Crawford, eds, *The Naval War of War: A Documentary History*, 3 vols, Annapolis: Naval Institute Press, 1985, 1992, 2004.

Dumouriez, Charles François, *La Vie et les Mémoires du Général Dumouriez, Avec des notes et éclairissements historiques par M. M. Berville et Barière*, 4 vols, Paris: Baudoins Frères,1822–3.

Dupont, Andre, ed., *Archives Parlementaires de 1787 à 1860: Recueil complet des débats législatifs et politiques des chambres Françaises*, 127 vols, Paris: Bibliothèque Nationale de France, 1879–1913.

Fletcher, Ian, ed., *In the Service of the King: The Letters of William Thornton Keep*, Staplehurst: Spellmount, 1997.

Gleig, George Robert, *A Narrative of the Campaigns of the British Army at Washington and New Orleans under Generals Ross, Pakenham, and Lambert, in the Years 1814 and 1815*, London: John Murray, 1826.

Gleig, George Robert, *The Subaltern*, London: T. Cadell, 1925.

Gore, John, ed., *The Thomas Creevey Papers*, New York: Macmillan, 1904.

Grattan, William, *The Adventures of a Connaught Ranger from 1808 to 1814*, London: Henry Colburn, 1847.

Greig, James, ed., *The Farington Diary*, 8 vols, London: Hutchinson, 1922.

Greville, Charles, *The Greville Memoirs: A Journal of the Reigns of King George IV and William IV and Queen Victoria*, ed. H. Reeve, 8 vols, London: Longmans, 1888.

Gurwood, Colonel, ed., *The Dispatches of Field Marshall the Duke of Wellington*, 8 vols London: Park, Furnivall, and Parker, 1944.

Hamilton, Sir Richard Vessey, ed., *The Letters and Papers of Admiral of the Fleet Sir Thomas Byam Martin*, 3 vols, London: Navy Records Society, 1903.

Hansard, T.C., ed., *The Parliamentary Debates from the Year 1803*, London: T.C. Hansard, 1812.

Harcourt, L.V., ed., *The Diaries and Correspondence of the Right Hon. George Rose*, London: Richard Bentley, 1860.

Harris, Nicolas, ed., *The Dispatches and Letters of Vice-Admiral Lord Viscount Nelson*, 7 vols, Cambridge: Cambridge University Press, 2011.

Hart, Lindell, ed., *The Letters of Private Wheeler*, New York: Houghton Mifflin, 1952.

Hathaway, Eileen, ed., *Benjamin Harris: A Dorset Rifleman*, London: Shinglepicker Press, 1995.

Hibbert, Christopher, ed., *Recollections of Rifleman Harris*, London: Cassell Military, 2007.

Hopkins, James F., and Mary Hargreaves, eds, *The Papers of Henry Clay*, 10 vols, Lexington: University of Kentucky Press, 1959–88.

Howell, Thomas, *Journal of a Soldier of the Seventy-First Regiment from 1806 to 1815, Memorials of the Late War, vol. 1*, Edinburgh: Balfour and Clarke, 1828.

Jennings, Louis J., ed., *The Croker Papers: The Correspondence and Diaries of John Wilson Croker, Secretary to the Admiralty from 1809 to 1830*, 3 vols, London: John Murray, 1885.

Kerautret, Michel, ed., *Les Grand Traités de l'Empire (1799–1804): Documents Diplomatiques du Consulat et de l'Empire*, Tome 1, Paris: Nouveau Monde Editions/Fondation Napoléon, 2002.

Kerautret, Michel, ed., *Les Grand Traités de l'Empire (1804–1810): Documents Diplomatiques du Consulat et de l'Empire*, Tome 2, Paris: Nouveau Monde Editions/Fondation Napoléon, 2004.

Kincaid, John, *Adventures in the Rifle Brigade*, London: Richard Drew Publishing, 1909.

Las Cases, Emmanuel Auguste Dieudonne, *Memoirs of the Life, Exile, and Conversations with the Emperor*, New York: Worthington Company, 1890.

Larpent, George, ed., *The Private Journal of Judge Advocate F.S. Larpent, attached to lord Wellington's Headquarters, 1812–14*, London: Richard Bentley, 1853.

Leach, John, *Rough Sketches of an Old Soldier*, London: John Murray, 1833.

Leech, Samuel, *Thirty Years from Home: or A Voice from the Main Deck, Being Six Years in a Man-of-War*, Boston: J.M. Whittemore, 1847.

Lentz, Thierry et al., eds, *Napoléon Bonaparte Correspondance Generale*, Vols 1–9, Paris: Fayard, 2004–12.

Lipscomb, Andrew A., ed., *The Writings of Thomas Jefferson*, 20 vols, Washington DC: Thomas Jefferson Memorial Association of the United States, 1905.

Londonderry, Charles William Vane, Marquis of, ed., *The Correspondence, Despatches, and Other Papers of Viscount Castlereagh, Second Marquis of Londonderry*, 12 vols, London: John Murray, 1848–53.

McGuffie, Thomas, ed., *Peninsula Cavalry General: The Correspondence of Lieutenant General Robert Ballard Long*, London: Harrap, 1951.

Maitland, Sir Frederick Lewis, *The Surrender of Napoleon*, London: H. Colbum, 1826.

Malmesbury, James Harris, Earl, *The Diaries and Correspondence of James Harris, the First Earl of Malmesbury*, 4 vols, London: Richard Bentley, 1845.

Marchand, Louis, *Mémoires de Marchand, Premier Valet de Chambre et Exécuteur testamentaire de l'Empereur*, 2 vols, Paris: Plon, 1952–5.

Mitchell, B.R., and Phyllis Deane, *Abstract of British Historical Statistics*, Cambridge: Cambridge University Press, 1962.

Monick, Stanley, ed., *Douglas's Tale of the Peninsula and Waterloo, 1808–1814*, London: Pen & Sword, 1997.

Morley, Stephen, *Memoirs of a Sergeant of the Fifth Regiment of Food, containing an Account of his Services in Hanover, South America, and the Peninsula*, Ashford: Ken Trotman, 1999.

Muir, Rory, ed., *The Letters of Lieutenant Colonel Alexander Gordon, 1808–1815*, London: Sutton, 2003.

Napier, William F.P., ed., *The Life and Opinions of General Sir Charles James Napier*, 4 vols, London: John Murray, 1858.

O'Meara, Barry E., *Napoleon in Exile, or a Voice from St. Helena: The Opinions and Reflections of Napoleon on the Most Important Events of His Life and Government in His Own Words*, New York: Worthington, 1890.

Page, John, ed., *Intelligence Officer in the Peninsula: The Letters and Diaries of Major the Honourable Edward Charles Cocks, 1786–1812*, London: Hippocrene Books, 1986.

Pellew, George, ed., *The Life and Correspondence of the Right Hon. Henry Addington, 1st Viscount Sidmouth*, 3 vols, London: John Murray, 1897.

Perrin, W.G., ed., 'The Journal of Surgeon Charles Chambers of H.M. Fireship Prometheus,' in *Naval Miscellany III*, London: Navy Records Society, 1928.

Pettigrew, Thomas, ed., *Memoirs of the Life of Vice-Admiral Lord Viscount Nelson*, 2 vols, London: T and W. Boone, 1849.

Pitt, William, *The Speeches of the Right Hon. William Pitt in the House of Commons*, 3 vols, London: Longman, Hurst, and Orne, 1817.

Raymond, John, ed., *The Reminiscences and Recollections of Captain Gronow*, 2 vols, London: Bodley Head, 1964.

Report on the Manuscripts of J.B. Fortescue, esq., preserved at Dropmore, Vols 1–10, London: Historical Manuscripts Commission, 1892–1927.

Ross, Charles, ed., *The Correspondence of Charles, First Marquis, Cornwallis*, 3 vols, London: John Murray, 1859.

Ross-Lewin, Henry, *With the Thirty-Second in the Peninsula and other Campaigns*, Dublin: Hodges, Figgis, and Company, 1904.

Rutland, Duke of, *Correspondence between the Right Hon. William Pitt and Charles, Duke of Rutland*, London: R. Spottiswoode, 1842.

Sabine, Edward, ed., *The Letters of Lieutenant Colonel Sir Augustus Simon Frazer, K.C.B., Commanding the Royal Horse Artillery in the Army under the Duke of Wellington Written During the Peninsular War and Waterloo Campaign*, London: John Murray, 1858.

Scott, James, *Recollections of a Naval Life*, London: Richard Bentley, 1834.

Scott, Winfield, *The Memoirs of Lieut.-General Scott, L.L.D., Written by Himself*, 2 vols, New York: Sheldon, 1864.

Smith, G.C.M., ed., *The Autobiography of Sir Harry Smith, 1787–1819*, London: John Murray, 1902.

Stanhope, Philip Henry, First Earl, *Miscellanies: Collected and Edited by Earl Stanhope*, London: John Murray, 1872.

Stanhope, Philip Henry, Fifth Earl, *Notes of Conversations with the Duke of Wellington, 1831–1851*, London: John Murray, 1885.

Strafford, Alice, Countess, ed., *Personal Reminiscences of the Duke of Wellington by Francis, the First Earl of Ellesmere*, New York: E.F. Dutton, 1903.

Sturgis, John, ed., *A Boy in the Peninsular War: The Services, Adventures, and Experiences of Robert Blakeney, Subaltern in the 28th Regiment*, London: John Murray, 1899.

Temperley, Harold, and Lillian Penson, eds, *The Foundations of British Foreign Policy*, London: Frank Cass and Company, 1966.

Verner, William, ed., *A British Rifleman: The Journals and Correspondence of George Simmons during the Peninsular War and Campaign of Waterloo*, London: A.C. and Black, 1899.

Wraxall, Nathaniel, ed., *The Historical and Posthumous Memoirs of Sir Nathaniel William Wraxall, 1772–1784*, London: Bickers & Sons, 1884.

Webster, C.K., ed., *British Diplomacy: Select Documents dealing with the Reconstruction of Europe, 1813–15*, London: G. Bell, 1921.

Webster, Charles, ed., *Some Letters of the Duke of Wellington to his Brother, William Wellesley Pole*, Camden Miscellany, Royal Historical Society, Vol. 18, 1948.

Wellington, Duke of, *The Supplementary Despatches, Correspondence, and Memoranda of Field Marshall Arthur, Duke of Wellington*, 15 vols, London: John Murray, 1858–72.

Wellington, Gerald, ed., *The Conversations of the First Duke of Wellington with George William Chad*, Cambridge: St Nicholas Press, 1956.

Whinyates, F.A., ed., *William Swabey, Diary of the Campaigns in the Peninsula for the Years 1811, 12, and 13*, London: Ken Trotman, 1984.

Wood, George, *The Subaltern Officer: A Narrative*, London: Septimus Prowett, 1825.

Wood, Sarah, ed., *William Hay: Reminiscences under Wellington, 1808–1815*, London: Simpkin, Marshall, Hamilton, Kent and Company, 1901.

Secondary Sources

Acerra, Martine, and Jean Meyer, *Marine et Revolution*, Rennes: Edition Ouest France, 1988.

Adams, Michael, *Napoleon and Russia*, London: Hambledon Press, 2006.

Adkin, Mark, *The Waterloo Companion: The Complete Guide to History's Most Famous Battle*, Mechanicsburg: Stackpole Books, 2001.

Adkins, Roy, and Lesley Adkins, *The War for all the Oceans: From Nelson at the Nile to Napoleon at Waterloo*, New York: Viking, 2006.

Albion, R.G., *Forests and Sea Power*, Cambridge, Mass.: Harvard University Press, 1926.

Altoff, Gerard, *Deep Water Sailors, Shallow Water Soldiers*, Put-in-Bay: Perry Group, 1993.

Anderson, David D., 'The Battle of Fort Stephenson: The Beginning of the End of the War of 1812 in the Northwest,' *Northwest Ohio Quarterly*, Vol. 33 (Spring 1961), 81–90.

Baird, David, *The life of General the Right Honorable Sir David Baird*, 2 vols, London: Richard Bentley, 1832.

Bamford, Andrew, *Sickness, Suffering, and the Sword: The British Regiment on Campaign, 1808–1815*, Norman: University of Oklahoma Press, 2013.

Bartlett, Thomas, *The Fall and Rise of the Irish Nation: The Catholic Question, 1691–1830*, New York: Barnes and Noble Books, 1992.

Battesti, Michèle, *La Bataille d'Aboukir*, Paris: Economica, 1998.

Battisti, Michèle, *Trafalgar: Les Aléas de la Stratégie Navale*, Paris: Editions Napoléon Ie, 2004.

Bayly, C.A., *Empire and Information: Intelligence Gathering and Social Communications in India, 1780–1880*, Cambridge: Cambridge University Press, 1996.

Behrens, C.B.A., *Society, Government, and the Enlightenment: The Experiences of Eighteenth Century France and Prussia*, London: Harper and Row, 1985.

Bennett, Geoffrey, *Nelson the Commander*, New York: Scribners' Sons, 1972.

Berton, Pierre, *The Invasion of Canada, 1812–1813*, Toronto: McClelland and Stewart, 1980.

Berton, Pierre, *Flames Across the Border: The Canadian-American Tragedy, 1813–1814*, Boston: Little, Brown, 1981.

Black, Jeremy, *British Foreign Policy in an Age of Revolution, 1783–1793*, Cambridge: Cambridge University Press, 1994.

Black, Jeremy, and Philip Woodfine, eds, *The British Navy and the Use of Naval Power in the Eighteenth Century*, Leicester: Leicester University Press, 1998.

Blanning, T.C.W., *The Origins of the French Revolutionary Wars*, London: Routledge, 1986.

Blanning, T.C.W., *The French Revolutionary Wars, 1787–1802*, New York: Arnold, 1996.

Boileau, John, *Half-Hearted Enemies: Nova Scotia, New England, and the War of 1812*, Halifax: Formac, 2005.

Bond, Gordon C., *The Grand Expedition: the British Invasion of Holland in 1809*, Athens: University of Georgia Press, 1979.

Borneman, Walter R., *1812: The War that Founded a Nation*, New York: Harper, 2004.

Bowden, Scott, *The Armies at Waterloo: A Detailed Analysis of the Armies that Fought History's Greatest Battles*, Arlington: Empire Games Press, 1983.

Brégeon, Jean-Joël, *L'Egypte Française au Jour le Jour*, Paris: Perrin, 1991.

Bret, Patrice, *L'Egypte: Au Temps de l'Expédition Bonaparte, 1798–1801*, Paris: Hachette, 1998.

Brewer, John, *The Sinews of Power: War, Money, and the English State, 1688–1783*, New York: Alfred A. Knopf, 1988.

Brown, Howard G., *War, Revolution, and the Bureaucratic States: Politics and Army Administration in France, 1791–1799*, New York: Oxford University Press, 1995.

Bryant, Arthur, *The Great Duke or the Invincible General*, New York: William Morrow and Company, 1972.

Bryant, Arthur, *The Great Duke: A Brilliant Biographical Narrative of Wellington the Soldier*, New York: William Morrow and Company, 1975.

Burne, Alfred H., *The Noble Duke of York: The Military Life of Frederick Duke of York and Albany*, London: Staples Press, 1948.

Cannadine, David, ed., *Admiral Lord Nelson: Context and Legacy*, Houndmills, Basingstoke: Palgrave Macmillan, 2005.

Chandler, David, *The Campaigns of Napoleon: The Mind and Method of History's Greatest Soldier*, New York: Macmillan, 1966.

Chickering, Roger, and Stig Forster, eds, *War in an Age of Revolution, 1775–1815*, New York: Cambridge University Press, 2010.

Childs, John, *Armies and Warfare in Europe, 1648–1789*, Manchester: Manchester University Press, 1982.

Clarke, James, and John McArthur, *The Life of Admiral Lord Nelson*, 2 vols, London: T. Cadell and W. Davies, 1809.

Clift, Glen G., *Remember the Raisin! Kentucky and Kentuckians in the Battles and Massacres at Frenchtown, Michigan Territory, in the War of 1812*, Frankfort: Historical Society, 1961.

Coad, J., *The Royal Dockyards, 1690–1815: Architecture and Engineering Works of the Sailing Navy*, Aldershot: Scolar Press, 1989.

Coats, Ann Veronica, and Philip Macdonald, *The Naval Mutinies of 1797: Unity and Perseverance*, London: Boydell Press, 2011.

Cochrane, Alexander, *The Fighting Cochranes: A Scottish Clan over Six Hundred Years of Naval and Military History*, London: Quiller Press, 1983.

Cole, Juan, *Napoleon's Egypt: Invading the Middle East*, New York: Palgrave Macmillan, 2008.

Coles, Harry L., *The War of 1812*, Chicago: University of Chicago Press, 1965.

Cookson, J.E., *The British Armed Nation, 1793–1815*, Oxford: Oxford University Press, 1997.

Coleman, Terry, *The Nelson Touch: The Life and Legend of Horatio Nelson*, New York: Oxford University Press, 2002.

Colley, Linda, *Britons: Forging the Nation, 1707–1837*, New Haven: Yale University Press, 2009.

Cormack, William S., *Revolution and Political Conflict in the French Navy, 1789–1793*, Cambridge: Cambridge University Press, 1995.

Corrigan, Gordon, *Waterloo: A New History, Wellington, Napoleon, and the Battle that Saved Europe*, New York: Pegasus Books, 2014.

Corvisier, Andre, *Armies and Society in Europe, 1494–1789*, Bloomington: University of Indiana Press, 1976.

Coss, Edward J., *All the King's Shilling: The British Soldier under Wellington, 1808–1814*, Norman: University of Oklahoma Press, 2010.

Cranwell, John Philips, and William Bowers Crane, *Men of Marque: A History of Private Armed Vessels out of Baltimore during the War of 1812*, New York: W.W. Norton, 1940.

Crowe, Kate Elizabeth, 'The Walcheren Expedition and the New Army Medical Board: A Reconsideration,' *English Historical Review*, Vol. 88, 1973, 770–885.

Crowhurst, Patrick, *The French War on Trade: Privateering, 1793–1815*, London: Scolar Press, 1989.

Curtin, Nancy J., *The United Irishmen: Popular Politics in Ulster and Dublin, 1791–1798*, Oxford: Oxford University Press, 1994.

Dallas, Gregor, *The Final Act: The Roads to Waterloo*, New York: Henry Holt, 1996.

Darling, Anthony D. *Red Coat and Brown Bess*, Bloomfield: Museum Restoration Service, 1993.

Davies, Huw J., *Wellington's Wars: The Making of a Military Genius*, New Haven: Yale University Press, 2012.

Dewar, Donald, and Paul Hutchinson, *The Battle of Beaverdams: The Story of Thorold's Battle in the War of 1812*, St Catherines: Slabtown Press, 1996.

Dickson, David, Daire Keogh, and Kevin Whelan, eds, *The United Irishmen: Republicanism, Radicalism, and Rebellion*, Dublin: Irish Academic Press, 1993.

Dillon, Richard, *We Have Met the Enemy: Oliver Hazard Perry: Wilderness Commodore*, New York: Harper and Row, 1965.

Doyle, William, *The Oxford History of the French Revolution*, New York: Oxford University Press, 1989.

Dudley, Wade G., *Splintering the Wooden Wall: The British Blockade of the United States, 1812–1815*, Annapolis: Naval Institute Press, 2003.

Duffy, Christopher, *The Military Experience in the Age of Reason, 1715–1789*, New York: Barnes and Noble, 1987.

Dunfermline, James, Lord, *Lieutenant-General Sir Ralph Abercromby, 1793–1801: A Memoir by his Son*, London: Naval & Military Press, 1861.

Edmunds, R. David, *Tecumseh and the Quest for Indian Leadership*, New York: Little, Brown, 1984.

Ehrman, John, *The Younger Pitt: The Reluctant Transition*, London: Constable, 1983.

Eisenhower, John S.D., *Agent of Destiny: The Life and Times of General Winfield Scott*, New York: Free Press, 1997.

Elliot, Marianne, *Partners in Revolution: The United Irishman and France*, New Haven: Yale University Press, 1982.

Elliot, Marianne, *Wolfe Tone: The Prophet of Irish Independence*, New Haven: Yale University Press, 1989.

Elting, John R., *Amateurs to Arms!: A Military History of the War of 1812*, New York: Da Capo Press, 1995.

Elting, John R., *Swords around a Throne: Napoleon's Grande Armée*, New York: Da Capo, 1997.

Esdaile, Charles, *The Peninsular War: A New History*, New York: Palgrave Macmillan, 2003.

Esdaile, Charles J., *Fighting Napoleon: Guerrillas, Bandits, and Adventurers in Spain, 1808–1814*, New Haven: Yale University Press, 2004.

Esdaile, Charles, *Napoleon's Wars: An International History, 1803–1815*, New York: Viking, 2007.

Esposito, Vincent J., and John R. Elting, *A Military Atlas of the Napoleonic Wars*, London: Greenhill Books, 1999.

Feibel, Robert M., 'What Happened at Walcheren: The Primary Sources,' *Bulletin of the History of Medicine*, Vol. 42, 1968, 62–79.

Fernyhough, Thomas, *The Military Memoirs of Four Brothers engaged in the Service of their Country*, London: William Sams, 1829.

Fleishman, Théo, *L'Expédition Anglaise sur le Continent en 1809*, Brussels: La Renaissance du Livre, 1973.

Fletcher, Ian, *Galloping at Everything: The British Cavalry in the Peninsular War and at Waterloo, 1808–15*, Mechanicsburg: Stackpole Books, 1999.

Fletcher, Ian, *The Waters of Oblivion: The British Invasion of the Rio de Plata, 1806–07*, London: Spellmount, 2006.

Forczyk, Robert, *Toulon 1793: Napoleon's First Great Victory*, London: Osprey, 2006.

Forrester, C.S., *The Naval War of 1812*, London: Landsborough Publications, 1958.

Fortescue, John, *A History of the British Army*, London: Macmillan, 1910.

Fosten, Bryan, *Wellington's Heavy Cavalry*, London: Osprey Books, 1982.

Fosten, Bryan, *Wellington's Light Cavalry*, London: Osprey Books, 1982.

Franceschi, Michel Verge, *La Marine Française au XVIIIe Siècle*, Paris: Sede, 1996.

Fredericksen, John C., 'The Pittsburgh Blues and the War of 1812: The Memoir of Private Nathaniel Vernon,' *Pennsylvania History*, Vol. 56 (July 1989), 196–212.

Fredericksen, John C. *The War of 1812 Eyewitness Accounts: an Annotated Bibliography*, Westport: Greenwood Press, 1997.

Fremont-Barnes, Gregory, *Waterloo 1815: The British Army's Day of Destiny*, London: History Press, 2015.

Gallo, Klaus, *Great Britain and Argentina: From Invasion to Recognition, 1806–1826*, London: Palgrave, 2001.

Galpin, W.F., 'The American Grain Trade to the Spanish Peninsula, 1810–1814,' *American History Review*, Vol. 28 (October 1922), 24–44.

Gardiner, Robert, *The Campaign of Trafalgar, 1803–05*, London: Chatham Publishing, 1997.

Gardiner, Robert, ed., *The Naval War of 1812*, London: Caxton Publishing, 2001.

Gardyne, C.G., *The Life of a Regiment: The History of the Gordon Highlanders from its formation in 1794 to 1816*, London: Medici Society, 1929.

Garitee, Jerome R., *The Republic's Private Navy: The American Privateering Business as Practiced by Baltimore during the War of 1812*, Middletown: Wesleyan University Press, 1977.

Gat, Azar, *The Origins of Military Thought From the Enlightenment to Clausewitz*, New York: Oxford University Press, 1989.

Gates, David, *The Napoleonic Wars, 1803–1815*, London: Arnold Press, 1997.

Gee, Austin, *The British Volunteer Movement, 1794–1814*, Oxford: Oxford University Press, 2003.

Geggus, D., 'The British Government and the Saint Domingue Slave Revolt, 1791–1793,' *English Historical Review*, Vol. 96 (1981), 285–305.

George, Christopher T., *Terror on the Chesapeake: The War of 1812 on the Bay*, Shippensburg: White Mane Books, 2000.

Gillet, Jean-Claude, *La Marine impériale: Le Grand Rêve de Napoléon*, Paris: Bernard Giovanangeli Editeur, 2010.

Gilpin, Alec R., *The War of 1812 in the Old Northwest*, East Lansing: Michigan State University Press, 1958.

Gleig, George Robert, *The Life of Arthur Duke of Wellington*, London: Longman Green, 1889.

Glover, Gareth, *Waterloo: Myth and Reality*, London: Pen & Sword Press, 2014.

Glover, Michael, *Wellington as Military Commander*, New York: Penguin, 2001.

Glover, Richard, *Peninsula Preparation: The Reform of the British Army, 1795–1809*, Cambridge: Cambridge University Press, 1988.

Goldenberg, Joseph A., 'The Royal Navy's Blockade in New England Waters, 1812–1815,' *International History Review*, Vol. 6 (1984), 424–7.

Gough, Hugh, and David Dickson, eds, *Ireland and the French Revolution*, Dublin: Irish Academic Press, 1990.

Graham, Gerard S., and R.A. Humphreys, eds, *The Navy and South America, 1783–1820*, London: Navy Records Society, 1962.

Grainger, John D., *The Amiens Truce: Britain and Bonaparte, 1801–1803*, Rochester, New York: Boydell Press, 2004.

Grattan, William, *Adventure with the Connaught Rangers, 1809–1814*, London: Henry Colburn, 1847.

Griffith, Paddy, *The Art of War of Revolutionary France, 1789–1802*, Mechanicsburg: Stackpole Books, 1998.

Griffiths, Arthur, *The Wellington Memorial, His Comrades and Contemporaries*, London: G. Allen, 1897.

Guy, Alan James, *The Road to Waterloo: The British Army and the Struggle against Revolutionary and Napoleonic France*, London: National Army Museum, 1990.

Gwyn, Julian, *Frigates and Foremasts: The North American Squadron in Nova Scotia Waters, 1745–1815*, Vancouver: University of British Columbia Press, 2003.

Hall, Christopher D., *Wellington's Navy: Sea Power and the Peninsular War, 1807–1814*, London: Chatham Publishers, 2004.

Hallaman, E., *The British Invasion of Ohio – 1813*, Columbus: Ohio Historical Society, 1958.

Harding, Richard, *The Evolution of the Sailing Navy, 1509–1815*, Basingstoke: Palgrave Macmillan, 1995.

Harding, Richard, *Seapower and Naval Warfare, 1650–1830*, Annapolis: Naval University Press, 1999.

Harding, Richard, *British Admirals of the Napoleonic Wars: The Contemporaries of Nelson*, London: Chatham, 2005.

Harrison, James, *The Life of Horatio Lord Viscount Nelson*, 2 vols, London: Ranelagh Press, 1806.

Hayes–McCoy, G.A., *Irish Battles: A Military History of Ireland*, New York: Barnes and Noble, 1969.

Haythornthwaite, Philip, *The Napoleonic Source Book*, London: Arms and Armour, 1990.

Haythornthwaite, Philip, *British Cavalrymen, 1792–1815*, London: Osprey Books, 1994.

Haythornthwaite, Philip J., *The Armies of Wellington, London*: Brockhampton Press, 1996.

Haythornthwaite, Philip, *Wellington: The Iron Duke*, Washington DC: Potomac Books, 2007.

Haythornthwaite, Philip, and Michael Chappell, *Uniforms of the Peninsular War, 1807–1814*, London: Arms and Armour, 1995.

Haythornthwaite, Philip, and Christopher Warner, *Uniforms of the French Revolutionary Wars*, London: Arms and Armour, 1997.

Heidler, David S., and Jeanne T. Heidler, *Old Hickory's War: Andrew Jackson and the Quest for Empire*, Mechanicsburg: Stackpole Books, 1996.

Henderson, James, *The Frigates: An Account of the Lighter Warships of the Napoleonic Wars, 1793–1815*, London: Leo Cooper, 1994.

Herold, J. Christopher, *Bonaparte in Egypt*, New York: Pen & Sword, 2005.

Hervey, Robert, *Cochrane: The Life and Exploits of a Fighting Captain*, New York: Da Capo, 2001.

Hibbert, Christopher, *Wellington: A Personal History*, Reading, Mass.: Perseus Books, 1997.

Hickey, Donald R., 'The Monroe-Pinkney Treaty of 1806: A Reappraisal,' *William and Mary Quarterly*, Vol. 44, No. 1, January 1987, 65–88.

Hickey, Donald R., *The War of 1812: A Forgotten Conflict*, Urbana: University of Illinois Press, 1990.

Hickey, Donald R., 'The War of 1812: Still a Forgotten Conflict?' *Journal of Military History*, Vol. 65, No. 3, July 2001, 741–69.

Higginson, Francis John, *Naval Battles of the Century*, London: W.W. Chambers, 1903.

Hilton, Boyd, *A Mad, Bad, & Dangerous People?: England, 1783–1846*, New York: Oxford University Press, 2008.

Hitsman, J. Mackay, *The Incredible War of 1812: A Military History*, Toronto: Robin Brass Studio, 1996.

Horsman, Reginald, *The War of 1812*, London: Eyre and Spottiswoode, 1969.

Houlding, J.A., *Fit for Service: The Training of the British Army, 1715–1795*, Oxford: Oxford University Press, 1981.

Humbert, J.M., and B. Ponsonnet, *Napoléon et la Mer: Un Rêve d'Empire*, Paris: Seuil, 2004.

Ingram, Edward, *Commitment to Empire: Prophecies of the Great Game for Asia, 1797–1800*, Oxford: Oxford University Press, 1981.

Ireland, Bernard, *The Fall of Toulon: The last Opportunity to Defeat the French Revolution*, London: Cassell Military Paperbacks, 2005.

James, William, *Naval History of Great Britain, 1793–1820*, 5 vols, London: Richard Bentley, 1822–4.

Johnston, Edith M., *Ireland in the Eighteenth Century*, Dublin: Gill and Macmillan, 1974.

Jones, Stuart, *An Invasion that Failed: The French Expedition to Ireland, 1796*, Oxford: Oxford University Press, 1950.

Kagan, Frederick W., *The End of the Old Order: Napoleon and Europe, 1801–1805*, New York: Da Capo, 2006.

Kaufman, William W., *British Policy and the Independence of Latin America, 1804–1814*, New Haven: Yale University Press, 1951.

Kelly, James, *Prelude to Union: Anglo-Irish Politics in the 1780s*, Cork: Cork University Press, 1992.

Keogh, Daire, *The French Disease: The Catholic Church and Irish Radicalism, 1790–1800*, Dublin: Irish Academic Press, 1993.

Knight, Roger, *Britain against Napoleon: The Organization of Victory, 1793–1815*, Norman: University of Oklahoma Press, 2013.

Latimer, John, *1812: War with America*, Cambridge, Mass.: Harvard University Press, 2009.

Laurens, Henry, *Les Origines Intellectuelles de l'Expédition d'Egypte: L'Orientalisme Islamisant en France, 1698–1798*, Paris : Editions Isis, 1987.

Laurens, Henry, et al., *L'Expédition d'Egypte, 1798–1801*, Paris: A. Collins, 1989.

Lavery, Brian, *Nelson's Navy: The Ships, Men, and Organization, 1793–1815*, Annapolis: Naval Institute Press, 1989.

Leggiere, Michael V., *The Fall of Napoleon: The Allied Invasion of France, 1813–14*, New York: Cambridge University Press, 2007.

Lémery, Henri, *La Révolution française à la Martinique*, Paris: Larose, 1936.

Lentz, Thierry, *Nouvelle Histoire du Premier Empire: Napoléon et la Conquête de l'Europe, 1804–1810*, Paris: Fayard, 2002.

Lewis, Michael, *A Social History of the Navy, 1783–1815*, London: Allen and Unwin, 1960.

Lincoln, Margarette, *Representing the Royal Navy: British Sea Power, 1750–1815*, Burlington: Ashgate, 2002.

Lloyd, Christopher, *St. Vincent and Camperdown*, London: Macmillan, 1963.

Longford, Elizabeth, *Wellington: Years of the Sword*, New York: Harper and Row, 1969.

Luthi, Jean-Jacques, *Regards sur l'Egypte au Temps de Bonaparte*, Paris: Harmattan, 1999.

Lynn, John A., *The Bayonets of the Republic: Motivation and Tactics in the Army of Revolutionary France, 1791–1794*, Urbana: University of Illinois Press, 1984.

McDowell, R.B., *Ireland in the Age of Imperialism and Revolution, 1760–1801*, Oxford: Oxford University Press, 1979.

McGuffie, T.H., 'The Walcheren Expedition and the Walcheren Fever,' *English Historical Review*, Vol. 62, 1947, 191–202.

McKay, Derek, and H.M. Scott, *The Rise of the Great Powers, 1648–1815*, London: Routledge, 1983.

Mackesy, Piers, *Statesmen at War: The Strategy of Overthrow, 1798–1799*, London: Longman, 1974.

Mackesy, Piers, *War without Victory: The Downfall of Pitt, 1799–1802*, Oxford: Oxford University Press, 1984.

Mackesy, Piers, *British Victory in Egypt: The End of Napoleon's Conquest*, New York: Tauris Parke Paperbacks, 2010.

Mahan, Alfred T., *Sea Power in Its Relations to the War of 1812*, Boston: Little, Brown, 1905.

Mainwaring, G.F., and Bonamy Dobree, *Mutiny: The Floating Republic*, London: Pen & Sword, 2004.

Malcomson, Robert, *The Lords of the Lake: The Naval War on Lake Ontario*, Annapolis: Naval Institute Press, 1998.

Marcus, G.J., *The Age of Nelson*, London: Allen and Unwin, 1971.

Marine, W.M., *The British Invasion of Maryland, 1812–1815*, Hatboro: Tradition Press, 1965.

Marshall, P.J., ed., *The Problems of Empire: Britain and India, 1757–1813*, London: Allen and Unwin, 1968.

Martray, J., *La Destruction de la marine Française par la Révolution*, Paris: France Empire, 1988.

Maxwell, Sir Herbert, *The Life of Wellington*, 2 vols, London: Sampson, Low, Marston, 1899.

Monarque, M., *Trafalgar*, Paris: Tallandier, 2005.

Moody, T.W., and W.E. Vaughan, *A New History of Ireland: Eighteenth Century Ireland, 1691–1800*, Oxford: Oxford University Press, 1986.

Moore, James, *A Narrative of the Campaign of the British Army in Spain Commanded by His Excellency Lieut. General Sir John Moore*, London: Joseph Johnson, 1809.

Morriss, Roger, *The Royal Dockyards during the Revolutionary and Napoleonic Wars*, Leicester: Leicester University Press, 1983.

Morriss, Roger, *Cockburn and the British Navy in Transition: Admiral Sir George Cockburn, 1772–1852*, Exeter: University of Exeter Press, 1997.

Mostert, Noel, *The Line Upon a Wind: The Great War at Sea, 1793–1815*, New York: W.W. Norton, 2007.

Munch-Petersen, Thomas, *Defying Napoleon: How Britain Bombarded Copenhagen and Seized the Danish Fleet in 1807*, London: Sutton Publishing, 2007.

Nelson, Larry L., *Men of Patriotism, Courage, and Enterprise! Fort Meigs and the War of 1812*, Westminster, Mary. Heritage Books, 2003.

Nester, William R., *Titan: The Art of British Power during the Age of Revolution and Napoleon*, Norman: University of Oklahoma Press, 2016.

Nettels, Curtis P., *The Emergence of a National Economy, 1775–1815*, New York: Harper and Row, 1969.

Nosworthy, Brent, *The Anatomy of Victory: Battle Tactics, 1689–1763*, New York: Hippocrene Books, 1992.

Nosworthy, Brent, *With Musket, Cannon, and Sword: Battle Tactics of Napoleon and His Enemies*, New York: Da Capo Press, 1996.

O'Brien, Gerard, *Anglo-Irish Politics in the Age of Grattan and Pitt*, Dublin: Irish Academic Press, 1987.

O'Connell, M.R., *Irish Politics and Social Conflict in the Age of the American Revolution*, Westport: Greenwood, 1976.

Ott, Thomas, *The Haitian Revolution, 1789–1801*, Knoxville: University of Tennessee Press, 1973.

Owlsley, Frank Lawrence, *The Struggle for the Gulf Borderlands: The Creek War and the Battle of New Orleans, 1812–1815*, Gainesville: University of Florida Press, 1981.

Pack, A.J., *The Man Who Burned the White House: Admiral Sir George Cockburn, 1772–1853*, Emsworth: Kenneth Mason, 1987.

Padfield, Peter, *Broke and the Shannon*, London: Hodder and Stoughton, 1968.

Padfield, Peter, *Maritime Power and the Struggle for Freedom: Naval Campaigns that Shaped the Modern World, 1788–1851*, London: John Murray, 2003.

Pakenham, Thomas, *The Year of Liberty: The Story of the Great Irish Rebellion of 1798*, London: Hodder and Stoughton, 1969.

Palmer, Richard, 'Lake Ontario Battles: Part 3; The Battle of Sandy Creek,' *Inland Seas*, Vol. 53 (1997), 282–91.

Parker, Geoffrey, *The Military Revolution: Military Innovation and the Rise of the West, 1500–1800*, New York: Cambridge University Press, 1996.

Parkinson, C. Northcote, *Britannia Rules: The Classic Age of Naval History, 1793–1815*, London: Alan Sutton Publishing, 1994.

Perkins, Bradford, *Prologue to War: England and the United States, 1805–1812*, Berkeley: University of California, 1963.

Perkins, Bradford, *Castlereagh and Adams: England and the United States, 1812–1823*, Berkeley: University of California Press, 1964.

Pettrie, Donald A., *The Prize Game: Lawful Looting on the High Seas in the Days of Fighting Sail*, Annapolis: Naval Institute Press, 1999.

Pitch, Anthony S., *The Burning of Washington: The British Invasion of 1814*, Annapolis: Naval Institute Press, 1998.

Pivka, Otto von, *Navies of the Napoleon Era*, London: D. & C. Newton Abbot, 1980.

Pivka, Otto von, *The Portuguese Army of the Napoleonic War*, London: Osprey, 1977.

Pullen, H.F., *The Shannon and the Chesapeake*, Toronto: McClelland and Stewart, 1970.

Reilly, Robin, *The British at the Gates: The New Orleans Campaign in the War of 1812*, New York: G.P. Putnam's Sons, 1974.

Remini, Robert, *The Battle of New Orleans: Andrew Jackson and America's First Military Victory*, New York: Penguin Books, 1999.

Roberts, Andrews, *Napoleon and Wellington: The Battle of Waterloo and the Great Commanders Who Fought It*, New York: Simon and Schuster, 2001.

Robertson, Ian C. *Wellington Invades France: The Final Phase of the Peninsular War, 1813–14*, London: Greenhill Books, 2003.

Rodger, A.B., *The War of the Second Coalition, 1798 to 1801: A Strategic Commentary*, Oxford: Oxford University Press, 1964.

Rodger, N.A.M., *The Wooden World: An Anatomy of the Georgian Navy*, New York: W.W. Norton, 1986.

Rodger, N.A.M., *The Command of the Ocean: A Naval History of Britain, 1649–1815*, New York: W.W. Norton, 2006.

Ross, Steven T., *Quest for Victory: French Military Strategy*, New York: Barnes and Company, 1978.

Sale, Nigel, *The Lie at the Heart of Waterloo: The Battle's Last Half Hour*, London: History Press, 2015.

Saul, Norman E., *Russia, and the Mediterranean, 1797–1807*, Chicago: University of Chicago Press, 1964.

Schama, Simon, *Citizens: A Chronicle of the French Revolution*, New York: Alfred A. Knopf, 1989.

Schoeder, Paul, *The Transformation of European Politics, 1763 to 1848*, New York: Oxford University Press, 1994.

Schom, Alan, *Trafalgar: Countdown to Battle, 1803–1805*, New York: Oxford University Press, 1990.

Schom, Alan, *One Hundred Days: Napoleon's Road to Waterloo*, New York: Oxford University Press, 1992.

Schom, Alan, *Napoleon Bonaparte*, New York: HarperCollins, 1997.

Scott, Samuel F., *The Response of the Royal Army in the French Revolution: The Role and Development of the Line Army, 1787–1793*, Oxford: Oxford University Press, 1978.

Ségéric, J.J., *Napoléon Face à la Royal Navy*, Paris: Marine Editions, 2008.

Severn, John, *Architects of Empire: The Duke of Wellington and His Brothers*, Norman: University of Oklahoma Press, 2007.

Shepard, Elihu H., *The Autobiography of Elihu H. Shepard, Formerly Professor of Languages in St. Louis College*, St Louis: George Knapp, 1869.

Sherwig, John W., *Guineas and Gunpowder: British Foreign Aid in the Wars with France, 1793–1815*, Cambridge, Mass.: Harvard University Press, 1969.

Simms, Brendan, *Three Victories and a Defeat: The Rise and Fall of the British Empire*, New York: Basic Books, 2009.

Simms, Brendan, *The Longest Afternoon: The 400 Men Who Decided the Battle of Waterloo*, New York: Basic Books, 2015.

Skagg, David, and Gerard Altoff, *A Signal Victory: The Lake Erie Campaign, 1812–1813*, Annapolis: Naval Institute Press, 1997.

Smith, Digby, *The Greenhill Napoleonic Wars Data Book: Actions and Losses in Personnel, Colours, Standards, and Artillery, 1792–1815*, London: Greenhill Books, 1998.

Smyth, Jim, *The Men of No Property: Irish Radicals and Popular Politics in the Late Eighteenth Century*, Basingstoke: Palgrave Macmillan, 1992.

Sobel, David, *Longitude: The True Story of a Lone Genius Who Solved the Greatest Scientific Problem of His Time*, New York: Penguin, 2006.

Southey, Robert, *The Life of Nelson*, London: Longman Green, 1896.

Sugden, John, *Tecumseh: A Life*, New York: Henry Holt, 1998.

Thomas, Donald, *Cochrane: Britainnia's Sea Wolf*, London: Cassells, 2001.

Toll, Ian W., *Six Frigates: The Epic History of the Founding of the U.S. Navy*, New York: W.W. Norton, 2006.

Tunstall, Brian, *Naval Warfare in the Age of Sail: The Evolution of Fighting Tactics, 1650–1815*, Annapolis: Naval Institute Press, 1990.

Turner, Wesley B., *British Generals in the War of 1812: High Command in the Canadas*, Montreal: McGill University Press, 1999.

Voltaire, *Candide*, New York: Dover Publications, 1991.

Warner, Oliver, *Nelson's Battles*, London: Pen & Sword Books, 2003.

Weigley, Russell F., *The Age of Battles: The Quest for Decisive Warfare from Breitenfeld to Waterloo*, Bloomington: Indiana University Press, 1991.

Weller, Jac, *Wellington in the Peninsula*, Mechanicsburg: Stackpole Books, 1992.

Weller, Jac, *Wellington in India*, London: Frontline Books, 2013.

Welsh, William, and David Skaggs, eds, *The War on the Great Lakes: Essays Commemorating the 175th Anniversary of the Battle of Lake Erie*, Kent: Kent State University Press, 1991.

Western, John R., *The English Militia in the Eighteenth Century: The Story of a Political Issue, 1660–1802*, London: Routledge, 1965.

Wilkinson, Clive, *The British Navy and the State in the Eighteenth Century*, London: Boydell Press, 2004.

Woodman, Robert, *The Victory of Sea Power: Winning the Napoleonic War, 1806–1814*, London: Chatham Publishing, 1998.

Yapp, M.E., *Strategies of British India: Britain, Iran, and Afghanistan, 1798–1850*, Oxford: Oxford University Press, 1980.

Zamoyski, Adam, *Rise of Peace: The Fall of Napoleon and the Congress of Vienna*, New York: Harper Press, 2007.

Zimmerman, James F., *The Impressment of American Seamen*, New York: Columbia University Press, 1925.

Index